PROGRAMMING
THE 8086/8088
For the IBM PC and Compatibles

PROGRAMMING THE 8086/8088
For the IBM PC and Compatibles

Michael Thorne
University College, Cardiff

THE BENJAMIN/CUMMINGS PUBLISHING COMPANY INC.

Menlo Park, California · Reading, Massachusetts · Wokingham, England
Don Mills, Ontario · Amsterdam · Bonn · Sydney
Singapore · Tokyo · Madrid · San Juan

The programs presented in this book have been included for their instructional value. They have been tested with care but are not guaranteed for any particular purpose. The publisher does not offer any warranties or representations, nor does it accept any liabilities with respect to the programs.

Cover design by 20/20 Graphics.
Typeset by Columns, Reading.
Printed in Great Britain at The Bath Press, Avon

First printed in 1986. Reprinted 1987 and 1988.

Library of Congress Cataloging-in-Publication Data
Thorne, Michael.
    Programming the 8086/8088 for the IBM PC and compatibles.

    Includes index.
    1. Intel 8086 (Microprocessor)–Programming.
2. Intel 8088 (Microprocessor)–Programming.
3. Assembler language (Computer program language)
4. IBM Personal Computer–Programming.   I. Title.
QA76.8.I292T458   1986   005.265   86–20690
ISBN 0–8053–5004–7

Contents

Preface

The object of this book is to provide an introduction to programming the 8086/8088 family of microprocessors at the assembly language level, suitable for undergraduates majoring in Computer Science, Electrical Engineering and related disciplines – though computer hobbyists may also find the contents of interest. The reader is assumed to have a fairly good knowledge of a high-level language such as Pascal. By means of carefully chosen examples, he or she is acquainted with the whole 8086/8088 instruction set. Each chapter has a plentiful supply of exercises which form an integral part of the text: assembly language programming is far too complicated to learn without actually writing and debugging some programs.

In the real computing world it is modern practice to avoid programming in assembly language whenever possible, since it takes so much longer than using a high-level language and the result, being much more complex, is considerably less trustworthy. Unfortunately, the microcomputer industry has clouded an otherwise clear-cut distinction between tasks best solved using high-level languages and those for which assembly language has, unfortunately, to be used, simply because of inadequate memory resources or machine efficiency considerations.

But the philosophy of this book is that undergraduates should learn about assembly language programming, not just in its own right but, more importantly, for the insight this can give into the code generation phase of a compiler and into the relationship between the (instruction-set) architecture of a microprocessor and the implementations of high-level languages using that architecture. To summarize, our aims are:

 i) Introduce the reader to assembly language programming.

 ii) Introduce the reader to the 8088 microprocessor architecture.

iii) Reinforce and supplement the reader's Pascal (or other, similar, high-level language) programming experience.

iv) Further the reader's progress in understanding and employing more advanced data structuring and data typing facilities.

 v) Introduce the reader to the relationship between high-level language and machine languages from the compiler writer's point of view.

Chapter 1 explains what assembly language is, and its relationship to high-level languages such as Pascal, and discusses when and when not to use it. It also summarizes the background knowledge concerning computer hardware and binary and hexadecimal arithmetic which is assumed in the book. The chapter concludes with a brief introduction to the 8088 family.

By the end of Chapter 2 the reader should be able to write some simple programs in 8088 assembly language and know how to use the technique of tracing to locate errors. Chapter 3 contains the remaining details which are required before a program can actually be assembled and debugged using the PC-DOS DEBUG program. A worked example demonstrates how this is done.

Writing any reasonably large program involves structuring the task if time is not to be wasted and if an end product is required which is quickly assimilable by another programmer not involved in its creation. Chapter 4 concerns techniques for structuring assembly language programs: sub-routines (with and without parameters) and the use of pseudo-Pascal in the stepwise refinement of program outlines. It also shows how to access the PC-DOS functions for reading in and printing out characters, and how to return control to PC-DOS after one of our own programs has finished execution.

To illustrate the practical use of this methodology, Chapter 5 uses most of the 8088 arithmetic instructions to build a calculator simulator. The complete program is given in Appendix I and the exercises invite the reader to extend and improve on the bare essentials given there. Chapter 6 likewise concerns a large program, this time a simple text editor, which affords us a natural opportunity to discuss the 8088 string manipulation instructions.

In Chapter 7 our attention turns to details of the 8088 particularly relevant to the implementation of compilers for high-level languages such as Pascal. The focus is on the various 8088 addressing modes and their use in implementing Pascal array and record types. We also look at 8088 instruction formats, the implementation of recursive routines, and the construction of programs using modules which are later joined together by the linker into a single executable unit.

Chapter 8 covers the 8088 instructions for performing arithmetic on numbers represented in BCD form – a form which saves much of the conversion overhead during input and output of decimal numbers and which easily allows us to represent numbers of arbitrary precision.

Chapters 9 and 10 present some of the more advanced features of the PC-DOS assembler MASM. All of the material up until these chapters would work equally with MASM's smaller cousin ASM, but here we meet features – macros, STRUC and RECORD for example – unique to MASM. The features discussed which are common to ASM and MASM include data definition, program linkage and memory pseudo-ops, controlling assembler printout, and certain facilities for conditional assembly.

PC-DOS allows the programmer to handle disk storage via operating system function calls. Chapter 11 contains several complete program examples to demonstrate their use, including: a program to dump the contents of a file onto the display screen; a program to store keyboard input in a disk file; a file copy utility; and a random access read utility.

The final chapter drops down a level from PC-DOS functions and involves the reader in writing programs to control a printer, the IBM PC keyboard, the black and white display, the PC speaker and the colour/graphics display. Fundamental to this is the 8088 interrupt mechanism, which is explained in detail.

This book grew out of the many, many courses I have given on assembly language programming to undergraduates, adult education classes and to groups of teachers over the past six years. For their lively and uncompromising feedback all of those students must be thanked. Andrew Bell of the University College Cardiff Computer Centre read several early drafts and his careful criticism has substantially improved the final text, as did the comments of the first of three anonymous reviewers. Maureen Evans typed the manuscript under considerable pressure but managed to remain in good spirits throughout. Acknowledgement must also be made of the patience of my long-suffering family who have endured neglect as cheerfully during this project as they have with others in the past. You see, the cups of tea were appreciated!

Michael Thorne
University College, Cardiff

Acknowledgement

The publishers wish to acknowledge International Business Machines Corporation for permission to reproduce material appearing in Appendix IV (8088 instruction set summary) and Appendix V (8088 instruction set encoding).

1 Introduction

AIMS

This first chapter explains what assembly language is, its relationship to high-level languages such as Pascal, and discusses when and when not to use it. We also summarize the background knowledge concerning computer hardware and binary and hexadecimal arithmetic which is assumed in this book, and describe the various ways of representing numeric and text data in binary form. Finally we introduce the concept of a microprocessor in general and the particular microprocessor on which the IBM PC is based, the Intel 8088. Since much of what we say in this book applies to other members of the 8088 family of microprocessors which are used by some advanced models of the IBM PC and several 'look-alikes', we shall also outline the relationship between them and the 8088.

1.1 ASSEMBLY LANGUAGE

Most computer programs these days are written in high-level languages such as BASIC, COBOL and Pascal. Writing programs in any of these is quicker and easier (and therefore cheaper if you're paying somebody to do it) than in the machine's own language – machine code. There are some occasions, however, when a high-level language just can't be used. Pascal may be able to do the job from a logical point of view but the machine code generated from it may be too slow for the application in question. For example, when a computer is being used to control a nuclear reactor in a power station, if the controlling program cannot respond very quickly to changes in the reactor's state the reactor may go critical and there will be danger of an explosion. Also, if it happens to be your lot to write programs to control peripherals such as disk drives, then a high-level language such as Pascal will neither work fast enough to give users the rapid response they expect nor will it give you close enough control over the hardware to do the job efficiently. Indeed, using a high-level language in this sort of context is often like trying to eat a bar of chocolate with a knife and fork whilst wearing a thick pair of mittens – just about possible but not much fun if you have to do it every day.

Regrettably, then, there are occasions when the programmer must program at the machine's own level though very few programmers actually use machine code, the language of 0s and 1s which the computer's circuits understand directly. Machine code programs are tedious to write and highly error prone. Imagine the errors likely to arise from an inter-departmental telephone conversation about the following machine code program:

```
0010101111000011
1000101111001000
1011101000000000000000000
```

In situations where a high-level language is inappropriate we avoid working in machine code most of the time by making the computer do more of the work. We humans write our programs in a more readable form – assembly language – and then get the computer to turn this assembly language program into machine code. The above machine code program was produced by a computer from the following assembly language version:

```
SUB AX,BX
MOV CX,AX
MOV DX,0
```

Here, as you may guess, the **mnemonic** (i.e. memory aid) SUB is short for SUBtract and MOV represents a MOVe instruction. It is much easier to remember SUB AX,CX than 0010101111000011 – the actual instruction code the machine uses.

Assembly languages are an intermediate step between high-level languages and machine code. For example, the actual execution of a Pascal program is sometimes achieved by automatically converting the program into assembly language form and then finally converting that into machine code which is executed. This process is illustrated in Fig. 1.1. Conversion between these languages is performed at each stage by computer programs: from high-level language to assembly language by a **compiler** and from assembly language to machine code by an **assembler**.

Pascal programmers work in a cushioned environment as do most high-level language programmers. Assembly language and machine code cannot automatically handle most of the data types high-level languages provide. Thus, in Pascal, variables can be of **integer**, **real**, **char** or **record** types – or even one of the programmer's own defined types – but machine code has just binary numbers. Pascal allows the automatic creation of arrays with elements of any of the permitted data types: in assembly language, the programmer has to arrange these. Moreover, Pascal compilers check that variables of one type (for example, **real**) are not assigned to values of an alien type (for example, **char**). In assembly language, no such checks are made.

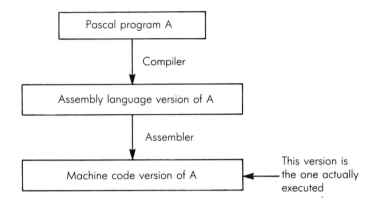

Fig. 1.1   The relationship between high-level languages and machine code.

This all makes writing big programs in assembly language harder and more error prone than high-level language programming. Unfortunately assembly language sometimes *has* to be used because of the loss of speed experienced when using a compiled language such as Pascal. Thus, in a commercial environment, assembly language is used only when no other higher level programming language is deemed able to give the necessary performance from the hardware. But then there is an even greater penalty for using assembly language than the extra high costs involved. Assembly language programs are very much more dependent upon the precise design of the computer they are to run on than their high-level language equivalents. In consequence, it is usually much easier to get a Pascal program, written originally for machine A, up and running on machine B than it is to transport an assembly language program from machine A to machine B. Indeed, if the architecture of machine B differs in any considerable way from that of machine A, virtually a complete rewrite may be necessary.

More often than not, operating systems have to be written in assembly language as do programs to control external devices such as printers and plotters. But even this use of assembly language may be avoided by using high-level languages such as C in which the vast majority of the Unix operating system – originally written for the DEC PDP/11 series of computers – including even the disk drive controllers is written. Within a Pascal type of programming environment, C allows programmers the efficient access to actual memory locations – and hence hardware devices – denied them by Pascal.

If C is not available to the programmer for some reason, it may be that linking assembly language modules in with a high-level language main program is the best way to avoid doing the whole job in assembly language. Different versions of the same high-level language vary enormously in the provision they make for doing this and in the complexity involved in making it all work, but overall this will almost certainly be quicker than developing a large program entirely in assembly language.

Hopefully the message is clear: for real life problems use assembly language only as a last resort. Sometimes you don't have any choice, as is the case if you want to modify an operating system already written in assembly language. From now on we assume that circumstances force you to read this book (!) and it is now time to commence our detailed study of assembly language.

1.2   NUMBER SYSTEMS USED IN ASSEMBLY LANGUAGE

As we remarked earlier, binary numbers are the only data type available in machine code. Assembly language frees us from this constraint in some respects by allowing us to work with one of three number systems – binary, decimal or hexadecimal – the assembler making any necessary conversions into binary. Thanks to our ten fingers and ten toes the decimal number system is the one with which we are all most familiar. Unfortunately assembly language cannot allow us just to stick to decimal numbers: computer designers have seen to that! Also, letters of the alphabet and punctuation marks have to be coded up into numeric form so that text can be processed by assembly language programs. In this section we present a brief overview of these three number systems and the ASCII text coding system which has become the de facto standard on microcomputers. It is intended only as a summary and a reader familiar with this material can move directly on to Section 1.3. Readers needing more information on these topics should consult *Introduction to Computer Science* by Neil Graham, West Publishing Co., St. Paul, Minnesota, 1985.

Binary numbers

As we learnt at school, the decimal number 294 means

$$
\begin{aligned}
&2 \text{ hundreds} + 9 \text{ tens} + 4 \text{ units} \\
&= 2*100 \quad\quad + 9*10 \quad + 4*1 \\
&= 2*10^2 \quad\quad + 9*10^1 \quad + 4*1^0
\end{aligned}
$$

All that's different about the binary number system is that only the digits 0 and 1 are used and each place to the left represents a higher power of 2 (instead of 10). Thus the binary number 11011 is

$$
\begin{aligned}
&1*2^4 + 1*2^3 + 0*2^2 + 1*2^1 + 1*2^0 \\
&= 16 \quad + 8 \quad + 0 \quad + 2 \quad + 1 \\
&= 27
\end{aligned}
$$

in decimal.

To avoid any possible confusion between the decimal number 10 and the binary number 10 (which is just 2 in decimal) we shall in future write the letter B after a binary number and D after a decimal number where there is any possible ambiguity. Thus 10B = 2D and 11011B = 27D as we saw above.

The number 11011B contains five binary digits (or **bits**). Since computers are largely concerned with performing arithmetic on binary numbers and with moving such numbers from one place in memory to another, it simplifies matters greatly if a fixed number of bits is moved each time. The IBM PC moves data around in multiples of 8 bits, a collection of 8 bits being called a **byte**. Often two bytes are moved at once so we call any group of two bytes a **word**.

a bit	0
4 bits	1011
a byte	11100010
a word	1010111001110010

In a byte or word (for example, 1010110001110010) the right-most digit is referred to as the **least significant digit** (in the example it's a 0) and the left-most digit is referred to as the **most significant digit** (1 in the above example).

Amongst the programming instructions for the 8088 microprocessor are several concerned with performing arithmetic, including those with mnemonics ADD, SUB, MUL and DIV. Arithmetic can be performed between either two bytes or two words, whichever the programmer chooses. Moreover, just as a programmer must decide whether to represent a numerical quantity by an integer or real variable in Pascal, in assembly language programmers choose whether to represent a value in a byte or word and whether as a **signed** or **unsigned** binary number. Unsigned binary numbers are the ones we have met so far and, whilst they do not admit the possibility of representing negative decimal numbers such as -8147 and -1 in binary, they are adequate for many purposes. Signed numbers allow both positive and negative numbers to be represented, but every signed number must be given a sign. This is done by taking the most significant digit in a byte or word as corresponding not to 2^7 or 2^{15} respectively, but to -2^7 or -2^{15}. Thus, as a **signed** number the byte 10110000 is, in decimal,

$$1*(-2^7)+0*2^6 + 1*2^5 + 1*2^4 + 0*2^3 + 0*2^2 + 0*2^1 + 0*2^0$$
$$= -128 + 32 + 16 = -80$$

and as a **signed** number the byte 00110000 is, in decimal,

$$0*2^7 + 0*2^6 + 1*2^5 + 1*2^4 + 0*2^3 + 0*2^2 + 0*2^1 + 0*2^0$$
$$= 32 + 16 = 48$$

It follows that the most significant digit of a byte or word representing a signed number will be 0 if the number is positive and 1 if it's negative.

The signed representation of a negative number can be found in the following way. If x is positive, $-x$ is represented by $2^{16}-x$ (word) or 2^8-x (byte) ignoring the most significant bit of the result of the subtraction. In binary the necessary arithmetic is surprisingly easy. For example, to represent the decimal -42 in signed 16-bit form we subtract 42 from 2^{16} as follows:

$$2^{16} = \quad 10000000000000000$$
$$42 = \quad 0000000000101010$$
$$\text{Difference} = \quad (0)\ 1111111111010110$$

and hence the 16-bit signed representation of -42 is 1111111111010110. This is called the **two's complement** representation of -42.

Another way of working out the two's complement of a number is to carry out the following procedure on its positive equivalent: change all the 0s to 1s and all the 1s to 0s; then add 1 to the result forgetting any carry digit which goes beyond the number of bits in the representation you are seeking. Thus $+37$ in signed 8-bit form is 00100101 so -37 in the same form is $11011010 + 1 = 11011011$ and -2 is 11111110 so $+2$ is $00000001 + 1 = 00000010$. If you're not familiar with two's complement representation, check the entries in Table 1.1 using both methods.

The range of **signed** numbers which can be held in a byte goes from -128 to $+127$ as follows:

-128	10000000
-127	10000001
	.
-37	11011011
	.
-2	11111110
-1	11111111
0	00000000
$+1$	00000001
$+2$	00000010
	.
$+37$	00100101
	.
$+126$	01111110
$+127$	01111111

Table 1.1 Examples of two's complement representations.

Decimal	One byte signed binary representation	Two's complement of binary no. in column 2	Decimal
0	00000000	00000000	0
$+1$	00000001	11111111	-1
$+2$	00000010	11111110	-2
$+3$	00000011	11111101	-3
$+4$	00000100	11111100	-4

For a word the corresponding range is as follows:

−32768	100000000	00000000
−32767	100000000	00000001
.		
.		
−2	11111111	11111110
−1	11111111	11111111
0	00000000	00000000
+1	00000000	00000001
+2	00000000	00000010
.		
.		
+32766	01111111	11111110
+32767	01111111	11111111

For unsigned numbers the ranges are 0 to 255 (byte) and 0 to 65535 (word). It is interesting to compare signed and unsigned representations, as shown in Table 1.2.

In general a given byte or word can represent one of two decimal numbers depending on whether it is to be regarded as signed or unsigned. Consequently, for each numeric data item in a program, the programmer must take a decision to use either a signed or unsigned representation and must stick to that choice: the two forms must not be mixed. This is rather like deciding in Pascal whether to store a date of birth as a number or as a string: both may be of use for certain applications but the two cannot be used interchangeably!

Hexadecimal numbers

Given that 0000000000000111 is one of the possible forms in which the computer handles the 'harmless' decimal number 7, there is a strong motivation for a shorthand for all those 0s and 1s. An essential feature of any shorthand is that it must be easy to go from the full form to the shorthand and vice versa. This is why we introduce a third number system, hexadecimal.

Table 1.2 Comparison of signed and unsigned numbers.

Binary		Value in decimal	
		Unsigned	Signed
01000110		70	70
11000110		198	−58
00101101	10001100	11660	11660
10101101	10001100	44428	−21108

Table 1.3 Hexadecimal conversion table.

Decimal	Binary	Hexadecimal
0	0000	0
1	0001	1
2	0010	2
3	0011	3
4	0100	4
5	0101	5
6	0110	6
7	0111	7
8	1000	8
9	1001	9
10	1010	A
11	1011	B
12	1100	C
13	1101	D
14	1110	E
15	1111	F

In the hexadecimal number system we use the ordinary decimal digits 0, 1, 2, 3, . . . , 9 together with the first six letters of the alphabet – A, B, C, D, E and F. A stands for 10 in decimal, B for 11 and so on up to F which stands for 15 in decimal. Otherwise everything works in the same way as for decimal and binary except that, in this case, each place to the left represents a higher power of 16. Thus the hexadecimal number 3FA04 is equivalent to the decimal

$$3*16^4 + F*16^3 + A*16^2 + 0*16^1 + 4*16^0$$
$$= 3*16^4 + 15*16^3 + 10*16^2 + 0*16^1 + 4*16^0$$
$$= 196608 + 61440 + 2560 + 0 + 4$$
$$= 260612$$

At first sight the idea of a number with letters in it may appear rather strange, but it should always be borne in mind that the letters stand for numbers which in decimal require two digits (Table 1.3).

Conversion between hexadecimal and binary is very easy. To convert *from* hexadecimal *to* binary involves replacing each hexadecimal digit by its binary equivalent written as a 4-bit number. Thus, to represent hexadecimal 3FA04 in binary:

3	F	A	0	4
0011	1111	1010	0000	0100

so the binary equivalent of 3FA04 is 00111111101000000100. Going the other way is just as easy:

1011	0110	0011	1001	1110
B	6	3	9	E

so that the hexadecimal equivalent of binary 10110110001110011110 is B639E. Hopefully this justifies the use of the hexadecimal number system as a shorthand for binary.

Pronunciation

If you're not sure how to pronounce hexadecimal numbers such as 1A, 1B . . . etc. you could always follow Bilbo Baggins and refer to 1A as onety-A and so on. More often than not, however, hexadecimal numbers like B639E are read as 'bee-six-three-nine-ee'.

Converting decimal to hexadecimal

To convert a decimal number to hexadecimal we repeatedly divide the decimal number by 16 until a zero quotient is obtained. The remainders from the divisions then give you the equivalent hexadecimal number, the last remainder obtained being the highest order digit of the hexadecimal number. For example, the conversion of decimal 1103 to hexadecimal looks like:

$$1103 \div 16 = 68 \text{ remainder F}$$
$$68 \div 16 = 4 \text{ remainder 4}$$
$$4 \div 16 = 0 \text{ remainder 4}$$

so that the hexadecimal equivalent of decimal 1103 is 44F.

Converting decimal numbers to binary is carried out in a similar fashion except that you divide by 2 each time. Thus, to find the binary equivalent of decimal 46:

$$46 \div 2 = 23 \text{ remainder 0}$$
$$23 \div 2 = 11 \text{ remainder 1}$$
$$11 \div 2 = 5 \text{ remainder 1}$$
$$5 \div 2 = 2 \text{ remainder 1}$$
$$2 \div 2 = 1 \text{ remainder 0}$$
$$1 \div 2 = 0 \text{ remainder 1}$$

so the binary equivalent of decimal 46 is 101110.

For future use, equivalences between decimal and hexadecimal numbers are shown in Table 1.4. As an exercise in converting decimal numbers to hexadecimal form we invite the reader to verify as many of the entries as time allows.

Table 1.4   Decimal and hexadecimal equivalence table.

Decimal	Hexadecimal
1	1
10	0A
100	64
1000	3E8
10000	2710
100000	186A0
1000000	F4240
10000000	989680

Further practice in conversion from hexadecimal to binary can be obtained by converting the right-hand entries to binary and then checking that the decimal value of the binary numbers obtained is that given in the left-hand column. For instance, 3E8 in hexadecimal is 001111101000 in binary which is $512 + 256 + 128 + 64 + 32 + 8 = 1000$ in decimal so that row four of Table 1.4 is verified.

Representing text

Computers are able to handle non-numeric data as well as numbers. In fact, most 'real world' computer use at the moment involves non-numeric computing, such as searching a file of accounts to find all outstanding invoices in the name of J. S. Gruntfuttock. The ability to handle text derives from coding the alphabet and punctuation marks into numbers. For example we could use the number 41H as a code for the letter A, 42H for the letter B, 43H for the letter C, 2CH for the symbol ',' (comma), 3BH for the symbol ';' (semicolon), etc. Given a numerical code, the processing of text is reduced to processing numbers. Thus searching a file for an invoice under the name SMITH actually involves searching for an invoice beginning with 53H, 4DH, 49H, 54H, 48H.

In microcomputers such as the IBM PC the code most often used is the ASCII (pronounced ASS-KEY) code – the American Standard Code for Information Interchange – from which the above examples were taken. The complete ASCII code is given in Appendix I for ease of reference. By the time you have finished reading this book that appendix will be well-thumbed. Take a first look at it now and verify that the examples given above conform to the ASCII code.

Besides the alphabetic characters A, B, C, . . . , Z, a, b, . . . , z and punctuation marks, the ASCII code also includes codes for certain characters which never get printed but rather are used to control devices external to the main computer, such as a printer. Other codes are used to control communications between the computer and a remote device, rather like the 'over and out' communications protocol used by aeroplane pilots.

Thus there is an ASCII code to get a printer to move onto a new line – LF (Line Feed) in the table; to send the printing head back to the beginning of the line – CR (Carriage Return) in the table; to signal an ENQuiry – ENQ in the table; and to signal the End Of Transmission – EOT in the table.

Originally ASCII codes contained just 7 bits and could thus be used to represent 128 (2^7) characters. When placing data in memory, multiples of 8 bits are used and so it is natural to use a single byte for each character. The additional eighth bit (added at the most significant end of the code) is put to use in two different ways.

First, in order to extend the range of characters which the PC can display on its screen, IBM has extended the ASCII code by using this eighth bit to represent an additional 128 characters. This permits such weird and wonderful display characters as Greek letters, playing-card suits, square root signs and smiling faces to be represented.

Second, when data is transmitted over relatively long distances – for example over telephone lines – there is the possibility of corruption due to electrical noise. The eighth bit can be used to afford protection against such data corruption by setting it to 0 or 1 as necessary to ensure that the code for every character has an even number of bits set to 1 (**even parity**) or to ensure that every character's code has an odd number of bits set to 1 (**odd parity**).

For example, the 7-bit ASCII code for the letter A is 1000001. If even parity is used this becomes 01000001 while odd parity would give 11000001. Hardware can be designed to check for parity discrepancies. Thus, if we were using odd parity and 11000011 were received by the computer over a telephone line, the hardware would detect that this cannot be the code of any real data (since it contains an even number of bits set to 1) and signal an error.

To summarize, inside the PC itself the eighth bit is used to give extra characters. When communicating with external devices – another computer or a printer perhaps – the eighth bit can be used to guard against transmission errors if we don't want to transmit or receive these extra characters.

EXERCISES 1.1

1. Complete the following table:

16-bit binary (unsigned)	4-digit hexadecimal	Decimal
0000000000011111	001F	31
0101010101010101		
	AE2B	
0001110001110000		
	1E1E	
	2345	
	ABCD	

2. Complete the following table:

16-bit (signed)	Decimal
1000000000111111	
1000111000111001	
0000100100100000	
0100000000000000	
1100000000000000	

3. Find the two's complement of the 16-bit signed number 0110110110110111. If the result is a binary number x, find the two's complement of x.

4. Decipher the following ASCII-coded secret message:

02 4D 45 65 54 20 6D 45 20 41 74 20 43 41 52 4E 45
67 49 65 20 48 41 6C 4C 20 31 34 2E 33 30 20 03

1.3 MICROPROCESSORS AND THE 8088 FAMILY

Inside any computer the basic arrangement of the main components is the same as shown in Fig. 1.2. Information is sent from one main component to another along the communication channel, which is often called a 'bus' by electrical engineers. Since you can put information 'on the bus' at the keyboard and get it off again at the processor or memory or . . . the analogy is quite a good one.

Both programs and data are stored in the memory, the processor fetching new instructions or data as necessary. It is also the processor's job to interpret or decode instructions, to perform memory address calculations, to route results to their proper destinations and to perform arithmetic.

In any microcomputer, the processor is entirely contained on a single silicon chip – a **microprocessor**. There are many different kinds of microprocessor just as there are different makes of microcomputer.

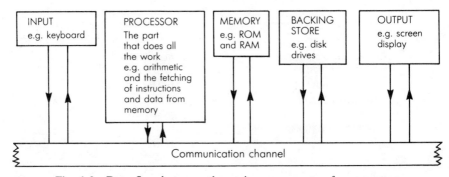

Fig. 1.2 Data flow between the main components of a computer.

Table 1.5 gives a short list of some popular microcomputers and the type of microprocessor each uses. Incidentally, microprocessors tend to have mysterious sounding names like QB99*4; just as the name of a car tells you little about the car itself, so it is with microprocessors.

This book is concerned with the 8088 microprocessor and other members of the same family, in particular, the 8086. From the programmer's point of view these two are virtually indistinguishable. In fact, programs which will run on one will run on the other. However, the 8086 has a somewhat higher performance capability. Its communication channel is 16 bits wide (a 16-decker bus?) whereas the 8088 has only an 8-bit wide communication channel and, consequently, the 8088 takes longer when fetching 16 bits from memory.

Both the 8086 and the 8088 are able to queue up instructions fetched from memory whilst other instructions not involving memory access are being executed. The 8086 can queue up a total of 6 bytes of instructions in this way whereas the 8088 can queue only 4 bytes. At any one time the processor can only fetch one item (be it data or instruction) from memory or store one item of data in memory. Hence, queuing instructions in this manner means that if the instruction just completed involved storing something in memory, then the 8086 or 8088 can get ready to execute the next instruction in the queue at the same time as the memory store is going on. Taken together, these two differences between the 8086 and the 8088 make the 8086 up to 20% more powerful than its sibling rival.

Synchronizing operations within a computer is an electronic clock which sends out pulses much like an army drill sergeant shouts left-right-left-right to synchronize a parade. For the 8086 and 8088 the maximum clock rate is 5 million pulses per second – a 5 MegaHertz (5 MHz) clock. The 8086 family also includes the 8086-2 microprocessor which is identical to the 8086 but allows a clock rate of up to 8 million pulses per second (8 MHz). There are three other members of the family, all of them more powerful still.

Table 1.5 Microcomputers and the microprocessors on which they are based.

Microcomputer	Microprocessor it uses
IBM Personal Computer	8088
IBM PC AT	80286
Research Machines Nimbus	80186
DEC Rainbow	8088 and Z80
ORION	8086
Apricot	8086
Apple Macintosh	68000
ACT Sirius	8088
Olivetti M-20	Z8000
CORVUS CONCEPT	68000

These are the 80186, the 80188 and the 80286 and their features are summarized in Table 1.6.

Table 1.6   Newer members of the 8086 family.

Micro-processor	Width of communication channel (bits)	Instruction queue length (bytes)	Maximum clock rate (MHz)	Notes
80186	16	6	8	Runs all 8086 and 8088 software but has ten new instructions
80188	8	4	8	Functionally identical to 80186, lower performance
80286	16	6	10	Runs all 8086 and 80186 programs but has extra instructions. Several times more powerful than the 8086

1.4 SUMMARY

Assembly language is a last resort for most programming tasks. High-level languages offer environments in which the programming of a task can proceed much more efficiently. Since assembly language has only two data types – binary signed or unsigned numbers – all data items for a given problem have to be coded into numeric form before they can be represented in an assembly language program. In particular, text is represented using the ASCII code.

The IBM PC is based on the 8088 microprocessor, one of a family sharing the same basic instruction set, though advanced members of the family have additional specialized instructions. In the next chapter we begin to study 8088 assembly language instructions and write our first programs.

2 Some Simple 8088 Instructions

AIMS

By the end of this chapter the reader should be able to write some simple programs in the assembly language of the 8088 microprocessor found in the IBM PC and know how to use the technique of **tracing** to locate errors. Details of how to have these programs executed by the computer will follow in Chapter 3.

2.1 REGISTERS

Since we have now covered all the necessary background we can start to explore 8088 instructions, remembering that much of what we say also applies to other members of the 8088 family – though each individual machine will have its own version of 8088 assembly language. The majority of these instructions involve **registers** in some way or other and it is to a description of four of the 8088 registers that we turn first.

My pocket calculator is one of the simplest and cheapest available. To get it to add two numbers, say 3 and 2, you have to follow the three steps of Fig. 2.1.

A calculator display is a good model for a **register** in a microprocessor. Registers are places where data can be processed particularly quickly. The 8088 is very well endowed in this respect. One of its registers is called the AX register and the AX register can be used to add 3 and 2 in much the same way as for the simple calculator discussed above. Here is the program:

```
MOV AX,3 ;put 3 into register AX
ADD AX,2 ;add 2 to contents of register AX
```

(Here, anything appearing after a semicolon (;) is a 'comment' to help humans understand the program. Only the instructions to the left of the ; are obeyed by the 8088 microprocessor.) As was the case with the calculator example above, the answer (5!) would be left in the register AX.

Actually the 8088 has 4 general purpose registers: AX, BX, CX and

15

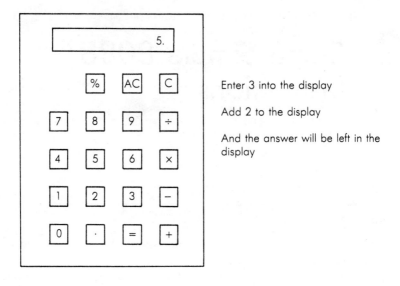

Enter 3 into the display

Add 2 to the display

And the answer will be left in the display

Fig. 2.1 A simple calculator.

DX, each of which holds one 16-bit number. Our simple addition program could have used any one of these four by replacing AX with the name of one of the other registers throughout. Moving data between registers is accomplished by the MOV instruction. Appending the following instructions to the above addition program would result in the value 5 being put into all the registers AX, BX, CX and DX.

```
MOV BX,AX ;copy what's in register AX into register BX
MOV CX,AX ;copy what's in register AX into register CX
MOV DX,CX ;copy what's in register CX into register DX
```

So often in programming do we want to add 1 to the contents of a register that the 8088 provides an instruction specially for that purpose: viz., the INC instruction. Thus,

```
INC DX
```

would add 1 to the current contents of register DX.

But we can do more than just add! Subtraction and three sorts of multiplication and division are possible as well. Consider the following little program:

```
MOV AX,5 ;put 5 into the AX register
MOV BX,4 ;put 4 into the BX register
SUB AX,2 ;subtract 2 from the AX register
MUL BX   ;multiply the number in the BX
         ;register by the number in the
         ;AX register and leave the answer
```

```
;in the DX and AX registers, DX
;containing the binary digits
;corresponding to 2^8 = 256D and
;higher powers of 2
```

It will calculate $(5-2)*4$ and leave the answer (12 in decimal, C in hexadecimal) in register AX. The stages of the calculation are illustrated in Fig. 2.2 in which we have adopted the convention which will often be followed, namely, the contents of registers are given in hexadecimal notation.

Note that in the MULtiply instruction, AX is one of the operands even though the assembly language mnemonic doesn't mention it: MUL BX causes the 8088 to work out BX times AX. It would be a reasonable criticism of the PC 8088 instruction mnemonics to say that each and every instruction should have explicit operands. Some versions of 8088 assembly language do follow this convention.

Removing ambiguity

Calculators work in decimal of course, but microprocessors use binary arithmetic. Thanks to assembly language we can write instructions like

```
MOV AX,7
```

and leave it to the assembler to convert the number 7 into its appropriate binary equivalent. However, there is now the possibility of ambiguity. For example, does

```
MOV AX,26
```

refer to the decimal number 26, or hexadecimal 26 ($2*16^1 + 6*16^0 = 38$ in decimal)?

To remove any ambiguity as far as the assembly language conversion is concerned we write 26H for hexadecimal 26 and 26D for decimal 26. Likewise 10B is binary, 10D is decimal and 10H is hexadecimal. Actually the PC assembler assumes any number is in **decimal** unless it is told

	AX	BX	CX	DX
	?	?	?	?
MOV AX,5	5	?	?	?
MOV BX,4	5	4	?	?
SUB AX,2	3	4	?	?
MUL BX	C	4	?	0

Fig. 2.2 Stages of the calculation of $(5-2)*4$. ? denotes a value which we do not know in advance. (Before our program starts the registers will contain whatever the previous program left in them.)

otherwise by adding a code letter after the number. For the time being it is better always to add a letter explicitly indicating which sort of number it is that you are talking about. In this way you will become used to thinking about the problem of ambiguity of meaning.

Size of registers

Given the benefits of assembly language, we still cannot ignore completely the fundamental reliance of microprocessors upon the binary number system. A pocket calculator has a limit to the number of decimal digits you can enter – mine accepts 98765432 (8 digits) but not 198765432 (9 digits), for example. Likewise the registers AX, BX, CX and DX are limited to 16 binary digits (bits) so that in an instruction

```
MOV AX,n
```

the number n must not need more than 16 bits for its binary representation, i.e. in decimal n must be less than or equal to 65535 for an unsigned number or between -32768 and 32767 for a signed number. This also means that all four registers are limited to 4 hexadecimal digits.

Unlike most pocket calculators, the number entered into AX, BX, CX or DX *must* consist of exactly 16 binary digits. Thus, the assembly language

```
MOV AX,7H
```

would actually be converted to the machine code equivalent of

```
MOV AX,0000000000000111B
```

since the binary for 7H is 111. Fortunately this is done for you automatically.

EXERCISES 2.1

1. What will be the contents of the AX, BX, CX and DX registers after executing each of the following program fragments?

a) ```
MOV CX,3
ADD CX,5
MOV BX,CX
INC BX
MOV AX,BX
MOV DX,CX
```

b) ```
MOV DX,8
MOV AX,9
SUB DX,4
MUL DX
MOV CX,DX
INC CX
SUB CX,1
MOV BX,CX
```

2. Write a program to leave the result of $5*(7+1)-6$ in register CX.

2.2 THE FLAGS REGISTER

The 8088 has a special 16-bit register called the **flags register** because the individual bits are used as flags to indicate the result of executing certain instructions. Thus, just as the British flag flies above Buckingham Palace when the Queen is in residence, so the **Z-flag** in the 8088 flags register can be set to 1 by any of a certain group of instructions to indicate that the result of executing that instruction was zero.

Altogether, five of the bits in the flags register are used to indicate the results of arithmetic and related operations and are referred to as the **arithmetic flags**. These are the O-flag (overflow), the S-flag (sign), the Z-flag (zero), the A-flag (auxiliary carry) and the C-flag (carry). The P-flag indicates the parity of a result and three other bits are used to control processor actions like the direction in which movements of large blocks of data is to take place. The rest of the bits in the flags register are unused (Fig. 2.3).

Some instructions (but not all) affect the flags register. For example, the program fragment

```
MOV AX,2
SUB AX,2
```

would set the Z-flag to 1 indicating that the result of SUB AX,2 was 0 whereas

```
MOV AX,3
SUB AX,2
```

would set the Z-flag to 0 indicating that the result of SUB AX,2 was not 0. Remember:

If the Z-flag = 0 it means that the result of the last instruction which affected the Z-flag was not 0.

If the Z-flag = 1 it means that the result of the last instruction which affected the Z-flag was 0.

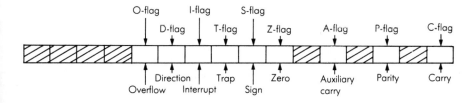

Fig. 2.3 The flags register.

Testing if registers CX and DX both contained the same number would therefore involve subtracting the contents of one register from the other and checking to see if the result was 0, this latter check being carried out by inspecting the Z-flag.

The sign flag or S-flag is set to 1 by certain instructions if the result produced is negative, otherwise it is set to 0. Thus, the program fragment

```
MOV AX,2
SUB AX,5
```

would set the S-flag to 1 and the Z-flag to 0. The carry flag, or C-flag, records whether certain instructions produce a number which was too big (or too small) to be held in the specified register or memory location. Thus, after

```
MOV AX,0FFFFH
ADD AX,2H
```

the C-flag will be set to 1.

Some instructions do not affect *any* of the flags; others affect all the flags we have mentioned. Remembering which instructions affect which flags comes with practice since there is no obvious pattern: ADD and SUB affect all the arithmetic flags but INC and DEC affect all of them except the carry flag; MOV affects *none* of the flags. Full details of which instructions affect which flags can be found in Appendix IV.

2.3 JUMPS

Jump instructions allow the 8088 to take decisions according to information provided by the flags register. For example, if registers AX and BX contain the ASCII code for the same letter then do one thing, if not then do another.

Generally speaking, instructions in an assembly language program are obeyed one after another. Jumps enable execution to continue either from an instruction further on in the program:

```
              :
          MOV AX,3
          SUB BX,AX
          JZ   MISSLOTS
          INC DX      ;obey this and the following
              :       ;instructions only if BX and AX
              :       ;do not contain the same value
MISSLOTS: MOV CX,DX
              :
```

or to continue from an earlier instruction:

```
               :
               :
BACKAGAIN: MOV BX,DX
               :
               :
               :
           SUB DX,AX
           JZ  BACKAGAIN
           INC DX
               :
               :
               :
```

In each case the jump instruction is of the form

JZ <label>

which means 'if the Z-flag is set to 1, then jump to the instruction labelled <label> and continue execution from there.' Another interpretation is 'jump to <label> if the result of the last instruction to affect the Z-flag was 0.'

The <label> is a luxury facility available thanks to assembly language. In machine code jump instructions you must *either* specify the precise place in the computer where the instruction you want to jump to can be found *or* indicate how many instructions before or after the current one you want to jump. During the conversion process from assembly language to machine code all the <label>s in jump instructions are replaced by the appropriate numbers. To make this conversion possible, there are certain rules concerning the way in which <label>s are made up. A <label> must contain only alphabetic characters (A, B, . . . , Z, a, b, . . . , z), digits (1, 2, 3, 4, . . . , 9) or underline characters (_) and begin with an alphabetic character. <label>s can be as long as you like though the assembler cannot differentiate between two labels both beginning with the same 31 characters. Thus,

```
process_gr
remove_12
step_19
list56
```

are allowable <label>s but

```
3rdmonth
tues+weds
mylabelwhichcontains;asemicolon
```

are not.

An example program using jump instructions

Let us write an assembly language program for the 8088 to compare the contents of registers AX and BX. If they both contain the same number we'll put a 1 in register DX; otherwise we'll put a 0 in DX. Further, suppose that the contents of both AX and BX is to be unaltered at the end of the program. The following satisfies our design constraints. (It is certainly not the best program possible but has been chosen to illustrate the use of jump instructions.)

```
        MOV CX,AX  ;take a copy of the contents of AX as the next
                   ;instruction will destroy what's in AX
        SUB AX,BX
        JZ  MAKE1  ;if AX and BX contain the same code, the previous
                   ;instruction will set the Z-flag to 1 and so
                   ;this instruction will cause execution to
                   ;continue from the instruction labelled MAKE1
        MOV DX,0   ;otherwise execution continues sequentially, so
                   ;set DX to 0 indicating that the contents of AX
                   ;and BX were different
        JMP RESET  ;jump unconditionally to the instruction labelled
                   ;RESET (this is to avoid obeying the
                   ;following instruction automatically)
MAKE1:  MOV DX,1   ;we only obey this instruction if the contents
                   ;of AX and BX were the same
RESET:  MOV AX,CX  ;restore the original contents of AX from CX
```

The 8088 has 18 different kinds of conditional jump instructions allowing the execution sequence to be altered depending on whether the result of the last instruction was zero, non-zero, above zero, below zero, less than or equal to zero and so on. These are summarized in Table 2.1. It is not always necessary to remember what each jump instruction looks for in the flags register before deciding whether to jump or not since the mnemonics give the effect of each one. Thus JA is Jump if Above zero.

In the table, CF stands for the Carry Flag, ZF for the Zero Flag and so on. Under 'flags tested' an entry of the form

(CF or ZF) = 0

means that the jump is made if either one of CF and ZF is currently set to 0.

EXERCISES 2.2

1. Write an assembly language program fragment which puts the ASCII code for the letter Y in register DX if the sum of the contents of registers AX and BX is the same as the current contents of register CX. If not, put the ASCII code for N in register DX. Lastly, put 0 in registers AX, BX and CX.

Table 2.1 8088 conditional jumps and the flags tested by them.

	Flags tested	Jump if
JA/JNBE	(CF or ZF)=0	Above/not below or equal
JAE/JNB	CF=0	Above or equal/not below
JB/JNAE/JC	CF=1	Below/not above or equal/carry
JBE/JNA	(CF or ZF)=1	Below or equal/not above
JE/JZ	ZF=1	Equal/zero
JNC	CF=0	No carry
JNE/JNZ	ZF=0	Not equal/not zero
JNO	OF=0	Not overflow
JNP/JPO	PF=0	No parity/parity odd
JNS	SF=0	No sign/positive
JO	OF=1	Overflow
JP/JPE	PF=1	Parity/parity even
JS	SF=1	Sign
JG/JNLE	ZF=0 and SF=OF	Greater/not less nor equal
JGE/JNL	SF=OF	Greater or equal/not less
JL/JNGE	SF< >OF	Less/not greater nor equal
JLE/JNG	(ZF=1)or(SF< >OF)	Less or equal/not greater
JCXZ	none	CX is equal to zero

2. Given that on entry register AX contains 3H and register BX contains 4H, what will be the contents of registers AX, BX and CX after execution of the following program fragment:

```
        MOV CX,0
AGAIN:  ADD CX,AX
        DEC BX
        JZ  DONE
        JMP AGAIN
DONE:   MOV AX,0
        MOV BX,0
```

If registers AX and BX contained 2H and 5H respectively, can you say what registers AX, BX and CX would contain after execution of the above program fragment without doing any more work?

3. Write an assembly language program which will examine the contents of register AX and leave 0 in register DX if the contents of AX is less than or equal to 47H and leave 0FFH in register DX otherwise. The program should preserve the contents of register AX, i.e. after the program has been run the contents of AX should be the same as at the beginning.

2.4 EIGHT 'NEW' REGISTERS

Actually, this section could have been entitled 'New Lamps for Old' because the promised eight new registers actually come from our four familiar ones, AX, BX, CX and DX. We already know that each of these is a 16-bit register, but the 8088 allows each of them to be used as two 8-bit registers as well. The left-most eight bits of AX form an 8-bit register, AH, and the right-most eight bits of AX form an 8-bit register, AL. Similarly, we get BH and BL from BX, CH and CL from CX, and DH and DL from DX (see Fig. 7.1).

One can use instructions like: MOV AL,BH; MOV DL,CL; MOV BH,3; ADD BL,DH; and ADD DL,DH, which have effects similar to those for their 16-bit register equivalents. However, any instruction must either operate entirely with 8-bit registers or entirely with 16-bit registers. Thus, MOV AX,DL is NOT allowed. (By the way, the H in AH stands for High and the L in AL stands for Low since if AX contains a 16-bit number, AH will contain the highest order bits and AL the lowest.)

Danger – ambiguity

There is now the risk of confusion as to whether

```
MOV DL,AH
```

means 'copy the contents of register AH into register DL' or 'put the hexadecimal number A into register DL'. To eliminate such ambiguity there is a rule in assembly language programming that all hexadecimal numbers beginning with a letter (e.g. A123H and E1FCH) must be written with a zero preceding them (so that our examples become 0A123H and 0E1FCH). Hence 'copy the contents of register AH into register DL' is now unambiguously

```
MOV DL,AH
```

and 'put the hexadecimal number A into register DL' becomes

```
MOV DL,0AH
```

2.5 GETTING AT THE INDIVIDUAL BITS OF A REGISTER

We have seen that the contents of a register like AX can be thought of as a signed or unsigned number and as the ASCII code for some character. There is a third important way of viewing the 16 binary digits in a register where each bit gives certain information depending on its position in the register. For example, the 16 bits could represent the result of an electronic quality control test on 16 product items – a 1 in a particular position indicating that the corresponding item was satisfactory, a 0 indicating failure. Thus, if the contents of AX was

0000100100000010

then items 5, 8 and 15 were faulty (numbering from the left-hand side). Accessing individual bits is also useful when the microcomputer containing the 8088 is being used to control an external device – a set of traffic lights, for example.

The logical family

The 8088 has several instructions which enable one to process information of this kind including AND, OR, NOT, XOR and TEST. An instruction

```
AND AX,BX
```

changes the contents of register AX in the following way. The contents of registers AX and BX are combined bit by bit. If in a given position both AX and BX contain a 1 then the result of AND AX,BX will have a 1 in that position, otherwise there will be a 0. For example,

Contents of AX	0000101011100011
Contents of BX	1001100000100001
Contents of AX after AND AX,BX	0000100000100001

(the result has a 1 only in those
positions in which both AX and BX
contain a 1)

The AND instruction affects all the arithmetic flags and can be used to check if the bit in a particular position is 0 or 1. To check if the bit in position 9 of register AX is a 1 we would first put 0000000010000000B into register BX and then execute an AND AX,BX instruction. Because of all the 0s in register BX the result of the AND can have at most one non-zero entry – in position 9. If AX contains a 1 in that position, so will the result which will then be 0000000010000000B, otherwise the result will be 0. Hence, if after AND AX,BX register AX is 0 (in which case the Z-flag will be set to 1) then there was a *0* in position 9 of register AX initially and if not then there was a *1* in that position.

This is an instance of a general technique called **masking**. As another example, let us consider the problem of recouping the numeric value from the ASCII code for a digit. Consider Table 2.2 and notice the correlation between the last two columns.

Whenever a digit is typed in at a computer keyboard, the ASCII code for that digit will end up in a register which we will suppose to be register CX. Before the value of that digit can be used in a calculation it must be transformed from ASCII into a numeric format. One method of effecting this transformation would be to enter 0000000000001111B into register BX and execute an AND CX,BX which will leave the numerical value of the

Table 2.2   Recouping a numeric value from an ASCII code.

Decimal digit	ASCII code		16-bit unsigned number with same value as the decimal digit
	Hex	Binary	
0	30H =	0011 0000	0000 0000 0000 0000
1	31H =	0011 0001	0001
2	32H =	0011 0000	0000
3	33H =	0011 0011	0011
4	34H =	0011 0100	0100
5	35H =	0011 0101	0101
6	36H =	0011 0110	0110
7	37H =	0011 0111	0111
8	38H =	0011 1000	1000
9	39H =	0011 1001	0000 0000 0000 1001

digit in register CX. For example, if register CX contains the ASCII code for the digit 7:

Contents of CX	00000000 0011 0111
Contents of BX	00000000 0000 1111
Contents of CX after AND CX,BX (an unsigned binary number equivalent to decimal 7)	00000000 0000 0111

As advertised earlier, there are two other bit manipulating instructions which we would like to mention at this point – OR and NOT. An instruction OR AX,BX changes the contents of register AX in the following way. The contents of registers AX and BX are compared bit by bit. If in a given position either AX or BX contains a 1 then the result of OR AX,BX will have a 1 in that position, otherwise a 0. For example,

Contents of AX	0011001101011010
Contents of BX	0101010100000111
Contents of AX after OR AX,BX	0111011101011111

Whilst the AND and OR instructions operate with two registers, NOT requires only one. NOT BX, for example, simply changes every bit in BX which is a 1 to a 0 and every 0 to a 1:

Initial contents of BX	0101111100001001
Contents of BX after NOT BX	1010000011110110

The format of the XOR instruction is exactly the same as that of the OR. An instruction

```
XOR AX,BX
```

changes the contents of register AX in the following way. The contents of registers AX and BX are combined bit by bit. If in a given position both AX and BX contain a 1 or both AX and BX contain a 0 then the result of XOR AX,BX will have a 0 in that position, otherwise there will be a 1. In other words, after XOR AX,BX register AX will have a 1 in a given position if either AX or BX has a 1 in that position, but not both (XOR stands for eXclusive OR). For example,

Contents of AX	0010001001001111
Contents of BX	1010111000110001
Contents of AX after XOR AX,BX	1000110001111110

The TEST instruction is very similar to the AND instruction in that they both have the same format and both perform the same operation between their operands but TEST only changes the flags. Thus,

	AH	*DL*	*Z-flag*
Before	01010011	10001100	?
After AND DL,AH	01010011	00000000	1
After TEST DL,AH	01010011	10001100	1

Uses of the logical family instructions – a summary

Table 2.3 summarizes the uses of the logical family instructions.

The shift family

Because the 8088 works with binary numbers, it can easily provide facilities for multiplying and dividing a signed or unsigned number by 2. As we shall see in the final section of Chapter 4 – which deals with issues of efficiency – it turns out that these special facilities work much faster than using the ordinary multiply and divide instructions.

The principle used is an easy one. Consider Table 2.4. In the binary column, the first three entries differ only in that entry 2 is the first entry shifted left one bit and entry 3 is the second entry shifted left one bit. From the decimal column we see that the decimal equivalents of these binary entries double after each left shift. On the other hand, binary column entries 4 to 8 (inclusive) differ only by a shift right of one bit and the corresponding decimal values are halved after each right shift.

There are two different sets of 8088 shift instructions, one set for doubling and halving unsigned binary numbers, the other for doubling and halving signed binary numbers. The instructions which perform the doubling and halving of unsigned numbers are SHL (SHift Left) and SHR (SHift Right). SHL doubles an unsigned number by shifting all bits one position to

Table 2.3 Logical family instructions.

Instruction	Uses
AND	Setting specified bit position of the first operand to 0, the other operand specifying the bit positions. Thus, AND BH,00011100B will set bits 1, 2, 3, 7 and 8 of BH to 0 leaving the others unchanged.
OR	Setting specified bit positions of the first operand to 1, the other operand specifying the bit positions. Thus, OR CL,11000000B will set bits 1 and 2 of CL to 1 leaving the others unchanged.
NOT	Changing every bit in its operand to the opposite of what they were initially.
XOR	Changing specified bits of its first operand to the opposite of their current settings, the other operand specifying the bit positions. Thus, XOR AH,00000011B will change bits 7 and 8 of AH to the opposite of their previous setting and leave the others unchanges.
TEST	Testing whether specified bit positions of the first operand are set to 0, the other operand specifying the bit positions. Thus, TEST DL,01010101B will set the Z-flag to 1 only if bits 2, 4, 6 and 8 of DL are all 0.

the left and filling in the vacated right-most bit with a 0. In order to test if the doubling has resulted in a number which is too big to be represented in the number of bits available in the particular register or memory location being operated on, the bit which is shifted out of the left-hand end is moved into the carry flag.

The general form of the SHL instruction is:

SHL register/memory,1

Example 1

a) Suppose that register AL contains 01001010B and that we execute the 8088 instruction:

```
SHL AL,1
```

After execution the contents of AL will be 10010100B and the carry flag will be set to 0.

b) If register CX contains 1001001001101110B, then after execution of

```
SHL CX,1
```

CX will contain 0010010011011100B and the carry flag will be set to 1.

Table 2.4 Binary and decimal equivalents.

Entry	Binary	Decimal
1	00010101	21
2	00101010	42
3	01010100	84
4	00110000	48
5	00011000	24
6	00001100	12
7	00000110	6
8	00000011	3

Halving unsigned numbers is carried out via the SHR instruction which has the general form:

SHR register/memory,1

and operates by shifting all bits one position to the right, filling the then vacated left-most position with a 0 and placing the bit that was shifted off the right-hand end into the carry flag. In this case, the carry flag being set to 1 indicates that the number just halved was not even (and therefore that the 'halving' is only approximate).

Example 2

a) If register DX contains 0101000010000110B before execution of

   SHR DX,1

   then after execution DX will contain 0010100001000011B and the carry flag will be set to 0.

b) With register BL containing 01100111B, the execution of

   SHR BL,1

   will leave 00110011B in BL and the carry flag will be set to 1 (01100111 in binary is equivalent to decimal 207).

Doubling and halving signed numbers involves the slight extra complication of ensuring that the sign of the number does not get changed. Thus, doubling +8 (00001000) should result in +16 (00010000) and doubling −20 (111101011) should result in −40 (111010110). Likewise, halving +6 (00000110) should give +3 (00000011) and halving −120 (10001000) should give −60 (11000100). SAL (Shift Arithmetic Left) doubles signed numbers and SAR (Shift Arithmetic Right) halves them. These instructions have the general form:

SAL register/memory,1
SAR register/memory,1

SAL operates in precisely the same way as SHL, since the sign bit of a positive signed number is 0. It is up to the programmer to ensure that the result of such doubling is in range (for otherwise doubling a positive signed number like 01101100 may well result in a negative signed number, namely 11011000). In general, it is better if the programmer plans in advance to avoid such an eventuality, but on occasions planning ahead is impossible. In these cases the S-flag (the Sign flag) enables detection of the phenomenon, for when the SAL or SAR instruction is executed the S-flag is set to 0 or 1 corresponding to the sign of the result.

SAR halves signed binary numbers by shifting all bits one position to the right but at the same time leaving the sign bit unchanged (see Table 2.5).

Quadrupling, octupling and all that

All four instructions have another form which allows shifting arbitrarily many places left or right at a time. Shifting left two bits corresponds to multiplying by 4D and shifting left 5 bits to multiplying by 32D. Shifting right two bits corresponds to dividing by 4D and shifting right 6 bits to dividing by 64D. In each case the only change to the instruction format is the addition of a register to hold the (unsigned) number of places to shift. This register must be CL:

    SHL register/memory,CL
    SHR register/memory,CL
    SAL register/memory,CL
    SAR register/memory,CL

Table 2.5   Effect of SAR.

Contents of AL before execution of SAR AL		Contents of AL after execution of SAR AL	
Binary	Decimal	Binary	Decimal
01101100	+108	00110110	+54
00101011	+43	00010101	+21
10000010	−126	11000001	−63
10101111	−81	11010111	−41
11000010	−62	11100001	−31

Notice that halving a signed number always results in a signed number which is less than or equal to half the given number. Hence, when an odd number like +43 is halved via an SAR instruction the result is +21, and similarly halving −81 gives −41.

EXERCISES 2.3

1. Write and test an 8088 assembly language program to multiply the unsigned number in the AL register by 10D using shift instructions. Assume that the result can be represented as an 8-bit unsigned number. (Hint: calculate eight times the contents of AL and twice the contents of AL and add.)

2. Expand the program you developed for Exercise 1 so that the result is left as an unsigned 16-bit number in AX and the program works for any unsigned number in AL. (Hint: shift one bit at a time and use the carry flag to make decisions about the contents of AH after each shift.)

3. Repeat Exercises 1 and 2 for division by 8D.

The rotate family

When a 4-bit shift left is performed, the 4 left-most bits 'fall off the end' and are lost forever (one of them may possibly end up in the carry flag). There are occasions when we do not wish to throw away information with such abandon. The rotate family of instructions provides the ability to rearrange bits without losing information. ROL (Rotate Left) and ROR (Rotate Right) permit left or right rotation of the bits respectively and the bit which falls off one end is rotated around to fill the vacated position at the other end. Thus, if AL contains 01010111 then execution of ROR AL,1 will leave 10101011 in AL.

Because the flags are not involved in the rotation it is difficult to keep track of a particular bit and so there are alternative forms of the rotate

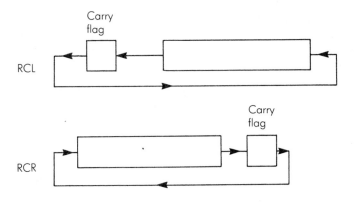

Fig. 2.4 The RCL and RCR instructions.

instructions involving the carry flag. Thus, RCL (Rotate through Carry Left) and RCR (Rotate through Carry Right) include the carry flag in the rotation: the bit that falls off one end goes into the carry flag, the bit that was in the carry flag goes into the vacated bit (Fig. 2.4). The rotate family instructions take the following general forms:

RCL memory/register,1
RCL memory/register,CL
RCR memory/register,1
RCR memory/register,CL

(and similarly for ROL and ROR).

2.6 MAKING TRACES

Following through the execution of any assembly language program consisting of more than a couple of lines can be a difficult undertaking. It helps to keep a **trace** of register contents. As a demonstration of this technique we now give an assembly language program involving AND, OR and NOT together with a trace of its execution. In the trace, an entry '?' will denote a value which we don't know. Thus, the contents of all four registers are indicated as '?' at the beginning of the trace when a particular

Program	Trace			
	AX	BX	CX	DX
	?	?	?	?
MOV AX,0110110110111111	0110110110111111	?	?	?
MOV BX,1010111101010111	0110110110111111	1010111101010111	?	?
MOV CX,0	0110110110111111	1010111101010111	0	?
AND AX,BX	0010110100010111	1010111101010111	0	?
OR AX,BX	1010111101010111	1010111101010111	0	?
JZ EXIT	1010111101010111	1010111101010111	0	?
NOT BX	1010111101010111	0101000010101000	0	?
AND AX,BX	0000000000000000	0101000010101000	0	?
JZ CHANGE				
MOV DX,1				
JMP EXIT				
CHANGE:MOV DX,0	0000000000000000	0101000010101000	0	0
EXIT: MOV CX,1	0000000000000000	0101000010101000	1	0

Fig. 2.5 Making a program trace.

program makes no assumption about the contents of registers before it is executed.

To make the trace we simply write down the contents of each of the registers before the program starts and then again after each instruction has been executed (Fig. 2.5).

EXERCISES 2.4

1. By making a careful trace determine the contents of all the registers involved in each of the following program fragments.

a)
```
         MOV AX,0001110001110001B
         MOV BX,1110001110001111B
         AND AX,BX
         NOT AX
         OR  AX,BX
         NOT BX
         JZ  NEWTRY
         AND BX,AX
         NOT BX
         JMP EXIT
 NEWTRY: AND AX,BX
   EXIT: NOT AX
```

b)
```
         MOV AX,38H
         MOV BX,2ABH
         MOV CX,10ABH
         AND AX,BX
         AND BX,CX
         NOT CX
         OR  CX,BX
```

(Hint: first work out the binary form of what goes into AX, BX and CX at the beginning.)

c)
```
         MOV AL,0H
         MOV BL,34H
         MOV CL,35H
         MOV DL,0FH
         AND BL,DL
         AND CL,DL
  AGAIN: ADD AL,BL
         DEC CL
         JZ  DONE
         JMP AGAIN
```

```
        DONE:  ADD  BL,30H
               ADD  CL,30H
```

Can you describe the action of this program fragment in words?

d)
```
               MOV  CX,1H
               MOV  DX,1H
               MOV  AX,0AH
        LOOP:  ADD  CX,DX
               DEC  AX
               ADD  DX,CX
               DEC  AX
               JNZ  LOOP
```

By inspection of the successive contents of registers CX and DX can you deduce what this program has got to do with rabbits?

2.7 INSTRUCTIONS WHICH AFFECT MEMORY

So far our programs have only used some of the 8088 registers and flags. Any 'real' program will necessitate the use of memory to store (possibly large amounts of) data. Computer memory is best thought of as a collection of numbered pigeon holes (called **locations**), each capable of storing 8 binary digits (i.e. a byte), as in Fig. 2.6.

Data can be retrieved from memory one or two bytes at a time. The instruction

```
    MOV  AL,[20H]
```

will transfer the *contents* of location 20H into register AL whereas the instruction

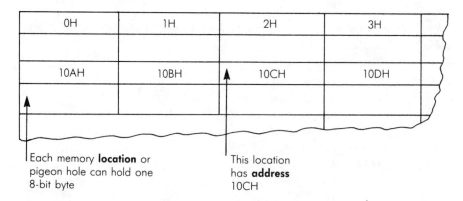

0H	1H	2H	3H	
10AH	10BH	10CH	10DH	

Each memory **location** or pigeon hole can hold one 8-bit byte

This location has **address** 10CH

Fig. 2.6 Computer memory. (Notice that the pigeon holes are numbered from zero onwards.)

```
MOV BX,[20H]
```

will transfer the contents of locations 20H and 21H into BX. The symbol [20H] is read as 'the contents of location 20H' to distinguish between

```
MOV AL,20H    (put the hexadecimal number 20H in AL)
```

and

```
MOV AL,[20H] (put the contents of location 20H in AL)
```

Storing data in memory can also be done one or two bytes at a time. MOV [20H],CL would copy the contents of register CL into location 20H; MOV [20H],DX would copy the contents of register DX into locations 20H and 21H. If register AX contained 2A8BH and the instruction

```
MOV [20H],AX
```

were executed, location 20H would contain 8BH and location 21H would contain 2AH. It is rarely the case that the programmer needs to be aware of this as moving data the other way – from memory to register – reverses this 'swap', as in Fig. 2.7.

Changing addresses

Varying an address whilst a program is running involves specifying the location concerned in a register. The following program adds 1 to each of the 8-bit numbers stored in locations 200H–202H inclusive. At the core of the program is the instruction

```
MOV AL,[BX]
```

which moves into AL the contents of the location whose address is given in register BX, and its counterpart

```
MOV [BX],AL
```

which saves what's in register AL as the contents of the location whose address is given in BX.

Once again this isn't necessarily the best or easiest way of going about the task – our choice of instructions has been dominated by the desire to explain.

```
             MOV BX,200H      ;BX will specify the location to
                              ;be worked on
             MOV CX,3H        ;CX will maintain a count of how
                              ;many more locations to be done
ALTER_NEXT: MOV AL,[BX]
             INC AL
             MOV [BX],AL      ;the preceding 3 instructions
                              ;add 1 to the contents of the
```

```
                              ;location whose address is given
                              ;in BX
          INC BX              ;advance BX to the next location
          DEC CX              ;one less location to be done
                              ;now
          JNZ ALTER_NEXT      ;do some more unless none left
                              ;to do
```

Assuming that before this program is run locations 200H–202H have the contents

Location	200H	201H	202H
Contents	2A	B4	51

then a trace of the execution of the program will look like Fig. 2.8.

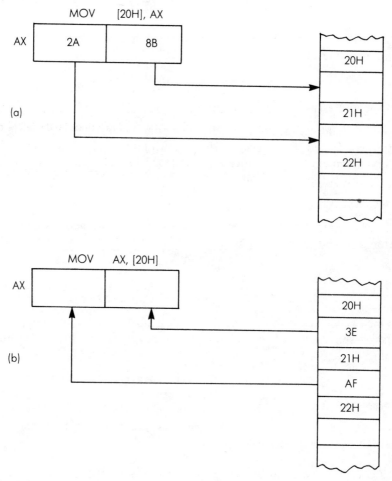

Fig. 2.7 Storing data in memory: (a) MOV [20H],AX; (b) MOV AX,[20H].

				Location	
AL	BX	CX	200H	201H	202H
?	200	?	2A	B4	51
?	200	3	2A	B4	51
2A	200	3	2A	B4	51
2B	200	3	2A	B4	51
2B	200	3	2B	B4	51
2B	201	3	2B	B4	51
2B	201	2	2B	B4	51
B4	201	2	2B	B4	51
B5	201	2	2B	B4	51
B5	201	2	2B	B5	51
B5	202	2	2B	B5	51
B5	202	1	2B	B5	51
51	202	1	2B	B5	51
52	202	1	2B	B5	51
52	202	1	2B	B5	52
52	203	1	2B	B5	52
52	203	0	2B	B5	52

Fig. 2.8 Trace of program to increment the contents of locations 200H–202H by 1.

There are corresponding instructions whereby two bytes are moved instead of one. For example,

```
MOV AX,[BX]
```

transfers two bytes, one from the location whose address is given in register BX and one from the location after that.

2.8 PROGRAMS WHICH AFFECT MEMORY – SOME EXAMPLES

Example 1

A program to swap the contents of locations 20H and 21H is:

```
MOV AL,[20H]
MOV BL,[21H]
MOV [20H],BL
MOV [21H],AL
```

Example 2

A program to store 0 in locations 200H–300H inclusive. (This is part of a technique used to test if the memory chips in a microcomputer are working

	AX	BX	CX	DX
MOV BX,200H	?	200	?	?
MOV CX,28H	?	200	28	?
MOV DX,0	?	200	28	0
NEXTLOC: MOV AX,[BX]	B52A	200	28	0
SUB AX,127H	B403	200	28	0
JNZ MISSING_COUNT				
INC DX	B403	201	28	0
MISSING_COUNT: INC BX	B403	202	28	0
INC BX	B403	202	27	0
DEC CX	0127	202	27	0
JZ DONE	0	202	27	0
JMP NEXTLOC	0	202	27	1
DONE:				
	0	203	27	1
	0	203	26	1
	1B6C	203	26	1
	1A45	203	26	1
	1A45	205	26	1
	1A45	206	26	1
	1A45	206	25	1
	etc.			

Fig. 2.9 Program and trace to count occurrences of 16-bit numbers.

properly. Every location is filled with 0 and then after a fraction of a second pause the content of each location is checked to verify it is still set at 0. If not, then one of the chips is malfunctioning.)

Since locations 200H–300H inclusive are to be filled, there are 101H locations to fill. (Compare this with being asked to deliver mail to addresses 0 to 7 – if you do you'll visit 8 houses in total.)

```
                MOV BX,200H      ;BX records the address of the next
                                 ;location to be done
                MOV CX,101H      ;CX will keep a count of the
                                 ;number of locations left to do
DO_ANOTHER:     MOV [BX],0H      ;fill the location
                INC BX           ;move on to the next address
                DEC CX           ;one less to do now
                JNZ DO_ANOTHER
```

Example 3

Counting the number of occurrences of a given 16-bit number. If locations 200H–24FH inclusive contain 28H 16-bit numbers (i.e. 28H numbers having

		AX	BX	CX
	MOV AX,0	0	?	?
	MOV BX,500H	0	500	?
	MOV CX,28H	0	500	28
ADD_IN_NEXT:	ADD AX,[BX]	100	500	28
	INC BX			
	INC BX	100	501	28
	DEC CX	100	502	28
	JNZ ADD_IN_NEXT	100	502	27
		200	502	27
		200	503	27
		200	504	27
		200	504	26
		0E2	504	26
		0E2	505	26
		02E	506	26
		etc.		

Fig. 2.10 Program (and trace) to total 16-bit numbers stored in memory.

4 hexadecimal digits), the program below will count the number of them which are equal to 0127H.

In order to give part of a trace for the program we will assume that the contents of locations 200H–205H are as follows:

Location	200	201	202	203	204	205
Contents	2A	B5	27	01	6C	1B

Thus, as far as the 8088 is concerned, the 16-bit number in locations 200H and 201H is 0B52AH; that in 202H and 203H is 0127H; and that in 204H and 205H is 1B6CH (Fig. 2.9).

Example 4

Making a total of 16-bit numbers stored in memory. If locations 500H to 54FH contain 28H 16-bit numbers, the program below will add up these numbers and leave the total in register AX.

The program makes use of the instruction

```
ADD AX,[BX]
```

which takes the two bytes stored at the address given in register BX as a 16-bit number (stored back to front) and then adds that number to the contents of register AX leaving the answer in AX.

		Location	Location
Before	AX: 0115	2011	2012
	BX: 2011	3A	1B
After	AX: 1C4F		
	(since 0115H + 1B3AH = 1C4FH)		

In order that a partial trace of the execution of the totalling program (Fig. 2.10) can be given we assume that the contents of locations 500H–505H before execution are as follows:

Location	500	501	502	503	504	505
Contents	00	01	00	01	E2	00

Example 5

The next example is a bit academic but illustrates how 16-bit numbers are stored in memory. The program will store 0H as a 16-bit number in locations 200H,201H; 2H in locations 202H,203H; 4H in locations 204H,205H; and so on, up until 200H has been stored in 400H and 401H (Fig. 2.11).

					Memory locations					
		BX	AX	CX	200	201	202	203	204	205
	MOV BX,200H	200	?	?	?	?	?	?	?	?
	MOV AX,0H	200	0	?	?	?	?	?	?	?
	MOV CX,100H	200	0	100	?	?	?	?	?	?
NEXT_LOC:	MOV [BX],AX	200	0	100	0	0	?	?	?	?
	INC BX									
	INC BX	201	0	100	0	0	?	?	?	?
	INC AX	202	0	100	0	0	?	?	?	?
	INC AX	202	1	100	0	0	?	?	?	?
	DEC CX	202	2	100	0	0	?	?	?	?
	JNZ NEXT_LOC	202	2	0FF	0	0	?	?	?	?
		202	2	0FF	0	0	2	0	?	?
		203	2	0FF	0	0	2	0	?	?
		204	2	0FF	0	0	2	0	?	?
		204	3	0FF	0	0	2	0	?	?
		204	4	0FF	0	0	2	0	?	?
		204	4	0FE	0	0	2	0	?	?
		204	4	0FE	0	0	2	0	4	0
				etc.						

Fig. 2.11 Program and trace storing 16-bit numbers in memory.

EXERCISES 2.5

Write 8088 assembly language program fragments to achieve each of the following tasks.

1. Fill locations 200H, 202H, 204H, . . . , 300H inclusive with 0FFH.

2. Swap the contents of location 200H with those of location 300H, those of 201 with 2FFH, etc. Thus:

	Location	Contents		Location	Contents
	200	2A		200	3F
	201	56		201	AB
Before	:	:	After	:	:
	2FF	AB		2FF	56
	300	3F		300	2A

3. Count the number of locations in the range 200H–300H inclusive which contain the ASCII code for the letter X.

4. Locations 200H–03FFH inclusive contain 100H 16-bit numbers. Leave in register AX the number of them which are equal to 1984H.

5. Store 500H in locations 200H,201H
         4FEH   "   "   202H,203H
         4FCH   "   "   204H,205H
         :   :
         302H   "   "   3FEH,3FFH

2.9 ADDRESSING MEMORY AND THE DS REGISTER

The 8088 can address a total of 1,048,576 bytes (1 Megabyte) of memory with locations numbered from 0 to 1,048,575. Rather than representing each address as a 20-bit unsigned number, memory is thought of as being divided up into **segments** each of which contains 2^{16} locations. In this way an address can be thought of as consisting of two parts: a 16-bit segment address and a 16-bit **offset** from the start of that segment. Thus, 020A:1BCD denotes offset 1BCDH from segment 020AH. The actual address it refers to is obtained in the following way:

1. Add a zero to the right-hand side of the segment address.   020A0H

2. Add to this the offset.   1BCDH

                                  Total: 03C6DH

Hence the actual address referred to by 020A:1BCD is 03C6DH.

In respect of instructions which address memory we have to admit to telling a little white lie. The actual address from which data is fetched when an instruction like

```
MOV AL,[200H]
```

is obeyed is not location 200H but location 200H *relative to the contents of the Data Segment register.* Any explicit address specified in an 8088 instruction is, in fact, taken relative to the Data Segment (DS) register contents. Loading the DS register cannot be done in the same way as loading any other register; DS must be loaded indirectly. Thus,

```
MOV BX,500H
MOV DS,BX
```

would set the DS register to 500H. Usually the computer's operating system sets the DS register to a suitable value before a program is run. It (the operating system!) decides where in memory to locate our programs. By setting the DS register with a MOV instruction like the one above it is possible to insist on using a collection of specific locations but it is rare that one wants to do this. On the contrary, at this stage of our knowledge of the 8088 we are only too grateful for all the help the operating system can provide.

To calculate the actual address used by the second instruction of

```
MOV BX,500H
MOV DS,BX
MOV AL,[200H]
```

we proceed as follows:

1. Add a zero to the right-hand side
    of the contents of the DS register.   5000H
2. Add to that the address given.   200H
                                              ———————
                                        Total: 5200H

Thus, the actual location accessed by the MOV AL,[200H] instruction is 5200H in this case. In the following program fragment, the right-hand column shows in parentheses the actual location(s) addressed by each instruction in hexadecimal.

```
MOV BX,1275H
MOV DS,BX
MOV AX,5H
MOV DX,17H
MOV BH,[100H]    (12750 + 100   = 12850)
MOV BL,[30H]     (12750 +  30   = 12780)
MOV CX,[BX]      (12750 +  17   = 12767 and
                  12750 +  18   = 12768)
ADD BX,CX
```

```
ADD AX,BX
MOV [75H],AX      (12750 +   75   = 127C5 and
                   12750 +   76   = 127C6)
MOV [204H],BL     (12750 +  204   = 12954)
MOV [31A5H],BH    (12750 + 31A5 = 158F5)
```

The operating system also decides where in memory our machine code programs will be stored. Storage of instructions is done relative to the CS (Code Segment) register in the same way that data is stored relative to the DS register. At any instant, the address of the next instruction to be executed is given in a 16-bit register, the IP (Instruction Pointer) register, relative to the contents of CS. In normal execution of a program instructions are automatically fetched from memory by the 8088 so we don't have to worry about CS and IP.

BX is special

There's no equivalent of the [BX] part of instructions like

```
MOV CX,[BX]
```

for registers AX, CX and DX. For example,

```
MOV CX,[DX] ;is illegal
```

is not allowed because of the [DX]. Only register BX may be used in this way.

EXERCISE 2.6

For each of the following pairs of addresses given in segment:offset form, decide if the two addresses correspond to the same memory location.

a) 74D6:0100   74C6:0110

b) 4E50:F10F   4C50:0FF0

c) 1234:1234   1358:0040

d) 0500:ABCD   0EB0:10CD

2.10 SUMMARY

In this chapter we have met the four main 16-bit registers of the 8088 (AX, BX, CX, and DX) and their 8-bit counterparts (AH, AL, etc.) and just over a dozen instructions summarized in Table 2.6. We have seen that these are sufficient to write programs with practical applications and have traced the execution of several programs by hand.

Experienced assembly language programmers use hand tracing only as a last resort, viz., when they think an error in one of their programs has been caused by misunderstanding the manner in which the 8088 executes a given instruction. PC-DOS provides an automatic facility for tracing the execution of machine code programs as part of a general purpose tool for finding errors called DEBUG. This will be described in detail in the next chapter along with details of how to assemble and run assembly language programs on the IBM PC.

Table 2.6 Summary of the effect on the flags by instructions introduced (see also Appendix IV)

Instruction	Flag affected				
	Z-flag	C-flag	S-flag	Overflow	Aux./Carry
ADD	Yes	Yes	Yes	Yes	Yes
SUB	Yes	Yes	Yes	Yes	Yes
INC	Yes	No	Yes	Yes	Yes
DEC	Yes	No	Yes	Yes	Yes
AND	Yes	0	Yes	0	Yes
OR	Yes	0	Yes	0	Yes
NOT	Yes	0	Yes	0	Yes
JMP					
JZ					
JNZ	All jump instructions have *no* effect.				
JA					
JB					
MOV	MOV instructions have no effect on flags.				

3 Running and Debugging Programs

AIMS

On completion of this chapter, the reader should be able to get an 8088 assembly language program converted to machine code and executed by the IBM PC and be able to use DEBUG, the PC tool for locating errors in machine code programs. In order to perform the conversion, the PC assembler must be given information other than just the raw 8088 instructions for the task to be carried out. This extra information is given via assembler **pseudo-ops**, several of which are introduced in this chapter.

3.1 RUNNING ASSEMBLY LANGUAGE PROGRAMS

We have already covered enough of the instruction set of the 8088 to enable the reader to write some powerful programs, but we have yet to describe how to get programs into the computer and actually executed by the machine. Neither have we discussed the mechanisms by which a program in assembly language can be tested. Experience with other languages such as Pascal should indicate that programs of any reasonable length will not work first time – a little 'fine tuning' is invariably necessary. With assembly language programming, matters are actually a little worse in that a slight change in the contents of a register may be the only outcome of a program. Without a device which tells you what's going on in the registers and memory it will therefore be impossible to determine if your program has worked! Consequently PC-DOS provides a special tool for debugging assembly language or machine code programs.

When you have written your 8088 assembly language program, three steps are involved in actually getting the program converted to machine code and then executed in such a way that you can check it has performed according to plan:

Step 1   In order that the assembler knows where to store the program and any data, extra statements will have to be added to the bare 8088 instructions. Having added these extra assembler directives, run the assembler program with your prepared assembly language program as input. The output from the assembler will be a machine code version of your assembly language original.

Step 2   As with high-level language programs, a large machine code program is best developed in modules which can be independently tested and then linked together to provide the final desired result. The linking together is done by a program known as the **linker**. Because the assembler outputs machine code in a form suitable for the linker but not ready for immediate execution, even a single program module must be submitted to the linker for final conversion into executable form.

Step 3   Run the executable machine code form of your program under the control of the PC-DOS debugger DEBUG.

Step 1 – preparing for the assembler

MASM and ASM

IBM supply two assemblers for the IBM PC, MASM and ASM. ASM runs on a PC with smaller memory than MASM which requires at least a 92K memory because of the comprehensive facilities it provides. The two are entirely compatible, save that MASM allows the incorporation of **macros** into assembly language programs (see Chapter 9). Henceforth we shall use MASM since it provides more helpful error messages, and assume that the reader's IBM PC has a sufficiently large memory. Users of systems with small memories may use ASM wherever we use MASM, except in a few clearly marked special cases.

File names

MASM requires that your assembly language program is already in a disk file. We shall assume that the reader already knows how to organize this. Using MASM is easiest when the file containing your assembly language program has the second name ASM. Thus you should put programs for conversion into files called

```
EXAMPLE.ASM
CALCS123.ASM
TEST.ASM
```

but *not* in files called

```
JUNK.TYP
WROT37.AB4
DONT.TRY
```

Should you want to, it is possible to over-ride this convention. For details see the IBM Macro Assembler manual.

Extra information for the assembler

When any computer program is executed, both the program and any necessary data must be in memory. Assembly language gives the programmer absolute control over the memory so that exactly where both program and data are stored is the programmer's choice. Normally one would have the program and data stored in completely separate areas of memory so that there is less chance of the program interfering with the data. There are occasions, however, where program and data can be mixed to advantage. To allow for this possibility, MASM insists that what is a program (or **code**) segment of the assembly language be clearly labelled. The **data** segments (in which the allocation and, if necessary, initialization of data storage space is made) must be similarly identified.

Code segments and data segments are distinguished by including assembler **pseudo-ops** in the assembly language program. These aren't 8088 instructions. Rather they are instructions to the assembler itself. Thus in MASM the pseudo-ops SEGMENT. . .ENDS tell the assembler that everything which they enclose belongs to the same segment. In addition, each segment must be given a name following the convention for label names given in Chapter 2. Thus, for example,

```
MYPROGRAM SEGMENT
          MOV AX,4H
          SUB AX,5H
            :
            :
            :
MYPROGRAM ENDS
```

could be the bare bones of a code segment with name MYPROGRAM.

MASM must also be told to which segment register a segment belongs. This is achieved via the ASSUME pseudo-op. Hence, if our program had segments called MYPROGRAM and MYDATA, then

```
ASSUME CS:MYPROGRAM
ASSUME DS:MYDATA
```

would inform MASM that the CS register must be used to calculate all addresses in the MYPROGRAM segment (i.e. MYPROGRAM is a code segment) and that the DS register must be used for address calculation in the MYDATA segment (i.e. MYDATA is a data segment). The alternative form

```
ASSUME CS:MYPROGRAM,DS:MYDATA
```

has the same effect.

Most large programs require temporary working storage and this is provided by means of a **stack** in which items are stored on a **last in, first out** basis, rather like the storage of plates in a cafeteria plate dispenser (see Fig. 3.1). The linker insists that every program has a STACK segment, whether it requires working space or not.

Before   After

Fig. 3.1 The operation of a cafeteria plate dispenser models that of a stack: the plates are removed in the reverse order from that in which they were inserted.

Selection of stack size depends on the particular program. All the programs in this book will be adequately served by a 100H word stack which we shall conventionally allocate in a segment called SSEG. Allocation of storage in any segment is carried out by the **define** pseudo-ops which allow multiples of one (DB – Define Byte), two (DW – Define Word), four (DD – Define Doubleword), eight (DQ – Define Quadword) or even ten (DT – Define Tenbytes) bytes of storage to be allocated and initialized at one time. Thus,

```
DB 16H     ;allocates one byte of store with initial value 16H

DB ?       ;allocates one byte of store with indeterminate initial
           ;value

DB 'Z'     ;allocates one byte of store with initial value the
           ;ASCII code for the letter Z

DB 'HELLO'   ;Allocates five bytes of storage in exactly the
             ;same way as DB  'H'
             ;             DB  'E'
             ;             DB  'L'
             ;             DB  'L'
             ;             DB  'O'

DB 21H,45H,73H, 'A' , 'B' ,11H, 'Z'
                          ;allocates 7 bytes, with
                          ;initial values determined
                          ;just as if 7 separate DB
                          ;pseudo-ops had been used
                          ;one after the other
```

```
DW 1,10,100,1000,10000      ;allocates ten bytes of storage,
                            ;initialized to the signed 16-bit
                            ;forms of 1D, 10D, 100D, 1000D and
                            ;10000D

DD 1294967295D              ;allocates four bytes of storage, MASM
                            ;automatically converting 1294967295D into
                            ;signed 32-bit form and initializing the
                            ;four bytes to that value
```

The DUP(. . .) pseudo-op permits multiple initializations to the same value. Thus we have:

```
DB 10H DUP('A')             ;allocates the next 10H locations with
                            ;initial value 41H (the ASCII code for A)

DB 80H DUP(?)               ;allocates the next 80H locations with
                            ;initial value indeterminate

DW 50H DUP(100D)            ;the next 50H words are set to 0064H
                            ;(the signed 16-bit form of 100D)
```

The stack segment of our programs will have addresses relative to a new segment register – the **SS** register – because 8088 instructions which operate on the stack (see Chapter 4) use SS to calculate actual addresses. Thus, the working store in our programs will be achieved by

```
SSEG SEGMENT STACK
DW    100H DUP(?)
SSEG ENDS
```

and the pseudo-op ASSUME SS:SSEG.

Contents of the assembly language file

Putting all this together, the contents of the file containing the assembly language program to be converted should be as follows:

```
DSEG SEGMENT
Insert here any necessary allocation
and/or initialization of data storage
DSEG ENDS

SSEG SEGMENT STACK
DW    100H DUP(?)
SSEG ENDS

CSEG SEGMENT
ASSUME DS:DSEG,SS:SSEG,CS:CSEG
Insert here the 8088 instructions
to perform the task which is to be
```

carried out
```
CSEG ENDS
END
```

The END pseudo-op denotes the end of the text which MASM is to process.

Conversion to machine code

We now assume that your assembly language program (with all the necessary pseudo-ops) is contained in a file of the right type. For the purposes of illustration we'll assume the file is called IBMEX.ASM. Remember that it's just the name of the file *type* which must be fixed; you can choose the file's first name.

Is everything on the right disk?

It simplifies matters considerably if your assembly language program and the assembler program which is going to do the conversion are both on the same disk in drive A. For practical purposes it's a good idea to make yourself up a disk with MASM, DEBUG, an editor program (EDIT, WORDSTAR or whatever you use) and LINK all on the same disk before you start trying to work in assembly language. (Check that this doesn't break anyone's copyright – one day you may be a software author yourself and value every cent of royalties). From now on we shall assume that this is the case. Moreover we shall assume that you have this disk in disk drive A. Thus, if you issue a DIR A: command to PC-DOS, the response should at least include the following files together with an editor or word-processing program:

```
MASM.EXE
LINK.EXE
DEBUG.COM
```

Invoking the assembler is easy. You type the name of the assembler after the A> operating system prompt, then a space, and then the first name of the file containing your assembly language program and a few extra characters at the end:

```
A>MASM IBMEX,,;
```

Table 3.1   Contents of files created by MASM IBMEX,,;

Name of file	Contents of the file
IBMEX.LST	A printout showing your assembly language program, its machine code equivalent in hexadecimal notation and a list of any errors detected in your assembly language.
IBMEX.OBJ	The machine code equivalent of your assembly language program, not quite in a state in which it can be executed.

Once the assembler has finished its job the 'A>' prompt will be displayed again and two new files will have been created because of the MASM options selected by the two commas and semicolon. The contents of these files are described in Table 3.1.

Step 1 reviewed

Starting with the simple assembly language program

```
MOV AX,67H
MOV BX,51H
ADD AX,BX  ;works out 67H + 51H!!
SUB BX,AX
```

we shall now illustrate the first step in detail. Adding the pseudo-ops needed by MASM gives us:

```
DSEG SEGMENT
DSEG ENDS
SSEG SEGMENT STACK
DW   100H DUP(?)
SSEG ENDS
CSEG SEGMENT
ASSUME DS:DSEG,SS:SSEG,CS:CSEG
      MOV  AX,67H
      MOV  BX,51H
      ADD  AX,BX  ;works out 67H + 51H!!
      SUB  BX,AX
CSEG ENDS
END
```

Putting this into a file of the right type (we'll call it EXAMPLE.ASM), we next invoke the assembler:

```
A>MASM EXAMPLE,,;
```

(PC-DOS supplies the A> prompt. It is only necessary to type in the rest of this command line.) As the conversion proceeds, the messages shown in Fig. 3.2 are printed on the display.

```
The IBM Personal Computer MACRO Assembly
Version 1.00 (C) Copyright IBM Corp 1981

Warning Severe
Errors  Errors
   0       0
```

Fig. 3.2 Messages displayed during conversion of assembly language program to machine code.

```
The IBM Personal Computer MACRO Assembler 01-01-80 Page 1-1

  0000                              DSEG SEGMENT
  0000                              DSEG ENDS

  0000                              SSEG SEGMENT STACK
  0000 0100 [                       DW   100H DUP(?)
                    ????
                        ]

  0200                              SSEG ENDS

  0000                              CSEG SEGMENT
                                    ASSUME DS:DSEG,SS:SSEG, CS:CSEG
  0000 B8 0067                        MOV AX,67H
  0003 BB 0051                        MOV BX,51H
  0006 03 C3                          ADD AX,BX ;works out 67H + 51H!!
  0008 2B DB                          SUB BX,AX
  000A                              CSEG ENDS

                                    END
```

Fig. 3.3 A complete record of the assembler's work.

When the conversion is complete, the 'A>' prompt will be displayed. The file EXAMPLE.LST now contains a complete record of the assembler's work, as shown in Fig. 3.3.

This shows, among other things, that the machine code equivalent of ADD AX,BX is 03 C3 in hexadecimal notation or 00000011 11000011 in binary and that this instruction is to be stored in locations 6H and 7H relative to the program's starting point. Page 2 of the contents of the file EXAMPLE.LST is not very meaningful to us at this stage but at least it says there are no errors. It is shown in Fig. 3.4.

Assembling large programs

Most assemblers have a limit to the number of instructions they can handle in any one assembly language program. Often this limit is dependent upon the amount of main memory the computer has available. Since the programs we shall write in this book are never extremely large, this problem should not arise. However, if the computer's memory is as small as 64K there may be a problem when the assembler is generating the .LST file, since the printout may involve more characters than the memory has capacity to store. If this happens it is normally possible to tell the assembler not to produce a .LST file. Using the format

```
The IBM Personal Computer MACRO Assembler 01-01-80 Page Symbols-1

Segments and groups:

                Name         Size    Align    Combine Class

    CSEG...............      000A    PARA     NONE
    DSEG...............      0000    PARA     NONE
    SSEG...............      0200    PARA     STACK


    Warning Severe
    Errors  Errors
      0        0
```

Fig. 3.4   Page 2 of the contents of the file EXAMPLE.LST.

```
A>ASM EXAMPLE;
```

stops the creation of a .LST file and any errors detected in the assembly language program would then be displayed on the screen as assembly proceeds.

Step 2 – invoking the linker

To convert the 'rough and ready' machine code version the assembler has produced into its final form, just one more command is needed:

```
A>LINK IBMEX,,,,
```

The linker produces two more files, IBMEX.MAP and IBM.EXE. IBMEX.MAP contains a list of the starting and finishing addresses of the various program segments, relative to a zero initial location:

Start	Stop	Length	Name	Class
00000H	00009H	000AH	CSEG	
00010H	00010H	0000H	DSEG	
00010H	0020FH	0200H	SSEG	

In our present context, the actual locations used for a program and its data are determined by DEBUG (see Section 3.2) or PC-DOS but the relative displacements in the linker's .MAP file are preserved.

The file IBMEX.EXE contains the EXEcutable machine code version with which debugging can now begin.

Step 3 – running a program under debug control

To commence debugging you type

```
A>DEBUG IBMEX.EXE
```

and the next thing you see will be an introductory message together with a debugger prompt which is just a dash at the edge of the screen.

Taking a look at your program and/or data in memory, modifying either of them and actually running the program are all handled by debugger commands, the most important of which we shall describe in the next section.

3.2 DEBUGGER COMMANDS

DEBUG is the IBM PC software tool for running machine code programs in such a way that the programmer can observe the changes a program makes to the 8088 registers and memory. In this section we describe the action of some of the most important DEBUG commands. Section 3.3 illustrates their use during an actual debugging session.

All DEBUG commands are obeyed once the RETURN key has been pressed to indicate the end of the command. Moreover, DEBUG assumes that all numbers are in hexadecimal so there is no need to type H (for hexadecimal) when entering numbers. (If you do you will get an error message.)

R   Display the contents of Registers

The R command can be used on its own, in which case the contents of every 8088 register is displayed on the screen. The display will be similar to the following:

```
AX=0000 BX=0000 CX=0000 DX=0000 SP=0200 BP=0000 SI=0000 DI=0000
DS=04B5 ES=04B5 SS=04D9 CS=04C5 IP=0000 NV UP DI PL NZ PE NC
```

Here, the current setting of register CX is 0000H and CS is set to 04C5H. SP, BP, SI, DI and ES are registers we have yet to use and NV, UP etc. are abbreviations for the current flag settings as given in Table 3.2. For example, NG means that the sign flag has been set to 1 by the last instruction to affect it.

Table 3.2 Flag name abbreviations in DEBUG.

Flag name	Flag set to one	Flag set to zero
Overflow	OV	NV
Direction	DN	UP
Interrupt	EI	DI
Sign	NG	PL
Zero	ZR	NZ
Auxiliary carry	AC	NA
Parity	PE	PO
Carry	CY	NC

The other form of the R command is used to inspect and/or change the contents of a single register. If, for example, you type RCX after the DEBUG prompt

```
-RCX
```

DEBUG responds by typing out the current contents of register CX, for example

```
CX 2347
:
```

and then waits for you either to type in the new value after the colon (followed by the return key) or just to press return, indicating that you don't want to change the contents of the CX register.

Un   Unassemble the contents of memory from location *n*

The memory locations containing your program store the full binary version of the instructions. When the debugger prints out what's in each location under this option, the assembly language format is reconstituted. The actual memory location from which the listing starts is obtained from the contents of the CS register and the offset address *n* in the usual way. Thus if the CS register contains 7BA4, then U23A in DEBUG would list from 7BA40 + 23A = 7BC7A. Normally one doesn't have to bother about the CS register at all since DEBUG sets this automatically. Given the way in which we prepared our raw assembly language programs for the assembler, all of our programs will begin at location 0 relative to the automatically determined contents of the CS register. Consequently our programs may be listed directly after entering the debugger by U0. Typically a listing similar to the following will be obtained:

```
04C5:0127 51        PUSH CX
04C5:0128 52        PUSH DX
04C5:0129 B8C900    MOV  AX,00C9
04C5:012C BB2D01    MOV  BX,012D
04C5:012F 58        POP  AX
04C5:0130 58        POP  BX
04C5:0131 03C2      ADD  AX,DX
04C5:0133 83EB7B    SUB  BX,+7B
04C5:0136 BBC601    MOV  BX,01C6
04C5:0139 49        DEC  CX
04C5:013A 4B        DEC  BX
04C5:013B 0000      ADD  [BX+SI],AL
04C5:013D 0000      ADD  [BX+SI],AL
04C5:013F 0000      ADD  [BX+SI],AL
04C5:0141 0000      ADD  [BX+SI],AL
04C5:0143 0000      ADD  [BX+SI],AL
04C5:0145 0000      ADD  [BX+SI],AL
```

As described in Chapter 2, the notation 04C5:0129 denotes the actual address

04C50 + 0129 = 04D79

which, the above listing tells us, is the first of three locations where the instruction MOV AX,00C9 is stored. The same notation is also used in the more general formats illustrated by:

i) CS:12AB

ii) DS:F02A

If the CS register currently contains 39F2 and the DS register 81EC then the actual address referred to by i) is 39F20 + 12AB = 3B1CB and by ii) is 81EC0 + F02A = 90EEA. Thus

UCS:12AB

would cause DEBUG to list the assembly language instructions stored at absolute address 3B1CB and following.

Dn Display memory contents in hexadecimal and as ASCII codes

This command option gives two listings of memory contents at the same time. The content of each location is displayed in hexadecimal form on the left-hand side of the display screen. If a given location contains the ASCII code for a printable character then that character is displayed on the right-hand side of the screen. If not then a dot (.) is displayed in the appropriate place. The actual address from which the listing commences is obtained by combining the contents of the DS register with the offset given in the command. Thus if the DS register contains 12E3 then the DEBUG command D27A4 would begin listing from memory location 12E30 + 27A4 = 155D4.

PC-DOS initializes the DS register to 10H below the contents of the CS register, so to get a hexadecimal listing of our program the command D100 should be used (remember that the 10H difference is effectively 100H because the contents of CS and DS registers always have an extra 0 added at the right-hand end in any calculations).

Some typical output from such a command is shown in Fig. 3.5.

Ga Go and execute up to the instruction at address a

This command causes execution to begin at the instruction contained in location CS:IP and stop just before executing the instruction at address a. The address of the stop instruction is taken relative to the current contents of the CS register which DEBUG sets automatically. To run the first eight instructions of the following program fragment:

These entries correspond;
51H is the ASCII code for the letter Q ⌐
(see Appendix I)

```
04C5:0100 B8 67 00 3B 51 00 03 43-2B 58 00 00 00 00 00 00  .g.;Q..C+X......
04C5:0110 00 00 0A 01 C5 04 07 03-2A 17 FF 76 0A FF 76 08  ........*..v..v.
04C5:0120 B0 FF 50 E8 A4 F9 89 46-FA A0 2A 17 8B 5E FA 88  ..P....F..*..^..
04C5:0130 87 2B 18 B4 00 89 C3 8A-4E 0A 88 8F 2C 17 D1 E3  .+......N...,...
04C5:0140 8B 46 08 89 87 70 08 80-F9 F7 73 49 B5 00 D1 E1  .F...p....sI....
04C5:0150 89 CB 3B 87 20 0D 72 0D-B8 14 02 50 B8 1E 00 50  ..;. .r....P...P
04C5:0160 9A BC 01 E7 05 8A 5E 0A-B7 00 D1 E3 8B 87 1E 15  ......^.........
04C5:0170 89 46 F8 83 F8 FF 75 09-B8 27 27 50 9A 12 02 E7  .F....u..''P....
```

These entries correspond; 89H is not
a printable ASCII code
(see Appendix I)

Location 04C50 + 0140 = 04D90 contains 8B
Location 04C50 + 0141 = 04D91 contains 46
Location 04C50 + 0142 = 04D92 contains 08 etc.

Fig. 3.5 Typical output from a command D*n*. (*Note*: All these numbers are in hexadecimal notation.)

```
04C5:0127 51       PUSH CX
04C5:0128 52       PUSH DX
04C5:0129 B8C900   MOV  AX,00C9
04C5:012C BB2D01   MOV  BX,012D
04C5:012F 58       POP  AX
04C5:0130 58       POP  BX
04C5:0131 03C2     ADD  AX,DX
04C5:0133 83EB7B   SUB  BX,+7B
04C5:0136 BBC601   MOV  BX,01C6
04C5:0139 49       DEC  CX
04C5:013A 4B       DEC  BX
04C5:013B 0000     ADD  [BX+SI],AL
04C5:013D 0000     ADD  [BX+SI],AL
04C5:013F 0000     ADD  [BX+SI],AL
04C5:0141 0000     ADD  [BX+SI],AL
04C5:0143 0000     ADD  [BX+SI],AL
04C5:0145 0000     ADD  [BX+SI],AL
```

it is first necessary to set the IP register correctly. This is done with the R command as described above. One types RIP after the DEBUG prompt

—RIP

and DEBUG responds by typing out the current contents of register IP

```
IP 2347
:
```

and then waits for you to type in the new value followed by the return key. We require 0127:

```
:0127
```

and now we check that IP has been correctly set:

```
—R
AX=0000 BX=01C6 CX=0147 DX=0000 SP=0008 BP=0000 SI=0000 DI=0000
DS=04B5 ES=04B5 SS=04D9 CS=04C5 IP=0127 NV UP DI PL NZ PE NC
04C5:0127 51 PUSH CX
—
```

Since it has and since the CS register has been set automatically by DEBUG, the command:

```
G 136
```

will cause the execution of the desired eight instructions. After execution, DEBUG prints the address of the next instruction and an assembly language version of that instruction:

```
04C5:0136 BBC601 MOV BX,01C6
—
```

Checking that the instructions have had the desired effect now involves examining the contents of memory and registers using the D, R and U commands.

T*n*   Trace the execution of *n* instructions

DEBUG provides facilities for making traces much as we did by hand in Chapter 2. The instruction has the format T*n* where *n* is the number of instructions (in hexadecimal) to be obeyed before tracing stops. The new state of all the registers is displayed *after* each instruction is obeyed. The address of the first instruction to be obeyed in a T command is taken to be CS:IP so it is generally necessary to set the IP register before beginning a trace.

E*a*   Enter the contents of memory location *a* directly

If a program requires data to be held in memory it is important to be able to change that data when testing a program (so that special cases can be tried out, for example). The command we shall describe in this section allows you to alter the contents of a memory location by typing in a new value in hexadecimal form. Changing the contents of location *a* relative to the

current contents of the CS register involves giving DEBUG the command
E*a* after the prompt, whereupon DEBUG prints the current contents of that
location and waits for the new value to be typed in.

Q   Quit using DEBUG and return to PC-DOS

Type Q and then press the RETURN key.

3.3   A SAMPLE DEBUGGING SESSION

We now demonstrate DEBUG in action, applied to the little program
assembled earlier:

```
MOV AX,67H
MOV BX,51H
ADD AX,BX   ;works out 67H + 51H!!
SUB BX,AX
```

Following all the necessary preparations, we shall assume that the
executable machine code version of this program now lies in the file
EXAMPLE.EXE.

Debugging the machine code program in the file EXAMPLE.EXE is
initiated by typing DEBUG EXAMPLE.EXE after the 'A>' operating
system prompt. DEBUG responds with a prompt:

–

Our program should be in location 0 and following (relative to the contents
of the CS register), so let's check:

```
–U0
04C5:0000 B86700     MOV AX,0067
04C5:0003 BB5100     MOV BX,0051
04C5:0006 03C3       ADD AX,BX
04C5:0008 2BD8       SUB BX,AX
04C5:000A 0000       ADD [BX+SI],AL
04C5:000C 0000       ADD [BX+SI],AL
04C5:000E 0000       ADD [BX+SI],AL
04C5:0010 0000       ADD [BX+SI],AL
04C5:0012 0000       ADD [BX+SI],AL
04C5:0014 0000       ADD [BX+SI],AL
04C5:0016 0000       ADD [BX+SI],AL
04C5:0018 EC         INC DX
04C5:0019 1A8A1E2A   SBB CL,[BP+SI+2A1E]
04C5:001D 17         POP SS
04C5:001E B700       MOV BH,00
```

–

(Only the first four instructions are significant. The U command always prints out about a dozen or so instructions and those at the end of our program were left in memory by a previous program or are the result of random memory settings which occurred when the computer was switched on.)

To have our program executed, we must first set the IP register to the address (relative to the CS register) of the first instruction (0 in this case). To do this we use the R command:

```
-RIP
```

DEBUG responds by typing the current setting of the IP register

```
IP 0000
:
```

and normally we would then type in the desired setting. Since IP is already correctly set in this case we simply press the RETURN key. To check all this we use the R command again:

```
-R
AX=0000 BX=0000 CX=0000 DX=0000 SP=0200 BP=0000 SI=0000 DI=0000
DS=04B5 ES=04B5 SS=04C6 CS=04C5 IP=0000 NV UP DI PL NZ NA PO NC
04C5:0000 B86700        MOV    AX,0067
-
```

We discovered from the output of the U command that the last instruction in our program resides in locations 8 and 9 (relative to the CS register) so we want to stop execution just before the instruction in location 000A is obeyed. Thus, to run our program we use the command

```
-G 000A
```

which, when execution has stopped, displays the current register contents and the next instruction to be executed:

```
AX=00B8 BX=FF99 CX=0000 DX=0000 SP=0200 BP=0000 SI=0000 DI=0000
DS=04B5 ES=04B5 SS=04C6 CS=04C5 IP=000A NV UP DI NG AC PE CY
04C5:000A 0000           ADD    [BX+SI],AL
```

Since 67H + 51H = B8H, register AX should contain B8H after execution of our program, so we can see from this display that at least that much of our program has behaved according to plan.

The final instruction in our little example program should have left the result of 51H–B8H in register BX. It is necessary to check that FF99H is the signed 16-bit form of −67H therefore. As observed in Chapter 1, the positive equivalent of FF99H can be obtained by forming its two's complement. Thus

FF99H = 1111 1111 1001 1001B

so taking the two's complement gives

0000 0000 0110 0111B

which is 0067H, and the value of BX is verified.

3.4 AUTOMATIC TRACING

For the sake of illustration we shall now trace the execution of our program. As a first step we must once again set the IP register to the address of the location (relative to the CS register) containing the instruction from which the trace of execution is to commence:

```
─RIP
IP 000A
:
```

We now type in the desired setting for IP, namely 0

```
:0
─
```

and once again use the R command to check:

```
─R
AX=00B8 BX=FF99 CX=0018 DX=0000 SP=0008 BP=0000 SI=0000 DI=0000
DS=04B5 ES=04B5 SS=04C6 CS=04C5 IP=0000 NV UP DI NG NZ AC PE CY
04C5:0000 B86700    MOV    AX,0067
─
```

Now we can begin the trace proper. First we trace a single step. After executing that step DEBUG prints out the new state of the registers:

```
─T1
AX=0067 BX=FF99 CX=0000 DX=0000 SP=0200 BP=0000 SI=0000 DI=0000
DS=04B5 ES=04B5 SS=04C6 CS=04C5 IP=0003 NV UP DI NG NZ AC PE CY
04C5:0003 BB5100    MOV    BX,0051
─
```

(MOV BX,0051 is the next instruction to be executed.) Let's do another step:

```
─T1
AX=0067 BX=0051 CX=0000 DX=0000 SP=0200 BP=0000 SI=0000 DI=0000
DS=04B5 ES=04B5 SS=04C6 CS=04C5 IP=0006 NV UP DI PL NZ NA PE NC
04C5:0008 2BD8      ADD    AX,BX
─
```

and finally, two more steps to finish off:

```
─T2
AX=00B8 BX=0051 CX=0000 DX=0000 SP=0200 BP=0000 SI=0000 DI=0000
DS=04B5 ES=04B5 SS=04C6 CS=04C5 IP=0008 NV UP DI PL NZ NA PE NC
04C5:0008 2BD8      SUB    BX,AX
```

```
AX=00B8 BX=FF99 CS=0000 DX=0000 SP=0200 BP=0000 SI=0000 DI=0000
DS=04B5 ES=04B5 SS=04C6 CS=04C5 IP=000A NV UP DI NG NZ AC PE CY
04C5:000A  0000          ADD     [BX+SI],AL
```

EXERCISES 3.1

1. Using your own machine, assemble and run under debugger control the following assembly language program:

```
MOV AX,7H
SUB AX,3H
MOV BX,AX
MOV CX,AX
MOV DX,AX
```

Try tracing the machine code version, one instruction at a time, and also execute the whole program in one go using the G command.

2. Using your own machine, assemble and run

```
     MOV AH,0
LOOP:INC AH
     JMP LOOP
```

Trace 10H steps of the execution of this program to check that you understand how it works. Then discover what happens when you obey INC AH and the contents of AH is 0FFH.

3. Try to assemble the erroneous

```
MOV AX,4K
MOV AH,AX
SUB AX,2
SUB AH,0123456H
MOV BX,AX
ADD AX,BL
SUB 3,AX
```

and see what error messages you get. Can you say what has caused each error?

3.5 THE DEBUGGING CYCLE

It is indeed rare that an assembly language program will assemble and eventually run as predicted at the first attempt. Typically several approximations to the truth will have to be made before a final working program is produced, and the following scheme is nearly always adopted:

While the machine code program (if any) does not match the desired specification:

1. Write or amend the raw assembly language program (as necessary) and submit it to the assembler.

2. While the assembly language program contains things the assembler can't understand, correct it by editing the file which contains the program and resubmit the corrected program to the assembler.

3. Now that a version has been obtained which contains no errors of assembly language, assemble and link it. Run the executable machine code version under debugger control.

3.6 IF IT ALL HANGS UP

Once things go radically wrong with a machine code program – which is often the case – it is all too easy to 'kill off' the operating system completely. The main symptom is the keyboard going dead – it will accept neither debugger commands nor any control keys such as CTRL-ALT-DELETE to restart PC-DOS. If this happens there is just the slightest chance that one of your disk files could be spoilt, but generally speaking it's nothing to worry about. Remove your disks from the disk drives, switch off the computer and then reboot the operating system as at the beginning of a normal session. You may then turn to the task of finding out why it all happened in the first place.

There are a variety of possible causes of such a system crash. Sometimes a loop that's designed to stop after a certain number of executions never actually stops because the terminating condition is never satisfied (BX never gets to zero, or AX never gets more than 37H or . . .). Perhaps the terminating address given to the G debugger command was wrong – often one instruction too many – or perhaps the IP register had not been set to the correct value to start with. Are all the jump instructions aimed at the right place? (Checking this is easier from the assembly language listing. Look out for JZ which should be JNZ and vice versa.)

3.7 SPECIFYING ACTUAL ADDRESSES

In a large payroll program written in Pascal it is better to declare the rates of tax as constants at the beginning of the program and then refer to them via the corresponding variable names than to use the actual values. For then, if the tax rates change (as they inevitably will!), updating the program would simply involve changes to the dozen or so constant declarations rather than searching through the entire 30000 lines of Pascal for every occurrence of a tax rate (and inevitably missing several).

Similarly, having written a large assembly language program which makes some complicated calculations based on the contents of a certain group of memory locations, if we avoid using actual numeric addresses in the program itself, changing the program to work on a different group of locations will be much easier. Consequently, MASM does not allow addresses of the form [200] as in the perfectly valid 8088 instruction MOV AX,[200] – all addresses must be represented by **variables** which are assigned to the locations to which they refer in the appropriate segment of the program. No small example can show the positive gains to which this approach can lead (on the contrary, for a small program we have to do more work!), but we next give an example of how this is done in practice.

An example

The following little program swaps the contents of locations 200H and 201H (relative to the start of the data segment of our program). We get at these specific locations by using the ORG pseudo-op which tells MASM to continue the allocation of storage to instructions or data as if it had already got to the location specified in the ORG command. Thus the combination

```
ORG 200H
FIRST_LOCATION DB ?
```

in a segment addressed by the DS register makes the variable FIRST_LOCATION refer to location 200H relative to the start of the data segment DSEG. Notice the difference between a label (which ends with a colon) and a variable (which does not). Otherwise, names for variables and labels are constructed in exactly the same way.

We must now initialize DS so that it points to the beginning of DSEG. As you will see if you examine the 8088 registers before running a program loaded under DEBUG, PC-DOS initializes DS to 100H locations below CS: typically, CS might be initialized to 0915H and DS to 0905H. In Chapter 11 we'll see that this is a helpful thing to do.

The true start of our program's data segment, DSEG, is easily accessed since the segment name DSEG has the relevant address as one of its attributes:

```
MOV AX,DSEG
MOV DS,AX
```

Notice that we cannot load DS directly since segment registers can only be loaded from a register *other* than a segment register.

```
DSEG SEGMENT
     ORG 200H
     FIRST_LOCATION DB ?
     ORG 201H
     SECOND_LOCATION DB ?
DSEG ENDS

SSEG SEGMENT STACK
DW   100H DUP(?)
SSEG ENDS
```

```
CSEG SEGMENT
     ASSUME DS:DSEG,SS:SSEG,CS:CSEG
     MOV  AX,DSEG
     MOV  DS,AX                 ;set DS to program data segment
     MOV  AL,FIRST_LOCATION
     MOV  BL,SECOND_LOCATION
     MOV  FIRST_LOCATION,BL
     MOV  SECOND_LOCATION,AL
CSEG ENDS
END
```

Put this program into a file called SWAP.ASM, assemble and link it, and then run the resulting program under debugger control.

It is rarely necessary to modify absolute locations in memory. Should this become necessary then DS must be loaded with an appropriate value so that the specific locations can be accessed. For example, to swap the contents of actual locations 9FF00H and 9FF01H we could load DS with 9FF0 via

```
MOV AX,9FF0H
MOV DS,AX
```

and then swap the contents of locations 0 and 1 relative to DS. However, care must be taken when using absolute addresses in this way as it is possible to overwrite PC-DOS or DEBUG (or both) and have the system hang up on you.

EXERCISES 3.2

1. Write and assemble an assembly language program which leaves in register AX the sum of the contents of the absolute locations 5000H and 5001H. Having assembled the program, use the E debugger command so that locations 5000H and 5001H contain 2 and 3 respectively. Run your program under debugger control and check that it works correctly. Then change the contents of locations 5000H and 5001H to 0FFH and 1H respectively. Run the program again and account for what happens.

2. Make the necessary changes to each of the little example programs given in Section 2.8 and thus assemble and test them using MASM, LINK and DEBUG.

3.8 THE JUMP MECHANISM

There are three basic forms of 8088 jump instruction. The first can be illustrated with reference to conditional jumps like the instruction JZ <label>. If the instruction indicated by the <label> is within +127 or −128 locations of the JZ instruction itself, the assembler replaces the <label> with the appropriate actual number. When the JZ is executed, that number is added to the contents of the IP register. If in JMP <label> the <label> points to an instruction between 0 and 0FFFFH locations from the last of those containing the JMP instruction itself, the assembler can replace the <label> by the unsigned 16-bit form of the distance between the two. On execution of the JMP, that unsigned 16-bit displacement is added to the IP register. The following extract from an assembler listing demonstrates both these possibilities:

```
3000 8B C3              MOV  AX,BX
3002 74 0B              JZ   NEAR_BY
     .                       .
     .                       .
     .                       .
300E B1 02     NEAR_BY: MOV  CL,2
3010 03 C3              ADD  AX,BX
3012 2A C1              SUB  AL,CL
3014 E9 E9 0F           JMP  FAR_AHEAD
     .                       .
     .                       .
     .                       .
4000 8A C3     FAR_AHEAD: MOV AL,BL
```

Here, we see that location 3002H contains 74H and 3003H contains 0BH. 74H is the machine code form of the JZ instruction. 0BH specifies that the target for the jump – the instruction labelled NEAR_BY – IS JUST 0BH locations ahead of the JZ instruction itself, in locations 300EH and 300FH.

Similarly, location 3014H contains the machine code form of the JMP <label> instruction, 0E9H, and the next two locations contain the unsigned 16-bit displacement of the instruction labelled FAR_AHEAD, namely 0FE9H.

The third basic form of jump instruction is:

JMP memory/register

where, for example, JMP [BX] would cause the word stored at the memory locations specified by [BX] to be moved into IP. Program execution will now continue from the address that was stored in memory.

MASM assumes that all jumps are **intra-segment**, i.e. within the same segment (or, what is the same thing, never more than 0FFFFH locations between the location being jumped from and the location to which you are jumping) unless a label has been specifically declared as a FAR away label via the LABEL pseudo-op. Thus,

```
LONG_WAY_OFF LABEL FAR
```

in conjunction with

```
JMP LONG_WAY_OFF
```

would mean that the JMP would be coded into the **inter-segment** form in which the target address would be specified by four bytes (as for CALL in Section 4.6).

3.9 SUMMARY

In this chapter we learned how to assemble, link and finally run machine code programs under DEBUG control and that pseudo-ops provide vital information for the assembler.

Assembly language programming is highly prone to errors because so much detailed work is involved. DEBUG provides facilities for locating errors, and a summary of the DEBUG commands introduced in this chapter is given in Table 3.3.

As ever, prevention is better than cure. In the next chapter, therefore, we look into programming techniques specifically aimed at minimizing the number of errors in an assembly language program.

Table 3.3   A summary of DEBUG commands introduced in this chapter.

Command	Purpose	Format
R	Display the contents of all registers.	R
	Alter the contents of a register.	R register_name
U	List the instructions contained in the given address and following in assembly language form (the address is relative to the contents of the CS register).	U address
D	Display the contents of memory in hexa-decimal format and as ASCII characters, starting with the address given (the address is relative to the contents of the DS register).	D address
G	Execute the instructions starting with the one in address CS:IP and stop just before execut-ing the instruction in the stop_address (the address is relative to the contents of the CS register).	G stop_address
E	Enter values into memory, starting with start_address.	E start_address
Q	Finish this session with DEBUG.	

4 Controlling Program Development

AIMS

This chapter describes a method the reader can use to develop his or her own assembly language programs. The method helps to contain the occurrence of errors by mimicking some of the facilities of a structured programming language like Pascal. Furthermore, we introduce the functions PC-DOS provides for reading in and printing out characters, as well as explaining how to automatically return to operating system control after the execution of one of our programs is complete.

4.1 STRUCTURED ASSEMBLY LANGUAGE PROGRAMMING

Experience has shown that it is possible to contain the number of errors in an assembly language program if program development is carried out in a controlled manner. Indeed, a systematic approach to program development is essential for the efficient production of software which is verifiable, reliable and understandable by programmers other than its author. Pascal is rich in control structures and data types which make this easier to achieve than is possible with assembly language, but it is possible to mimic some of these facilities quite readily.

For any given problem we first map out a solution using the normal combination of top-down and bottom-up methodologies as appropriate and the language pseudo-Pascal. Pseudo-Pascal contains *ad hoc* extensions to the Pascal programming language to allow us to make a more or less statement by statement assembly language implementation of the pseudo-Pascal original. Thus a **repeat . . . until** loop in pseudo-Pascal:

repeat *action 1*
       action 2
       action 3
       :
       :

> :
>
> *action n*
>
> **until**   *<condition>*

could be implemented by assembly language of the form:

> START_REPEAT: implementation of action 1
>   implementation of action 2
>   implementation of action 3
>   :
>   :
>   :
>   implementation of action *n*
>   test <condition> and jump to START_REPEAT
>   if not satisfied

and an **if** . . . **then** . . . **else** statement of the form:

> **if** *<condition>* **then** *action 1* **else** *action 2*

could be implemented by assembly language of the form:

>   test <condition>
>   if satisfied jump to DO_ACTION_2
>   implementation of action 1
>   JMP NEXT_INSTRUCTION
> DO_ACTION_2:   implementation of action 2
> NEXT_INSTRUCTION:

Apart from the relatively easy transition from pseudo-Pascal to assembly language, the main advantage of this approach is that use of pseudo-Pascal enforces a structured approach to the assembly language programming task. Moreover, if the pseudo-Pascal is used to comment the assembly language program, a high standard of program documentation is assured.

We shall now illustrate these advantages by working through the solution to a specific example problem. If the reader needs convincing at this stage, he or she should try the problem to be tackled without this methodology.

Since pseudo-Pascal is – by its very definition – a rather ephemeral object, we shall henceforth drop the grandiose prefix *pseudo* from general use and often simply refer to Pascal whether we mean the real thing or the more flexible relative. Hopefully, the context will always make it clear to which of the two we are referring.

The problem

We are given as data the ASCII codes for an extract from the book *David Copperfield* by Charles Dickens. All punctuation except full stops has been removed from the extract and the words of the text are separated by single ASCII space characters (code 20H). When represented in this manner the complete extract is contained within the memory segment specified by the DS register.

An assembly language program is required which will leave in register AX the length of the longest sentence (in characters, including spaces) and in CX the starting address of that sentence (relative to DS). The maximum length of any sentence is 255 characters (including spaces) and an ASCII code for a $ sign indicates the end of the extract.

Imagine solving a corresponding problem in Pascal. One of the first things to do is to decide which variables are required and of what type they should be. Since we shall have to examine the length of each sentence in the extract in relation to the lengths of previous sentences, variables are required to record the maximum sentence length so far and the length of the sentence currently being examined. Similarly, variables are needed for the starting address of the current sentence and the starting address of the sentence having the maximum length amongst those already considered. Also we need a variable to hold each character of the text as we examine it for ends of sentences and the end of the text.

In Pascal, the next stage would be to decide on the type of these variables – should they be integer, real or char? A corresponding set of decisions has to be made in assembly language: for example, should the variables occupy a byte or a word and should signed or unsigned representations be used for numeric work?

For the problem under consideration both variables representing

Table 4.1 Allocation of registers to variables for the text processing problem.

Variable	Register	Comment
maxaddress	CX	Start address of sentence of maximum length encountered so far.
max	AL	Length (in characters) of the sentence of which the starting address is given in CX (i.e. length of the sentence so far considered to be the longest).
address	BX	Start address of the sentence currently under consideration.
linecount	DH	The number of characters encountered in a given sentence so far.
char	DL	The particular character being examined.

addresses must be unsigned 16-bit numbers, and, since we were told that the maximum length of any sentence is 255 characters, unsigned 8-bit numbers will be adequate for the sentence length variables. The variable which holds each character of the text as it is inspected will occupy one byte. It remains to decide whether to use registers or memory locations to store these variables. In this instance all the variables could be stored in registers, so that is what we shall do, given that the two answers to the problem must be left in AX and CX. Table 4.1 gives our allocation of registers to variables.

Using these variables, it is easy to give a complete solution to the problem in Pascal:

```
address := address of first character in text;
max := 0; maxaddress := address; read (char);
while char < > '$' do
    begin
    (*count to the end of this sentence*)
    linecount := 0;
    while char < > '.' do
        begin
        linecount := linecount + 1;
        address := address + 1;
        read(char)
        end;
    (*compare length with biggest so far*)
    if linecount > max then
        begin
        max := linecount;
        maxaddress := address − linecount
        end;
    (*now at the end of a sentence, so read on*)
    address := address + 1;
    read(char)
    end
```

Thus, if we can implement **while** loops in assembly language a complete solution will be easy. But by definition of a Pascal **while** loop:

```
while <condition> do begin
                action 1
                action 2
                :
                :
                action n
                end
```

this is roughly equivalent to the assembly language structure:

START: test <condition> and jump to STOP if not satisfied
　　　　action 1
　　　　action 2
　　　　　:
　　　　　:
　　　　　:
　　　　action *n*
　　　　JMP START
STOP:

We can now use this to finish the solution, assuming that the start of the text has been associated with a variable by a pseudo-op of the form:

```
START_OF_TEXT DB............
```

and using the pseudo-op OFFSET to extract from the variable START_OF _TEXT its offset from DS so that:

```
MOV BX,OFFSET START_OF_TEXT
```

in effect, loads BX with the actual starting address (relative to DS) of the start of the text.

A solution

Here is a solution to the *David Copperfield* problem.

```
                ;set up data segment address in DS
                        MOV AX,DSEG
                        MOV DS,AX
                ;address := address of first character in text
                        MOV BX,OFFSET START_OF_TEXT
                ;max := 0; maxaddress := address;
                        MOV AX,0  ;zeros AH and AL
                        MOV CX,BX
                ;read(char)
                        MOV DL,[BX]
                ;while char <> '$' do
                    ;begin
            CHECK_DOLLAR_SIGN: CMP DL,'$'
                            JZ  END_OF_TEXT
                    ;count to the end of this sentence
                    ;linecount := 0
                            MOV DH,0
                    ;while char <> '.' do
                        ;begin
                    CHECK_FULL_STOP: CMP DL,'.'
                            JZ  END_OF_SENTENCE
```

```
                ;linecount := linecount + 1
                        INC DH
                ;address := address + 1
                        INC BX
                ;read (char)
                        MOV DL,[BX]
                ;end
                        JMP CHECK_FULL_STOP
        ;compare length with biggest so far
        ;if linecount > max then
    END_OF_SENTENCE: CMP DH,AL
                    JB  NEXT_SENTENCE
                ;begin
                ;max := linecount
                        MOV AL,DH
                ;maxaddress := address-linecount
                        MOV CX,BX ;copy address into maxaddress
                        MOV DL,DH ;convert linecount to
                        MOV DH,0  ;unsigned 16-bit form
                        SUB CX,DX ;subtract
                ;end of comparison with biggest so far
        ;now at the end of a sentence, so read on
        ;address := address + 1; read(char)
    NEXT_SENTENCE: INC BX
                    MOV DL,[BX]
        ;end of dealing with a sentence
                    JMP CHECK_DOLLAR_SIGN
    ;end of whole text
    END_OF_TEXT: HLT
```

(HLT is an 8088 instruction which causes the 8088 to HaLT completely. Once a HLT instruction has been obeyed, the IBM PC will have to be switched off and PC-DOS reloaded, since the HLT suspends operation and cannot be over-ridden by software.)

EXERCISES 4.1

1. Add the necessary pseudo-ops to the above fragment so that it can be assembled by MASM and run the result under DEBUG control. Use the following extract from *David Copperfield* as test data.

   I could think of the past now gravely but not bitterly and could contemplate the future in bright spirit. Home in its best sense was for me no more. She in whom I might have inspired a dearer love I had taught to be my sister. She would marry and would have new claimants on her tenderness and in doing it would never know the love for her that had grown in my heart. It was right that I should pay the forfeit of my headlong passion. What I reaped I had sown.$

You can either type the data in every time you do a test run via DEBUG (laborious!) or use DB pseudo-ops in the assembly language program and enter it just once.

2. Use the above method (preparing an outline solution in Pascal and then mimicking the resulting Pascal-like fragment in assembly language) to solve the following problems. Test your solutions carefully.

a) You are given two strings of characters, which we shall refer to as X and Y. Write an assembly language program which will count the number of occurrences of the string X in the string Y, leaving the result in AL. Assume that both X and Y are at most 255 characters long.

Thus, if X were the string 'on' and Y were the string 'once upon a time' your program should leave 2 in AL.

b) Write an assembly language program which, given a pattern P and a piece of ASCII coded text T, will count the number of those words in T which match P. The pattern P contains letters and two special characters: ? matches any single character; * matches any sequence of characters (including the empty string).

For example, the pattern DOG matches the word DOG, the pattern D?G matches the words DOG, DUG and DIG, the pattern D?G* matches the words DOG, DOGS, DIG, DIGS and DOGGEREL.

4.2 SUBROUTINES

In Pascal, **procedures** make it possible to break a large program down into smaller pieces so that each piece can be shown to work correctly without reference to any of the others. In this way the final program is built up out of lots of trusty bricks and is easier to debug since, if there is an error, it can only be caused by the interlinking of the bricks. In 8088 assembly language the nearest equivalent to Pascal's procedures are **subroutines**.

Making a sequence of assembly language instructions into a subroutine is easy – we simply label the first instruction in the sequence as if we were going to make it the object of a jump instruction, and add the 8088 instruction RET to the end of the sequence. Consider the example below, which contains an 8088 program fragment which leaves the sum of the unsigned 16-bit numbers in AX, BX, CX and DX (assuming this sum can be represented in 16-bit form) in SI, a 16-bit register, new to us, the special purpose of which will be introduced in Chapter 5.

```
MOV SI,0
ADD SI,AX
ADD SI,BX
ADD SI,CX
ADD SI,DX
```

Here we have made this into a subroutine called REGISTER_ SUMMATION:

```
REGISTER_SUMMATION: MOV SI,0
                    ADD SI,AX
                    ADD SI,BX
                    ADD SI,CX
                    ADD SI,DX
                    RET
```

Having done so, we can call the subroutine into action via the 8088 CALL instruction, thus: CALL REGISTER_SUMMATION. This causes the 8088 microprocessor to begin executing the instruction sequence starting with the label REGISTER_SUMMATION until a RET instruction is encountered, at which point execution RETurns to the instruction next in sequence after the CALL instruction itself (see Fig. 4.1).

In the program segment below, comments show the sequence of values taken by SI during the execution of the given program fragment:

```
MOV AX,0
MOV BX,0
MOV CX,0
```

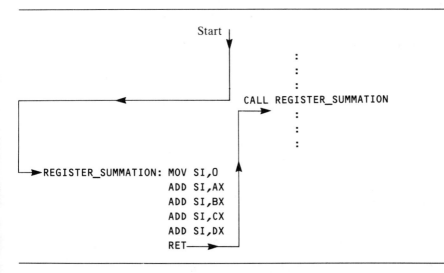

Fig. 4.1 Execution of a subroutine.

```
MOV DX,1
CALL REGISTER_SUMMATION
                        ;SI set to 1
MOV AX,2
CALL REGISTER_SUMMATION
                        ;SI set to 3
MOV BX,3
MOV CX,4
CALL REGISTER_SUMMATION
                        ;SI set to 0AH
```

EXERCISE 4.2

Make a hand trace of the execution of the following program fragment, assuming that the subroutine PRINT_ON_SCREEN prints on the display screen the character whose ASCII code is in register AL. Give a clear indication of what appears on the display screen.

```
                 MOV   CX,5H
                 MOV   AX,40H
   NEXT_STEP:    INC   AX
                 CALL  PRINT_ON_SCREEN
                 CALL  CODE_AND_PRINT
                 DEC   CX
                 JNZ   NEXT_STEP
                 HLT

CODE_AND_PRINT:  MOV   BX,1AH
                 SUB   BX,AX
                 ADD   BX,41H
                 MOV   CX,AX    ;save the value of AX
                 MOV   AX,BX
                 CALL  PRINT_ON_SCREEN
                 MOV   AX,CX    ;restore the value to AX
                 RET

PRINT_ON_SCREEN:   .
                   .
                   .
                   .
                 RET
```

Notice that, as with procedures in Pascal, one subroutine may call another.

4.3   THE STACK AND ITS ROLE IN THE SUBROUTINE MECHANISM

As stated in Chapter 3, a stack is a group of locations in memory which the programmer reserves for the (temporary) storage of important items of data. The mechanism by which subroutines are implemented in the 8088 uses a stack. Briefly, when a subroutine is called up, the address of the instruction following the call is saved on a stack until the RET instruction in the body of the subroutine is encountered. Then execution continues from the instruction following the CALL by retrieving the return address from that stack. Before examining the mechanism in detail, a thorough discussion of 8088 stack implementation is necessary, and it is to that which we now turn.

The stack

The method by which the 8088 provides a stack facility is a common one. It assumes that the programmer using a stack normally specifies a starting address for the stack well away from the area of memory in which the program and any fixed data are stored. Typically the programmer's stack would start at a location near the end of available memory and would grow backwards in memory as demand warranted, as shown in Fig. 4.2.

Copies of the contents of registers can be stored on and retrieved from a stack thanks to the PUSH and POP instructions, which have the general forms:

PUSH 16-bit register name e.g. PUSH AX
POP   16-bit register name e.g. POP DX

(PUSH stores the copy in memory, and POP loads it back again), or, for the flags register, PUSHF stores and POPF retrieves.

In order that PUSH and POP can operate successfully it is necessary only to specify how big a memory stack is required and to set the 16-bit SP

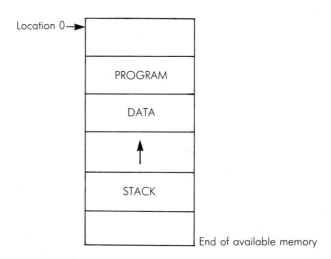

Fig. 4.2 Typical memory allocation when using a stack.

(Stack Pointer) register to the address of the top of the stack (which is where items are added and removed – compare with the dinner plate dispenser model of Chapter 3). All addresses within the stack are taken to be relative to the contents of another new 16-bit register, the SS (Stack Segment) register. It, and SP, are initialized automatically by MASM thanks to the pseudo-ops:

```
SSEG SEGMENT STACK
        DW 100H DUP(?)
SSEG ENDS
```

which instruct the linker to set SS to a value compatible with the memory allocation plan of Fig. 4.2 and to initialize SP to the top of stack value (200H, relative to SS). Of course, reserving more words of store for the stack – up to 64 Kbytes is allowed – will alter the value to which MASM initializes SP.

Let us suppose that the stack pointer register, SP, has been initialized to 0200H (relative to the SS register) and consider the effect of the instruction PUSH BX in detail. Suppose further that register BX contains 1A9EH. Then the action of PUSH BX is as follows:

1. The SP register is decremented by 1.
2. The high-order byte of BX is stored in the memory location addressed by SP (relative to the SS register).
3. The SP register is decremented by 1.
4. The low-order byte of BX is stored in the memory location now addressed by SP (relative to the SS register).

(Notice that SP is thus left pointing to the last element stored in the stack – i.e. to the top of the stack.)

Before			After		
	SP	0200		SP	01FE
	BX	1A9E		BX	1A9E
01FE		??		01FE	9E
01FF		??		01FF	1A
0200		??		0200	??

On the other hand the action of an instruction such as POP DX releases memory from the stack, in that the SP register is incremented. Its action is as follows:

1. Copy the byte stored at the address given in the SP register (relative to SS) into DL.
2. Increment the SP register by 1.
3. Copy the byte now pointed to by the SP register (relative to SS) into DH.
4. Increment the SP register by 1.

Assuming that the SP register currently contains 009EH, and that locations 009EH and 009FH relative to the SS register contain 0A2H and 0B3H respectively, then the effect of POP DX will be to put 0B3A2H into DX and to change the contents of the SP register to 00A0H.

PUSH and POP in daily use

Once everything is initialized, PUSH and POP can be used freely wherever temporary storage is required. It is necessary to remember just two points:

i) It is essential that any subroutine should leave the stack in the same state as when that subroutine started using the stack. Otherwise, strange things may happen when your program is executed since, for example, a value which you have PUSHed but not POPped could be taken as the return address for that subroutine – see Section 4.5.

ii) The last item put on the stack is the first off. Thus:

```
PUSH AX ;copy AX onto stack
PUSH BX ;copy BX onto stack
POP  AX ;copy the item currently on the top
        ;of the stack into register AX and
        ;then remove that item from the stack
POP  BX ;copy what's on the top of the stack
        ;into register BX and then remove
        ;that item from the top of the stack
```

effectively swaps the contents of registers AX and BX.

EXERCISE 4.3

Make a detailed trace of the execution of the following program fragment, giving the contents of the registers and memory locations involved. Assume that the SS register contains 1000H, and the SP register 0200H, and that the contents of AX, BX, CX and DX are (respectively) 0200H, 123AH, 0FE1BH and 0A981H.

```
PUSH  AX
PUSH  BX
PUSH  CX
POP   DX
POP   CX
PUSH  DX
POP   AX
POP   BX
```

4.4 A COMPLETE PROGRAM USING SUBROUTINES

To make matters absolutely clear, in this section we shall give a complete assembly language program which uses subroutines and which prints a small message on the display screen of the IBM PC. The actual printing on the screen is done by one of the PC-DOS operating system **functions**.

PC-DOS functions

PC-DOS provides a whole range of functions which can be called up by assembly language programs. These functions work by allowing the programmer to interrupt the normal, line by line execution of an assembly language program. It is then possible to branch into the operating system's own machine code instructions. Within the operating system are routines to read a character from the keyboard, print a character on the screen, read some data from a disk, etc. After the execution of one of these routines, control is returned to the program which caused the interruption. Execution then resumes on the usual line by line basis.

The 8088 instruction which allows this to happen is the INT instruction (INT is short for INTerrupt). Altogether 256 different sorts of interruption are allowed, so it is necessary to specify which one is required. The interrupt instruction which allows operations such as reading a character from the keyboard, printing a character on the display screen and handling files on disk is number 21H. Other software interrupts are discussed in Chapter 12.

Thus executing the instruction INT 21H gives you access to a whole range of input and output functions. Specifying which function you want involves putting a code number in register AH. Table 4.2 specifies the effects of a dozen of the functions available under software interrupt 21H. The remainder are listed in Chapter 11.

It is now easy to write a subroutine which will print the character whose ASCII code is held in register DL.

Table 4.2   Specifications of PC-DOS functions available under software interrupt 21H.

Function number	Description	What it does
1	Keyboard input	Wait until a character is typed at the keyboard and then put the ASCII code for that character in register AL. Whatever is typed is also printed on the display screen.
2	Output on display screen	Print on the display screen the character whose ASCII code is contained in register DL.

Table 4.2 (*continued*)

Function number	Description	What it does
3	Asynchronous input	Waits for a character to be input via the asynchronous communications adapter card and places the received character in AL.
4	Asynchronous output	The character in DL is sent to the asynchronous communications adapter card.
5	Print character	The character in DL is sent to the printer.
6	Keyboard input/ character display	If DL = 0FFH, the Z-flag is set to zero if a keyboard character is ready and the character is placed in AL. If no character is available ZF is set to 1. No waiting takes place. If DL< >0FFH the character in DL is displayed.
7	Keyboard input/ no display	Waits for an input character from the keyboard and, when it arrives, places it in AL. The character is not automatically printed on the display screen. CTRL-BRK cannot be used to return to PC-DOS.
8	Keyboard input/ no display	As in function 7 except that normal CTRL-BRK service is provided.
9	Display string	Print a whole series of characters stored in memory starting with the one in the address given in DX (relative to DS). Stop when a memory location containing the ASCII code for a $ sign is encountered. Don't print the $ sign.
A	Keyboard string	A character string is read into store beginning at the address given in DS:DX. The first byte typed by the user specifies the length of the string. The actual characters of the string are now read in and stored in the third and following bytes of the designated group of locations until either the ENTER key is pressed or one less than the stated number of locations has been filled. If the ENTER key is pressed, then the second byte of the store area is set to the number of characters read (excluding CR). The last byte of the string is set to CR. Extra characters are ignored and the bell is rung if an overflow condition is about to occur.
B	Keyboard status	AL is set to 0FFH if a character is available from the keyboard. Otherwise AL is set to zero. A check for CTRL-BRK is made.
C	Keyboard buffer clear	The keyboard buffer within the keyboard is cleared, and the INT 21H function (only 1, 6, 7, 8 and A are allowed) specified in AL is performed.

```
PRINTCHAR: MOV AH,02H ;function number 2
           INT 21H    ;of INTerrupt 21H
           RET
```

Note that each time something is printed, printing continues from wherever it finished last time.

Printing new lines

When using a typewriter, starting a new line involves two operations: returning the carriage which holds the paper to the beginning of the line (carriage return) and moving the paper up one line (line feed). The display of text on a computer's screen has been designed to emulate this, so taking a new line involves 'printing' the ASCII codes for line feed and carriage return. Since we already have a subroutine printing a single character on the screen, we can use that to create a PRINT_NEWLINE subroutine.

```
PRINT_NEWLINE: MOV  DL,0AH    ;a carriage return
               CALL PRINTCHAR
               MOV  DL,0DH    ;a line feed
               CALL PRINTCHAR
               RET
```

(As with a typewriter, the operations of carriage return and line feed can be done in either order, but there may be problems with some makes of printer if the carriage return is not done first.)

EXERCISE 4.4

Printing a message using PC-DOS functions

Below is a complete program which uses the subroutine PRINTCHAR to print the three-letter message IBM on the screen. Type it into your machine and verify that it works. Try to amend it so that the message printed out is ABC and check your work by re-assembling your amended version.

In the program we have used two new MASM pseudo-ops, EQU and COMMENT. EQU admits a facility in some ways similar to the **constant** data type of Pascal. Thanks to EQU, a program heavily dependent on certain numerical values need not be spattered with those values, since they can be declared as constants at the beginning of a program. In this way, a tax calculation program can be amended to accommodate a new rate of tax by altering one single EQU statement rather than (possibly) tens of individual instructions.

COMMENT lets you enter comments about your program without having to precede each comment line with a semicolon. Instead, the actual comment is enclosed by the first non-blank character after the COMMENT pseudo-op and the next occurrence of that character.

```
COMMENT         *This program prints a three-letter message on
                the PC screen. The message can be changed by
                altering the values of FIRSTLETTER,
                SECONDLETTER and THIRDLETTER.*

FIRSTLETTER  EQU 49H ;49H is the ASCII code for the letter I
SECONDLETTER EQU 42H ;42H is the ASCII code for the letter B
THIRDLETTER  EQU 4DH ;4DH is the ASCII code for the letter M
PRINTFUN     EQU  2H
CHARFNS      EQU 21H

DSEG SEGMENT
DSEG ENDS

SSEG SEGMENT STACK
        DW 100H DUP(?)
SSEG ENDS

CSEG   SEGMENT
ASSUME CS:CSEG,DS:DSEG,SS:SSEG
        MOV  DL,FIRSTLETTER
        CALL PRINTCHAR
        MOV  DL,SECONDLETTER
        CALL PRINTCHAR
        MOV  DL,THIRDLETTER
        CALL PRINTCHAR
        HLT

PRINTCHAR: MOV AH,PRINTFUN
           INT CHARFNS
           RET

CSEG ENDS
END
```

To stop the main program we have used the 8088 HLT instruction. As was pointed out earlier, this HaLTs the whole computer until the system is re-booted. When trying out these programs under debugger control, therefore, it's a good idea to stop execution just before the HLT instruction is obeyed. (You could do this using the G command of DEBUG.)

EXERCISE 4.5

Amend the program in Exercise 4.4 so that the message printed is:

```
IBM
RULES
OK !!
```

4.5   CALL AND RET – THE MECHANISM OF THE BASIC (INTRA-SEGMENT) FORMS

As pointed out in Chapter 2 (Section 2.9) it is from the IP register (relative to the contents of the CS register) that the 8088 gets the address of the *next* instruction to be obeyed. Generally speaking, the programmer does not access the IP register directly. Before execution of a program the operating system initializes IP to the first of the locations containing that program. After execution of any particular instruction, IP is automatically incremented to point to the address of the next instruction. CALL and RET disturb this mechanism by changing the contents of the IP register (and sometimes the CS register).

As a specific example let's consider the following extract from the listing of an assembler:

```
                          .
                          .
                          .
010B 8B C1                MOV    AX,CX
010D E8 01 00             CALL   A_SUB
0110 F4                   HLT
0111 F7 EB      A_SUB:    IMUL   BX
0113 8B D0                MOV    DX,AX
  .                          .
  .                          .
0124 C3                   RET
```

By the time these instructions come to be executed the assembler will have replaced the label A_SUB in CALL A_SUB with one of two things. If the subroutine with first instruction labelled A_SUB is stored within 0FFFFH locations of the CALL instruction, then the label A_SUB is replaced by a 16-bit unsigned number specifying the actual displacement of the start of the subroutine from the CALL instruction. Thus, in this case, the label in CALL A_SUB will be replaced by 0001, since the IP register will automatically have been incremented to point to the instruction after the CALL, and the subroutine starts one location further on than that. This is shown in Fig. 4.3.

When CALL 0001 is executed, the 16-bit unsigned number following the code for the CALL instruction itself (0E8H) is added to the current contents of the IP register. Since the next instruction to be obeyed will be taken from the location specified by the IP register (relative to the contents of CS), the next instruction executed will indeed be that labelled A_SUB. But this is not the only effect of CALL. In order that a return to the main program can be effected once a RET instruction is encountered, CALL also pushes the address of the instruction which follows it onto the stack. Execution of the RET instruction simply entails popping the top 16-bit element of the stack

	Before		*After*
		CALL 0001	
IP	010DH		0111H
SP	01E4H		01E2H
01E1H	??		??
01E2H	??		10H
01E3H	??		01H
01E4H	??		??
		RET	
IP	0125H		0110H
SP	01E2H		01E4H
01E1H	??		??
01E2H	10H		10H
01E3H	01H		01H
01E4H	??		??

Fig. 4.3 The effect of CALL and RET on the contents of the IP register.

into the IP register. Provided as many PUSHes as POPs have occurred within the body of the subroutine, the word at the top of the stack will be the address of the instruction following the CALL.

CALL and RET instructions of this type are known as **intra-segment** (or within segment) instructions, since the body of the subroutine is in the same segment (i.e. in the same collection of 10000H memory locations) as the CALL.

Intra-segment CALL and RET – a summary

CALL <label>

- The <label> following the instruction is replaced by an unsigned 16-bit number which is the difference between the address of the first location after those containing the CALL instruction and the address of the first location containing the body of the subroutine (both relative to CS).

- When the CALL instruction is executed, the unsigned 16-bit number is added to the contents of the IP register and the address of the instruction following the CALL instruction is pushed onto the stack.

RET

- When the RET instruction is executed, the top of the stack is popped into the IP register.

4.6   THE INTER-SEGMENT SUBROUTINE MECHANISM

If the instruction following CALL and the body of the subroutine called are more than 0FFFFH locations apart, the **inter-segment** form of both CALL and RET must be used. Fortunately MASM keeps track of which form is necessary so we never actually have to count locations ourselves. The format of the CALL instruction does not change but CALL <label> where the <label> refers to a subroutine in another segment will be translated by MASM into the form CALL <address> where the <address> is a 4-byte quantity representing the address of the body of the subroutine. Of these four bytes, the first two are the offset of the subroutine from the CS register and the second two the setting of the CS register for the segment containing the CALL instruction. When the intersegment CALL instruction is executed the full (4-byte) address of the instruction following the CALL is placed onto the stack, CS value first. Then the 4-byte address in the CALL instruction itself is transferred to the IP and CS registers so that the next instruction to be executed will be the first in the appropriate subroutine.

To return from an inter-segment subroutine a different form of the RET instruction is used. On execution it pops the top two stack bytes into IP and the next two bytes into the CS register.

In order to know in advance whether a given CALL is to be converted into the machine code form of an inter-segment CALL or an intra-segment CALL, MASM insists that the programmer who wants to work in several segments must cloak each part of the program in such a way that what is *near* and what is *far* is obvious to the assembler. Otherwise it assumes that all CALL and RET instructions are intra-segment.

Thus, inter-segment CALLs and RETs are achieved thanks to the idea of a PROCedure, which is simply a subroutine labelled in a careful way and given one of the attributes *near* or *far*. Thus:

```
i) MY_SUBROUTINE: MOV AX,4
                  INC BX

                    .
                    .
                  RET
```

```
ii) MY_SUBROUTINE PROC NEAR
        MOV AX,4
        INC BX

          .
          .
        RET
    MY_SUBROUTINE ENDP
```

```
iii) MY_SUBROUTINE PROC FAR
         MOV AX,4
         INC BX
```

```
      .
      RET
MY_SUBROUTINE ENDP
```

all result in exactly the same machine code, except that the RET instruction in i) and ii) will be coded as intra-segment and that in iii) as inter-segment (and likewise CALL MY_SUBROUTINE in the first two cases will be translated into an intra-segment CALL whereas CALL MY_SUBROUTINE in case iii) will be inter-segment).

DEBUG uses different names for the CALL and RET instructions if inter-segment operation is involved. Thus CALLF is used to CALL a Far away subroutine and RETF to RETurn from a Far away subroutine.

4.7 RETURNING TO THE OPERATING SYSTEM

PC-DOS provides a mechanism whereby a program can be called into action in such a way that, when the program has been executed, control can once again be returned to the operating system. Of course, this is very similar to the mechanism for calling up a subroutine from a main program: when execution of the subroutine has finished, control returns to the main program. It is so similar, in fact, that the PC-DOS operating system actually runs other programs by executing a CALL <address> instruction where the <address> is the 4-byte address of the start of the user's program. As usual with a CALL instruction of this type, the address of the instruction following the CALL (i.e. of the next instruction in the operating system program itself) is put onto the stack. Provided that the user's program does not reset the SS and SP registers and that when the program finishes the stack is left clear (i.e. the program contains the same number of PUSH and POP instructions), then execution of an inter-segment RET will return control to the operating system.

At the time of the transfer of control from PC-DOS to the user program, the first four bytes in the Data Segment give the address for return. Hence, we push DS and the unsigned 16-bit form of zero onto the stack before the main body of the program. As a result, control returns to PC-DOS when the final inter-segment RET is encountered.

The following example shows how this is carried out in a program:

```
CHARFNS      EQU 21H
PRINTSTRING  EQU 9H

DSEG      SEGMENT
MESSAGE   DB 'THIS IS HOW WE RETURN TO PC-DOS',0AH,0DH,'$'
DSEG      ENDS

SSEG      SEGMENT STACK
          DW 100H DUP(?)
SSEG      ENDS
```

```
CSEG    SEGMENT
ASSUME CS:CSEG,DS:DSEG,SS:SSEG
START PROC FAR
        PUSH DS        ;save restart segment address
        MOV   AX,0
        PUSH AX        ;save restart offset address
;establish data segment addressability
        MOV   AX,DSEG
        MOV   DS,AX
;main program
        MOV   DX,OFFSET MESSAGE
        MOV   AH,PRINTSTRING
        INT   CHARFNS
;return to PC-DOS
        RET             ;this is inter_segment because of 'proc far'
START ENDP
CSEG ENDS
END
```

EXERCISES 4.6

1. Write and test an 8088 assembly language program which asks its user to type in a name and then prints out:

   Roses are red
   Violets are blue
   How are you
   <the name typed in>?

   and then returns to the operating system.

2. Rewrite the program in Exercise 4.4 so that control returns to the operating system once the message has been printed.

4.8 SUBROUTINES WITH PARAMETERS

The PRINTCHAR subroutine of Section 4.4 was an example of the technique of using registers to pass a parameter across to a subroutine: register AL contained the ASCII code for the character to be printed by PRINTCHAR. In this way, general purpose registers can be used to hold the parameters themselves or they may hold the addresses where parameters are located in memory. The main advantages of such an approach are that it is relatively easy to pass a small number of parameters and that, when a register is used to pass the initial (or **base**) address of a group of memory locations, the calling subroutine does not need its own copy of the data.

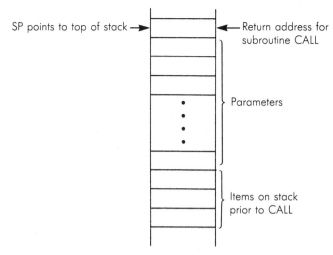

SP points to top of stack ——►

◄—— Return address for
subroutine CALL

Parameters

Items on stack
prior to CALL

Fig. 4.4   Accessing parameters placed on the stack cannot easily be done using PUSH and POP.

Since the number of general purpose registers is limited (really there are just four – AX, BX, CX and DX), if it is required to pass several parameters the stack must be used. Before the subroutine CALL the parameters are simply PUSHed onto the stack, but because the CALL then stores its own return address also on the stack, these parameters cannot easily be retrieved by PUSH and POP instructions (see Fig. 4.4).

The problem is overcome by using the BP register, a 16-bit register which can be used to access the contents of memory locations in the same way as BX. Addresses accessed via BP, however, are taken relative to the SS register, whereas BX works relative to the DS register. Both BX and BP have a further property, namely they can both be used as base registers. Thus, while the instruction:

```
MOV AX,[BP]
```

loads AX with the word at the address (relative to SS) given in BP,

```
MOV AX,[BP+2]
```

loads AX with the word at the address (relative to SS) formed by taking what's in BP and adding 2 to it. In general,

MOV register,[BP + n]
MOV [BP + n],register

(where n is either a signed 8-bit number or an unsigned 16-bit number) will transfer the contents (byte or word as appropriate) from or to the location having address (relative to SS) found by adding n to the contents of BP.

Similarly – though less often useful as one normally needs the BX register for other duties – the instructions

    MOV register,[BX + n]
    MOV [BX + n],register

perform equivalent transfers, though all addresses are taken relative to the DS register in this case.

Returning now to the problem of passing subroutine parameters placed on the stack before the subroutine was called, an easy solution is provided by setting BP to the same value as SP (so that BP now also points to the top of the stack) and then using instructions

```
MOV ...,[BP+2]
MOV ...,[BP+4]
MOV ...,[BP+6]
```

and so on to access the parameters (see Fig. 4.5).

MASM allows the use of instructions of the form

```
MOV AX,[BP+'A'] ;equivalent to MOV AX,[BP+41H]
MOV CX,[BP+'b'] ;equivalent to MOV CX,[BP+62H]
MOV BX,[BP+'W'] ;equivalent to MOV BX,[BP+57H]
```

so that, for example, one parameter could be specified for every letter of the alphabet, or for each printable character in the ASCII code.

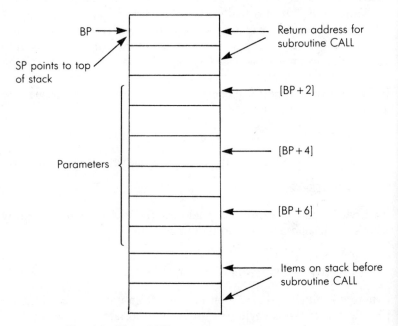

Fig. 4.5 Use of BP to access parameters.

Local variables can be provided through BP under these circumstances
by instructions of the form

```
MOV AX,[BP-2]
MOV DX,[BP-4]
```

and so on, provided that local use of the stack (i.e. use within the subroutine
itself) does not interfere with this.

After execution of a subroutine which accesses its parameters in this
way, upon return to the calling program the top items on the stack will be
these very same parameters. Quite often, the parameters are no longer
required after the execution of the subroutine and so must be POPped and
discarded. To make such discarding of parameters easier, there is a special
form of both intra- and inter-segment RET instructions:

RET x

which allows return from a subroutine in the normal manner, but
which – after the return – increments SP by x, where x is an unsigned 16-bit
number (see Fig. 4.6).

To illustrate much of this we shall now give a complete example
program which uses BP and RET x. The program adds a fixed value to each
element of an array of values and then returns to PC-DOS. It most certainly
does not follow the best method of accomplishing this task, but is, rather,
intended to illustrate subroutine parameter passing using the stack without
masses of other details getting in the way. In the program we have used the
pseudo-op .RADIX which allows one to set the default radix, assumed by
MASM to be any number between 2 and 16 (inclusive). Thus, after a

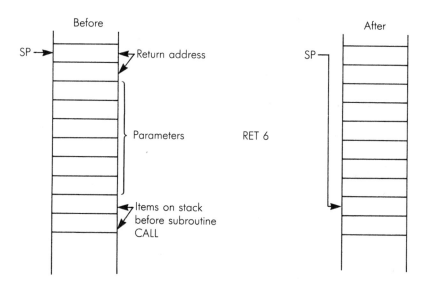

Fig. 4.6 The effect of RET 6.

.RADIX 16 pseudo-op, all numbers not explicitly marked as being in a certain base are assumed by MASM to be hexadecimal. Nevertheless, it is still necessary that every number begins with a digit (possibly 0), so that there is no chance of confusion between labels, variables, registers and numbers.

Adding a fixed value to each element of a numerical array

Here is the program using BP and RET *x*.

```
      .RADIX 16
ADDNUMBER   EQU    12
ARRAY_SIZE  EQU    9
DSEG SEGMENT
TEST_ARRAY     DW   3A,4A,5A,6A,7A,1234,5678,9ABC,0DEF
DSEG ENDS
SSEG  SEGMENT STACK
        DW  100 DUP(?)
SSEG  ENDS
CSEG SEGMENT
ASSUME CS:CSEG,DS:DSEG,SS:SSEG
MAIN PROC FAR
      PUSH DS
      MOV  AX,0
      PUSH AX              ;set up for the return to PC-DOS
      MOV  AX,DSEG
      MOV  DS,AX           ;set the DS register to initial value
      MOV  AX,OFFSET TEST_ARRAY
      PUSH AX
      MOV  AX,ADDNUMBER
      PUSH AX
      MOV  AX,ARRAY_SIZE
      PUSH AX
      CALL ARRAY_INC
      RET                  ;to PC-DOS
MAIN ENDP
ARRAY_INC PROC NEAR
                MOV BP,SP            ;initialize BP to value of SP
                MOV CX,[BP+2]        ;CX is the size of the array
                MOV AX,[BP+4]        ;AX is the number to be added
                MOV BX,[BP+6]        ;BX is the start address
ALTER_THIS_LOC:MOV DX,[BX]           ;bring contents of next location
                ADD DX,AX            ;add the increment to it
                MOV [BX],DX          ;store away again
                ADD BX,2             ;set BX to next address
```

```
            DEC CX                  ;reduce count
            JNZ ALTER_THIS_LOC
            RET 6                   ;if done, return and add 6 to SP
ARRAY_INC EDNP

CSEG ENDS
END
```

EXERCISES 4.7

1. Write a subroutine which adds up the five unsigned 16-bit numbers which have been placed on the stack and leaves their total in AX. (Assume that this total can be accurately represented in unsigned 16-bit form.) Write also a main program which calls up your subroutine, and test the complete program carefully.

2. Write a subroutine which will add together the corresponding entries in two arrays, each containing 10D signed 16-bit numbers, and leave the result in a third similar array, assuming in every case that the result of the addition is accurately represented in signed 16-bit form. Your subroutine should take its parameters from the stack, given that they were *placed* on the stack in the following order:

   starting address of first array
   starting address of second array
   starting address of array to hold the sums

   Write a main program to accompany the subroutine so that it can be properly tested.

3. Repeat Exercise 2 but with the subroutine in this case swapping the elements of the two given arrays. Use two local variables accessed via BP to effect the swap.

4.9 EFFICIENCY

In a commercial programming environment the single most expensive resource is programming staff. Efficient working in this case involves maximizing the amount of correct programming they can get done in a given period of time. The best way of achieving this is to ensure that programs are developed in small, independent blocks which are then glued together – as promoted earlier in this chapter. Locating errors in programs is thus speeded up by the ability to trust previously proven blocks to work exactly according to their specification.

Some practical applications of computing may require a minimum speed of execution, my favourite illustration of this fact being the ultimate in computerized cash dispensing machines, which could give you all sorts of information about Wall Street share prices as well as your own bank account, but which was famous for keeping some people waiting for their own money for 20 minutes! Other applications can involve restrictions on the amount of memory available, possibly to contain costs in a commercial product. Just because the 8088 can address more than one million locations, it doesn't mean that a computer system based on that microprocessor will necessarily have more than a few bytes of memory.

In the commercial world, then, writing a program for a particular task may involve a trade-off between the amount of time required to write the program in a particular way (which influences the cost of producing the program radically), the speed at which the program executes (which must conform to the user's desired minimum) and the amount of memory occupied by the program. Minimizing the memory used by a program often comes down to giving careful thought to the way any graphics are implemented. However, there are some considerations which can save more than the odd byte or two, the most important being to choose a good algorithm and related data structures for the program. After that the programmer must resort to dirty tricks, but because these make a program hard to read for a person not directly involved in its production, these are eschewed in commercial programming environments. A good algorithm is also the basis of producing a program which performs within certain speed constraints. If the best possible algorithm is already in use and speed requirements are still not satisfied, it may be that a more careful choice of 8088 instructions can solve the problem.

Before we examine a specific example, it is necessary to remind the reader that the IBM Personal Computer system clock works at 4.77 million pulses a second. Each 8088 instruction takes a certain number of clock pulses or **cycles** to be executed. The details of the number of cycles each instruction takes to execute can be found in Appendix V. RET takes just eight cycles, RCR CX,1 takes two; the NOP (No OPeration) instruction does nothing and takes three cycles – it is normally used to enable a program to wait for a certain amount of time before continuing; MUL BX takes between 118 and 133 cycles.

Cycle times give us a means, should we really need to, of comparing the speed of two program fragments. Let us prove that a program which uses shift instructions to perform multiplication by powers of two executes faster than it would if using the 8088 multiplication instructions. Consider the program fragment:

```
        CALL  MULT_BY_8
              .
              .
              .
MULT_BY_8:    MOV   CL,3
```

```
        SAL AX,CL
        RET
```

The MULT_BY_8 subroutine takes up five bytes of store when converted to machine code, and the CALL instruction another three bytes. It takes 19 cycles to execute the CALL and 32 cycles for the subroutine itself. On the other hand, consider:

```
        CALL   TIMES_8
              .
              .
              .
TIMES_8:  SAL AX,1
          SAL AX,1
          SAL AX,1
          RET
```

This takes up two extra bytes of storage but executes in a mere 14 cycles.

Use of 8088 multiplication instructions such as MUL is slower in all cases since these instructions require a minimum of 71 cycles to execute. However all 8088 multiplication instructions occupy just two bytes of store for the instruction itself and two bytes for the MOV instruction to initialize a register to 8. Thus, if memory were very short, the obvious choice of MUL (or an equivalent – see Chapter 5) would be the correct one as it would be in all but the most execution-time critical applications.

4.10 SUMMARY

This chapter has been concerned with the artefacts of good assembly language programming technique: a controlled program development methodology, mimicking the sophisticated features for structured programming which are found in languages such as Pascal; the use of subroutines – with and without parameters – so that difficult, large programs can be built up out of smaller, proven building blocks; and the realization that, in these days of high labour costs, it is the actual programming process which is the key to efficiency rather than the execution speed of a particular program fragment. The next chapter will apply this methodology to produce a complete example program.

5 An Example of Large Program Development – Simulating a Simple Calculator

AIMS

In this chapter we illustrate the use of the program development methodology outlined in Chapter 4 to produce a substantial machine code program which simulates the operation of a simple four-function electronic calculator. This will simultaneously afford us the opportunity of introducing the remaining 8088 instructions for addition, subtraction, multiplication and division (Table 5.4 at the end of the chapter gives a complete summary of 8088 arithmetic instructions). The final exercises in this chapter assume that the reader has become sufficiently familiar with the architecture of the calculator simulating program to make modifications and extensions to its basic structure.

5.1 SPECIFICATION

Users of our calculator simulator will have to enter their sums in one of the following formats:

      number + number =
  or number − number =
  or number * number =
  or number / number =

and the simulating program will then print the answer after the equals sign. Once it has been started up our simulator will do sums forever, or at least until the computer is switched off.

Only positive decimal whole numbers will be accepted. Each such number may be preceded or followed by any number of spaces but will be terminated by the first non-digit character encountered. Also, there must be at least one digit before and after the operation sign (+, −, * or /, whichever it is). Thus:

      24+   96=
       22+317=
    9148   *   8866 =

are allowed but

```
3   7  −    1   4 =
         −  999     =
  +2169 * 417   =
  4.16/2.72      =
```

are *not* allowed.

If either of the numbers typed in is too big we will display the message

```
NUMBER TOO BIG — RESTART CALCULATION
```

on the computer's screen and expect the person using our calculator simulator to enter the whole of that sum again. If an illegal character is entered due to mistyping (or malice!) we shall display

```
ILLEGAL CHARACTER — RESTART CALCULATION
```

and once again demand that the user start afresh. (As far as our simulator is concerned the only characters which are legal are the digits 0, 1, 2, . . . , 9; the operation signs +, −, *, /; the equals sign =; and spaces).

Division by zero is not allowed: an attempt to divide by zero will gain the system response:

```
DIVISION BY ZERO NOT ALLOWED
```

and the whole of that calculation will be ignored. For a successful division, the answer will be printed in quotient and remainder form. Thus:

```
13/2=6R1
```

5.2 PROGRAM DESIGN

Step 1 – choose data structures and types

We have only to deal with numbers, so data structuring is not a problem. Only whole numbers of up to 4 decimal digits are allowed, so the biggest number which can be entered into our calculator is 9999. This means that the biggest number of digits in an answer will come from 9999 * 9999 = 99980001. If we use signed 16-bit numbers in the program the biggest number we can have is 0111111111111111B, i.e. 32767D. Thus signed 16-bit numbers are quite adequate for storing our 4-digit, positive, decimal whole numbers. The answer which results from combining two such decimal numbers can similarly be accommodated as a 32-bit signed number, since the largest positive number representable in that form is 2147483647D.

Step 2 – top-down program design

A basic outline of the program is easy to write:

> **repeat**
>> *read in a decimal number and an operator;*
>> *store the decimal number in AX;*
>> *store the operator in DL;*
>> *read in a second decimal number and store it in BX;*
>> *when the user has typed an equals sign then*
>> *print the result of the operator applied to AX and BX*
> **forever**

However, a few attempts at producing the next stage of refinement so that errors can be dealt with easily leads one to introduce a subroutine:

GET_OK_NUM_AND_TERM_NON_SPACE_CHAR

This subroutine performs the following functions:

> **repeat**
>> *digits_read* := 5;
>> **while** *digits_read* = 5 **or** *code* < > 1 **do**
>>> **begin**
>>> *print(newline);*
>>> *call get_ok_num_and_term_non_space_char;*
>>> **if** *digits_read* = 5 **then** *print(too_long);*
>>> **if** *code* < > 1 **then** *print(illegal_character);*
>>> **if** *digits_read* = 0 **then**
>>>> **begin**
>>>> *print(illegal character);*
>>>> *code* := 0
>>>> **end**
>>> **end;**
>> PUSH AX (*to preserve the operator on the stack*)
>> PUSH BX (*save user's first decimal number on stack*)
>> *call get_ok_num_and_term_non_space_char;*
>> **if**   *digits_read* = 5 **then begin** POP AX; POP BX; *print(too_long)* **end**
>> **else if** *digits_read*>0 **and** *code* = 2 **then**
>>> **begin**
>>> POP AX ; (*restore first user number*)
>>> POP DX ; (*restore operator to DL*)
>>> **case** DL **of**
>>> '+' : *call doplus;*
>>> '−' : *call dosub;*
>>> '*' : *call domult;*
>>> '/' : *call dodivision;*
>>>> **end**
>>> **end**
>> **else begin** POP AX; POP BX; *print(illegal character)* **end**
> **forever**

Fig. 5.1   Outline of the calculator simulator program.

Fig. 5.2 For a signed 32-bit number register DX contains the higher order bits.

1. Skips preceding and trailing spaces in the user's input.
2. Waits for the user to type in a single decimal number of not more than four digits at the keyboard.
3. Leaves in CL a code:
    1. signifying that the first non-space character typed after the decimal number was one of +, −, *, /
    2. signifying that the first non-space character typed after the decimal number was =
4. Leaves in BX the binary form of the decimal number entered (if it was valid).
5. In AL leaves the ASCII code for the terminating non-space character.

Using this subroutine we can develop a version of the program which is sufficiently refined to identify the building-block subroutines of the final program. This is shown in Fig. 5.1.

From Fig.5.1 it follows that we must write the following subroutines:

1. Wait for a character to be typed at the keyboard and leave its ASCII code in AL.
2. Print the character whose ASCII code is in a register – we shall use DL.
3. Using the subroutine in 2, print error messages on the screen as follows:
    a) `NUMBER TOO BIG — RESTART CALCULATION`
    b) `ILLEGAL CHARACTER — RESTART CALCULATION`
    c) `DIVISION BY ZERO NOT ALLOWED`
4. Assuming the signed 16-bit forms of the two decimal numbers typed in by the user are in AX and BX (AX containing the first number typed), a routine to perform each of the four basic arithmetic operations on the contents of those registers. In every case the answer will be left as a signed 32-bit number in registers CX and DX with DX containing the higher order bits, as shown in Fig. 5.2.

    The operations performed will be as follows:

    a) Addition
    b) Subtraction
    c) Multiplication
    d) Division

5. Implement the subroutine GET_OK_NUM_AND_TERM_NON_SPACE_CHAR.

6. Convert the signed 32-bit binary number held in registers CX and DX into a decimal number and print it on the screen.

5.3   READING AND PRINTING CHARACTERS

1 – Reading a character from the keyboard (READCHAR)

Thanks to function number 1 provided by INTerrupt 21H there's very little work to do.

```
READCHAR: MOV AH,1H
          INT 21H
          RET
```

(Function 1 also causes the character corresponding to the key which was pressed to be printed on the display screen.)

2 – Printing a character on the display screen (PRINTCHAR)

Exactly the same subroutine as that introduced in Chapter 4 will do:

```
PRINTCHAR: MOV AH,2H
           INT 21H
           RET
```

3 – Printing the error messages

The combination

```
MOV DX,starting address of message
MOV AH,09H
INT 21H
:
:
```

will print the characters whose ASCII codes are stored in the locations with the given starting address (relative to the DS register) and following until the ASCII code for a $ sign is encountered (see Section 4.4). At this point the INTerrupt will cease and execution will continue as normal from the instruction after INT 21H. When the user of our calculator simulator goes wrong we want to be able to print out helpful messages such as NUMBER TOO BIG and ILLEGAL CHARACTER. All that remains is i) to put the message into an appropriate place in memory, and ii) to specify its starting address. To do this, in the code segment CSEG we must add the subroutine:

```
ILLEGAL_CHAR: CALL PRINT_NEWLINE
              MOV  AH,09H
              MOV  DX,OFFSET ILLEGAL_MESS
              INT  21H
              RET
```

and in the data segment DSEG:

```
ILLEGAL_MESS DB 'ILLEGAL CHARACTER — RESTART CALCULATION', 0AH,0DH,'$'
```

Appendix II gives a complete listing of the calculator simulator program. It would be worth glancing through this appendix at this point to see the subroutines we have developed so far in their actual places in the final program. To encourage you to do this we shall present here neither the bodies of the other two subroutines which print error messages – TOO_LONG and DIVISION_BY_ZERO – nor the necessary data pseudo-ops. Instead you are requested to turn to the appropriate appendix.

EXERCISES 5.1

1. The following fragment is part of a program which will wait for 10D characters to be typed at the keyboard and then print those characters in reverse order. Complete the program, type it into your computer and assemble and run it. Modify the program so that once the 10D characters have been typed in they are printed out with at least each pair of characters in the correct order. Thus, if the 10D characters typed were A, then B, then C, . . . , and then J, the output from the modified program would be IJGHEFCDAB.

```
READ_NEXT:CALL READCHAR
          PUSH AX
          DEC  BX        ;read another if BX
          JNZ  READ_NEXT ;not zero yet
          MOV  BX,0AH     ;set up new count for printing
PRINT_NEXT:POP AX        ;restore the last item stacked
          MOV  DL,AL      ;transfer the character ready
          CALL PRINTCHAR  ;for printing
          DEC  BX
          JNZ  PRINT_NEXT ;done 10D yet?
          HLT
```

2. Write an assembly language program to read in four letters (A, B, . . . , Z) from the keyboard, print a space (ASCII code 20H) and then print the four letters in reverse order followed by a new line. Keep the four letters typed in registers BH, BL, DH and DL.

3. Write an assembly language program to read in a letter (A, B, . . . , Z) from the keyboard, print a new line, and then print the alphabet

up to and including that letter. (Hint: use the fact that the hexadecimal numbers 41H, 42H, 43H, . . . , 59H represent the letters A, B, C, . . . , Z).

5.4   SUBROUTINES FOR SIGNED 16-BIT ARITHMETIC

4a – Addition of two signed 16-bit numbers, both between 0 and 9999D

This requires the following procedure:

1.   Given the first signed 16-bit number in AX, call it a.
2.   Given the second signed 16-bit number in BX, call it b.
3.   Then the sum $a + b$ is to be left in signed 32-bit form in CX and DX, DX to contain the higher order bits (Fig. 5.3).

Fig. 5.3   The sum of AX and BX is stored in CX and DX in signed 32-bit form.

We already know all the necessary instructions for this so the implementation is easy:

```
ADDITION: ADD AX,BX
          MOV CX,AX
          MOV DX,OH
          RET
```

Testing this little block involves going through the procedure described in Chapter 3 for obtaining a machine code version and then using a debugger to enter various values in registers AX and BX. When doing test runs it is important to stop execution before the RET instruction is obeyed. Otherwise the 8088 will try to return to the 'main' program and there isn't one yet!

With any program which does arithmetic (or even just counts things!) it is the extreme values which are most likely to cause failure so these should be checked carefully. In this particular case, 9999D + 9999D = 19998D is much less than the biggest positive signed 16-bit number, 32767D, so there is no doubt that the answer to our sum will fit into register AX.

4b – Subtraction of two signed 16-bit numbers both between 0 and 9999D

This requires the following procedure:

1.   Given the first signed 16-bit number in AX, call it a.

2. Given the second signed 16-bit number in BX, call it *b*.

3. The difference, *a–b*, is to be left in signed 32-bit form in CX and DX, DX to contain the higher order bits

```
SUBTRACTION: SUB AX,BX
             CWD           ;sign extend AX into DX
             MOV CX,AX
RESULT_POSITIVE: RET
```

The CWD instruction stores 0FFFFH in DX if the highest order bit of AX (i.e. the sign bit in a signed 16-bit representation) is 1 and stores 0000H in DX otherwise. This ensures that DX,CX contains the signed 32-bit form of the result of the subtraction, even when this is negative.

If the result of the subtraction is negative the sign flag (first introduced in Chapter 2) will be set to 1, otherwise it will be set to 0. Since the RET instruction does not affect any of the flags, the sign flag will still indicate whether the result of the subtraction was negative or not even after the return to the main program has been effected. We shall use this fact when writing the routine which prints out the result of the subtraction, for we shall want to print a minus sign only if the result is negative.

4c – Multiplication of two signed 16-bit numbers both between 0 and 9999D

Whilst the ADD and SUB instructions will work with both signed and unsigned numbers, the 8088 provides separate instructions for the multiplication of signed and unsigned numbers.

Multiplication of signed numbers

The instruction takes one of the forms:

IMUL register

or

IMUL memory location

Thus IMUL CX will multiply the signed 16-bit number in register AX by the signed 16-bit number in register CX and leave the signed 32-bit result in registers AX and DX, DX containing the higher order bits. (Multiplying a 16-digit number by another 16-digit number gives a product with 32 digits.) Similarly

```
IMUL [200H]
```

would multiply the signed 16-bit number in register AX by the signed 16-bit number in locations 200H, 201H (relative to the DS register) and leave the signed 32-bit result in AX and DX.

Multiplication of unsigned numbers

In this case the formats are:

MUL register

or

MUL memory location

Both of these work in exactly the same way as the corresponding IMUL instruction but the 32-bit result is unsigned.

Returning now to the multiplication building block for our calculator simulator, we require:

1. A signed 16-bit number in AX, call it a.
2. A signed 16-bit number in BX, call it b.
3. The product $a*b$ to be left in signed 32-bit form in CX and DX, DX to contain the higher order bits.

```
MULTIPLICATION: IMUL BX
                MOV  CX,AX
                RET
```

4d – Division of two signed 16-bit numbers, both between 0 and 9999D

As for multiplication, there are separate instructions for signed and unsigned division – IDIV and DIV respectively. Moreover, both IDIV and DIV allow the alternatives of dividing an 8-bit number into a 16-bit number or of dividing a 16-bit number into a 32-bit one. Both do primary school 'long division with whole numbers' so that dividing 7D into 36D would give a quotient of 5D and a remainder of 1D.

The instructions take one of the forms:

DIV register
DIV memory location

or

IDIV register
IDIV memory location

and both DIV and IDIV operate according to whichever of the following schemes the programmer chooses:

1. The 32-bit number in registers DX and AX (DX containing the higher order bits) is divided by the contents of the specified 16-bit register (or the 16-bit number stored at the given location) and the result left in registers AX and DX: quotient in AX, remainder in DX (see Fig. 5.4a).

2. The 16-bit number in register AX is divided by the contents of the specified 8-bit register or memory location and the result left in registers AL and AH: quotient in AL, remainder in AH (see Fig. 5.4b).

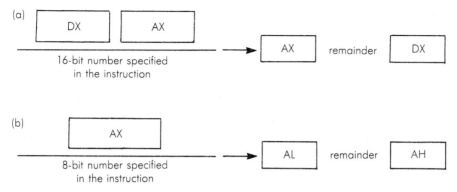

Fig. 5.4 Signed and unsigned division: (a) dividing a 32-bit number by a specified 16-bit number; (b) dividing a 16-bit number by a specified 8-bit number.

Warning – division by zero

Any attempt to divide by zero will cause your computer to resort to all manner of strange behaviour – exactly what will depend on the particular make – and you'll probably have to switch it off and start running your program all over again. Consequently, great care must be taken within a program to ensure that division by zero is never attempted. (To be completely honest, the disastrous results of dividing by zero can be brought under programmer control – see Chapter 12).

For the division routine of our calculator simulator we shall assume that a check for division by zero has been made before it is entered from the main program. Our working specification is therefore:

1. Given a signed 16-bit number in AX, call it *a*.
2. Given a signed 16-bit number in BX, guaranteed not zero, call it *b*.
3. If $a/b = x$ remainder y, then x is to be left in signed 32-bit form in DX and CX, DX to contain the higher order bits; and y is to be left in signed 32-bit form in AX and BX, BX to contain the higher order bits.

```
DIVISION: MOV    DX,0
          IDIV   BX
          MOV    CX,AX
          MOV    AX,DX
          MOV    DX,0
          MOV    BX,0
          RET
```

EXERCISE 5.2

Write and test under debugger control, assembly language programs for each of the following tasks:

i) Leave in register AX the sum of the contents of all four general purpose registers AX, BX, CX and DX.

ii) Leave in register AX the value of $(a - b)/(c - d)$ where a, b, c, d denote the contents of AX, BX, CX and DX respectively and where we assume that $c - d$ is not zero.

iii) Leave the average value $(a + b + c)/3$ in register DX where a, b, c are as in ii) above.

iv) Leave the value of $(b*c)/a$ in register DX where a, b, c are as in ii) above and it is assumed that the contents of AX are not zero.

5.5 READING AND CONVERTING DECIMAL NUMBERS TO SIGNED 16-BIT FORM

5 – The GET_OK_NUM_AND_TERM_NON_SPACE_CHAR subroutine

Characters are read from the keyboard one at a time, so whilst we think of typing in the number 7231 the computer actually gets a stream of single digits: first a 7, then a 2, then a 3 and then finally a 1. What we have to organize is the conversion of this stream of digits into a number (actually a binary number) stored in one of the 8088 registers.

Retrieving the binary form of any one digit is easy. Our READCHAR subroutine will be used to read the digit from the keyboard and it leaves the ASCII code for that digit in register AL. The ASCII codes for the digits $0, 1, \ldots, 9$ are as shown in Table 5.1.

Each ASCII code is precisely 30H bigger than the actual numerical value of the digit concerned. Hence, if in register AL we have the ASCII code of a digit, subtracting 30H from register AL will leave the digit's numerical value in that register.

Table 5.1 ASCII codes for digits 0–9.

Digit	ASCII code
0	30H
1	31H
2	32H
3	33H
4	34H
5	35H
6	36H
7	37H
8	38H
9	39H

So much for single digits. Here now is how we deal with a stream of digits (for example, 7 then 2 then 3 then 1). First initialize register BX to 0. Then, having read the first digit 7 and converted the resulting ASCII coded contents of AL to the numeric value 7, we add that to the current contents of BX. If there's another digit to be read we now multiply the contents of BX by ten and add in the numeric value of the next digit. (At this stage in our example, register BX contains the binary for decimal 72.) Again, if there's another digit to be read we now multiply the contents of BX by ten and add in the numeric value of the next digit (BX now contains the binary for decimal 723). And so on until there are no more digits to be read in. (In our example, multiplying the contents, 723, of BX by ten and adding in the numeric value of the last digit read, 1, leaves the desired result – 7231 – in binary form in register BX.)

Now we can give a structured outline of the subroutine GET_OK_NUM _AND_TERM_NON_SPACE_CHAR:

> $BX := 0$;
> $digits\_read := 0$;
> **repeat** *read(char)* **until** *char* <> ' '; (*skip spaces*)
> **while** *char* **in** ['0' . . '9'] **and** *digits_read* <> 4 **do**
>   **begin**
>   *digits_read* := *digits_read* + 1;
> $BX := BX * 10 + binary\_value\_of(char)$;
>   *read(char)*
>   **end**;
> **while** *char* = ' ' **do** *read(char)*; (*skip trailing spaces*)
> **if** *char* **in** ['0' . . '9'] **then** *digits_read* := *digits_read* + 1
> **else if** *char* **in** ['+', '−', '*', '/'] **then** $CL := 1$
> **else if** *char* = '=' **then** $CL := 2$

Here are the three instructions we shall use to skip over any spaces which precede a numeric input to our calculator simulator:

```
SKIP_SPACES: CALL READCHAR
             CMP  AL,' '
             JZ   SKIP_SPACES
```

Only when a character has been read whose ASCII code is different from that for a space will the instructions following the JZ instruction be obeyed. The CMP (CoMPare) instruction does not change the value of any of the 8088 registers. Generally it has one of the following forms (where we assume that comparisons are always made betweeen numbers of the same size):

CMP register,number
CMP register,register
CMP [address],number
CMP register,[address]
CMP [address],register

Table 5.2 Assignment of registers.

Register	Variable
BX	binary value of user's decimal number
CH	digits_read
AL	char – each character read from the keyboard
CL	the code indicating the type of the terminating non-space character

and only the flags are affected by it. For example, CMP AL,23H will set the Z-flag to 1 if the current content of AL is 23H. In fact the flags are set as they would be by a SUB AL,23H instruction but CMP AL,23H does not change the value of AL. In CMP AL,'x' the assembler will look up the ASCII code for the letter x (let's suppose it is n) and then assemble the whole instruction into machine code as if it had been CMP AL,n in the first place.

The implementation of the above outline will use registers for the variables as shown in Table 5.2.

First, we initialize variables, skip over any preceding spaces and form the body of the main **while** loop:

```
GET_OK_NUM_AND_TERM_NON_SPACE_CHAR: MOV BX,OH
;digits_read := 0;
     MOV CH,0
;repeat read(char) until char <> ' ';
SKIP_SPACES: CALL READCHAR
             CMP   AL,' '
             JZ    SKIP_SPACES
;while char in ['0' .. '9'] and digits_read <> 4 do
CHECK_NUMERIC: CMP AL,'0'
               JB  MISS_TRAIL_SPACES
               CMP AL,'9'
               JA  MISS_TRAIL_SPACES
               CMP CH,4
               JZ  MISS_TRAIL_SPACES
               ;begin

                     .
                     .
                     .

               ;end
               JMP CHECK_NUMERIC
MISS_TRAIL_SPACES:
```

Once the body of this **while** loop has been filled in, that leaves us with a **while** loop to skip any trailing spaces and an **if** statement to set CL and digits_read appropriately. Let us complete these last two statements first:

```
;while char = ' ' do read(char)
  MISS_TRAIL_SPACES: CMP  AL,' '
                     JNZ  IS_THIS_FIFTH_DIGIT
                     CALL READCHAR
                     JMP  MISS_TRAIL_SPACES
;if char in ['0' .. '9'] then digits_read := digits_read + 1
IS_THIS_FIFTH_DIGIT: CMP  AL,'0'
                     JB   TRY_OPERATOR
                     CMP  AL,'9'
                     JA   TRY_EQUALS
                     INC  CH
                     JMP  DONE_THIS
;else if char in ['+', '-', '*', '/'] then CL := 1
      TRY_OPERATOR:  CMP  AL,'+'
                     JZ   GOT_OPERATOR
                     CMP  AL,'-'
                     JZ   GOT_OPERATOR
                     CMP  AL,'*'
                     JZ   GOT_OPERATOR
                     CMP  AL,'/'
                     JZ   GOT_OPERATOR
;else if char = '=' then CL := 2
        TRY_EQUALS:  CMP  AL,'='
                     JNZ  DONE_THIS
                     MOV  CL,2
                     JMP  DONE_THIS
      GOT_OPERATOR:  MOV  CL,1
        DONE_THIS:   RET
```

EXERCISE 5.3

Work through the two parts of the above outline of GET_OK_NUM_AND_TERM_NON_SPACE_CHAR for each of the following calculator simulator inputs:

  i)   17+2138=

  ii) 4   2   −   181 =

  iii) + 16 − 4 =

State clearly what will be in registers AL, BX, CH and CL at the end of each call.

The numeric conversion on input

Our requirement is for instructions which will multiply the contents of register BX by 10D and add into BX the numeric value of the character whose ASCII code is in register AL. The contents of register CH should be the same at the end of the conversion as they were at the beginning.

```
;BX := BX * 10D + binary_value_of(char)
MOV   CL,AL   ;copy the contents of AL for safe keeping
MOV   AX,10D
IMUL  BX
MOV   BX,AX   ;BX now contains 10D times its previous contents
MOV   AL,CL   ;restore AL
SUB   AL,30H  ;retrieve numeric value from character
MOV   AH,OH   ;prepare AX for 16-bit addition
ADD   BX,AX
```

Even though the result of IMUL BX is held in registers DX and AX, DX cannot be non-zero since the largest decimal number we are to read in is 9999 which is easily represented in signed 16-bit form. Thus we can ignore the contents of DX after the multiplication instruction has been executed. Figure 5.5 gives the complete GET_OK_NUM_AND_TERM_NON_SPACE_CHAR subroutine.

EXERCISES 5.4

1. Write an assembly language program which will accept a 2-digit decimal number typed at the keyboard and then print out a new line followed by the remainder when that decimal number is divided by 9.

2. Write an assembly language program which will read in a 3-digit decimal number and print a new line followed by whichever of the following messages is appropriate: ABOVE 100, EQUAL 100, or BELOW 100.

```
GET_OK_NUM_AND_TERM_NON_SPACE_CHAR: MOV BX,OH
;digits_read := 0;
      MOV   CH,O
;repeat read(char) until char <> ' ';
SKIP_SPACES: CALL READCHAR
             CMP   AL,' '
             JZ    SKIP_SPACES
;while char in ['0' .. '9'] and digits_read <> 4 do
CHECK_NUMERIC: CMP   AL,'0'
               JB    MISS_TRAIL_SPACES
               CMP   AL,'9'
               JA    MISS_TRAIL_SPACES
```

Fig. 5.5 The GET_OK_NUM_AND_TERM_NON_SPACE_CHAR subroutine.

```
                    CMP   CH,4
                    JZ    MISS_TRAIL_SPACES
                    ;begin
                    ;digits_read := digits_read + 1;
                    INC   CH
                    ;BX := BX * 10D + binary_value_of(char)
                    MOV   CL,AL   ;copy the contents of AL for safe
                                  ;keeping
                    MOV   AX,10D
                    IMUL  BX
                    MOV   BX,AX   ;BX now contains 10D times its
                                  ;previous contents
                    MOV   AL,CL   ;restore AL
                    SUB   AL,30H ;retrieve numeric value from character
                    MOV   AH,0H   ;prepare AX for 16-bit addition
                    ADD   BX,AX
                    ;read(char)
                    CALL READCHAR
                    ;end
                    JMP   CHECK_NUMERIC
;while char = ' ' do read(char)
MISS_TRAIL_SPACES: CMP   AL,' '
                    JNZ   IS_THIS_FIFTH_DIGIT
                    CALL READCHAR
                    JMP   MISS_TRAIL_SPACES
;if char in ['0' .. '9'] then digits_read := digits_read + 1
IS_THIS_FIFTH_DIGIT: CMP AL,'0'
                       JB  TRY_OPERATOR
                       CMP AL,'9'
                       JA  TRY_EQUALS
                       INC CH
                       JMP DONE_THIS
;else if char in ['+', '-', '*', '/'] then CL := 1
TRY_OPERATOR: CMP AL,'+'
              JZ   GOT_OPERATOR
              CMP AL,'-'
              JZ   GOT_OPERATOR
              CMP AL,'*'
              JZ   GOT_OPERATOR
              CMP AL,'/'
              JZ   GOT_OPERATOR
;else if char = '=' then CL := 2
   TRY_EQUALS: CMP AL,'='
              JNZ DONE_THIS
              MOV CL,2
              JMP DONE_THIS
GOT_OPERATOR: MOV CL,1
    DONE_THIS: RET
```

Fig. 5.5 (*continued*)

5.6   CONVERTING A SIGNED 32-BIT NUMBER

6 – Convert the contents of DX,CX into decimal and print

Our requirement is for a building block (which we shall call PRINTOUT) which will print on the display screen the decimal equivalent of the 32-bit signed number held in registers DX and CX (DX containing the higher order bits). Since the largest possible number we will have to print out is the result of 9999 * 9999 = 99980001, the method we shall adopt for determining the decimal digits of the number held in registers DX and CX is as follows.

Suppose for the sake of illustration that DX and CX contain 21030087D. Subtract 10000000D (7 zeros) from DX and CX until DX and CX is negative and count the number of subtractions. Thus:

21030087 − 10000000 − 10000000 − 10000000

is negative and we have subtracted three times. Hence the first *decimal* digit of the contents of DX and CX is 2 in this case. Now add the last 10000000D subtracted back again, so making the contents of DX and CX positive. This gives 1030087D in our example. Now subtract 1000000D (6 zeros) repeatedly until DX and CX becomes negative. Thus:

1030087 − 1000000 − 1000000

is negative and we have subtracted 2 times. Thus the next decimal digit of the decimal equivalent of the contents of DX and CX is 1. Now make DX and CX positive again by adding back the last 1000000 subtracted. This gives 30087D. Now subtract 100000 (5 zeros) until DX and CX becomes negative. Since:

30087 − 100000

is already negative and we have subtracted only once, the next decimal digit of DX and CX is 0. Add the 100000 back and then subtract 10000 (4 zeros) giving the next digit as 3. Add back and subtract 1000 (3 zeros) giving the decimal digit 0; add back to make DX and CX positive and then subtract 100 (2 zeros) and so on until finally subtracting 1 until DX and CX is negative. Since:

7−1−1−1−1−1−1−1−1

is negative, the final decimal digit of the decimal equivalent of the number in DX and CX is 7. (Notice that this method destroys the contents of DX and CX.)

Implementing this method in 8088 assembly language will require a subroutine which enables numbers such as the binary equivalent of 10000000D to be subtracted from DX and CX, and a corresponding subroutine for addition. These subroutines will be called BIG_SUB and BIG_ADD respectively.

BIG_ADD – signed 32-bit addition

This subroutine will treat the register pairs DX,CX and BX,AX as 32-bit registers (DX and BX containing the higher order bits). The current contents of the pair DX,CX as a 32-bit signed number will be added to the 32-bit signed number in BX,AX and the result left in DX,CX. After a call to the subroutine the pair BX,AX will be unaltered.

To implement the subroutine we follow the time-honoured primary school method for the decimal addition of, say, 37 + 15. Add the units, so that 7 add 5 is 2 down, carry 1. Then add the tens: 3 add 1 is 4 plus the carry makes 5. Hence the answer is 52. BIG_ADD will first add CX and AX leaving the result in CX. Next it will add DX and BX together with any carry from the previous addition.

```
BIG_ADD: CLC
         ADD CX,AX
         ADC DX,BX
         RET
```

The **CLC** instruction clears the carry flag before we begin the arithmetic. Addition of DX and BX together with any carry is then achieved by the ADC instruction which takes one of the general formats:

ADC register,register
ADC register,number
ADC register,memory location
ADC memory location,register.

ADC DX,BX adds the contents of register BX to the contents of register DX, then adds the current value of the carry flag to that and leaves the result in register DX. (In BIG_ADD the ADD CX,AX instruction will set the carry flag to 1 if there is a carry from adding the numbers in registers CX and AX and to 0 otherwise.)

BIG_SUB – signed 32-bit subtraction

This is very similar to BIG_ADD in that we follow the method of decimal subtraction which allows us to 'borrow then pay back'. For example, to work out 46 − 19 (in decimal) we borrow 10 and do 16 − 9 which leaves 7. Then we pay back 1 to the tens and do 4 − 2 which leaves 2, so that 46 − 19 is 27. BIG_SUB first clears the carry flag and then subtracts AX from CX. If the result is negative (i.e. a borrow was necessary) the carry flag is set to 1. Next the contents of BX is subtracted from the contents of DX once any borrow has been paid back.

```
BIG_SUB: CLC
         SUB CX,AX
         SBB DX,BX
         RET
```

The SBB instruction has the same general format as the ADC instruction described above. SBB DX,BX adds the current contents of the carry flag (0 or 1) to the contents of register BX and subtracts the resulting total from the contents of register DX, leaving the result in DX. (In BIG_SUB the SUB CX,AX instruction will set the carry flag to 1 if a borrow was necessary and to 0 otherwise.)

Powers of ten

According to our method for extracting the digits of the decimal equivalent of the contents of DX,CX we first repeatedly subtract 10000000; then 1000000; then 100000; and so on. Consequently we shall need the signed 32-bit equivalent of all these various powers of ten stored in memory. This is easily organized thanks to the DD (Define Doubleword) pseudo-op first mentioned in Chapter 3. We simply add the following pseudo-ops to the data segment of our program:

```
POWERS_TABLE DD 10000000
             DD 1000000
             DD 100000
             DD 10000
             DD 1000
             DD 100
             DD 10
             DD 1
```

and MASM does all the necessary conversions for us and stores the results in the location labelled POWERS_TABLE and following.

The SI register and indexing

When writing the body of the PRINTOUT subroutine we shall want to access the powers of ten one by one. To enable us to work through such a list it is convenient to use a new 16-bit register, the SI (Source Index) register. By initializing SI to the address of the first entry in the list:

```
MOV SI,OFFSET POWERS_TABLE
```

the first two bytes of the signed 32-bit equivalent of 10000000D can be loaded into AX by the instruction

```
MOV AX,[SI]
```

demonstrating that SI is similar to BX and BP in this respect. What is new, however, is that the instruction

```
MOV BX,2[SI]
```

will load BX with the 16-bit number to be found in the location 2 + (current value in the SI register). Together then, these three instructions accomplish the loading of the signed 32-bit form of 10000000D (the first power of ten on our list) into BX,AX ready for subtraction from DX,CX. When the time comes to load BX,AX with the next power of ten (1000000D) all we need do is obey an ADD SI,4 instruction and jump back to the MOV AX,[SI] instruction, and so on:

```
               MOV SI,OFFSET POWERS_TABLE
                 .
                 .
                 .
REMOVE_POWER: MOV AX,[SI]
              MOV BX,2[SI]
                 .
                 .
                 .
              ADD SI,4
              JMP REMOVE_POWER
              RET
```

Finishing the PRINTOUT subroutine

We can now complete the PRINTOUT subroutine by implementing the repeated subtraction plan. The only remaining complication is that we don't want to print zeros at the beginning of a number. Thus we prefer to print 1286 rather than 00001286. To achieve this we shall use a variable **digit_printed_yet** as an indicator of whether we've had a non-zero decimal digit to print yet. What happens after the next digit to be printed has been worked out depends on the setting, true or false, of this variable. If it is false and the digit just calculated is zero then we don't print the digit unless it is the very last to be printed. If it is the last digit to be printed, then the number in DX,CX must itself have been zero and we do print a zero in this case.

A structured outline for the PRINTOUT subroutine is given in Fig. 5.6.

The assignation of variables to registers in our implementation of this outline will be as shown in Table 5.3, and we begin by initializing registers:

```
;power := 7;
PRINTOUT:     MOV BP,7
              MOV SI,OFFSET POWERS_TABLE
;digit_printed_yet := false;
              MOV BH,0
;repeat count := 0
NEXT_POWER: MOV BL,0
```

The **while** loop which repeatedly subtracts off a power of ten is

```
power := 7;
digit_printed_yet := false;
repeat
    count := 0;
    while DX,CX >= 0 do
        begin
        DX,CX := DX,CX − 10^power;
        count := count + 1
        end;
    DX,CX := DX,CX + 10^power;
    count := count − 1;
    if count <> 0 then
        begin
        digit_printed_yet := true;
        print(count)
        end;
    if count = 0 and (digit_printed_yet or (power = 1)) then
        begin
        print(count);
        digit_printed_yet := true
        end;
    power := power − 1
until power = 0
```

Fig. 5.6 A structured outline for the PRINTOUT subroutine.

Table 5.3 Assignation of variables.

Register	Variable
BP	power
BH	digit_printed_yet (0 indicates FALSE, 1 indicates TRUE)
BL	count

straightforward, except that we need our powers of ten in BX,AX so that we can use BIG_SUB and BIG_ADD. It is necessary, therefore, to preserve the contents of BX on the stack before reading a power of ten into BX,AX. To test if DX,CX is negative we rotate the sign bit into the carry flag.

```
                ;while DX,CX >= 0 do
REMOVE_POWER:   MOV    AX,DX
                RCL    AX,1
                JB     ADD_BACK
           ;begin
```

```
;DX,CX := DX,CX-10^power;
            PUSH  BX
            MOV   AX,[SI]
            MOV   BX,2[SI]
            CALL  BIG_SUB
;count := count + 1
            POP   BX
            INC   BL
;end;
            JMP   REMOVE_POWER
```

If the result of the call to BIG_SUB is below zero then we are ready to add back and print this digit. If the digit is non-zero there are no complications.

```
          ;DX,CX := DX,CX + 10^power;
ADD_BACK: PUSH  BX
          MOV   AX,[SI]
          MOV   BX,2[SI]
          CALL  BIG_ADD
        ;count := count-1;
          POP   BX
          DEC   BL
        ;if count <> 0 then
          CMP   BL,0
          JZ    TRY_COUNT_ZERO
          ;begin
          ;digit_printed_yet := true;
              MOV   BH,1
          ;print(count)
```

The printing is easy: we need only convert the digit in BL to ASCII by adding 30H, and print the digit by a call to PRINTCHAR. Since PRINTCHAR assumes that the code for the thing to be printed is in register DL, we first preserve the contents of DX on the stack and then restore those contents after printing.

```
        ADD   BL,30H
        PUSH  DX
        MOV   DL,BL
        CALL  PRINTCHAR
        POP   DX
    ;end;
```

Finally we deal with the digits which are zero:

```
        ;if count = 0 and (digit_printed_yet or (power = 1)) then
TRY_COUNT_ZERO: CMP   BL,0
        JNZ   DONE_THIS_POWER
        CMP   BP,0
```

```
      .JZ    PRINT_THIS_ZERO
       CMP   BH,1
       JZ    PRINT_THIS_ZERO
       JMP   DONE_THIS_POWER
       ;begin
       ;print(count);
       PRINT_THIS_ZERO: PUSH DX
                 MOV   DL,BL
                 ADD   DL,30H
                 CALL  PRINTCHAR
                 POP   DX
       ;digit_printed_yet := true
                 MOV   BH,1
       ;end;
    ;power := power-1
DONE_THIS_POWER: ADD  SI,4
                 SUB  BP,1
;until power = 0
    JAE  NEXT_POWER
DONE_ALL_DIGITS: RET
```

EXERCISES 5.5

1. Work out a complete trace for a call to the PRINTOUT routine
with DX containing 0H and CX containing 27H. Record carefully
the data items stored on the stack and list each digit as it would be
printed by the call to PRINTCHAR under a column headed 'digits
printed'.

2. Suppose that locations 700H–79FH inclusive contain the exam
marks for 40D students in each of four subjects. Thus:

Location	700	701	702	703	704	705	706	707	708
Contents	41	63	22	38	4B	60	5A	1F	5C

would indicate that student number 1 got marks of 65D, 99D, 34D
and 56D for the four subjects, student 3 has the highest mark in
the first subject out of students 1, 2 and 3, and so on.

Here is a program fragment which leaves the total of each
student's marks in AX ready for printing by a subroutine call
PRINTMARK (the details of which do not concern us at the
moment).

```
              MOV   BX,0
              MOV   SI,700H
NEXT_STUDENT: MOV   AX,0
              ADD   AX,[SI]
```

```
            ADD   AX,1[SI]
            ADD   AX,2[SI]
            ADD   AX,3[SI]
            CALL  PRINTMARK
            ADD   SI,4
            INC   BX
            CMP   BX,28H   ;40D = 28H
            JNZ   NEXT_STUDENT
```

Produce a detailed trace of the execution of this program fragment for the first two students, using the exam marks specified above.

5.7 DOING THE ARITHMETIC

We now have all but four of the building blocks necessary for the outline in Fig. 5.1. The missing subroutines are DOPLUS, DOSUB, DOMULT and DODIVISION. DOPLUS is simple:

```
DOPLUS: CALL ADDITION
        CALL PRINTOUT
        RET
```

DOSUB is a little more complicated because we want to print a minus sign before a negative answer and because actually printing the answer when the result is negative cannot be done by just calling PRINTOUT into action on the contents of DX and CX. Our SUBTRACTION subroutine sets DX,CX to the signed 32-bit form of the result, but when PRINTOUT gets to work it assumes that the signed number in DX and CX is positive. Hence, if DX,CX is negative, we print a minus sign, convert DX,CX to its positive equivalent (by subtracting DX,CX from zero) and then use that as a parameter for PRINTOUT.

```
            DOSUB: CALL SUBTRACTION
        ;check if result was negative
                JNB   RESULT_NOT_NEG
        ;if so print minus sign
                PUSH DX
                MOV  DL,'-'
                CALL PRINTCHAR
                POP  DX
        ;then negate DX,CX
                MOV  BX,DX
                MOV  AX,CX
                MOV  DX,0
                MOV  CX,0
                CALL BIG_SUB
        ;now convert to decimal and print
```

```
RESULT_NOT_NEG: CALL PRINTOUT
                RET
```

DOMULT involves no special cases and is easy to handle:

```
DOMULT: CALL MULTIPLY
        CALL PRINTOUT
        RET
```

Before invoking our DIVIDE subroutine we must check for division by zero. If it is attempted then the user who perpetrated this crime must be admonished by a suitable error message. In between the quotient and remainder of the answer to a correctly posed division problem the specification said we were to print the letter R (for Remainder). After a call to DIVIDE, registers BX and AX contain the actual numeric remainder so their values have to be preserved on the stack before a call is made to PRINTOUT in order to print the quotient.

```
    DODIVISION: CMP  BX,0              ;check for division by zero
                JZ   DIVISION_ERROR
                ;otherwise do the division
                CALL DIVIDE
                ;print the quotient
                PUSH AX               ;preserve remainder
                PUSH BX               ;on stack
                CALL PRINTOUT
                MOV  DL,'R'
                CALL PRINTCHAR        ;print R for Remainder
                POP  BX
                POP  AX               ;now restore and print
                MOV  DX,BX            ;remainder
                MOV  CX,AX
                CALL PRINTOUT
                JMP  DONE_DIV
DIVISION_ERROR: CALL DIVISION_BY_ZERO ;prints error message
       DONE_DIV: RET
```

5.8 PUTTING IT ALL TOGETHER

At last we can complete the main program as outlined in Fig. 5.1. The only unusual feature is our first informal use of a CASE statement as a program development aid. A statement of the form:

case *variable* **of**
        value_1 : *action_1*
        value_2 : *action_2*
                :
                :

```
                    :
    value_n : action_n
                end
```

will be implemented by assembly language of the form:

```
                CMP  value,value_1
                JZ   action_1
                CMP  value,value_2
                JZ   action_2
                    :

                    :

                    :
                CMP  value,value_n
                JZ   action_n
                JMP  END_CASE
ACTION_1:           :

                    :
                JMP  END_CASE
ACTION_2:           :

                    :
                JMP  END_CASE
ACTION_3:           :

                    :
                JMP  END_CASE
ACTION_n:           :

                    :
END_CASE:
```

The main program begins with register initialization and a **while** loop:

```
;digits_read := 5;
      START: MOV CH,5
;while digits_read = 5 or code <> 1 do
      TEST: CMP CH,5
            JZ   READ_FIRST_DECIMAL
            CMP CL,1
            JNZ READ_FIRST_DECIMAL
            JMP READ_SECOND_DECIMAL
            ;begin
                :
                :
                :
            ;end;
END_FIRST_WHILE: JMP TEST
```

The body of the **while** loop is performed if we haven't read a valid first operand yet:

```
                        ;print(newline);
        READ_FIRST_DECIMAL: CALL  PRINT_NEWLINE
                             CALL  GET_OK_NUM_AND_TERM_NON_SPACE_CHAR
        ;if digits_read = 5 then print(too long);
                             CMP   CH,5
                             JNZ   TRY_CODE
                             CALL  TOO_LONG
        ;if code <> 1 then print(illegal character);
                   TRY_CODE: CMP   CL,1
                             JZ    NO_NUM_BEFORE_OPERATOR
                             CALL  ILLEGAL_CHAR
        ;if digits_read = 0 and code = 1 then
   NO_NUM_BEFORE_OPERATOR: CMP   CL,1
                             JNZ   END_FIRST_WHILE
                             CMP   CH,0
                             JNZ   END_FIRST_WHILE
                             ;begin
                             ;print(illegal character);
                                   CALL  ILLEGAL_CHAR
                             ;code := 0
                                   MOV   CL,0
                             ;end
   END_FIRST_WHILE: JMP   TEST
```

After successful execution of the program so far we're ready to process the user's second decimal number.

```
                        ;preserve operator and operand on the stack
                        ;call GET_OK_NUM_AND_TERM_NON_SPACE_CHAR
        READ_SECOND_DECIMAL: PUSH AX
                             PUSH BX
                             CALL GET_OK_NUM_AND_TERM_NON_SPACE_CHAR
        ;if digits_read = 5 then begin clear stack;print(too long) end
                             CMP   CH,5
                             JNZ   TRY_DO_SUM
                             POP   BX
                             POP   AX
                             CALL  TOO_LONG
                             JMP   REPEAT_LOOP
        ;else if digits_read <> 0 and code = 2 then begin
             TRY_DO_SUM: CMP   CH,0
                             JZ    NO_DIGITS
                             CMP   CL,2
                             JNZ   NO_DIGITS
        ;pop operand and operator
                             POP   AX
                             POP   DX              ;operand into DL
```

```
;case operator of ......
                  CMP   DL,'+'
                  JZ    PLUS
                  CMP   DL,'-'
                  JZ    MINUS
                  CMP   DL,'*'
                  JZ    STAR
                  CMP   DL,'/'
                  JZ    SLASH
                  JMP   REPEAT_LOOP
          PLUS: CALL DOPLUS
                  JMP   REPEAT_LOOP
         MINUS: CALL DOSUB
                  JMP   REPEAT_LOOP
          STAR: CALL DOMULT
                  JMP   REPEAT_LOOP
         SLASH: CALL DODIVISION
                  JMP   REPEAT_LOOP
;else begin clear stack; print(illegal character) end
NO_DIGITS: POP   AX
           POP   BX
           CALL ILLEGAL_CHAR
;forever
REPEAT_LOOP: JMP  START
```

And now we really have completed our first major assembly language program. You are invited to type it into your own computer, assemble it and then try it out under debugger control. At the very least you should turn to Appendix II where (as often advertised) you will find a complete listing of the program.

EXERCISES 5.6

1. If you did go to the trouble of typing in the whole calculator simulator program, try to make small alterations to the assembly language version which satisfy the following conditions. Reassemble and debug the resulting machine code programs.

   i) Change the error messages so that they are very rude to the user. (In general we know that the users of any computer program respond better if the error messages are Kind and Understanding but you can let your hair down here, just this once.)

   ii) Instead of just printing R for Remainder after a division print the whole word. Thus:

   ```
   110/9 = 12 REMAINDER 2
   ```

iii) Change the program so that multiple operators are allowed. Thus:

$$11 * 2 + 4 = 26$$
$$5 + 8 - 3 + 7 + 9 + 11 = 37$$
$$5 - 1 + 14 / 2 - 3 + 7 * 6 = 78$$

(Expressions are to be evaluated from left to right. Beware of numbers which are so large that they are no longer within the scope of the program. For example 9999 * 9999 * 9999 should cause an error message to be printed out.)

iv) As it stands, our simulator program could not be used by people unfamiliar with its constraints and limitations. Add instructions so that messages are printed out which make the program completely self-contained in this respect.

2. List in detail the changes you would have to make so that the simulator could handle up to twice the number of digits we discussed. If you're feeling energetic, have a go at implementing the changes.

3. Since the answers to the sums given to our calculator simulator needed more than 16 bits for a signed representation we were not able to make use of the 8088 instruction **NEG** which turns positive 8-bit and 16-bit signed numbers into their negative two's complement equivalent and vice versa (NEG is short for NEGate). Thus, if to begin with CX contains 00000000 00011001 (the 16-bit signed representation of +25), after the instruction NEG CX has been implemented, CX contains 11111111 11100111 (the 16-bit two's complement representation of −25). Similarly, if BX contains 11111111 11110001 (the 16-bit two's complement representation of −15), after NEG BX it will contain 00000000 00001111 (the 16-bit signed representation of +15).

Write an 8088 assembly language program which accepts a 4-digit decimal number from its user and then types out that number and its negative. Thus, if the user types 7291, the output from your program should be:

    7291   −7291

Use the NEG instruction to perform the actual negation and cannibalize as many of the calculator simulator routines as possible to keep your effort to a minimum.

5.9 RUNNING PROGRAMS WITHOUT A DEBUGGER

Once an assembly language program has been assembled, tested and finally knocked into shape so that it runs satisfactorily under debugger control, the next step is to be able to run the machine code version without having to use the debugger. Thanks to PC-DOS, this is easy. If your assembly language program was in a file called WORKING.ASM, then one of the files output by LINK will be a file WORKING.EXE. If you now type WORKING after the A> prompt, PC-DOS will cause the program in WORKING.EXE to be executed.

If all your program does is to change the contents of memory or some of the registers, you won't see very much happening without the assistance of the debugger. Worse, your program may affect the operating system so that the system 'hangs' and you have to restart the computer as if you had obeyed a HLT instruction or switched off. The calculator simulator program prints out messages and accepts information from the keyboard so there is plenty of external evidence that everything is working in its case.

EXERCISES 5.7

1. Write an assembly language program which when run will allow its users to type in a number M between 0 and 100D and then print out the M times table in the form:

   $$0 * M = 0$$
   $$1 * M = M$$
   $$2 * M = \ldots \ldots$$

   .
   .
   .

   $$10 * M = \ldots \ldots$$

2. Write an assembly language program to print out a conversion table from Centigrade to Fahrenheit for temperatures in the range -100 to 100 degrees centigrade inclusive, in steps of ten degrees. Set out the table as follows:

Centigrade	Fahrenheit
-100	-148
-90	-130
.	.
.	.
0	32
10	40
.	.
.	.
100	212

3. A collection of locations in memory contains signed 16-bit numbers. The first address of these locations is given in register AX and the final address in BX. Find the maximum positive number in those locations and print this number on the display.

4. The modulus of a negative number is the number you are left with when the minus sign is dropped. Thus the modulus of −71 is 71 and of −8 is 8. Find and print the negative number in the same range of locations as above which has maximum modulus. In each case, if the range specified does not contain a number of the given type print out a suitable message.

5.10 SUMMARY

This chapter has featured the 8088 arithmetic instructions (which are summarized in Table 5.4) and their use in a fairly large project. The next chapter examines the 8088 text handling instructions in some detail and provides another example of the use of our program development methodology.

Table 5.4 A summary of 8088 arithmetic instructions.

Instruction	Effect
Addition	
ADD op1,op2	op1 := op1 + op2. Allowed formats:

	op1	*op2*
	register	register
	memory	register
	register	memory
	register	number
	memory	number

Instruction	Effect
ADC op1,op2	ADd with Carry: if CF = 0, then ADD as above. If CF = 1, then op1 := op1 + op2 + 1.
INC op	INCrement: op := op + 1. The operand may be in either a register or memory.
Subtraction	
SUB op1,op2	op1 := op1 − op2. Allowed formats as in ADD above.
SBB op1,op2	SuBtract with Borrow: if CF = 0, then SUB as above. If CF = 1 then op1 := op1 − op2 − 1.
DEC op	DECrement: op := op − 1. The operand may be in either a register or memory.
NEG op	NEGate: op := 0 − op. Operand as in DEC.
CMP op1,op2	CoMPare: set flags according to the result of op1 − op2 but do not change either operand.

Table **5.4** (*continued*)

Instruction	Effect
Multiplication	
MUL op	MULtiplication (unsigned): if op is a byte, then AH,AL := op $*$ AL. If op is a word, then DX,AX := op $*$ AX. If the upper half of the result is zero then CF and OF are set to 1. op can be either in a register or in memory.
IMUL op	Integer MULtiplication (signed): as with MUL except that signed multiplication takes place.
Division	
DIV op	DIVision (unsigned): if op is a byte, then (AH,AL)/op = AL remainder AH. If op is a word, then (DX,AX)/op = AX remainder DX. If the quotient exceeds the capacity of AL or AX, then both quotient and remainder are undefined (and a type 0 interrupt is generated – see Chapter 12). op can be as in MUL above.
IDIV src	Integer DIVision (signed): as with DIV above except that a signed division takes place.
Sign extension	
CBW	Convert Byte to Word: the 8-bit signed number in AL is converted to 16-bit signed equivalent in AX.
CWD	The 16-bit signed number in AX is converted to a 32-bit signed equivalent in DX,AX with DX containing the higher order bits.

6 Text

AIMS

The vast majority of commercial computer use involves non-arithmetical work such as word processing, searching files for invoices relating to BLOGGS Ltd. and sorting payments received into customer file order. Consequently the 8088 is well endowed with instructions for handling text or, more precisely, **strings**. A string is any arbitrary sequence of characters, such as 12;"[[hhM<ABX or 123 or HELLO, HELLO, HELLO WHAT'S ALL THIS THEN. In the first part of this chapter we shall describe each of the 8088 string manipulation instructions in detail (and the related, special purpose, instructions CLD, STD, REP and LOOP) and illustrate their use via some short example programs. The second part is devoted to the construction of a simple text editor program using these instructions and the techniques of Chapter 4. This also provides us with a natural opportunity to introduce the XLAT table translation instruction, the XCHG (eXCHanGe) instruction and the MASM operator PTR.

6.1 PRIMITIVE STRING MANIPULATION INSTRUCTIONS

There are five primitive 8088 string manipulation instructions: MOVS, LODS, STOS, SCAS and CMPS. Using these instructions it is possible to move strings around in memory and to compare two strings to see if they are the same or to find the first place in which they differ. All of this could be done using the instructions we have already encountered but the special string manipulation instructions work much faster than anything we programmers could put together. Moreover, they facilitate the programming of tasks involving the manipulation of text. This has the commercial advantage that if the task is made easier, the time taken to carry it out will be reduced and so the cost will be lower.

Each of the string manipulation instructions enables a certain basic operation (such as moving one or two bytes from a certain place in memory to another location or locations) to be repeated without us having to organize lots of little details ourselves. It is possible, for example, to move the contents of locations 200H–300H (relative to the DS register) *en bloc* into locations 500H–600H. In addition, we can easily determine whether the move is to be done in the forwards direction (i.e. the contents of location 200H are moved to location 500H, then the contents of location 201H to 501H, etc. or in reverse (so that the contents of location 300H are first moved into location 600H, then the contents of 2FFH into 5FFH, etc.). The CLD – CLear Direction flag – instruction sets the direction flag to zero and thereby determines that any string instruction following it should work forwards through memory. STD – SeT the Direction flag – causes reverse order working.

The primitive string instructions are controlled with the CX, SI and DI registers. CX is used to keep a count of the number of locations left to be operated on and we think of SI as holding the Source Index and DI (a 16-bit register we haven't come across before), the Destination Index.

REP and MOVS

Given that register CX contains *n*, moving a sequence of *n* bytes starting at the address given in the SI register to the collection of locations whose first address is given in the DI register involves the following operations:

while $CX <> 0$ **do**
      1. *MOV register,[SI]*
      2. *MOV [DI],register*
      3. *INC SI*
      4. *INC DI*
      5. *DEC CX*

Actions 1–4 of the body of this **while** loop can be accomplished by a single 8088 instruction, namely MOVS. Better still, there is an instruction REP which, when used as a prefix for the MOVS instruction, implements the **while** loop and action 5 of its body. To emphasize: REP MOVS is equivalent to the complete **while** loop above.

We haven't given all the necessary details yet, however. In steps 1 and 2 above we must make it clear whether the MOV is to be an 8-bit move or a 16-bit move. Both are possible but a different form of the MOVS instruction is used for each. Thus if 8 bits are to be moved at a time we use the format MOVSB and if 16 bits are to be moved at a time we use the format MOVSW.

Another detail omitted so far is that MOVS (as do all the primitive string instructions) treats the address given in SI as being relative to the contents of the DS register, whereas that in DI is relative to the ES (Extra Segment) register. The extra segment register is the only 8088 register which remains to be introduced. It belongs to the family of segment registers which contains CS, DS and SS. Often we initialize DS and ES to the same value so that, for example, MOVS can be used to relocate a string within a program's data segment. In more advanced applications, however, the extra segment addressed by ES will be different from that addressed by DS.

(If your IBM PC is fitted with a monochrome display adapter card, up to 2000 characters may be placed on the screen using an 80 column by 25 line character grid. The screen display is then **memory mapped** so that placing the ASCII code for a character in one of the 4000 even-numbered locations starting with absolute location 0B0000H will cause that character to be displayed on the screen. In these circumstances we shall use ES to address the screen locations and DS to address the program's data segment proper. The details are given in Chapter 12.)

For reference purposes the properties of REP and MOVS are summarized as follows.

REP   Causes the primitive string instruction following it to be repeated *while CX is not zero*. After each step of the execution of the string instruction, CX is decremented.

MOVS   Moves 8 or 16 bits from the location whose address is given in the SI register (relative to the contents of DS) to the address given in the DI register (relative to the contents of ES). The SI and DI registers are then incremented if the direction flag is 0 or decremented if the direction flag is 1.

Example 1

The following little program copies the contents of the group of locations labelled FIRST_GROUP to those labelled SECOND_GROUP and following.

```
DSEG SEGMENT
     FIRST_GROUP  DB 56H DUP('A')
     SECOND_GROUP DB 56H DUP(?)
DSEG ENDS
SSEG SEGMENT STACK
     DW 100H DUP(?)
SSEG ENDS
CSEG SEGMENT
     ASSUME DS:DSEG,SS:SSEG,CS:CSEG
     MOV AX,DSEG
     MOV DS,AX                 ;address our program's data segment
     MOV ES,AX                 ;initialize ES to same value as DS
     MOV SI,OFFSET FIRST_GROUP  ;source address
     MOV DI,OFFSET SECOND_GROUP ;destination
     MOV CX,56H                ;there are 56H bytes to be moved
     CLD                       ;move them in the forward direction
     REP MOVSB
CSEG ENDS
END
```

As always, the reader is invited to type the program into a computer and to try it out.

A new DEBUG command

Testing programs such as that in Example 1 under debugger control is facilitated by the DEBUG command F (Fill). Using the F command a whole range of locations can be filled with a given value. Thus:

```
F 21A 324 41
```

would store the ASCII code for the letter A (41H) in each of locations 21AH, 21BH, . . . , 324H. Individual locations can, of course, be accessed more easily by the E command.

EXERCISE 6.1

Write an assembly language program with a data segment as follows:

```
START_OF_RANGE  DB 'AA'
ORIGINAL_STRING DB 100H DUP(?)
BEFORE_COPY     DB 'BB'
COPY_STRING     DB 100H DUP (?)
END_OF_RANGE    DB 'CC'
```

The program should copy the contents of the 100H locations starting with that labelled ORIGINAL_STRING into the locations starting with that labelled COPY_STRING. Test your program under DEBUG control by first using the F command to fill ORIGINAL_STRING with the ASCII code for the letter X, then run your program and verify that the locations in COPY_STRING have been set appropriately.

Next, test your program carefully at the end points of the range concerned (the places where things are most likely to go wrong, since programs often work with one location too few or one too many due to the programmer miscounting).

STOS

Filling blocks of memory with the same byte is one of the functions of the second primitive string operation, STOS. It stores the contents of AL (8-bit operation) or AX (16-bit operation) in the memory location addressed by the DI register (relative to the ES register) and then the DI register is incremented or decremented depending on the setting of the direction flag. As with the MOVS instruction, two formats, STOSB and STOSW, are used depending on whether an 8-bit (STOSB) or 16-bit (STOSW) store is to be performed.

Example 2

The following assembly language program fragment fills locations 200H–20FH (relative to the DS register) inclusive with 0H.

```
MOV DI,200H ;destination address
MOV CX,10H  ;number of locations to be filled
MOV AL,0H   ;fill them with 0H
CLD         ;fill them forwards
REP STOSB
```

EXERCISE 6.2

Add the necessary assembler directives to the program fragment in Example 2 and assemble and test the result under DEBUG control.

LODS

The LODS primitive string operation moves 8 (LODSB) or 16 (LODSW) bits at a time, from the location given in the SI register (relative to the contents of the DS register) into the AL or AX register as appropriate. The SI register is then incremented or decremented depending on the value of the direction flag.

REP is hardly ever used in conjunction with LODS. This is because it is unlikely that we should want to move the contents of a particular location into register AL and then straight away move the contents of the next location into the same register. On the other hand, LODS and STOS are often used together when we want to move a collection of bytes or words from one area of memory to another making changes during the move. In that case the number of repetitions is not controlled by a REP instruction but by the LOOP instruction. Indeed,

```
LOOP NEXT_LOCATION
```

is, in effect, equivalent to

```
DEC CX
JNZ NEXT_LOCATION
```

but the LOOP instruction affects none of the flags. The next example illustrates the combined use of STOS and LODS and shows the LOOP instruction in context.

Example 3

A glance at the table of ASCII codes in Appendix I will confirm that the lower case letters a, b, c, . . . , z all have ASCII codes which are 20H more than their upper case equivalents A, B, . . . , Z. The following program fragment moves the contents of locations 154H–27BH (relative to the DS register) to locations 300H–427H inclusive (relative to the ES register) and assumes that the bytes to be moved are all ASCII codes for upper case letters. During the move the entire text is converted to lower case.

```
          MOV    SI,154H ;source address
          MOV    DI,300H ;destination address
          MOV    CX,128H ;the number of bytes to be moved
          CLD            ;forwards direction
NEXTLOC: LODSB           ;move the next byte into AL
          ADD    AL,20H  ;convert into lower case
          STOSB          ;store it in the new location
          LOOP   NEXTLOC ;if more to do, go back and repeat
```

There are two other instructions in the LOOP family. These are: LOOPZ <label> (alias LOOPE) which decrements the CX register without affecting the flags and jumps to the <label> if CX<>0 *and* the Z-flag is 1; and LOOPNZ <label> (alias LOOPNE) which decrements the CX register without affecting the flags and jumps to the <label> if CX <> 0 *and* the Z-flag is 0.

CMPS and REPZ

We come now to an instruction for comparing two strings. CMPS subtracts the byte or word specified by the memory location whose address is given in the DI register (relative to the ES register) from the byte or word specified by the location whose address is given in the SI register (relative to DS) and sets the flags accordingly. (The contents of memory are not affected by the CMPS instruction.) Then both the SI and DI registers are incremented or decremented depending upon the current setting of the direction flag. CMPS takes the form CMPSB if two 8-bit quantities are to be compared and CMPSW when we are comparing two 16-bit quantities.

If we're searching through two strings in an attempt to determine if they're the same or not, the search can come to a halt in one of two ways. Either we've found a place where they differ or the strings agree because all the locations that needed to be checked have been. As usual, the REP instruction can be used to control the number of repetitions but in order to stop the search through the two strings once a difference between them has been identified we use a slightly modified form – REPZ.

When used in conjunction with any one of the five primitive string operations, REPZ causes that operation to be repeated while CX is not 0 and the Z-flag is 1. Thus

```
REPZ CMPSB
```

will stop for one of two reasons. The first possibility is that the count in CX has been reduced to zero. In this case the Z-flag will still be 1 since the subtractions performed by CMPS on each iteration will always have resulted in zero. On the other hand, REPZ CMPS may have stopped because the

Z-flag has been set to 0, indicating that the two strings being compared disagree at some point.

The only way of telling which of these two possibilities obtains is to test the Z-flag and jump accordingly after the REPZ CMPS instruction. Thus

```
            REPZ CMPS
            JNZ   STRINGS_DIFFER
            CALL PRINT_STRINGS_EQUAL
                    .
                    .
                    .
STRINGS_DIFFER:     .
```

makes the jump only if the strings disagree.

Example 4

The following program fragment compares the string in locations 200H–24FH inclusive (relative to the DS register) with that in locations 300H–34FH inclusive (relative to the ES register). If they're the same, the ASCII code for the letter Y is left in AL; if not then the ASCII for the letter N is left in AL.

```
                CLD                     ;forward direction
                MOV   CS,50H            ;length of the two strings
                MOV   SI,200H           ;start of first string
                MOV   DI,300H           ;start of second string
                REPZ CMPSB              ;compare the two strings
                JNZ   STRINGS_DIFFER
                MOV   AL,'Y'
                JMP   DONE
STRINGS_DIFFER: MOV   AL,'N'
          DONE: HLT
```


SCAS and REPNZ

SCAS is the primitive string instruction which enables us to scan memory for a particular byte or word, held in AL or AX. The memory byte or word specified by the address given in register DI (relative to the ES register) is subtracted from AL or AX and the flags set accordingly. (Neither the contents of the relevant memory location(s) nor the AL or AX register are affected.) Then the DI register is incremented or decremented depending on the value of the direction flag. The formats of the SCAS instruction are SCASB (when searching for an 8-bit object) and SCASW (when searching for a 16-bit object).

As with CMPS, repeated application of SCAS may stop for one of two reasons. Either the locations to be searched have been exhausted (i.e. CX has been reduced to zero) or the required byte or word has been found, in which case the Z-flag will be set to 1. Used in conjunction with a primitive string operation, REPNZ causes the operation which follows it to be repeated *while CX is not zero and the Z-flag is zero.*

Thus in

```
REPZ SCASB
JZ   FOUND
        .
        .
        .
FOUND:  .
```

the jump will only be made if the byte or word being searched for has been found.

Example 5

In the following program fragment, the contents of each location in the range 200H–400H inclusive (relative to the ES register) which contains the ASCII code for the letter X is replaced by the ASCII code for the letter Y. After the REPNZ SCASB instruction we test to see if the Z-flag has been set to 1, indicating that a location containing the ASCII code for the letter X has been found. If so, then we want DI to contain the address of this location in order that the STOS instruction can be used to store the ASCII code for Y there, afterwards. But the last repetition of SCASB will have incremented DI so we must decrement DI before the STOS instruction is executed. Similarly, CX will be reduced by REPNZ SCASB before it stops, having located the code for the letter X. Consequently CX must be incremented after replacement of X by Y if we are to loop back ready to search for another letter X without missing a location.

```
      CLD               ;forward direction
      MOV   DI,200H ;first location to be searched
      MOV   CX,201H ;the number of locations to be searched
NEXT: MOV   AL,'X'
      REPNZ SCASB   ;do the search
      JNZ   NEXT    ;more locations to check? Go check them!
      DEC   DI
      MOV   AL,'Y'
      STOSB           ;substitute 'Y'
      INC   CX        ;restore CX
      LOOP  NEXT      ;try to find another X if
                      ;all the locations haven't been
                      ;exhausted
```

Changing direction

This far, every one of our examples works independently of the direction in which the primitive string operation is performed. We could replace CLD by STD in any of them and still each program fragment would have its desired effect. There are occasions, however, when the ability to move the relevant bytes or words in reverse order is crucial.

Consider the problem of moving the string stored in locations 100H–120H to locations 102H–122H. Because of the overlap, it is impossible to make this move in a forward direction. The bytes at 100H and 101H are easily copied into locations 102H and 103H but when it comes to moving the byte originally at location 102H into 104H we find that we have just replaced the contents of location 102H!!

Moving in reverse order eliminates the problem since the bytes at 120H and 11FH are copied into 122H and 121H respectively and when we come to move the byte at 11EH into 120H the byte which was at 120H has already been moved into its new position.

Handling two bytes at a time

Whilst none of our examples has employed the 16-bit form of a string operation, the ability to move a word at a time or search for a given pair of bytes has advantages both in handling coded external data and in straight numeric work. The following program fragment, for example, searches locations 200H–24BH (each pair of which contains a 16-bit signed number) for 0128H and leaves the appropriate address in DI.

```
            MOV    AX,0128H ;search for 0128H
            MOV    DI,200H   ;the address of the first of them
            MOV    CX,26H    ;there are 26H 16-bit numbers to check
            REPNZ  SCASW
            JNZ    NOT_FOUND
            DEC    DI
                   .
                   .
                   .
NOT_FOUND:         .
```

REP and its variants

REPZ and REPNZ have aliases: REPZ can also be called REPE (REPeat while Equal to zero); REPNZ can also be called REPNE (REPeat while Not Equal to zero). Moreover, the illustrative examples above may have given the impression that REPZ can only be used with CMPS, and REPNZ only with SCAS, etc. In fact, the programmer is free to combine any of the

Table 6.1   8088 primitive string instructions.

MOVSB MOVSW	The byte or word at address DS:SI is moved to address ES:DI. If DF = 0, then SI := SI + X and DI := DI + X. If DF = 1, then SI := SI − X and DI := DI − X. X = 1 for byte moves, X = 2 for word moves.
REP	REPeat next string instruction while CX < > 0.
REPE/REPZ	REPeat next string instruction while CX < > 0 and ZF = 1.
REPNE/REPNZ	REPeat next string instruction while CX < > 0 and ZF = 0.
STOSB STOSW	STOre String – Byte; STOre String – Word. The byte or word in AL or AX is transferred to the address in ES:DI. SI and DI are modified as for MOVSB and MOVSW above.
LODSB LODSW	LOaD String Byte; LOaD String Word. The byte or word in address DS:SI is transferred to AL or AX. SI and DI are modified as for MOVSB and MOVSW above.
CMPSB CMPSW	CoMPare String – Byte; CoMPare String – Word. The byte or word in address ES:DI is subtracted from that at DS:SI and the flags are set accordingly. SI and DI are modified as for MOVSB and MOVSW above.
SCASB SCASW	SCAn String – Byte; SCAn String – Word. The byte or word at address ES:DI is subtracted from AL or AX and the flags are set accordingly. SI and DI are modified as for MOVSB and MOVSW above.

string primitives with REP, REPZ or REPNZ as the task in hand dictates. Since MOVS, LODS and STOS have no effect on the flags it is unlikely that one would want to use REPZ or REPNZ in conjunction with those instructions, but it is not forbidden.

Table 6.1 gives a summary of the 8088 string manipulation instructions.

EXERCISES 6.3

Write assembly language programs to carry out the following tasks. Test the programs thoroughly with strings addressed by the variables FIRST, SECOND and THIRD as necessary.

1. In a certain string of known length, replace every occurrence of the string LTD with the string PLC. (Hint: use the string operations to locate the letter L and then check if the next two locations contain T and D. Then repeat.)

2. At the first place where two strings of known (and equal) length differ, insert the string YES in each of them. (Obviously this will involve increasing the length of each string.) If the two strings are identical then leave them both unchanged.

3. Leave a copy of the FIRST string in the SECOND string but with the characters in reverse order. Thus if the original string begins ONCE ... and ends ... UNLIKELY, the copy will begin YLEKILNU ... and end ... ECNO.

6.2 TRANSLATION TABLES AND XLAT

Replacing one character in a string with another according to a corresponding entry in a table is, like comparing and moving strings, a frequently required operation. For example, before sending details of a customer's account along telephone lines from a branch to head office, a bank will encode the account details to prevent fraud and infringement of privacy. The 8088 provides the XLAT instruction to facilitate translation between one character code and another, and to enable tasks involving table look-up to be carried out efficiently.

If the starting address of a table is held in the location specified by register BX, and a particular entry in the table is specified by giving a number in AL relative to the start of the table (for example, entry 0, 1, 2, 3, ...) the XLAT instruction will load the AL register with the contents of the address obtained by adding what's in AL to what's in BX (relative to the DS register). Thus XLAT is equivalent to the ILLEGAL move instruction:

```
MOV AL,[BX+AL]   ;illegal instruction
```

The EBCDIC code is a way of coding textual material into binary, most often used in big, mainframe computers. It begins as shown in Table 6.2.

By way of example, suppose locations 400H–41AH contain the 8-bit EBCDIC codes for the letters A, B, C, ... , Z in alphabetical order. To

Table 6.2 EBCDIC coding.

Letter	EBCDIC code	Letter	EBCDIC code	Letter	EBCDIC code
A	C1	J	D1	S	E2
B	C2	K	D2	T	E3
C	C3	L	D3	U	E4
D	C4	M	D4	V	E5
E	C5	N	D5	W	E6
F	C6	O	D6	X	E7
G	C7	P	D7	Y	E8
H	C8	Q	D8	Z	E9
I	C9	R	D9		

convert the ASCII code of a given letter held in register AL into EBCDIC we would obey the instructions

```
MOV   BX,400H
SUB   AL,41H
XLAT
```

which would leave the EBCDIC code for the given letter in register AL.

EXERCISE 6.4

In a certain Secret Society a secret code is used for all communications. Under the code, each letter of the alphabet is replaced by another letter arrived at by considering the diagram in Fig. 6.1. A given letter is substituted by the letter which is five places further round the circle in a clockwise direction. Write an assembly language program to encode messages under this procedure using the XLAT instruction.

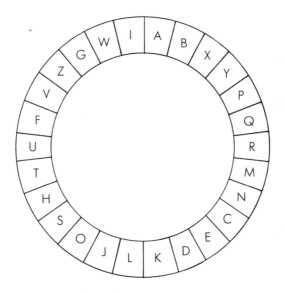

Fig. 6.1 Encoding diagram for a Secret Society.

6.3 A SIMPLE TEXT EDITOR

The remainder of this chapter is devoted to the construction of a simple text editor. It will allow the user to type in a text and modify it in various ways – by adding a new line or deleting an existing one, for example. Since the mechanisms for copying data held in memory onto disk and for copying from disk into memory will not be described until Chapter 11, our text editor will lack many features vital to a real editor program. In particular, the user will not be able to save text on disk. Thus our text editor will be a long way from being a practical tool; indeed, even its basic design is not appropriate for a real editor. However, our aim is to illustrate the use of the 8088 string manipulation instructions introduced in the first part of this chapter in an appropriate environment, rather than to compete with professionally produced products.

Specification

Our text editor will handle up to nine lines of text at any one time. These will be stored in memory and may each contain up to 72D characters. Editor commands will have one of the formats:

> P*n*
> D*n*
> N
> S*nm*
> F%any string%
> P
> E

where the letter (P, D, N, S, F, E) specifies the type of command and *n* and *m* are single digits (1, 2, . . . , 9) which specify to which line or lines that command is to be applied. Commands are typed straight after the editor's prompt character – an asterisk (*). Each command is obeyed when the person using the text editor presses the RETURN key after entering that command. Table 6.3 summarizes the commands and the actions they cause.

If the RETURN key is not pressed immediately after a command the message

A COMMAND MUST BE TERMINATED BY PRESSING THE RETURN KEY

will be displayed and that command ignored. Indeed, if anything is wrong with the format of a command, then that command is ignored. To simplify the printing out of the text we shall assume that no line of text entered by the user contains a dollar sign ($). This is not essential to the design of the text editor and in due course it will be an exercise for the reader to eradicate this restriction.

Text storage – the strategy

As in Chapter 5, we shall break the task down into independent building blocks. Before we do, however, it is necessary to decide on a strategy for storing the text in memory. Once again we depart from practical considerations and allow ourselves the luxury of reserving separate groups of memory locations for each of the nine lines of text. The first location of

Table 6.3 Command summary for the text editor program.

N*m*	This command allows the user to specify New text for line *m*. The previous line *m* is completely eliminated by this command.
	Once the RETURN key has been pressed for the N command to be obeyed, a colon (:) is printed as a prompt to the user. The line of text typed by the user after the colon prompt then becomes the new line number *m*. If *m* is not one of 1, 2, . . . , 9 then the error message
	NO SUCH LINE EXISTS. ILLEGAL CHARACTER IN LINE NUMBER?
	is printed out. If the new line of text contains more than 72D characters, the old text is retained and the error message
	STRING TOO LONG
	is displayed.
D*m*	This is the editor command to Delete the *m*th line of text. Again, if *m* is not one of 1, 2, . . . , 9 then the message
	NO SUCH LINE EXISTS. ILLEGAL CHARACTER IN LINE NUMBER?
	is displayed.
P*m*	Print the *m*th line of text. If *m* is out of range then the same error message as for the N and D commands is displayed.
P	This is a short form of the Print command which causes all nine lines of text to be printed out.
S*mn*	This allows the user to Swap lines *m* and *n* of the text. The command is abandoned if *m* or *n* is out of range (and the usual error message is printed). There must be no spaces between the first line number, *m*, and the second, *n*.
F%any string%	Finds all the lines which contain the string inside the percent signs (%). (This string must not itself contain percent signs – it will be an exercise for the reader later on to remove this restriction.) The line number of each line containing the search string is printed on the display. If one (or both) of the percent signs is (are) missing the error message
	%SIGN(S) MISSING IN FIND COMMAND
	will be displayed.
E	End the editing session and return to the operating system. (Since we are not yet able to save the text on a disk, the text stored in memory will be lost after this command.)

the first line of text will be labelled START_OF_TEXT and for each line we shall reserve a total of 75D locations (i.e. 72D maximum for the actual text, to which we shall then add CR and LF characters and finally a $ sign, so that each line can be printed out by using the operating system 'print string' function).

START_OF_TEXT text of line number 1 .... 0A 0D $
                      text of line number 2..0A 0D $......................
                                      ↓
                      text of line number 9 .... 0A 0D $..........

Since 9 * 75D = 675D, the first pseudo-op in the data segment of our program will be

```
START_OF_TEXT DB 675D DUP(?)
```

If the N (New text) command is called up it must then prompt the user with a colon to indicate that the user may now type in the new text. If we were to replace the old text by the new as each character was typed in by the user, we would run the risk of having ruined the old text despite the fact that the new line is too long and therefore unacceptable. Consequently we read the proposed new text into a **buffer** (or temporary store) and move it into place only when we know everything is as it should be.

Since the maximum allowed length of any text line in our editor is 72D characters, we shall know that the maximum has been exceeded if 73D characters have been entered by the user and the last one is not a carriage return (CR) character. Hence we reserve 50H bytes for the buffer (more than we actually need) by adding the directive:

```
READ_LINE_BUFFER DB 50H DUP(?)
```

to the data segment of our program.

After a new line of text has been entered we want to calculate and record its length once and for all so that the same calculation is not necessary every time we call up the F(ind) command. To record the lengths of the nine lines of text as signed 8-bit numbers we use the directive

```
LINE_LENGTHS DB 0,0,0,0,0,0,0,0,0
```

in the data segment of our program. This initializes the nine lengths to zero in each case since each line of text will be set to blank at the beginning of the program (actually each line will consist of just a CR and LF character but we don't count these in line length calculations).

PTR – a MASM operator

The first step in the main body of our text editor program will be to call up a subroutine – INITIALIZE – to create the nine blank lines in the appropriate places. They could be initialized in other ways – for example, by means of DB pseudo-ops – but by adopting a different method we are able to introduce the MASM operator PTR (PoinTeR) which is used to change the type of its operand.

An instruction such as

```
MOV [SI],0AH
```

is ambiguous. It is not clear whether the single byte 0AH should be stored at the location whose address is in SI or whether the word 000AH should be stored in that location and the next. But in

```
MOV BYTE PTR [SI],0AH
```

precisely one byte is stored whereas

```
MOV WORD PTR [SI],0AH
```

would cause two bytes to be stored.

The INITIALIZE subroutine uses PTR to store CR, LF and a $ sign in the first three storage locations allocated to each of the nine lines. Its basic structure is a simple **for** loop:

for $i := 1$ **to** 9 **do** *line*[i] := (*CR,LF,'$'*);

Normally a **for** loop of the form

for $i := start$ **to** *finish* **do** <*action(s)*>

would be implemented by assembly language of the form

```
                MOV CX,finish
                MOV AX,start
                SUB  CX,AX
                ADD CX,1
                JBE   FOR_DONE
NEXT_ACTION:         :
                     :
                <action(s)>
                     :
                LOOP NEXT_ACTION
     FOR_DONE:
```

so that (finish >= start) is verified before any action(s) are carried out. In our more restricted circumstances we shall use:

```
                MOV CX,number of repetitions
NEXT_ACTION:         :
                     :
                <action(s)>
                     :
                LOOP NEXT_ACTION
```

where the number of repetitions = (finish−start) + 1. This is the approach taken in INITIALIZE:

```
INITIALIZE PROC NEAR
;for i := 1 to 9 do line[i] := (CR,LF,'$');
           MOV   CX,9
           MOV   SI,OFFSET START_OF_TEXT
```

```
INIT_NEXT: MOV   [SI],BYTE PTR 0AH
           MOV   1[SI],BYTE PTR 0DH
           MOV   2[SI],BYTE PTR '$'
           ADD   SI,75D
           LOOP  INIT_NEXT
           RET
INITIALIZE ENDP
```

An outline of the text editor program

The only other variables which are required at this stage of the design are char1 and char2 to store the first two characters of an editor command (for E and the short form of P these are the only characters). Using these and assuming subroutines which carry out the effect of each command (with reasonably obvious names such as SWAP which corresponds to S, FIND which corresponds to F, and so on) it is fairly easy to write an outline of the program and this is given in Fig. 6.2.

6.4   IMPLEMENTING THE MAIN PROGRAM

For reading characters from the keyboard and printing characters on the display screen we shall use the READCHAR and PRINTCHAR sub-routines (respectively) of Chapter 5. Furthermore, we shall borrow the PRINT_STRING subroutine for printing strings on the display screen given

---

call initialize;
print(prompt);
read(char1, char2);
while *char1 <> E* **or** *char2 <> CR* **do**
    begin
    if *char1 = P* **and** *char2 = CR* **then** *call print_all_text*
    else if *char1 = P* **then** *call print_a_line*
    else if *char1 = S* **then** *call swap*
    else if *char1 = N* **then** *call new_text*
    else if *char1 = D* **then** *call delete*
    else if *char1 = F* **then** *call find*
    else *print(illegal command)*;
    print(newline);
    print(prompt);
    read(char1, char2)
    end;
return to PC-DOS

Fig. 6.2   Outline of the text editor program.

a starting address in DX. These apart, we have to write the subroutines PRINT_ALL_TEXT, PRINT_A_LINE, SWAP, NEW_TEXT, DELETE and FIND given in Fig. 6.2. Before attempting these, however, we shall code the main body of the program. The text editor program is a good example of a program wherein the subroutines to be written are completely independent but where testing can be facilitated by choosing a sensible order of implementation. Thus, if we implement PRINT_ALL_TEXT first it can be used in testing NEW_TEXT and so on.

Testing of our implementation of the skeletal main program is carried out by implementing all missing subroutines (not counting INITIALIZE and those for reading and writing stolen from Chapter 5) as a single RET instruction. For example, for the purpose of testing the main program, NEW_TEXT could be implemented as

```
NEW_TEXT PROC NEAR
         RET
NEW_TEXT ENDP
```

Fig. 6.3 gives our implementation. The complete text editor program can be found in Appendix III, which can be referred to for further clarification as and when the reader desires it.

6.5 PRINTING THE TEXT

Printing the whole text is carried out by the PRINT_ALL_TEXT subroutine and is relatively straightforward to implement using the PRINT_STRING subroutine.

```
PRINT_ALL_TEXT PROC NEAR
;for i := 1 to 9 do print(line[i]);
                CALL PRINT_NEWLINE
                MOV  CX,9
                MOV  DX,OFFSET START_OF_TEXT
    NEXT_LINE:  CALL PRINT_STRING
                ADD  DX,75D   ;set address pointer to next line
                LOOP NEXT_LINE
                RET
```

If just one line is to be printed, the subroutine which does the work must also check the format of the command and verify that the line number is valid. Since this verification is an essential part of carrying out many of the editor commands we shall put both of these functions into a subroutine called VERIFY_RANGE_AND_FORMAT.

VERIFY_RANGE_AND_FORMAT assumes that the ASCII code for the character typed by the user *after* the command letter is in AL. VERIFY_RANGE_AND_FORMAT returns three parameters in registers AH, BL and DX as follows:

```
CR     EQU OAH
LF     EQU ODH
STAR   EQU '*'
COLON EQU ':'
DSEG SEGMENT
ILLEGAL_MESS DB 'ILLEGAL CHARACTER IN INPUT',CR,LF,'$'
DSEG ENDS
SSEG SEGMENT STACK
           DW 100H DUP(?)
SSEG ENDS
CSEG SEGMENT
           ASSUME DS:DSEG,SS:SSEG,CS:CSEG
MAIN PROC FAR
;set up stack for return to PC-DOS
           PUSH DS
           MOV  AX,0
           PUSH AX

;address our program's data segment
           MOV AX,DSEG
           MOV DS,AX
           MOV ES,AX          ;for string manipulation instructions
;call initialize
   CALL INITIALIZE
;print(prompt)
   MOV  DL,STAR
   CALL PRINTCHAR
;read(char1, char2);
   CALL READCHAR
   MOV  CL,AL
   CALL READCHAR ;CL = char1, AL = char2
;while char1 <> E or char2 <> CR do
PROCESS: CMP   CL,'E'
         JNZ   NOT_END
         CMP   AL,CR
         JNZ   NOT_END
         JMP   DONE
      ;begin
      ;if char1 = P and char2 = CR
        NOT_END: CMP   CL,'P'
                 JNZ   TRY_LINE
                 CMP   AL,CR
                 JNZ   TRY_LINE
      ;then print all the text
                 CALL PRINT_ALL_TEXT
                 JMP   GET_COMMAND
```

Fig. 6.3 Implementation of the main program.

```
            ;else if char1 = P then print a line
            TRY_LINE: CMP   CL,'P'
                      JNZ   TRY_S
                      CALL  PRINT_A_LINE
                      JMP   GET_COMMAND
            ;else if char1 = S then call swap
               TRY_S: CMP   CL,'S'
                      JNZ   TRY_N
                      CALL  SWAP
                      JMP   GET_COMMAND
            ;else if char1 = N then call new_text
               TRY_N: CMP   CL,'N'
                      JNZ   TRY_D
                      CALL  NEW_TEXT
                      JMP   GET_COMMAND
            ;else if char1 = D then call delete
               TRY_D: CMP   CL,'D'
                      JNZ   TRY_F
                      CALL  DELETE
                      JMP   GET_COMMAND
            ;else if char1 = F then call find
               TRY_F: CMP   CL,'F'
                      JNZ   ILLEGAL
                      CALL  FIND
                      JMP   GET_COMMAND
         ;else print(illegal character);
           ILLEGAL: CALL ILLEGAL_CHARACTER
         ;print(newline);
       GET_COMMAND: CALL PRINT_NEWLINE
         ;print(prompt);
                      MOV   DL,'*'
                      CALL  PRINTCHAR
         ;read(char1, char2);
                      CALL  READCHAR
                      MOV   CL,AL
                      CALL  READCHAR
         ;end;
                      JMP   PROCESS
   ;return to PC-DOS
      DONE: RET

   MAIN ENDP

   ILLEGAL_CHARACTER PROC NEAR
         MOV   DX,OFFSET ILLEGAL_MESS
         CALL  PRINT_STRING
         RET
   ILLEGAL_CHARACTER_ENDP
```

Fig. 6.3 (*continued*)

AH Set to 0 to indicate format correct or set to 0FFH to indicate format error.

DX If there is a format error then DX is set to the offset address of a suitable error message.

BL If the format is correct BL contains the ASCII code for the number of the line which is to be affected by this command.

The first job of VERIFY_RANGE_AND_FORMAT is to check that the second character typed by the user (supplied to that subroutine as a parameter in AL) is a valid line number. If not, then we set register AH to 0FFH to denote an error, set register DX to the address of the NO_SUCH_LINE error message and exit from the subroutine.

Once we are sure that the line number is in range, we save its ASCII code in BL and read the next character. If that character is not a CR character then once again there's been an error so we set register AH to 0FFH and register DX to the address of the RETURN_ERROR message and exit. Otherwise we set register AH to 0 to indicate that all is well and we are done:

> **if** *char2 not in* ['*1*' . . '*9*'] **then**
> > **begin**
> > *DX* := *address of NO_SUCH_LINE message*
> > *AH* := *0FFH*
> > **end**
> **else begin**
> > *read(char3)*
> > **if** *char3* < > *CR* **then**
> > > **begin**
> > > *DX* := *address of RETURN_ERROR message*;
> > > *AH* := *0FFH*
> > > **end**
> > **else** *AH* := *0*;

Our implementation of this outline is given in Fig. 6.4.

Of course, we must also add the definition of the error messages to the data segment. They are as follows:

```
FORMAT_ERROR  DB 'SPACE MISSING AFTER COMMAND',CR,LF,'$'
NO_SUCH_LINE  DB 'NO SUCH LINE EXISTS.'
              DB 'ILLEGAL CHARACTER IN LINE NUMBER?',CR,LF,'$'
RETURN_ERROR  DB 'A COMMAND MUST BE TERMINATED BY '
              DB 'PRESSING THE RETURN KEY',CR,LF,'$'
```

To summarize: after a call to the VERIFY_RANGE_AND_FORMAT subroutine, register AH either contains 0FFH, indicating that an error has occurred, or it contains 0H, indicating that a valid line number followed by a CR have been read and the ASCII code for the line number is in register

```
VERIFY_RANGE_AND_FORMAT PROC NEAR
;if char2 not in ['1' .. '9'] then
        CMP    AL,'1'
        JB     OUT_OF_RANGE
        CMP    AL,'9'
        JBE    IN_RANGE
        ;begin
        ;set DX to address of error message
OUT_OF_RANGE: MOV   DX,OFFSET NO_SUCH_LINE
        ;set AH to indicate error
               MOV   AH,OFFH
        ;end
               JMP   RF_ERROR
;else begin
        ;read(char3)
    IN_RANGE: MOV   BL,AL     ;char2 now in BL
               CALL READCHAR
        ;if char3 <> CR then
               CMP   AL,CR
               JZ    RF_OK
               ;begin
               ;set DX to address of error message
                      MOV   DX,OFFSET RETURN_ERROR
               ;set AH to indicate error
                      MOV   AH,OFFH
               ;end
                      JMP   RF_ERROR
        ;else set AH to indicate OK
        RF_OK: MOV   AH,0
    RF_ERROR: RET
        VERIFY_RANGE_AND_FORMAT ENDP
```

Fig. 6.4 Implementation of VERIFY_RANGE_AND_FORMAT.

BL. If an error has occurred, register DX will be set to the address of a suitable error message.

Having done all this work in advance, completing the PRINT_A_LINE subroutine now comes down to calculating the starting address of the relevant line:

```
PRINT_A_LINE PROC NEAR
            CALL VERIFY_RANGE_AND_FORMAT
            CALL PRINT_NEWLINE
;if AH <> OFFH then DX := address of text_line[BL-30H];
            CMP   AH,OFFH
            JZ    PRINT_DONE
            SUB   BL,31H
```

```
                    MOV    AL,75D
                    IMUL   BL
                    MOV    DX,AX
                    ADD    DX,OFFSET START_OF_TEXT
        PRINT_DONE: CALL PRINT_STRING
                    RET
        PRINT_A_LINE ENDP
```

Notice that whilst subtracting 30H from the ASCII code for the line number would give the actual line number, what we want is rather the number of reserved blocks of store 75D bytes long from START_OF_TEXT where that line can be found. Hence we subtract 31H not 30H.

6.6 NEW_TEXT

The plan for the NEW_TEXT subroutine is relatively straightforward. NEW_TEXT is brought into action after the first command character has been entered and recognized as an N. Hence the first thing which must happen in the body of NEW_TEXT is a call to VERIFY_RANGE_AND_ FORMAT to check that the next character is a valid line number and that the command is terminated properly. If all is well, we print a colon prompt at the beginning of a new line and, using the STOS instruction, move the new text into the READ_LINE_BUFFER as it is typed. Reading finishes as soon as either more than 72D characters have been typed or a carriage return (CR) character is typed. If more than 72D characters have been typed and character number 73D is not a CR character, the new text line is too long and we print an error message and exit from the subroutine.

> call VERIFY_RANGE_AND_FORMAT;
> call PRINT_NEWLINE;
> **if** AH = 0FFH **then** print error message
>   **else begin**
>   print(colon prompt);
>   DI := address of READ_LINE_BUFFER;
>   CX := 73D;
>   **repeat** read(char); decrement CX;
>   store char in READ_LINE_BUFFER
>   **until** CX = 0 **or** char = CR;
>   **if** char < > CR **then** print(TOO_LONG)
>   **else begin**
>   append LF and $ to text in READ_LINE_BUFFER;
>   calculate start address of text's destination;
>   calculate and store length of text in LINE_LENGTHS;
>   move the text into place
>   **end**
>   **end**;

Much of the implementation of this is routine:

```
PROC NEW_TEXT NEAR
          CALL VERIFY_RANGE_AND_FORMAT
          CALL PRINT_NEWLINE
;if AH = 0FFH then print error message
          CMP   AH,0FFH
          JNZ   OBEY_NEW
          CALL PRINT_STRING
          JMP   NEW_LINE
    ;else begin
          ;print (colon prompt);
  OBEY_NEW:  CLD
            MOV   DL,':'
            CALL PRINTCHAR
          ;DI := address of READ_LINE_BUFFER
              MOV  DI,OFFSET READ_LINE_BUFFER
          ;CX := 73D
              MOV  CX,73D ;print the prompt
          ;repeat read(char);
  READ_MORE: CALL READCHAR
              ;store char in buffer
              STOS AL
          ;until CX = 0 or char = CR;
              CMP   AL,CR
              LOOPNZ READ MORE
              JZ    END_OF_LINE
          ;if char <> CR then print error message
              MOV   DX,OFFSET TOO_LONG
              CALL PRINT_STRING
              CALL PRINT_NEWLINE
              JMP   NEW_DONE
  END_OF_LINE: .
                .
                .
                .
    NEW_DONE: RET
```

When the new text is too long the error message to be printed out is specified by adding the following pseudo-op to the data segment:

```
TOO_LONG DB 'STRING TOO LONG',CR,LF,'$'
```

Assuming now that the new text in the buffer is within the allowed length we must ensure that there's a CR, LF, $ sequence at the end of it so that the complete new text line can be moved into its proper place by a MOVS instruction. Since the STOS instruction will have automatically incremented DI and will have stored the CR typed by the user at the end of the text in the buffer, it remains to add the LF and $ characters:

```
END_OF_LINE: MOV BYTE PTR [DI],LF
             INC DI
             MOV BYTE PTR [DI],'$'
```

All that remains to be done now is to calculate the starting address of the buffered text's destination (using the fact that the ASCII code for the appropriate line number is still in register BL) and to calculate and store the length of the text (not counting the CR, LF, $ sequence).

```
;calculate starting address of buffered text's destination
            SUB   BL,31H
            MOV   AL,75D
            IMUL  BL            ;address now in AX
;calculate the length of the text in READ_LINE_BUFFER
            MOV   DI,AX
            ADD   DI,OFFSET START_OF_TEXT
            MOV   SI,OFFSET READ_LINE_BUFFER
            MOV   DX,75D
            SUB   DX,CX         ;length now in DX
;store the text length in appropriate place
            MOV   CX,DX         ;save length for text move
            MOV   BH,0          ;BX now contains the line no.-1
            ADD   BX,OFFSET LINE_LENGTHS
            SUB   DL,3          ;remove CR, LF, $ from count
            MOV   [BX],DL       ;save the line length
;move the text into place
            REP   MOVSB
;end
;end
 NEW_DONE: RET
```

6.7 DELETE

The DELETE subroutine is somewhat similar in structure to NEW_TEXT:

call *VERIFY_RANGE_AND_FORMAT*;
call *PRINT_NEWLINE*;
if *AH = 0FFH* **then** *print error message*
    else begin
        find start address of line to be deleted;
        insert CR, LF, '$' at this address and following;
        reset entry in LINE_LENGTHS to zero;
        print deletion OK message
        end;

Once the deletion has been completed we print out the message DELETION COMPLETED by adding to the data segment the pseudo-op:

```
DELETE_OK DB 'DELETION COMPLETED',CR,LF,'$'
```

it being just as important to keep users of your programs informed when things go right as it is when they go wrong. (It is another exercise for the reader to modify previous subroutines in which this has not been done.)

```
DELETE PROC NEAR
        CALL VERIFY_RANGE_AND_FORMAT
        CALL PRINT_NEWLINE
;if AH = OFFH then print error message
        CMP   AH,OFFH
        JNZ   DO_DELETE
        MOV   DX,OFFSET NO_SUCH_LINE
        CALL PRINT_STRING
        JMP   DELETE_DONE
;else begin
        ;find start address of line to be deleted
   DO_DELETE:SUB   BL,31H ;our line is this many 75D blocks
                          ;from start
            MOV   AL,75D
            IMUL BL
            ADD   AX,OFFSET START_OF_TEXT
        ;start address now in AX
        ;insert CR, LF, $ at beginning of line with this address
            MOV   SI,AX
            MOV   BYTE PTR [SI],CR
            MOV   BYTE PTR 1[SI],LF
            MOV   BYTE PTR 2[SI],'$'
        ;reset line length to zero
            MOV   SI,OFFSET LINE_LENGTHS
            MOV   BH,OH
            ADD   SI,BX
            MOV   [SI],BH
        ;print deletion OK message
            MOV   DX,OFFSET DELETE_OK
            CALL PRINT_STRING
        ;end
DELETE_DONE: RET
DELETE ENDP
```

6.8 SWAP

The S(wap) command required two valid line numbers and our SWAP subroutine is to be called up once the S command has been identified. The second character typed by the user should be the ASCII code for a line number between 1 and 9. Having checked this, we preserve the ASCII code for the first line number in register CL and since we now expect another valid line number followed by a CR we can read the next character and call up VERIFY_RANGE_AND_FORMAT as usual.

The next step is to calculate the starting addresses of the actual text for the line numbers whose ASCII codes are in CL and BL and to swap the corresponding recorded line lengths. To keep the structure simple we relegate the actual instructions for this to a subroutine, LENGTH_SWAP, which swaps the line lengths of the lines whose offsets from the start of the LINE_LENGTHS block are given in registers BL and CL.

In order to effect the swap we move the string whose starting address is in AX into the READ_LINE_BUFFER, copy the string starting at the address in DX into the locations starting with that given in AX and then finally copy the contents of the READ_LINE_BUFFER into the locations starting with that given in DX.

> **if** *AL not in* ['1' . . '9'] **then** *print no such line*
> **else begin**
>   *MOV CL,AL*
>   *read(char);*
>   *call VERIFY_RANGE_AND_FORMAT;*
>   **if** *AH = 0FFH* **then** *print error message*
>   **else begin**
>   *call LENGTH_SWAP*
>   *DX := start address of line in CL;*
>   *AX := start address of line in BL;*
>   *move string addressed by AX into READ_LINE_BUFFER;*
>   *copy string addressed by DX into that addressed by AX;*
>   *copy READ_LINE_BUFFER string into that addressed by DX;*
>   *print(SWAP COMPLETED)*
>   **end**
> **end**

Here again, we inform the user once the editing command has been carried out, this time via the pseudo-op:

```
SWAP_OK DB 'SWAP COMPLETED',CR,LF,'$'
```

The complete SWAP subroutine follows:

```
SWAP PROC NEAR
;if AL not in ['1' .. '9'] then print NO SUCH LINE
        CMP   AL,'1'
        JB    TOO_LOW
        CMP   AL,'9'
        JBE   LINE_NO_OK
```

```
TOO_LOW: MOV   DX,OFFSET NO_SUCH_LINE
         CALL PRINT_STRING
         JMP   SWAP_DONE
;else begin
         MOV   CL,AL
     ;read(char)
         CALL READCHAR
         CALL VERIFY_RANGE_AND_FORMAT
     ;if AH = OFFH then print error message
         CMP   AH,OFFH
         JNZ   DO_THE_SWAP
         MOV   DX,OFFSET NO_SUCH_LINE
         CALL PRINT_STRING
         JMP   SWAP_DONE
     ;else begin
             ;swap the recorded line lengths
       DO_THE_SWAP: SUB   CL,31H
                    SUB   BL,31H
                    CALL LENGTH_SWAP
           ;DX := address of first text line
                    MOV   AL,75D
                    IMUL BL
                    ADD   AX,OFFSET START_OF_TEXT
                    MOV   DX,AX
           ;AX := address of second text line
                    MOV   AL,75D
                    IMUL CL
                    ADD   AX,OFFSET START_OF_TEXT
           ;move string addressed by AX into READ_LINE_BUFFER
                    MOV   SI,AX
                    MOV   DI,OFFSET READ_LINE_BUFFER
                    MOV   CX,75D
                    REP   MOVS AL,AL
           ;move string addressed by DX into locations addressed
           ;by AX
                    MOV   SI,DX
                    MOV   DI,AX
                    MOV   CX,75D
                    REP   MOVS AL,AL
           ;copy string in READ_LINE_BUFFER to locations
           ;addressed by DX
                    MOV   SI,OFFSET READ_LINE_BUFFER
                    MOV   DI,DX
                    MOV   CX,75D
                    REP   MOVS AL,AL
```

```
                     ;print(swap complete)
                             MOV  DX,OFFSET SWAP_OK
                             CALL PRINT_NEWLINE
                             CALL PRINT_STRING
                     ;end
             ;end
        SWAP_DONE: RET
        SWAP ENDP
```

The XCHG instruction

It remains to define the LENGTH_SWAP subroutine which provides a natural opportunity to illustrate the 8088 instruction **XCHG**. There are three basic forms:

  i) XCHG 16-bit register   e.g. XCHG BX
 ii) XCHG register,memory e.g. XCHG CX,[SI]
iii) XCHG register,register e.g. XCHG BL,CH

In form i), the contents of the specified register are swapped with the contents of AX; in forms ii) and iii) the contents of the register are swapped with the contents of the register or memory location(s). Thus XCHG CX,[SI] exchanges the contents of the CX register with the word stored at the location specified by SI (relative to DS).

Before giving the instructions for LENGTH_SWAP let's quickly recapitulate: we require a subroutine which swaps the recorded line lengths for the text lines whose offsets from the start of the LINE_LENGTHS block of memory are in registers BL and CL. Moreover, the subroutine must preserve the latter two registers. Since the flow of control through the subroutine is entirely linear we shall give the full version of it at once:

```
LENGTH_SWAP PROC NEAR
;preserve BL on the stack
     PUSH BX
     MOV  SI,OFFSET LINE_LENGTHS
     MOV  CH,0
     MOV  BH,0
     ADD  BX,SI   ;start address of 2nd line now in BX
     ADD  SI,CX   ;start address of 1st line now in SI
     MOV  AL,[SI]
     XCHG AL,[BX]
     MOV  [SI],AL
     POP  BX
     RET
LENGTH_SWAP ENDP
```

6.9   IMPLEMENTATION OF THE FIND SUBROUTINE

The structure of a F(ind) command line is a little different from that required by the other editor commands. For example, to search the text for the string HULLABALLOO the command line would be

```
F%HULLABALLOO%
```

Since our FIND subroutine is called up after the F command has been recognized, AL will contain the ASCII code for the character the user typed immediately after the F command itself. We must first verify that this was a % sign. If this is not the case we must display an appropriate error message via the addition of the pseudo-op

```
SEARCH_ERROR DB '%SIGN(S) MISSING IN FIND COMMAND',CR,LF,'$'
```

to the data segment of the program.

After the % sign we accept characters until another % sign is encountered or the RETURN key has been pressed or until 73 characters

---

if *AL* < > '%' then *DX* := *address of SEARCH_ERROR message*
else begin
    count := *73D*;
    repeat *read*(*char*);
        store char in next free location in READ_LINE_BUFFER;
        count := *count* − *1*
    until (*char* = '%') or (*count* = 0);
    if *count* = 0 then *DX* := *address of TOO_LONG message*
    else begin
        read(*char*);
        if *char* < > CR then *DX* := *address of RETURN_ERROR*
                                message
        else begin
            BX := *length of text in READ_LiNE_BUFFER*;
            if *BX* < > *0* then
                begin
                MOV BP,BX;
                CALL PRINT_NEWLINE;
                CALL LOCATE
                end
            end
        end
    DX := *address of FIND_OK message*
    end;
CALL PRINT_NEWLINE;
CALL PRINT_STRING

Fig. 6.5   Pseudo-Pascal outline of the FIND subroutine.

have been entered, the last of which is not a % sign. In the latter two cases an error has occurred (because we don't allow the RETURN character in the Find string or because the maximum length of a line – and hence of a string to be found – is 72D characters) and we display an appropriate error message. As the characters are entered we copy them into the READ_ LINE_BUFFER ready to begin the search if the command line is correct. Next we check that the command line is terminated with the RETURN key and then finally we can set things up for the search itself.

The actual search will be carried out by a subroutine LOCATE which searches the text for the string contained in the READ_LINE_BUFFER, the length of which will be passed to LOCATE in the BP register. Once the search has been completed we display the message SEARCH COMPLETED via the pseudo-op

```
FIND_OK DB 'SEARCH COMPLETED',CR,LF,'$'
```

Putting all this into pseudo-Pascal gives the outline in Fig. 6.5.

Using the outline of Fig. 6.5 it is now easy to complete FIND:

```
FIND PROC NEAR
;if AL <> '%' then DX := address of SEARCH_ERROR message
        CMP    AL,'%'
        JZ     READ_SEARCH_STRING
        MOV    DX,OFFSET SEARCH_ERROR
        JMP    FIND_DONE
;else begin
     ;count := 73D;
READ_SEARCH_STRING: MOV  CX,73D
        ;point DI to start of READ_LINE_BUFFER
         MOV   DI,OFFSET     READ_LINE_BUFFER
        ;repeat
   MORE_STRING: CALL READCHAR
             ;store char
              STOSB
        ;until char = % or count = 0;
        CMP     AL,'%'
        LOOPNZ MORE_STRING
        ;if count = 0 then DX := address of TOO_LONG message
        JZ    END_OF_STRING
        MOV   DX,OFFSET TOO_LONG
        JMP   FIND_DONE
             ;else begin
                ;read(char);
     END_OF_STRING: CALL    READCHAR
              ;if char <> CR then DX := addition of RETURN_ERROR
                CMP   AL,0DH
                JZ    START_SEARCH
```

```
                    MOV   DX,OFFSET RETURN_ERROR
                    JMP   FIND_DONE
                   ;else begin
                        ;BX := length of search text
              START_SEARCH:MOV   BX,73D
                         SUB     BX,CX
                         DEC   BX      ;ignore final %
                        ;if BX <> 0 then
                         CMP   BX,0
                         JZ    FIND_DONE
                            ;begin
                            MOV  BP,BX
                            CALL PRINT_NEWLINE
                            CALL LOCATE
                            ;end
                      ;end
                 ;end
        ;DX := address of FIND_OK message
  FIND_DONE:MOV   DX,OFFSET FIND_OK
        ;end;
CALL PRINT_NEWLINE
CALL PRINT_STRING
RET
FIND ENDP
```

6.10 THE LOCATE SUBROUTINE

The hard work is nearly over. It remains now to produce the subroutine
LOCATE which must print the line number of every text line containing the
string in the READ_LINE_BUFFER (which has length given in register
BP). Our strategy is simple-minded. Suppose we are searching for an
occurrence of the string HULLABALLOO in the text line, 'HULLO
HULLO WHAT'S ALL THIS THEN': we reposition HULLABALLOO
alongside the text until we either find a match or come to the end of the text
line:

```
HULLO HULLO WHAT'S ALL THIS THEN
HULLABALLOO
  HULLABALLOO
   HULLABALLOO
      .
      .
      .
                    HULLABALLOO
```

Once we've found a match, we print the relevant line number. If no match is
found, we try the next line – if there is one:

```
for i := 1 to 9 do
    begin
    found := false; j := 1
    while (not found) and
        (j <= (length(line[i])−length(search text) + 1)) do
            begin
            compare string in position j of line[i] with search text;
            if equal then begin print(i); found := true end
                else j := j + 1
            end
    end
```

In the LOCATE subroutine, DL is used to hold which of the nine lines of text is currently being searched, but instead of holding the actual line number, DL holds a number specifying how many blocks of 75D bytes that line is from the START_OF_TEXT. Ultimately, we want to use the CMPS instruction to compare the search string with various portions of each text line, so that SI is set to the address specified by the label READ_LINE_BUFFER and DI initially to that specified by START_OF_ TEXT.

```
for DL := 8 downto 0 do
    begin
    AX := length of line DL + 1;
    if AX <= length of search text then AX := 0
        else AX := max necessary number of scans of this text line;
    BX := start address of the (DL + 1)th line of text;
    found := false;
    while (not found) and (AX <> 0) do
        begin
        PUSH AX (*make AX and CX available*);
        PUSH CX (*as working registers*);
        CX := length of search string;
        set DI to start of text being searched;
        set SI to start of search text;
        compare the strings;
        if strings equal then
            begin
            print line number DL + 1;
            POP CX
            found := true;
            POP AX
            DEC AX
            end
                else begin
                        POP CX
                        POP AX
                        DEC AX
```

> **end**
> **end** (*of while loop*)
> **end** (*of for loop*);
> *set DX to address of completion message*;

Register CL will be set to 0FFH to represent the FALSE state of the pseudo-Pascal variable *found* and set to 0H to represent the TRUE state. The length of the search text is passed to LOCATE in register BP. With these two pieces of information we can now complete LOCATE:

```
LOCATE PROC NEAR
;for DL := 8 downto 0 do
             MOV   DL,8
         ;begin
         ;AX := length of line DL + 1
  SEARCH_NEXT_LINE: MOV   BX,OFFSET LINE_LENGTHS
                    MOV   AL,DL
                    XLAT  BX
                    MOV   AH,0
         ;if AX <= BP then AX := 0
                    CMP   AX,BP
                    JAE   SET_SCANS
                    MOV   AX,0
                    JMP   SET_ADDRESS
         ;else AX := max number of scans necessary of this line
  SET_SCANS: SUB   AX,BP
             INC   AX
         ;BX := start address of the (DL + 1)th line of text
  SET_ADDRESS: PUSH AX
               MOV   BL,DL
               MOV   AL,75D
               IMUL  BL
               ADD   AX,OFFSET START_OF_TEXT
               MOV   BX,AX
               POP   AX
         ;found := false
               MOV   CL,0FFH
         ;while not found and AX <> 0 do
  CHECK_THIS_LINE: CMP   AX,0
                   JZ    END_FOR
                   CMP   CL,0FFH
                   JNZ   END_FOR
             ;begin
                       PUSH AX
                       PUSH CX
             ;CX := length of search string
                       MOV   CX,BP
```

```
                ;set DI to start of text being searched
                ;DI := AX + BX - 1
                        DEC   AX
                        ADD   AX,BX
                        MOV   DI,AX
                ;set SI to start of search text
                        MOV   SI,OFFSET READ_LINE_BUFFER
                ;compare the strings
                        REPZ  CMPSB
                ;if strings equal then
                        JNZ   TRY_FURTHER_ALONG
                    ;begin
                    ;print line number DL + 1
                        ADD   DL,31H
                        CALL  PRINTCHAR
                        CALL  PRINT_NEWLINE
                        SUB   DL,31H
                    ;found := true
                        POP   CX
                        MOV   CL,0
                        POP   AX
                        DEC   AX
                    ;end
                        JMP   END_WHILE
                    ;else begin
            TRY_FURTHER_ALONG:POP   CX
                             POP   AX
                             DEC   AX
                             ;end
            ;end (*of while*)
            END_WHILE: JMP  CHECK_THIS_LINE
        ;end (*of for loop*)
        END_FOR: SUB   DL,1
                 JB    LOCATE_DONE
                 JMP   SEARCH_NEXT_LINE
    ;set DX to address of completion message
    LOCATE_DONE: MOV   DX,OFFSET FIND_OK
                 RET
    LOCATE ENDP
```

This completes our second major program. Once again, we invite the reader to inspect the full program in Appendix III, to type it into a computer and to verify that it does indeed work. Exercises 6.5 suggest some of the simpler improvements which could be made to the program.

EXERCISES 6.5

1. Make the improvements to our simple text editor which were suggested in the text. Namely:

   a) Remove the restriction that no line of text may contain a dollar sign ($).

   b) Display a message after the successful completion of every command.

2. Modify the simple text editor program so that an arbitrary number of spaces can be used in command lines (except inside the % signs of an F command).

3. Add an extra command called A to the simple text editor which allows the user to type nine new lines at once, each terminated by pressing the RETURN. The first line typed becomes the new text line number 1, the second becomes new text line number 2, and so on. Print out suitable error messages if things go wrong.

4. Make the text find and replacement facilities more like those available from your own particular text editor or word processing software.

7 Implementing High-level Language Constructs and Assemblers

AIMS

In this chapter our attention turns to details of the 8088 particularly relevant to the implementation of compilers and assemblers. The designers of the 8086 family of microprocessors had the convenient implementation of high-level language data types and control constructs as one of their major objectives. For example, the ability to access successive memory locations with a sequence of instructions such as

```
MOV   AX,[SI]
          .
          .
MOV   AX,1[SI]
          .
          .
MOV   AX,2[SI]
          .
          .
```

was provided specifically to assist in the setting up and manipulation of arrays. Accessing memory by using SI to provide an index in this way is one of seven **addressing modes** available from the 8088 micro-processor. In this chapter we shall study these addressing modes in relation to the problem of implementing the machine code generation phase of a compiler for a high-level language such as Pascal. We also study 8088 machine code instruction formats very briefly, since an understanding of these is vital to someone who has to produce an 8088 assembler or debugger. Next comes consideration of the 8088 assembly language implementation of recursive Pascal programs and of the creation of modules within the MASM 8088 assembly language. The chapter concludes with a short note on implementing floating point arithmetic.

7.1   REGISTER ADDRESSING

The 8088 has eight general purpose 16-bit registers, eight general purpose 8-bit registers, four segment registers and the IP register (which the programmer cannot access directly) as summarized in Fig. 7.1. Instructions which affect registers only (for instance, MOV CX,DX) execute faster than instructions involving memory access as no time is spent fetching operands. Consequently, a good Pascal compiler will endeavour to ensure that data items required in repeatedly executed sections of a program are held in registers whenever possible.

Thus, if *a* and *b* are identifiers corresponding to integer variables, by the time it comes to executing:

a := *4*; *b* := *3*
for *i* := *1* **to** *10000* **do**
    begin
    write (*i,a,b,a∗b*);
    a := *a* + *2*;
    b := *b* + *1*
    end

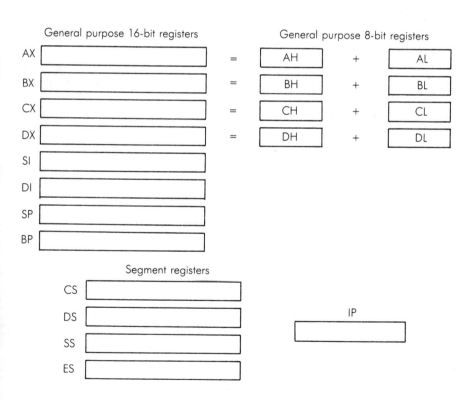

Fig. 7.1   A summary of 8088 registers.

a Pascal compiler would have already assigned memory locations to *i*, *a* and *b* but would try to arrange that the values of *i*, *a*, and *b* are moved into registers for the duration of the **for** loop execution.

7.2 IMMEDIATE ADDRESSING AND DIRECT ADDRESSING

With **immediate addressing** – for example, MOV CL,61H – the immediate *operand* 61H is stored as part of the instruction in memory. When that instruction comes to be executed, the immediate operand is thus fetched from memory at the same time as the instruction, once again reducing execution time.

Direct addressing is similar except that in this case the effective *address* of one of the operands is taken directly from the instruction. Thus in

```
MOV AX,TOTAL
```

where, for example, TOTAL is an assembly language variable correspond-ing to location 210H (relative to DS), the machine code version of the instruction is

```
A1 1002
```

so that TOTAL is addressed directly by the instruction since 1002 is the memory representation of 0210H.

Only one operand of an instruction may be directly addressed, so that if **total** and **item_sum** are identifiers of two Pascal integer variables which we assume are represented in signed 16-bit form then, for optimal execution speed not involving arithmetic in registers, the Pascal

$$total := total + item\_sum$$

could be coded by a compiler using two directly addressed instructions:

```
MOV AX,ITEM_SUM
ADD TOTAL,AX
```

(where ITEM_SUM and TOTAL are the locations corresponding to the identifiers **item_sum** and **total** respectively).

Also, given

const *taxrate = 30*;
var *total:integer*;
    ⋮
    ⋮
begin
    ⋮
    ⋮
end

the statement **total** := **taxrate** could be coded using direct and immediate addressing thus:

```
MOV TOTAL,30D
```

(where we assume that TOTAL is a word in memory corresponding to the Pascal integer **total**).

7.3 INDIRECT ADDRESSING

With **indirect addressing**, the effective address is found in either the BX, SI or DI registers, i.e. the effective address is not found directly from the instruction itself but *indirectly* by accessing a register, as in

```
SUB DX,[BX]
```

In a Pascal compiler, indirect addressing can be useful for matching formal parameters and actual parameters. For example, given declarations

proc *example*(**var** *f:integer*);
begin
  :
  :
end;
var *a:integer*;

the assembly language or machine code equivalent of **example** produced by a compiler cannot use any specific address corresponding to the variable *f* since this will not be known until a call such as

example(*a*)

occurs and the actual parameter (*a*) corresponding to the formal parameter (*f*) is known. If the address of the actual parameter is put into BX and indirect addressing is used to refer to *f* in the compiler's implementation of the body of **example**, the problem is solved.

7.4 INDEXED ADDRESSING

Consider implementing the Pascal assignment

account[*i*] := *total*

where we have

var
    i,total:integer;
    account,daily_balance:**array**[*1. .limit_constant*] **of** *integer*;

Suppose further that the array **account** is stored in consecutive locations corresponding to the variable ACCOUNT starting with account[1]; that the value of *i* is in register SI; and that the variable TOTAL corresponds to **total**. Then

```
MOV ACCOUNT[SI],TOTAL
```

is equivalent to

$account[i] := total$

Such array accesses are precisely the reason for the **indexed addressing** mode, where the effective address is calculated from 'index register + displacement'. An assignment of the form

$$account[i] := daily\_balance[j] \qquad (7.1)$$

requires two index registers (which is one reason why the 8088 has SI and DI), and if we assume the value of *j* in register DI, then

```
MOV AX,DAILY_BALANCE[DI]
MOV ACCOUNT[SI],AX
```

is the assembly language equivalent of 7.1 above. Similarly

for $i := 1$ **to** 10 **do** $balance[i] := balance[i] - credit[i] + debit[i]$;

could be implemented

```
                MOV   CX,10D
                MOV   SI,1
NEXT_BALANCE:   MOV   AX,BALANCE[SI]
                SUB   AX,CREDIT[SI]
                ADD   AX,DEBIT[SI]
                MOV   BALANCE[SI],AX
                INC   SI
                INC   SI
                LOOP  NEXT_BALANCE
```

Alternative forms

8088 assembly language actually requires index-addressed instructions to be written in the forms

```
MOV AX,[SI+BALANCE]
MOV [SI+BALANCE],AX
```

but MASM allows the alternative forms

```
MOV AX,BALANCE[SI]
MOV BALANCE[SI],AX
```

which we have used. Similarly, in later sections of this chapter

```
MOV AX,[BX+8]      is equivalent to MOV AX,[BX] 8
MOV AX,[BX+SI]     is equivalent to MOV AX,[BX][SI]
MOV AX,[BX+SI+4]   is equivalent to MOV AX,[BX][SI]4
```

7.5 BASED ADDRESSING

Given the Pascal declarations:

type *marks* = **record**
> *student_number:integer*;
> *maths:integer*;
> *french:integer*;
> *physics:integer*;
> *geography:integer*;
> *biology:integer*;
>> **end**;
> *exam* = **file of** *marks*;
> **var** *year1:exam*;

consider a Pascal program fragment to find the average biology mark in Year 1:

sum := *0*; *count* := *0*;
while not eof **do**
> **begin**
> *get(year1)*;
> *sum* := *sum* + *year1^.biology*;
> *count* := *count* + *1*
> **end**;
if *count* <> *0* **then**
> *writeln('average biology mark is'*, *sum/count*)

To access the record component **year1^.biology** in machine code equivalent to this fragment, **based addressing** is used. Registers BX and BP can be used in this mode, though addresses given in BX are taken relative to DS whereas those in BP are taken relative to SS.

The biology component of a marks record will be stored in the word eight locations from the start of that record (see Fig. 7.2). Hence, if BX is used to point to the beginning of successive records in the year1 file so that [BX] corresponds to **year1^**, then [BX+8] corresponds to **year1^.biology** and

sum := *sum* + *year1^.biology*

could be implemented as:

```
MOV AX,SUM
ADD AX,[BX+8]
MOV SUM,AX
```

7.6 BASED-INDEXED ADDRESSING

The 8088 **based-indexed** addressing mode is provided to assist in the accessing of records in a file which contain array fields. Consider the Pascal declarations

```
type classrecord = record
        student_number:integer;
                    age:integer;
    coursework_marks:array[1. .20] of integer;
            exam_average:integer
        end;
var class_file:file of classrecord;
```

and suppose that we want to find the average total coursework mark for all students whose details are held in class_file – see Fig. 7.3.

Assuming that, within each record, the array **coursework_marks** is held in bytes 5 to 45 (inclusive), then the body of the loop of

```
get(class_file); no_of_students := 0; sum := 0;
while not eof do
begin
    no_of_students := no_of_students + 1;
    for i := 1 to 20 do
        sum := sum + class_file^.course_work_marks[i];
    get(class_file)
end
```

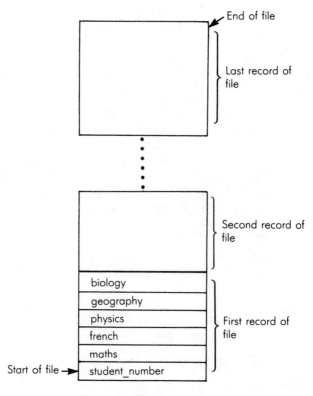

Fig. 7.2 The file year1.

could be implemented by having the base register BX to hold the starting address of this particular record (i.e. corresponding to **class_file^**), and having the index register SI point to each particular array element to be added, thus:

```
ADD AX,[BX+SI+4]
```

(see Fig. 7.3).

This completes our survey of 8088 addressing modes. Remembering which registers can be used in which mode takes practice, but the details are summarized in Table 7.1 which also contains information relating to the machine code equivalent of each instruction.

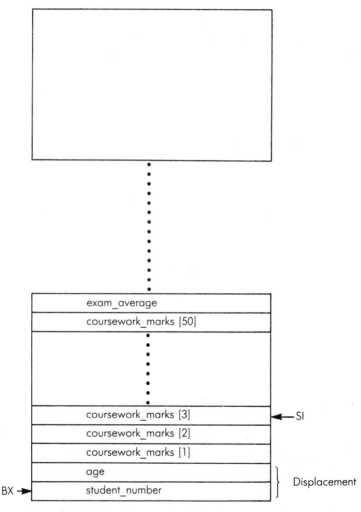

Fig. 7.3   ADD AX,[BX+SI+displacement] used to access elements of
a record of a file.

EXERCISES 7.1

1. Find a Pascal (or other, similar, high-level language) textbook and choose a few example programs spread throughout the book. For every executable statement in each of your chosen programs decide which would be the most appropriate addressing mode(s) for a compiler's 8088 code generation phase to adopt for that statement.

2. In Pascal or another, similar, high-level language with which you are familiar, write programs for each of the following tasks and then write, test and debug 8088 assembly language equivalents using addressing modes which a compiler's machine code generation phase might be expected to employ:

   a) Given a collection of ages in the range 0 to 100 terminated by the sentinel −99, print out the number of occurrences of each age.

   b) Input a series of dates expressed in the form ddmmyy and print the most frequently occurring year, month and day.

   c) Input a series of dates in the form ddmmyy and, for each date, the sales of each of 50 different products. For each product print the date on which sales of that product were highest. If the highest sales figure was achieved on more than one day, print the most recent date.

Table 7.1 Use of registers in direct and indirect addressing modes (d is a signed 8-bit number; n is an unsigned 16-bit number; and *address* is an unsigned 16-bit offset derived from a MASM variable).

				mod	
	00	01	10	11	
r/m				$w=0$	$w=1$
000	[BX+SI]	[BX+SI+d]	[BX+SI+n]	AL	AX
001	[BX+DI]	[BX+DI+d]	[BX+DI+n]	CL	CX
010	[BP+SI]	[BP+SI+d]	[BP+SI+n]	DL	DX
011	[BP+DI]	[BP+DI+d]	[BP+DI+n]	BL	BX
100	[SI]	[SI+d]	[SI+n]	AH	SP
101	[DI]	[DI+d]	[DI+n]	CH	BP
110	*address*	[BP+d]	[BP+n]	DH	SI
111	[BX]	[BX+d]	[BX+n]	BH	DI

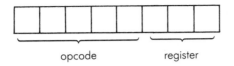

opcode   register

Fig. 7.4 Format of single operand instruction where the operand is in a 16-bit register.

7.7 INSTRUCTION FORMATS

In this section we take a brief look at 8088 machine code instruction formats. From the point of view of learning about the architecture of the 8088 this is interesting in its own right, but our inclusion of this section has two other motivating factors. First, the implementor of a new 8088 assembler or debugger (with, of course, all kinds of fancy programmer productivity aids not available in those supplied by the manufacturer) needs to know about them. Second, it does help to explain the decoding process – mnemonic to binary – carried out by MASM. Full details of the 8088 instruction set encoding are given in Appendix V.

Single operand instructions

Typical of 8088 assembly language instructions having a 1-byte machine code equivalent is the INC instruction used in register addressing mode (Fig. 7.4).

The first five bits are used as a code – 01000 – to denote the INC instruction used in this addressing mode and with a 16-bit operand. The REG field specifies which register is to be used as an operand according to Table 7.2. Thus the encoded form of INC BX is 01000011 or 43H.

As we know, in its most general form INC can increment any register (not just 16-bit registers) as well as the contents of directly and indirectly

Table 7.2 Encoding of the REG instruction field.

r/m	16-bit register operand	8-bit register
000	AX	AL
001	CX	CL
010	DX	DL
011	BX	BL
100	SP	AH
101	BP	CH
110	SI	DH
111	DI	BH

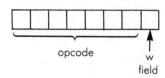
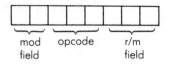

Fig. 7.5 General form of a single operand instruction where the operand is in a register or memory.

addressed memory locations. The encoding of this more general form can be found in Appendix V and occupies two bytes (Fig. 7.5).

In this case the opcode is split into two blocks, the first block of seven bits being contained in the first byte and the remaining three bits in the second byte. The **w** field specifies whether the operand is 8 (w = 0) or 16 (w = 1) bits (i.e. w specifies the *width* of the operand) whereas the **mod** field specifies whether the operand is in a register (mod = 11) or memory (mod <> 11). If the operand is in a register, the **r/m** field specifies which register, using the encoding in Table 7.2. For example, INC DH is encoded 11111110 11000110 (w = 1, mod = 11, r/m = 110 and INC opcode 1111111000).

If the operand is in memory (i.e. we are using direct or indirect addressing) the r/m field specifies base and index registers (as shown in Table 7.3) and the mod field specifies the displacement from a base or index register or from DS if direct addressing is being used (see Table 7.4).

To summarize:

w   specifies the width of the operand
mod   specifies whether the operand is in a register or memory
r/m   specifies which register or which addressing mode

Table 7.3 Encoding of the r/m field.

r/m		Base register	Index register
000		BX	SI
001		BX	DI
010		BP	SI
011		BP	DI
100		—	SI
101		—	DI
110	**if** mod = 00	BP	—
	else the instruction contains two additional bytes specifying an offset address from DS		
111		BX	—

Table 7.4   Encoding of the mod field.

Mod	Displacement
00	0000H
01	instruction contains an additional byte and the displacement is the 8-bit signed contents of that byte sign-extended to 16 bits
10	instruction contains two additional bytes specifying an unsigned 16-bit displacement

Thus, INC BYTE PTR [BX−4] is encoded as 0FE47FCH:

1111111	0	01	000	111	11111100
opcode	w	mod	opcode	r/m	additional third byte specifying displacement

and INC MY_LOCATION, where MY_LOCATION is a MASM byte variable with offset 01A3H from DS, as 0FE0601A3H:

1111111	0	00	000	110	00000001 10100011
opcode	w	mod	opcode	r/m	16-bit offset

Addressing modes field encoding is summarized in Table 7.1 above.

Two operands

Instructions such as MOV, ADD and TEST all take two operands. At the design stage of the 8088 it was decided to insist that, in any instruction requiring two operands, one of them would have to be a register. In this way the maximum length of an 8088 instruction was restricted to six bytes. The general format of ADD for a register to register addition is shown in Fig. 7.6. It contains a new encoding field – the **d** (destination) field.

The d field specifies whether the result should be stored back into the operand specified by the mod and r/m field (d = 0) or into the operand specified by the reg field (d = 1). Thus, the encoding of ADD BL,DH is 02DEH:

000000	10	11	011	110
opcode	dw	mod	reg	r/m

(the d field indicating that the result is to be placed in the operand referred

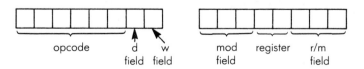

Fig. 7.6   General form of the ADD instruction for register addition.

to by the **reg** field) and the encoding of ADD MY_LOCATION,DX (where MY_LOCATION is a MASM variable having offset 0A2BCH from DS) is 0116A2BCH:

```
000000   01   00     010   110   10100010 10111100
opcode   dw   mod    reg   r/m   offset address
```

Two operand instructions have only one w field so the operands must either both be 8 bits or both be 16 bits wide. When arithmetic is being done, immediate operands are often representable in signed 8-bit form, so to reduce the length of some 8088 immediate-operand instructions, the s (sign-extend) field is used. The field only has significance for 16-bit operands (i.e. when w = 1) and specifies whether all 16 bits of the immediate operand are contained in the instruction (s = 0) or whether only the eight least significant bits are contained in the instruction (s = 1) which must therefore be sign-extended to a signed 16-bit equivalent. To summarize:

d = 0 result goes to operand specified by mod and r/m
d = 1 result goes to operand specified by reg

and if

w = 1 then
s = 0 indicates all 16 bits of the immediate operand are present
s = 1 sign-extend the eight given bits of the immediate operand to get
a full 16-bit operand.

Consider the general encoding of the SUB instruction in the case where the two operands are an immediate operand and a register (not AX) or memory operand, as shown in Fig. 7.7.

From this, it follows that the encoding of SUB BX,14H is

```
100000   11   11     101     011   00001110
opcode   sw   mod    opcode  r/m   immediate operand
```

and that the encoding of SUB WORD PTR MY_LOCATION,31H (where MY_LOCATION is a MASM variable with offset 0200H from DS) is

```
100000   11   00     101     110   00000010 00000000   00011111
opcode   sw   mod    opcode  r/m   address-offset      immediate
                                                       operand
```

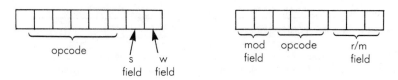

Fig. 7.7 Encoding of a SUB instruction.

EXERCISE 7.2

Appendix V contains a summary of 8088 instruction coding. Use it to encode the following program fragment. Check your answer using MASM.

```
          AND   BX,[BP+SI+14]
          MOV   CX,0
          INC   AH
          MOV   CL,4
          SUB   AH,CL
          MOV   MY_LOCATION,CX
          CALL  TEMP
          IDIV  AX
    TEMP: SBB   BX,MY_LOCATION
          SUB   CX,[BX]
          LOOP  TEMP
          RET
```

7.8 RECURSION

Recursion is a feature of many present-day high-level languages, but, thanks to the stack, the 8088 assembly language implementation of, for example, Pascal's recursive programming facility, is surprisingly straightforward. Consider a recursive implementation of the factorial function in Pascal:

function *fact (n:integer):integer*;
begin
if *n = 1* **then** *fact := 1*
else *fact := n * fact(n−1)*
end;

Thus,

fact(1)   returns 1
fact(2)   returns $2 = 2 * 1$
fact(3)   returns $6 = 3 * 2 * 1$
          $\vdots$
          $\vdots$

and

fact(10) returns $3628800 = 10 * 9 * 8 * 7 * 6 * 5 * 4 * 3 * 2 * 1$

In our 8088 assembly language version the input parameter is passed via BX and the result returned in AX:

```
          PROC FACT NEAR
          CMP  BX,1
          JNE  RECURSIVE_CALL
```

```
                    MOV   AX,1
                    JMP   DONE
RECURSIVE_CALL:     PUSH  BX
                    DEC   BX
                    CALL  FACT
                    POP   BX
                    IMUL  BX
        DONE:       RET
```

A trace of the execution of this subroutine with 3 as the contents of BX reveals how it works (see Fig. 7.8).

AX	BX	Stack
?	3	?
?	3	?3
?	2	?3
?	2	?3,2
?	1	?3,2
1	1	?3,2
1	2	?3
2	2	?3
2	3	?
6	3	?

Fig. 7.8   Trace of the execution of a recursive subroutine.

If we define the function Fib(n) (for n an integer and $n > 0$) so that Fib(1) = 1, Fib(2) = 2, and

Fib(n) = Fib($n-1$) + Fib($n-2$) (where $n > 2$),

then Fib(3) = 2 + 1 = 3, Fib(4) = 3 + 2 = 5, Fib(5) = 5 + 3 = 8, etc. and the value of Fib(n) is the nth Fibonacci number. A typical recursive implementation of this in Pascal is:

function *fib(n:integer):integer*;
begin
if *n = 1* **then** *fib := 1*
else if *n = 2* **then** *fib := 2*
else *fib := fib(n-1) + fib(n-2)*
end;

which, assuming that the input parameter is to be found in BX and the result returned in AX, can be implemented in 8088 assembly language as follows:

```
            PROC FIB NEAR
            CMP  BX,1
```

```
                JNE   TRY_TWO
                MOV   AX,1
                JMP   DONE
     TRY_TWO:   CMP   BX,2
                JNE   RECURSIVE_CALL
                MOV   AX,2
                JMP   DONE
RECURSIVE_CALL: DEC   BX
                PUSH  BX
                CALL  FIB
                ;AX now contains Fib(n-1)
                POP   BX
                DEC   BX
                PUSH  AX
                CALL  FIB
                ;AX now contains Fib(n-2)
                ;top of stack contains Fib(n-1)
                POP   DX
                ADD   AX,DX
        DONE:   RET
```

This time we encourage the reader to make his or her own trace of execution of the subroutine when it is entered with BX containing 4.

EXERCISES 7.3

1. In each case, describe in detail the restrictions on the values of the input parameter given in BX which are necessary to ensure that the result returned in AX by subroutines FACT and FIB is accurate.

2. Write and test 8088 assembly language implementations of the following recursive Pascal functions.

   a) **function** $h(x,\ n:integer):integer;$
      begin
      if $n <= 0$ **then** $h := 1$ **else**
      if $n = 1$ **then** $h := 2 * x$ **else**
      $h := 2 * x * h(x,\ n-1)-2 * (n-1) * h(x,\ n-2)$
      end;

   b) **function** $ack(m,n:integer):integer;$
      begin
      if $m = 0$ **then** $ack := n + 1$ **else**
      if $n = 0$ **then** $ack := ack(m-1,\ 1)$ **else**
      $ack := ack(m-1,\ ack(m,n-1))$
      end;

   c) **function** $gcd(m,\ n:integer):integer;$
      begin

        if $n = 0$ **then** $gcd := m$ **else**
        $gcd := gcd(n, m$ **mod** $n)$
        end;

7.9 PROGRAM MODULES

When writing an assembler or a compiler for a high-level language such as Pascal, certain routines have to be written which could be used in other applications. These include routines to calculate trigonometric functions such as SIN, COS and TAN, and formatted input and output routines. Whenever possible, these routines will be written in a high-level language. But if it has been found essential to write them in assembly language it is even more important that their use should not be confined to the application for which they were written. This is part of the fundamental philosophy of software engineering which favours the formation of new systems by integrating previously produced programs. Consequently, routines such as those mentioned above are often not built into a particular application program but, rather, are built as **modules** which can be used in the formation of many different programs. A module can be a part of a segment, a segment, parts of several segments, several segments, or a combination of these.

In our present context, this modularity is achieved through MASM pseudo-ops which communicate with the linker. A collection of assembly language statements assembled as a single unit is referred to as a **source module** which, after assembly, becomes an **object module**. The linker can then be told to 'join' together a certain named collection of object modules, thus forming a single, larger, executable module.

If the source module is in a file MYPROG.ASM then the object module created is called MYPROG.OBJ by default, but it is possible to override this by using the NAME pseudo-op. Thus

```
NAME RANDOMMODULE
```

would associate the name RANDOMMODULE with the object module created from the source module, regardless of the file in which it was contained.

Apart from the names of the files containing the modules it is to link together, the linker must also know the address of the first instruction to be executed. This information is determined by the assembler (which passes it to the linker through the object module) from the END pseudo-op. We have already met END in one of its roles, namely, to indicate the physical end of the assembly language statements in a module. But the END pseudo-op may optionally be followed by an expression which indicates the first instruction to be executed.

Thus

```
END FIRST_LOC
```

tells the assembler that execution is to begin at the instruction labelled FIRST_LOC. When several modules are linked together in this way only one END statement may specify the starting location of the combined module.

To allow one module to refer to labels and variables in another module, MASM provides the **EXTRN** (EXTeRNal) and **PUBLIC** pseudo-ops. Suppose, for example, that we wish to develop a program to add random numbers in the range 0 to 16D to the contents of a certain group of locations. In order that we can use it as a module in other programs let us suppose further that we want to have the random number generating subroutine in a separate module. Figures 7.9 and 7.10 show the contents of two files (ADDRANDS.ASM and RANDFUNC.ASM respectively) which contain the two source modules which are to be assembled separately and then combined by the linker.

The pseudo-random number generating subroutine RANDOM of Fig. 7.9 generates a new random number r_n (which is left in AX) from the previous one (or an initial seed), r_n-1 (also in AX), using the formula

$$r_n = ((r_{n-1} * 25173) + 13849) \bmod 2^{28}$$

RANDOM will be required by another module at link time, so the PUBLIC pseudo-op is used to inform the assembler of this fact.

The main module (Fig. 7.10) contains a small test program which adds a random number to the contents of each of four locations, the first of which

```
NAME RANDSMOD
SSEG SEGMENT STACK
            DB    100H DUP(?)
SSEG ENDS

CSEG SEGMENT
RANDOM PROC FAR
PUBLIC RANDOM
ASSUME CS: CSEG
            MOV   BX,25173D
            MUL   BX
            ADD   AX,13849D
            MOV   BX,0
            ADC   DX,BX
            MOV   AH,0
            AND   AL,0FH
            RET
RANDOM ENDP
CSEG ENDS
END
```

Fig. 7.9 Contents of the file RANDFUNC.ASM.

is identified by the variable LOCATIONS. Within the code segment, the EXTRN pseudo-op informs the assembler that there is a symbol which is not completely defined within the current module but whose definition will be provided at link time. Also, the END START_OF_MAIN_PROGRAM pseudo-op informs the linker that any program formed from modules combined with this one should begin execution at the instruction labelled START_OF_MAIN_PROGRAM.

After separate assembly in the normal manner, the modules are linked together via the command

```
LINK ADDRANDS+RANDFUNC,,,;
```

(the linker always requires *filenames*). Trial runs may then be carried out under debugger control via

```
DEBUG ADDRANDS.EXE
```

As usual the reader is urged to type in the two modules and to carry out this procedure at the earliest opportunity. Have a look, also, at the linker created file ADDRANDS.MAP.

```
NAME RANDS
DSEG SEGMENT
LOCATIONS DB 1,2,3,4
DSEG ENDS

SSEG SEGMENT STACK
DB 100H DUP(?)
SSEG ENDS

CSEG SEGMENT
ASSUME CS:CSEG,DS:DSEG,SS:SSEG
EXTRN RANDOM: FAR

START_OF_MAIN_PROGRAM: MOV   AX,DSEG
                       MOV   DS,AX
                       MOV   SI,OFFSET LOCATIONS
                       MOV   BX,3
                       MOV   AX,[BX+SI]
               NEXT LOC:PUSH BX
                       CALL RANDOM
                       POP   BX
                       ADD   [BX+SI],AX
                       DEC   BX
                       JNB   NEXT_LOC
                       HLT
CSEG ENDS
END START_OF_MAIN_PROGRAM
```

Fig. 7.10 Contents of the file ADDRANDS.ASM.

Sharing data between modules is organized along similar lines, as illustrated by the two modules in Figs. 7.11 and 7.12. When combined via LINK they form a program which calculates the tax payable on incomes stored as unsigned 16-bit numbers in the group of locations labelled TEST_VALUES. The tax payable is calculated at TAXRATE percent and the results left in corresponding locations labelled TEST_RESULTS.

The TAXCALCS module (Fig. 7.11) actually calculates the tax payable, accessing the variable TAXRATE from the main TAXPROG module to do so. Hence, in TAXCALCS, TAXRATE must be declared as EXTRN and the data segment in which this declaration is made must be on PUBLIC access.

In the TAXPROG module, on the other hand, TAXRATE must be declared PUBLIC after its definition, and once again the containing data segment made PUBLIC. Similar arrangements for accessing the subroutine CALCULATE_TAX must be made as for accessing RANDOM in the previous example.

When these are combined in the manner described above, the linker produces a file TAXPROG.MAP which contains the following information about the manner in which it has combined the modules:

Start	Stop	Length	Name
00000H	00020H	0021H	CSEG
00030H	0003FH	0010H	DSEG
00040H	0013FH	0100H	SSEG
00140H	0014BH	000CH	CSEG

Program entry point at 0000:0000

```
NAME TAXCALCS
DSEG SEGMENT PUBLIC
EXTRN TAXRATE:WORD
DSEG ENDS

CSEG SEGMENT
CALCULATE_TAX PROC FAR
            PUBLIC CALCULATE_TAX
ASSUME CS:CSEG,DS:DSEG
            MOV   BX,TAXRATE
            MUL   BX
            MOV   CX,100D
            DIV   CX
            RET
CALCULATE_TAX ENDP
CSEG ENDS
END
```

Fig. 7.11 The module TAXCALCS.

```
NAME TAXPROG
DSEG SEGMENT PUBLIC
TEST_VALUES DW 10000D,20000D,30000D
TEST_RESULTS DW ?,?,?

TAXRATE DW 33D
          PUBLIC TAXRATE
DSEG ENDS

SSEG SEGMENT STACK
          DB 100H DUP(?)
SSEG ENDS

CSEG SEGMENT
ASSUME CS:CSEG,DS:DSEG,SS:SSEG
          EXTRN CALCULATE_TAX:FAR
  COMMENCE: MOV   AX,DSEG
            MOV   DS,AX
            MOV   CX,3
            MOV   DI,OFFSET TEST_RESULTS
            MOV   SI,OFFSET TEST_VALUES
  NEXT_LOC: MOV   AX,[SI]
            CALL  CALCULATE_TAX
            MOV   [DI],AX
            ADD   SI,2
            ADD   DI,2
            DEC   CX
            JNE   NEXT_LOC
            HLT
CSEG ENDS
END COMMENCE
```

Fig. 7.12 The module TAXPROG.

EXERCISES 7.4

1. Write and test a module CONVERT which, given a length in inches in AX, will leave in BX the nearest equivalent length expressed as a whole number of centimetres. Thus, for example, if AX contained 123D then, after execution, BX would contain 312D (using 1 inch = 2.54 cm). Combine this with another module MAIN which, given a length of *m* feet and *n* inches, stores *m* in location FEET and *n* in location INCHES, converts (*m* feet, *n* inches) to inches, calls CONVERT to do a conversion to centimetres and leaves the result in location METRIC.

2. Write and, as far as is possible, test independently two modules which together allow the ratio of consonants to vowels in a given piece of text to be calculated. The main module should work out

and print the ratio from counts of consonants and vowels supplied by the other module.

3. Write and test a module which calculates the simple interest payable on a sum of m pounds at a rate of interest $n\%$ over r years (assume that m, n and r are whole numbers). Use this module in conjunction with another module to print tables showing the interest which could be earned on sums of £1000, £2000, . . . , £30 000 invested for 5 or 10 years at rates of interest of 10, 11 and 15%.

7.10 FLOATING POINT ARITHMETIC

Arithmetic between REAL variables in an 8088 Pascal compiler must be implemented in software, since the 8088 itself has no facilities for performing floating point arithmetic. Consequently, REAL arithmetic operations will be comparatively slow. For applications where this could be critical, the manufacturers of the 8088 – the Intel Corporation – designed the 8087 arithmetic co-processor which, if installed, works in tandem with the 8088 and provides the missing floating point operations and, of course, does them at hardware speeds. Full details on the Intel 8087 Numeric Data Processor can be found in the IAPX 86, 88 Users' Manual, Intel Corporation, Santa Clara, California, 1981.

A full discussion of software floating point arithmetic implementation is outside the scope of this book. There are more than a dozen different possible floating point data formats and various proposals for standards by the professional bodies like the IEEE. In the first instance, the interested reader is referred to *The Art of Computer Programming*, Volume 2, by D. E. Knuth, Addison-Wesley, Reading, Massachusetts, 1969. We conclude this chapter with an exercise which attempts to introduce the reader to some of the problems involved.

EXERCISE 7.5

The REAL number $m * 2^n$, $0 \leqslant m < 1$, can be represented in a single word if n is represented as a signed 8-bit number and m is represented as an 8-bit signed binary fraction. What range of real numbers is thus representable? Are there any gaps in this range? Write and test an 8088 assembly language program to add two real numbers thus represented.

8 8088 BCD Arithmetic Instructions

AIMS

This chapter introduces the 8088 instructions for performing arithmetic on numbers represented in **BCD** (Binary Coded Decimal) form. BCD can save us much of the trouble of converting decimal numbers into binary on input and has the advantage that it can easily represent numbers of arbitrary precision.

8.1 BCD REPRESENTATION

One of the disadvantages of reading in numbers as a series of ASCII codes for digits is that, before any arithmetic can be performed with such numbers, their binary equivalents have to be calculated. Thus, if the decimal number 37 were typed at the keyboard, the ASCII codes for 3 and 7 (33H and 37H respectively) would have to be converted to their corresponding binary equivalents, and then the binary equivalent of the first digit multiplied by ten and added to the second! (We had to do all this – and worse – in the GET_OK_NUM_AND_TERM_NON_SPACE_CHAR subroutine of Chapter 5.)

BCD is a way of representing numbers which avoids the need for conversions of this sort. The principle used is to encode each decimal digit separately and to use as many bits as necessary to represent the complete number exactly. To encode each of the digits 0, 1, 2, . . . , 9 their unsigned 4-bit equivalents are used (see Table 8.1). Thus, rather than adopt the above procedure, we can read the ASCII codes for 3 and 7 (33H and 37H respectively) and convert them to their BCD equivalents (3H and 7H) and store these instead of the signed or unsigned binary equivalent of decimal 37.

The remaining details of a BCD representation are left up to the programmer. Typically, one or more bytes will be used at the beginning of a representation to indicate the total number of BCD digits used. Another byte (or just four bits) may be used for the sign. Thus, one way of obtaining a BCD representation of a decimal number such as 125 is to first glue

Table 8.1 BCD representation of the digits 0, 1, . . . , 9.

Digit	BCD representation
0	0000
1	0001
2	0010
3	0011
4	0100
5	0101
6	0110
7	0111
8	1000
9	1001

together the BCD representation of each of its digits: 0001 0010 0101; then add a sign (coded, for example, as 0000 for a +, 0001 for a −): 0000 0001 0010 0101; and finally add on the number of digits in the representation (three!): 0011 0000 0001 0010 0101. Since we have packed two BCD digits into each byte this is known as a **packed** BCD representation.

Unpacked BCD representation involves storing one BCD digit per byte. Thus an unpacked BCD representation of −2619 might be:

0000 0100 0000 0001 0000 0010 0000 0110 0000 0001 0000 1001

In order to focus more specifically on the problems involved, in most of what follows we work with unsigned BCD numbers and leave the reader to produce equivalent versions of programs for signed BCD representations.

EXERCISES 8.1

1. Write a) packed and b) unpacked BCD representations of the decimals 29, −3091 and 11111111.

2. BCD is sometimes used in mainframe computer systems where there is a great deal of input and output to be done but only a relatively small amount of arithmetic processing. Consider, for example, a customer order handling system for a mail order company which offers its 500,000 customers in excess of 100,000 different products. In this case, BCD representation might be used for the quantity a given customer requires of a certain product and for the number of such a product in stock. In this way it would be hoped that the time taken to amend stock records, produce invoices, maintain a sales ledger etc. is not dominated by the time taken to convert successive streams of digits into signed or unsigned binary equivalents.

   Write a simulation to estimate the extra time taken by this

conversion on the IBM PC for 6-digit decimal whole numbers when compared with reading and storing such numbers in packed BCD form. What is the overall saving to be expected for 10,000 6-digit whole numbers?

8.2 ADDITION AND SUBTRACTION

We have already seen one disadvantage of representing numbers in BCD form – a BCD representation is generally less compact than the straight binary (signed or unsigned) form: decimal 125 is 000100100101 in unsigned packed BCD form compared with a signed 8-bit representation of 01111101. At first sight, another disadvantage is that, when we add two BCD representations, the result is not necessarily the BCD form of the sum of the two numbers represented. Consider the following addition. On the left-hand side we have written the decimal equivalent of the packed BCD numbers on the right.

24	0010 0100
13	0001 0011
37	0011 0111

Here, everything works. Adding the BCD form of 24 and 13 results in the BCD form of the correct answer, 37. But now consider:

19	0001 1001
24	0010 0100
3?	0011 1101

The problem is that 1101 is not the BCD for any digit. A 4-bit coding can represent up to 16 different things, but there are only ten decimal digits. This means that if we add the BCD form of any two digits which give a number in this range of non-codes (such as 9D + 4D or 1001 + 0100), the result cannot be correct.

All is not lost, however. If we add 6 to the sum in any digit position that steps into the forbidden range we compensate for the non-existent digits which must be passed over:

19	0001 1001	
24	0010 0100	
3?	0011 1101	
06	0000 0110	(adjust forbidden range digits)
43	0100 0011	

Consider next:

19	0001 1001
28	0010 1000
41	0100 0001

The answer is wrong! In this case the right-most digit passed completely through the forbidden range and so again we need to adjust by adding 6:

41	0100 0001	
06	0000 0110	(adjust for digits passing through forbidden range)
47	0100 0111	

It turns out that we need to add 6 whenever there's a carry resulting from the addition of two *digit* codes. If we are adding two BCD numbers in an 8-bit register, the carry flag indicates whether a carry has resulted from adding the two most significant BCD digits. The **auxiliary** carry flag is set to 1 if there was a carry from adding the two least significant BCD digits and to 0 otherwise. Thus, in

19	0001	1001
18	0001	1000
31	0011 (1)	0001

the auxiliary carry flag would be set to 1.

Although the above discussion has considered only packed BCD representations, there are corresponding problems with unpacked BCD representations. Thankfully, we don't have to worry about all these details in the course of normal programming, since there are 8088 instructions which do the adjusting for us. These are **DAA** (Decimal Adjust for Addition) which makes adjustments for packed representations, and **AAA** (ASCII Adjust for Addition) which makes adjustments for unpacked representations.

Based on the settings of the carry and auxiliary carry flags and on whether the sum of two digits has entered the forbidden range, DAA adds 6 to the appropriate BCD digit of the BCD number held in AL. Similar instructions – **DAS** (Decimal Adjust for Subtraction) and **AAS** (ASCII Adjust for Subtraction) – make the corresponding adjustments when subtracting two BCD numbers via the AL register.

Example 1 – adding and subtracting unpacked BCD numbers

```
MOV AL,52H
MOV BL,47H
ADD AL,BL
DAA
```

This program extract loads the AL register with the unpacked, unsigned BCD representation of the decimal 52 and the BL register with the corresponding BCD equivalent of 47 in decimal. The two numbers are added by an ordinary 8088 ADD instruction, leaving the result in AL. Finally DAA is used to adjust AL so that the sum is left in packed BCD form.

Subtraction of BCD numbers is carried out in a similar way. Thus:

```
MOV AL,56H
MOV BL,28H
SUB AL,BL
DAS
```

leaves 28H in register AL.

Of course, in each case the programmer would also have to ensure that the sign and number-of-digits fields of the BCD representation were manipulated appropriately.

Example 2 – adding two packed BCD numbers having lots of digits

Up to now the discussion has centred on BCD representations involving just two BCD digits. In practice, most BCD numbers we would want to handle will have more than two BCD digits and so we turn our attention to writing an 8088 program fragment which can add together two numbers represented in packed BCD form, each having the same number of BCD digits. There will be very little restriction on the number of BCD digits allowed in either of the BCD numbers to be added. As many as 131,072 BCD digits can be handled but, however many BCD digits are involved, there must be an even number of them. The reason for this comes from practical considerations best illustrated by an example.

The BCD number 123H requires at least 12 binary digits of storage (not counting the sign and number-of-digits fields). Since the 8088 is designed to handle multiples of 8 bits at a time, programmers normally arrange to store BCD numbers in a form which occupies an exact number of *bytes*. Thus, BCD 123H would be stored in the equivalent BCD form: 0123H. We shall follow this convention and therefore will be able to specify the length of a BCD number by stating the number of bytes it occupies. Thus a BCD number occupying five bytes has 10 BCD digits.

Our program fragment for adding two multi-digit BCD numbers will assume that both numbers occupy the same number of bytes and that this is given in register CX. The first BCD number is assumed to be stored in the collection of locations starting at that given in the SI register (relative to the contents of the DS register) and the second in the location given in the DI register (relative to DS) and following. Both BCD numbers are further assumed to have been stored with their least significant pair of BCD digits in the lowest address, the next least significant pair of BCD digits in the next lowest address, and so on. Within each location, the two BCD digits are stored as in our illustrative examples above: the most significant BCD digit occupies the most significant binary digits.

The sum of the two BCD numbers to be added will be left in the group of locations beginning with that given in the DI register and will be stored in the same form as each of the original two numbers. Thus, if before executing the program fragment we have:

	Location	Contents
CX : 0003H	400H	41
SI : 0400H	401H	98
DI : 0500H	402H	01
	403H	??
	.	.
	.	.
	500H	64
	501H	71
	502H	02
	503H	??

(? indicates 4 bits of a byte
whose contents are not known)

then after execution we would have

	Location	Contents
CX : 0000H	400H	41
SI : 0400H	401H	98
DI : 0500H	402H	01
	403H	00
	.	.
	.	.
	500H	05
	501H	70
	502H	04
	503H	00

since, as decimals, 019841 + 027164 = 047005.

The program fragment itself affords a natural opportunity to demonstrate that DAA and DAS can just as well be used with ADC and SBB (respectively) as with ADD and SUB. The method used is to sum two BCD digits at a time, adding in any BCD carry digit which resulted from the previous two digits. Thus to calculate the sum of the BCD numbers 1234H and 5678H the program fragment proceeds as follows. Given:

$$
\begin{array}{cc}
12 & 34 \\
56 & 78 \\
\hline
?? & ?? \\
\end{array}
$$

add the first pair of BCD digits:

$$
\begin{array}{c}
34 \\
78 \\
\hline
\end{array}
$$

(carry 1)   12

add the next pair of digits together with any previous carry:

$$
\begin{array}{r}
12 \\
56 \\
\text{previous carry:}\quad 1 \\
\hline
69
\end{array}
$$

Therefore the sum is:

$$69 \quad 12$$

In pseudo-Pascal this method is:

> *clear carry*;
> **repeat** *move next two digits of first number into AL*;
>   *add corresponding digits of second number*;
>   *add current carry*;
>   *do BCD adjustment*;
>   *save the sum digit*;
> **until**   *no more digits to do*;
> *save the final carry*;

Programming this method into 8088 assembly language under the afore-
mentioned assumptions we obtain the program fragment in Fig. 8.1.

```
            ;clear carry;
                    CLC
            ;repeat move next two digits of first number into AL;
NEXT_DIGITS: MOV AL,[SI]
                    ;add corresponding digits of second number;
                    ;add current carry;
                    ADC AL,[DI]
                    ;do BCD adjustment;
                    DAA
                    ;save the sum digit;
                    MOV [DI],AL
                    ;adjust pointers to positions of next digits;
                    INC SI
                    INC DI
            ;until no more digits to do;
                    DEC CX
                    JNZ NEXT_DIGITS
            ;save the final carry;
                    MOV AL,0
                    ADC AL,0
                    MOV [DI],AL
```

Fig. 8.1 Addition of two unsigned packed BCD representations.

EXERCISES 8.2

1. Two packed BCD numbers of the same length are stored in memory, one – let's call it x – starting at the address given in SI, the other – call it y – at the address given in DI (both relative to the DS register). The format in which these numbers are stored is the same as in Example 2 above. Write an 8088 assembly language program which will leave $x-y$ stored in BCD in the same format in the group of locations beginning at the address given in DI.

2. Incorporate the program fragment of Example 2 and your solution to Exercise 1 above into a program which will calculate the sum or difference of any two positive numbers typed in at the keyboard. Each number should be terminated by the user pressing the RETURN key. Both numbers should be stored in memory in packed BCD format, the appropriate answer calculated as a packed BCD number, and finally the decimal equivalent of the BCD number printed out on a new line. Make any reasonable simplifying assumptions you like. (*Hint*: work out the number of bytes, n, needed to store the largest of the two numbers in packed BCD format and then store both numbers as n-byte packed BCD numbers.)

3. Produce an equivalent program fragment to that given in Fig. 8.1 for packed, signed BCD representations.

4. Repeat Exercises 1 and 3 for *unpacked* BCD representations.

8.3 MULTIPLICATION

It is not possible to perform multiplication and division by using the ordinary 8088 multiply and divide instructions and then adjusting the result unless an *unpacked* BCD representation is used. In that case, multiplying two unpacked BCD digits, one in AL and the other in BL, is carried out by the two instructions:

```
MUL BL
AAM
```

MUL BL multiplies the two unpacked BCD digits in AL and BL as binary numbers, leaving the result in AX. **AAM** (ASCII Adjust for Multiplication) converts this result into two unpacked BCD digits and leaves the most significant digit in AH and the least significant in AL. Thus if AL contains 04H and BL contains 09H before execution of these two instructions, register AX would contain 0000001100000110 = 0306H, the unpacked BCD representation of 36D, after execution.

Example 3 – a subroutine to multiply unpacked BCD numbers

Any program which requires the multiplication of unpacked BCD numbers will almost certainly need a subroutine to multiply two such numbers with several digits, not just one. Our next example takes the first step towards providing such a subroutine; the reader is invited to complete the task in an exercise. Once again we confine our attention to unsigned BCD representations.

We shall construct an 8088 assembly language program fragment which will multiply an unpacked BCD number having a more or less arbitrary number of digits by a single unpacked BCD digit. As in Example 2, we shall assume that the first unpacked BCD number is stored at the sequence of locations beginning with the address given in the SI register (relative to the contents of DS) and that the BCD digits of this number are stored least significant digit in lowest address, next least significant digit in next lowest address and so on. We shall further assume that the number of the BCD digits of this number is in the CX register and that the DL register contains the single unpacked BCD digit by which the other number is to be multiplied. The result of the multiplication will be stored starting at the address given in DI (relative to DS) in the same form as the two multiplicands. Thus, if before executing the program fragment we have:

	Location	Contents
CX : 0004H	0400H	01H
DL : 06H	0401H	09H
DI : 0600H	0402H	02H
SI : 0400H	0403H	08H
	.	.
	.	.
	0600H	?
	0601H	?

then after execution we shall have

	Location	Contents
CX : 0000H	0400H	01H
DL : 06H	0401H	09H
DI : 604H	0402H	02H
SI : 404H	0403H	08H
	.	.
	.	.
	0600H	06H
	0601H	04H
	0602H	07H
	0603H	09H
	0604H	04H

since $8291 * 6 = 49746$.

Once again, the program fragment itself uses the schoolchild's multiplication algorithm, which applied to 8291 * 6 is:

1. 6 times 1 is 6 so write down 6 and carry 0;
2. 6 times 9 is 54, add the carry is 54, so write down 4 and carry 5;
3. 6 times 2 is 12, add the carry is 17, so write down 7 and carry 1;
4. 6 times 8 is 48, add the carry is 49, so write down 9 and since this is the last digit to be multiplied, write down 4 also.

Very informally in pseudo-Pascal this is:

last_carry := *0*;
repeat *move the next digit of the big number into AL*;
        multiply this by the contents of DL;
        adjust the result;
        add last_carry;
        adjust the result;
        save the sum digit as the current product digit;
        move pointers to next digits;
        last_carry := current carry
until *no more digits of the multiplicand left*;

This leads to the 8088 assembly language version given in Fig. 8.2.

```
            ;last_carry := 0;
                   MOV [DI],0
            ;repeat move the first digit of the big number into AL;
NEXT_DIGIT: MOV AL,[SI]
                   ;multiply this by the contents of DL;
                   MUL DL
                   ;adjust the result;
                   AAM
                   ;add last_carry;
                   ADD AL,[DI]
                   ;adjust the result;
                   AAA
                   ;save the sum digit as the current product digit;
                   MOV [DI],AL
                   ;move pointers to next digits;
                   INC DI
                   INC SI
                   ;last carry := current carry;
                   MOV [DI],AH
            ;until no more digits of the multiplicand left;
                   DEC CX
                   JNZ NEXT_DIGIT
```

Fig. 8.2 Multiplication of a multi-digit unsigned unpacked BCD number by a single unpacked BCD digit.

EXERCISES 8.3

1. Make a detailed trace of the execution of the program fragment given in Example 3 above for the following initial contents of registers and memory locations.

Register	Contents	Location	Contents
CX	0005H	0400H	4
DL	07H	0401H	1
SI	0400H	0402H	9
DI	0600H	0403H	2
		0404H	8

2. Use the program fragment in Example 3 to construct a subroutine which will multiply two unpacked BCD numbers – x and y – each having the number of BCD digits given in the CX register. Assume that x and y are stored in the same format as the multiple digit unpacked BCD number in Example 3, and that y is stored in the sequence of locations beginning with that having the address given in the BX register (relative to DS). Test your program carefully. (*Hint*: you may need to use a (slightly) modified version of the program fragment in Example 2.)

3. Construct equivalents for *signed*, unpacked BCD numbers of the program fragment in Fig. 8.2 and for the program you constructed in Exercise 2 above.

8.4 DIVISION

Division of two unpacked BCD digits can be accomplished by using the ordinary (binary) 8088 divide instruction after the dividend (the thing to be divided into) has been suitably adjusted. The **AAD** (ASCII Adjust for Division) instruction takes the unpacked two BCD digit number in AX and converts it to a form so that DIV may be used to leave an unpacked BCD quotient in AL and an unpacked BCD remainder in AH. Thus if AX contains 0604H and DL contains 09H then after execution of

```
AAD
DIV DL
```

register AL will contain 07H and register AH will contain 01H.

Example 4 – dividing a single unpacked BCD digit into an unpacked BCD number

Predictably, we shall now construct a program fragment which will divide one single unpacked BCD digit into an unpacked BCD number with (almost) arbitrarily many digits. As before, we shall assume that the SI register (relative to DS) points to the unpacked BCD number, the number of digits of which is recorded in register CX, and that this number is stored with its least significant digit in the lowest address, the next least significant digit in the next lowest address and so on. The quotient of the division will be stored in the same form as the dividend, but at the sequence of locations beginning with that having the address given in DI (relative to DS). AH will contain the remainder. DL will contain the single unpacked BCD digit divisor. Thus, if before execution of the program fragment we have:

Register	Contents	Location	Contents
SI	0400H	0400H	01H
DI	0600H	0401H	09H
CX	05H	0402H	09H
DL	08H	0403H	07H
AH	?	0404H	02H
		.	.
		.	.
		.	.
		0600H	?
		0601H	?
		0602H	?
		0603H	?
		0604H	?

then after execution we will have:

Register	Contents	Location	Contents
SI	03FFH	0400H	01H
DI	05FFH	0401H	09H
CX	0000H	0402H	09H
DL	08H	0403H	07H
AH	07H	0404H	02H
		.	.
		.	.
		.	.
		0600H	08H
		0601H	09H
		0602H	04H
		0603H	03H
		0604H	00H

Once again the algorithm used by the program fragment will mirror the schoolchild's method. For example, to divide decimal 231 by decimal 6: 6 into 2 won't go, so carry the 2 forward and try 6 into 23; 6 into 23 is 3 remainder 5 so write down 3 and carry the 5 forward; 6 into 51 is 8 remainder 3 so write down 8 and, since there are no more digits to divide into, 3 is the remainder for the whole division. Thus, 231 divide by 6 is 38 remainder 3.

This gives us the program fragment of Fig. 8.3 (in which register AH is

```
             MOV AH,0
     ;point SI to highest order BCD digit of dividend;
             ADD DI,CX
     ;point DI to highest order BCD digit of result;
             ADD SI,CX
     ;repeat move next unpacked digit into AL;
NEXT_DIGIT: MOV AL,[SI]
             DEC SI
             ;adjust AL and AH;
             AAD
             ;divide DL into AL; (*remainder now in AH,
             ;quotient in AL*)
             DIV DL
             ;store quotient at address pointed to by DI;
             MOV [DI],AL
             DEC DI
     ;until no more digits left;
             DEC CX
             JNZ NEXT_DIGIT
```

Fig. 8.3   Division of a multi-digit unsigned, unpacked BCD number by a single unpacked BCD digit.

used to contain the digit to be carried forward at each stage) and completes our discussion of the 8088 BCD instructions. For reference purposes, Table 8.2 contains a summary of all these instructions.

EXERCISES 8.4

1. Make a detailed trace of the execution of the program fragment in Example 4 for the following initial data:

						Locations				
AH	AL	CX	DL	DI	SI	400H	401H	402H	403H	404H
?	?	05H	07H	300H	400H	07H	04H	00H	02H	09H

   (Set out your trace across the page as we have done and make one trace entry for each instruction executed, except that AAD and DIV DL should be regarded as a single instruction.)

2. Devise, implement and thoroughly test a program which accepts two unsigned, unpacked BCD numbers typed in at the keyboard and divides the first number typed by the second and prints out the quotient and remainder. Assume that each of the two numbers is terminated by pressing the RETURN key. (Hint: try to imitate the schoolchild algorithm for long division.)

3. Using the routines you have developed in Exercises 8.2, 8.3 and Exercise 2 above as a basis, write a multi-length arithmetic equivalent to the calculator simulator of Chapter 5. In other words, your new version should accept non-negative whole numbers of up to, say, 1000 digits.

4. An alternative means of implementing multi-length integer arithmetic is to store each integer in signed binary form, allowing the maximum number of bits in the representation to be a multiple of 8 and to be determined by the integers with which you are calculating. Thus, to calculate 125784361 ∗ 5522110000193667832 both integers would first be represented in signed 64-bit form and the multiplication would be carried out between these signed representations. Write such subroutines for each arithmetic operation and compare execution times with their BCD equivalent.

Table 8.2 Summary of the 8088 BCD arithmetic instructions.

Operation	Mnemonic	Effect
Addition	AAA	ASCII Adjust for Addition: contents of AL are modified so that it contains a valid unpacked BCD number.
	DAA	Decimal Adjust for Addition: contents of AL are modified so that it contains a valid packed BCD number.
Subtraction	AAS	ASCII Adjust for Subtraction: if AL contains the result of subtracting two unpacked decimal digits, executing AAS modifies the contents of AL so that it contains a valid unpacked BCD digit.
	DAS	Decimal Adjust for Subtraction: if AL contains the result of subtracting two packed operands, executing DAS modifies AL so that it contains a valid packed BCD number.
Multiplication	AAM	ASCII Adjust for Multiply: if AX contains the result of multiplying two unpacked operands, executing AAM modifies AX so that AH and AL each contain a valid BCD digit.
Division	AAD	ASCII Adjust for Division: executing AAD *prior* to dividing two unpacked BCD operands modifies the contents of AL so that the quotient in AL after division is a valid unpacked BCD digit.

9 Assembly Language Features

9.1 STATEMENTS

MASM allows two kinds of assembly language statement which have the general forms:

> label   mnemonic   argument, . . . , argument ; comment

or

> name   pseudo-op   argument, . . . , argument ; comment

Names and **labels** can be up to 31 characters in length, consist of alphabetic characters (upper and lower case, though the assembler converts lower case to upper), digits and the characters ?, -, @ and $, but must *not* begin with a digit. In order to avoid confusion, names and labels must be different from the MASM reserved words which include standard 8088 instruction mnemonics (such as MOV, REP and ADD), register names (such as AH, DL and BP), assembler pseudo-op names (such as EQU and DB) and assembler operators (such as PTR).

A label represents a location which can be used in, for example, a JMP or CALL instruction. If a colon (:) is appended when the label is defined, MASM assumes that this label is to be referenced only from within the same segment (i.e. the NEAR form of JMP or CALL is assumed for any such instruction referring to that label). A name can be just a **symbol**, for example CR in

```
CR EQU 0AH ;ASCII line feed character
```

or a **variable**, for example RUN_ERROR in

```
RUN_ERROR DB 'COMMAND NOT UNDERSTOOD',CR,LF,'$'
```

Labels and variables have three attributes: segment, offset and type. MASM calculates appropriate values for these attributes which can be accessed via the SEG, OFFSET and TYPE operators. SEG is similar to OFFSET which we have often used in preceding chapters. Thus:

```
MOV BX,SEG RUN_ERROR
```

would be assembled by MASM into an instruction equivalent to

```
MOV BX,n
```

where n is the segment address of the variable RUN_ERROR. For a variable, TYPE returns the number of bytes occupied by that variable. Thus, given

```
NEW_CENTURY DW 2000D
```

then

```
MOV AX,TYPE MY_WORD
```

would be assembled into an instruction equivalent to

```
MOV AX,2
```

When used with labels, the TYPE operator returns -1 if the label is NEAR and -2 if it is FAR.

Statements which use the DUP operator as in

```
SALES_ARRAY DB  80H DUP(0)
DATES_ARRAY DW 100H DUP(1924D)
```

(used to initialize the contents of SALES_ARRAY to zero and DATES_ ARRAY to 1924) or which give multiple definitions as in

```
TEST_VALUES DB 2,4,6,8,0AH,0CH,0EH
```

can be referred to by the LENGTH and SIZE operators. LENGTH returns the total number of units allocated for the variable on which it operates. Thus

```
MOV AX,LENGTH SALES_ARRAY
MOV BX,LENGTH DATES_ARRAY
```

would be assembled into instructions equivalent to

```
MOV AX,80H
MOV BX,100H
```

The SIZE operator returns the product of LENGTH and TYPE. Thus

```
MOV AX,SIZE SALES_ARRAY
MOV BX,SIZE DATES_ARRAY
```

would be assembled into instructions equivalent to

```
MOV AX,80H
MOV BX,200H
```

By way of example, the program fragment below shows a simple utility which copies the string ASTRING into the string BSTRING, assuming suitable definitions of ASTRING and BSTRING.

```
MOV AX,DS
MOV ES,AX
MOV SI,OFFSET ASTRING
MOV DI,OFFSET BSTRING
MOV CX,LENGTH ASTRING
CLD
REP MOVSB
```

9.2 EXPRESSIONS

A MASM expression consists of a collection of operators which act on operands to produce a value at assembly time. Expressions can be used in certain selected statements. For example:

```
MOV AX,100H MOD 17D
MOV BX,0EFH SHL 2
```

would be assembled into instructions equivalent to

```
MOV AX,1
MOV BH,0BCH
```

since 100H MOD 17D is 1 and 0EFH shifted left two bits is 0BCH. In the case of

```
CO_ORD_ADDRESS DW OFFSET START_LOC+(22H*2)
```

the expression is OFFSET START_LOC+(22H*2), but logical and relational expressions are also allowed as in

```
MOV DL,3EH OR 0FEH
MOV DL,5EH GE 6EH
```

which would be assembled into instructions equivalent to

```
MOV DL,0FEH
MOV DL,0
```

since the result of the expression 3EH OR 0FEH is 0FEH (an ordinary logical OR), and the result of 5EH GE 6EH (is 5EH greater than or equal to 6EH ?) is false, represented by 0.

Table 9.1 summarizes the MASM operators which can be used in expressions. Many of the **logical** and **relational** expression operators are most useful in the context of conditional assembly, which is dealt with in Section 10.4. The MASM manual specifies the operands permissible with each operator in detail. For our purposes, it is enough to remark that an operation is acceptable if its results make sense. Thus, in

Table 9.1 Operators which MASM and ASM have in common (see Section 9.7 and following for operators unique to MASM).

Arithmetic	
HIGH, LOW	Produces the HIGH or LOW byte of an operand e.g. `MOV AL,LOW(0ABC1H); MOV AL,0C1H`
$*$, /, MOD	e.g. `CMP DX, (132*15)/3 MOD 4`
SHL, SHR	SHift Left (SHL) or SHift Right (SHR) the operand e.g. `CMP AH,14H SHR 6`
+, −	e.g. `MOV AL,RECORD_START+2`
Relational	
EQ, NE, LT LE, GT, GE	Return all 1s (true) or all 0s (false) e.g. `MOV AL,16 LT 17; MOV AL,0FFH`
Logical	
NOT	e.g. `MOV BH,NOT 15H`
AND	e.g. `MOV CL,22H AND 0ABH`
Value returning	
LENGTH, SIZE	Return the number of data items and number of bytes in a variable defined using DUP or containing multiple byte definitions.
SEG, TYPE, OFFSET	These operate on a variable or label and return the designated attribute.
Set or override attribute value	
Segment override	e.g. `MOV CL,ES:SCREEN_BYTE` `MOV CL,DISPLAY_SEG:SCREEN_BYTE`
PTR, THIS	Override the type (byte or word) of a previously defined variable or label.
SHORT	Request encoding of a SHORT jump instruction.

```
DATE    DW 1922
TIME    DB 60
SECONDS DB DATE*TIME ;error!
```

DATE*TIME is erroneous because MASM gives no meaning to such a quantity. (To which segment should it belong in general? That of the first or second operand?)

We have already seen the use of the PTR operator to remove ambiguity from an instruction such as

```
INC [BX] ;illegal ambiguous instruction
```

but PTR can also be used to override the type of a variable. Thus, given

```
MY_WORD DW 4142H
```

then

```
MOV AX,BYTE PTR MY_WORD
```

will be assembled so that its effect is the same as

```
MOV AX,41H
```

Another use of PTR is where a label has been defined to be of a particular type (say NEAR) but at some point in the program it becomes necessary to refer to the label as having the opposite type (FAR in this case). This is illustrated in the following program fragment, where NEAR_LOOP has type NEAR because of the appended colon:

```
NEAR_LOOP: ADD AX,BX
           MOV DX,AX
             :
             :
           JMP NEAR_LOOP
             :
             :
    FAR_LOOP EQU FAR PTR NEAR_LOOP
           JMP FAR_LOOP
```

It is also possible to override the *segment* associated with a variable or label with the MASM segment override operators. Thus

```
MOV AL,ES:ABYTE
```

would be assembled so that AL were filled from a location in the segment addressed by ES having the same offset from ES as ABYTE from the start of its segment of definition. Similarly:

```
MOV AL,MYSEGMENT:ABYTE
```

uses the segment name MYSEGMENT to achieve the same effect.

Two other operators complete the complement of MASM **attribute value** setting and overriding pseudo-ops, namely SHORT and THIS. SHORT specifically requests the assembler to encode a JMP instruction in the signed 8-bit form (see Section 2.3) rather than the unsigned 16-bit form. However, instructions such as

```
JMP SHORT NEXT_BLOCK_LABEL
```

which use SHORT are only permitted if NEXT_BLOCK_LABEL is in the same segment as the JMP instruction itself.

The MASM operators THIS WORD and THIS BYTE allow the redefinition to the assembler of variables already defined, rather like PTR allowed access to separate bytes of a word variable in our example above. Hence:

```
AB_WORD      EQU THIS WORD
FIRST_BYTE  DB   41H
SECOND_BYTE DB   42H
```

would allow the contents of the contiguous locations FIRST_BYTE and SECOND_BYTE to be accessed as a word. THIS can be used to define alternative labels for the same address, one being NEAR and the other FAR as, for example, in

```
FAR_LOOP EQU THIS FAR
NEAR_LOOP:ADD AX,2
```

Operator precedence

Expressions are evaluated in the normal way: highest precedence operators first, then left to right for equal precedence operators. Round brackets (and) can be used to alter precedence. Operators are listed in Table 9.2 in order of precedence, SHORT having lowest possible precedence and entries on the same line equal precedence.

Table 9.2 MASM operator precedence in order (SHORT has lowest precedence).

An entry in square [] or round () brackets
LENGTH, SIZE
A segment override operator (e.g. ES:)
PTR, OFFSET, SEG, TYPE, THIS
HIGH, LOW
*, /, MOD, SHL, SHR
+, − (both unary and binary)
EQ, NE, LT, LE, GT, GE
NOT
AND
OR, XOR
SHORT

EXERCISE 9.1

Rewrite the following program fragment so that it does not use any of the MASM operators in Table 9.1. Check your answer by assembling and running both your rewritten program and the given one.

```
DSEG SEGMENT
    INITIAL_VALUES EQU THIS WORD
    VALUE_COUNT      DB   LENGTH TEST_VALUES
    LETTER_COUNT     DB   LENGTH TEST_LETTERS
    TEST_VALUES      DB   2,4,6,8,0CH,0EH
    COUNT            EQU  168 MOD 16 + 2
    TEST_LETTERS     DB   20H DUP('A')
DSEG ENDS

SSEG SEGMENT STACK
    DB 100H DUP(?)
SSEG ENDS

CSEG SEGMENT
    ASSUME CS:CSEG,DS:DSEG,SS:SSEG
                MOV   AX,DSEG
                MOV   DS,AX
                MOV   AL,TYPE TEST_VALUES - 1
                MOV   CX,LENGTH TEST_VALUES * 10/COUNT
                MOV   BX,OFFSET TEST_VALUES
   NEXT_VALUE:  ADD   AL,[BX]
                INC   BX
                LOOP  NEXT_VALUE
                MOV   BX,0F0H SHL 4 AND 0ABH
                MOV   CX,OFFSET INITIAL_VALUES
                MOV   CL,CH
                MOV   CH,137*14 MOD 9 LT 14
                MOV   BP,OFFSET TEST_LETTERS
  NEXT_LETTER:  MOV   DL,DS:[BP]
                MOV   DH,0
                ADD   BX,DX
                INC   BP
                LOOP  NEXT_LETTER
                HLT
CSEG ENDS
END
```

9.3   DATA DEFINITION, MEMORY AND PROGRAM LINKAGE PSEUDO-OPS

Data definition

The most common data definition pseudo-ops are:

LABEL (defines a variable or label name);
DB, DW, etc.;
EQU; and
= (which defines a symbol which may be redefined).

LABEL and the operator THIS can be used to achieve essentially the same effects. Thus in

```
AB_WORD LABEL WORD
FIRST_BYTE   DB 41H
SECOND_BYTE DB 42H
```

AB_WORD can be used to access the contents of contiguous locations FIRST_BYTE and SECOND_BYTE as a word. More generally, given

```
ARRAYB LABEL BYTE
ARRAYA DW 100 DUP(?)
           :
           :
ADD AL,ARRAYB[99]
ADD AX,ARRAYA[49]
```

the first ADD instruction adds the contents of the 100th *byte* to AL whereas the second adds the contents of the 50th *word* to AX. Similarly in

```
FAR_LOOP   LABEL FAR
NEAR_LOOP:ADD AX,2
```

FAR_LOOP refers to the same address as NEAR_LOOP but FAR_LOOP has the attribute FAR whereas the colon (:) after NEAR_LOOP gives it the attribute NEAR.

We are, by now, very familiar with DB and DW of course. DD was used in Chapter 5 in one of its formats. Thus DD 10000000D initialized four locations to the 4-byte unsigned equivalent of 10000000D etc. But DW, DD, DQ and DT provide other facilities. Given

```
NEXT_LOC:MOV AX,BX
```
                                                                    (9.1)

then

```
        STORED_OFFSET_OF_NEXT_LOC DW NEXT_LOC
    STORED_FULL_ADDRESS_OF_NEXT_LOC DD NEXT_LOC
```

is equivalent to

```
STORED_OFFSET_OF_NEXT_LOC DW OFFSET NEXT_LOC
```

and replacing (9.1) with

```
STORED_FULL_ADDRESS_OF_NEXT_LOC LABEL FAR
NEXT_LOC: MOV AX,BX
```

As was pointed out in Chapters 7 and 8, DD, DQ and DT may also be used to initialize and label locations with contents different from unsigned numbers.

In its simplest form EQU allows a name or value to be defined. However, it can also be used to define your own mnemonics (though before such a tempting facility is used it should be borne in mind that this will make it harder for others to read your programs). For example, given

```
ENTER EQU MOV
ADDRESS EQU DS:[BP]
INITIALIZER EQU AX,DS
```

then

```
ENTER INITIALIZER
ENTER AX,ADDRESS
```

assembles as

```
MOV AX,DS
MOV AX,DS:[BP]
```

Wherever ENTER appears in the assembly language program containing the above EQU statement it will be replaced by MOV on assembly. Similarly every occurrence of ADDRESS and INITIALIZER will be replaced by DS:[BP] and AX,DS respectively.

A name defined by an EQU pseudo-op may not be subsequently redefined in the same program. If you want to be able to redefine a name in your program, the = pseudo-op must be used instead. For example:

```
CR = 0DH  ;Carriage Return
    :
    :
    :
    :
CR = 0H    ;Current Record
CR = CR+1  ;increase value of Current Record
```

is allowed but

```
CR EQU 0DH ;Carriage Return
    :
    :
    :
    :
CR EQU 0H      ;illegal redefinition
CR EQU CR + 1 ;illegal self reference
```

Memory pseudo-ops

The SEGMENT. .ENDS combination is used to define a logical unit called a segment. One segment may be combined with other segments in the same module and/or with segments defined in other modules. When combined, these segments will form the actual physical segments located in memory that are pointed to by the segment registers. In its most general form, the SEGMENT pseudo-op can be followed by up to three optional entries specifying an **align-type**, a **combine-type** and a **class-name**.

The combine-type specifies how this particular segment is to be combined with segments from other modules to form a single physical segment in the memory using the options in Table 9.3 (see also Fig. 9.1).

Of slightly more specialist interest is the align-type parameter, which specifies on which type of boundary in memory the linker should locate the segment. In effect, this poses conditions on the absolute address at which the given segment may be loaded, as shown in Table 9.4.

All of these derive from attempts to overcome one of the shortcomings of segmented memory. The last four bits of an absolute segment address are always zero (since segment addresses are left-shifted four bits to get absolute addresses) so memory segments always start on 16-byte boundaries. A segment can be up to 64 Kbytes long, but if a segment doesn't use all of its bytes, some other segment can start just beyond the last byte used by the first segment. But since the second segment must also start on a 16-byte

Table 9.3 Combine-type options for the SEGMENT pseudo-op.

Option	Comment
blank	Segment is non-combinable (this is the default option).
PUBLIC	All PUBLIC segments with the same name as this one are to be concatenated to form one physical segment when linked.
STACK	All STACK segments having the same name will be treated as if they were PUBLIC. The linker requires that a program has at least one STACK segment.
COMMON	All COMMON segments with the same name as this one are to begin at the same physical address and thus occupy common storage. The length of the single combined segment will be the length of the largest segment of that name.
MEMORY	A MEMORY segment is to be placed in memory at a higher address than all the other segments. If several segments having the MEMORY combine-type are being linked together then the first one encountered by the linker will be processed as such; the rest are processed as COMMON segments.
AT expression	The segment is placed AT the absolute equivalent of the segment address given in the expression.

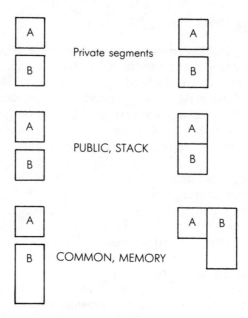

Fig. 9.1 SEGMENT combine-types.

Table 9.4 Align-type options for the SEGMENT pseudo-op.

Align-type	Effect	Form of absolute address at which segment may be loaded
PARA	(This is the default setting if this parameter is blank.) A PARA segment must begin on a paragraph boundary (i.e. with address divisible by 16D).	XXXX0H
PAGE	A PAGE segment must begin on a page boundary (i.e. with address divisible by 256D).	XXX00H
WORD	A WORD segment begins on a word boundary (i.e. at an even address where the least significant bit of the address equals zero).	XXXXYH (Y even)
BYTE	A BYTE segment can begin anywhere.	XXXXXH

boundary, there could be up to 15 bytes wasted between segments – which may be important in situations where memory is scarce. PAGE, WORD and BYTE give more control than the default (PARA) SEGMENT parameter in that they allow the linker to begin a segment at various absolute addresses, not just those with last hexadecimal digit zero. PAGE can be very useful when preparing 8088-based ROM programs. WORD is essential when using the 8086 processor since all segments must then begin on word, paragraph or page boundaries because all memory access starts on an even boundary.

The class-name parameter consists of a name enclosed in single quotes (e.g. 'TRIG') which tells the linker to group segments of the same class-name together in memory, one after the other. Within the memory allocation to a class, segments are loaded in the order that the linker encounters the segments in the object files. Thus, one might give the class-name 'code' to all program segments, 'data' to all data segments and 'stack' to all stack segments in various modules, depending on whether the combine-type implies that this would make sense.

EXERCISES 9.2.

1. With the module of Fig. 9.2 in a file EXMOD1.ASM and that of Fig. 9.3 in EXMOD2.ASM, the linker invocation

   ```
   LINK EXMOD1+EXMOD2,,,;
   ```

   produces an executable program in the file EXMOD1.EXE. By careful study of the two modules, predict what will be printed out if this program is run and then check your answer by typing in the modules, assembling and linking them, and finally actually running the program. You may find it helpful to consider the contents of the file EXMOD1.MAP produced by the linker:

Start	Stop	Length	Name	Class
00000H	0002AH	002BH	CSEG	CODE
00030H	0003DH	000EH	CSEG	CODE
00040H	0009DH	005EH	DSEG	
000A0H	003EFH	0350H	SSEG	OUR_STACK

   Program entry point at 0000:0000

2. By making a few changes to the pseudo-ops in these two modules (and in some cases to the STACK segment definitions), produce four paired versions of each of these modules so that when assembled and linked the contents of EXMOD1.MAP is as shown in i)–v) below. In each case, state the changes necessary *to the originals given in Figs 9.2 and 9.3*. State clearly what will be printed out when the modules are combined into a program and that program is run. Check your answers on the computer.

i)

Start	Stop	Length	Name	Class
00000H	0002AH	002BH	CSEG	CODE
00030H	0003DH	000EH	CSEG	CODE
00040H	0009DH	005EH	DSEG	
000A0H	0019FH	0100H	SSEG	SOME_STACK
001A0H	003EFH	0250H	SSEG	OUR_STACK

Program entry point at 0000:0012

ii)

Start	Stop	Length	Name	Class
00000H	0002AH	002BH	CSEG	CODE
00030H	0003DH	000EH	CSEG	CODE
00040H	000C8H	0089H	DSEG	
000D0H	0041FH	0350H	SSEG	OUR_STACK

Program entry point at 0000:0012

iii)

Start	Stop	Length	Name	Class
00000H	0002AH	002BH	CSEG	UTILITY
00030H	0008DH	005EH	DSEG	
00090H	003DFH	0350H	SSEG	OUR_STACK
003E0H	003EDH	000EH	CSEG	CODE

Program entry point at 0000:0012

iv)

Start	Stop	Length	Name	Class
00000H	0002AH	002BH	CSEG	CODE
00100H	0015DH	005EH	DSEG	
00160H	004AFH	0350H	SSEG	OUR_STACK
00500H	0050DH	000EH	CSEG	UTILITY

Program entry point at 0000:0012

v)

Start	Stop	Length	Name	Class
00000H	0002AH	002BH	CSEG	CODE
0002BH	00038H	000EH	CSEG	CODE
00039H	00096H	005EH	DSEG	
000A0H	003EFH	0350H	SSEG	OUR_STACK

Program entry point at 0000:0012

Memory pseudo-ops GROUP and ASSUME

The minimum memory supplied with an IBM PC is 64K. Thus, the GROUP pseudo-op enables the programmer to instruct the linker to collect together

```
DSEG SEGMENT PARA COMMON
MESSAGE_ONE DB 'HELLO. THIS IS MESSAGE ONE IN THE MAIN MODULE',CR,LF,'$'
MESSAGE_TWO DB 'THIS IS MESSAGE TWO IN THE MAIN MODULE (TWO)',CR,LF,'$'
CR EQU 0AH
LF EQU 0DH
PUBLIC CR,LF
DSEG ENDS

SSEG SEGMENT PARA STACK 'OUR_STACK'
DB 100H DUP(?)
SSEG ENDS

CSEG SEGMENT PARA 'CODE'
   ASSUME CS:CSEG,DS:DSEG,SS:SSEG
          EXTRN PRINT_STRING:FAR
START PROC FAR
        PUSH DS
        MOV  AX,0
        PUSH AX

        MOV  AX,DSEG
        MOV  DS,AX

        MOV  DX,OFFSET MESSAGE_ONE
        CALL PRINT_NEWLINE
        CALL PRINT_STRING
        CALL PRINT_NEWLINE
        RET
START ENDP

PRINT_CHAR PROC NEAR
        MOV  AH,2H
        INT  21H
        RET
PRINT_CHAR ENDP

PRINT_NEWLINE PROC NEAR
        PUSH DX
        MOV  DL,CR
        CALL PRINT_CHAR
        MOV  DL,LF
        CALL PRINT_CHAR
        POP  DX
        RET
PRINT NEWLINE ENDP

CSEG ENDS
END START
```

Fig. 9.2   Contents of the file EXMOD1.ASM

```
DSEG SEGMENT PARA COMMON
CR EQU 0AH
LF EQU 0DH
MESSAGE_ONE DB 'NOW THIS IS MESSAGE ONE, MODULE 2 (TWO)',CR,LF,'$'
DSEG ENDS

SSEG SEGMENT STACK 'OUR_STACK'
            DB 250H DUP(?)
SSEG ENDS

CSEG SEGMENT PARA 'CODE'
ASSUME CS:CSEG,DS:DSEG,SS:SSEG
PUBLIC PRINT_STRING

PRINT_STRING PROC FAR
            MOV   AH,9H
            INT   21H
            RET
PRINT_STRING ENDP

MAIN PROC FAR
            MOV   DX,OFFSET MESSAGE_ONE
            CALL PRINT_STRING
            RET
MAIN ENDP

CSEG ENDS
END
```

Fig. 9.3   Contents of the file EXMOD2.ASM.

a list of segments so that they all reside in one 64K physical segment (this limit is not checked by the assembler). For example, it is possible to have

```
SMALL_MEMORY GROUP CODESEG1,CODESEG2
     CODESEG1   SEGMENT
                ASSUME CS:SMALL_MEMORY
                   :
                   :
                   :
     CODESEG1   ENDS
     CODESEG2   SEGMENT
                ASSUME CS:SMALL_MEMORY
                   :
                   :
                   :
     CODESEG2   ENDS
  END
```

in one module and

```
    SMALL_MEMORY GROUP OTHER_MODULE_SEG
OTHER_MODULE_SEG SEGMENT
                ASSUME CS:SMALL_MEMORY
                    :
                    :
                    :
OTHER_MODULE_SEG ENDS
    END
```

in another module so that CODESEG1, CODESEG2 and OTHER_ MODULE_SEG are collected together into the same physical 64K segment of memory under the name SMALL_MEMORY. Once a group name has been defined in this way, it can be used like any segment name.

We are already familiar with the main purpose of the ASSUME statement, i.e. to inform the assembler of the association between segment registers and segments. At the very beginning of (or before) any segment containing 8088 instructions, we must tell the assembler what it should assume will be in the CS register when that segment of code is executed. Consider the program fragment of Fig. 9.4 and suppose we wish to copy the contents of the byte DATA_BYTE into the first entry of SCREEN_ DISPLAY. Then

```
MOV AL,DATA_BYTE
MOV SCREEN_DISPLAY,AL
```

will work, but only thanks to the ASSUME statements, since both instructions automatically use DS as the segment register for the data to be moved. In the case of MOV AL,DATA_BYTE that is just what we wanted, whereas in the case of MOV SCREEN_DISPLAY,AL it is not. Because of the presence of ASSUME ES:EXTRA and the definition of SCREEN_ DISPLAY in the EXTRA segment, when it sees MOV SCREEN_ DISPLAY,AL the assembler generates a segment override so that ES is used rather than DS. Hence our two instructions are assembled as

```
MOV AL,DATA_BYTE
MOV ES:SCREEN_DISPLAY,AL
```

In fact, it is not *essential* (though much easier in practice to do so) to provide an ASSUME pseudo-op to tell the assembler about DS, ES and SS. But if this is not done, we are forced to provide the assembler with the information on an instruction by instruction basis, using segment override instructions. For example, the copy of DATA_BYTE into SCREEN_DISPLAY could be made without ASSUME pseudo-ops as follows:

```
MOV AL,DS:DATA_BYTE
MOV ES:SCREEN_DISPLAY,AL
```

It is not always possible to know what will be in the segment registers when a particular instruction is executed. Referring again to Fig. 9.4, the first time the INC instruction is executed everything works out correctly:

```
DSEG SEGMENT
   DATA_BYTE DB 41H
DSEG ENDS

EXTRA SEGMENT
   SCREEN_DISPLAY DB 2000H DUP(?)
EXTRA ENDS

CSEG SEGMENT
       ASSUME CS:CSEG,DS:DSEG,ES:EXTRA
              MOV AX,DSEG
              MOV DS,AX
              MOV ES,AX
              MOV AL,DATA_BYTE
              MOV SCREEN_DISPLAY,AL
       ASSUME DS:DSEG,ES:DSEG
              :
              :
              :
NEXT_LETTER:INC DATA_BYTE
              :
              :
              :
              MOV AX,EXTRA
              MOV DS,AX
              JMP NEXT_LETTER
              :
              :
CSEG ENDS
END
```

Fig. 9.4   Program fragment to illustrate the ASSUME pseudo-op.

DATA_BYTE is in the segment currently addressed by DS, which is the default segment register for the INC instruction. However, subsequent instructions reset DS to point to the EXTRA segment, so that after the JMP is excuted we shall execute INC with DS incorrectly set. How can we prevent this happening? The problem comes from the association between DS and DSEG caused by ASSUME DS:DSEG. A special form of the ASSUME pseudo-op allows us to cancel this association. Thus in:

```
       ASSUME DS:NOTHING
NEXT_LETTER:INC DATA_BYTE
```

the problem is solved. ASSUME DS:NOTHING tells the assembler that from this point on DS is not to be assumed to refer to any particular named segment. On reaching INC DATA_BYTE after the ASSUME DS:NOTHING pseudo-op, MASM looks to see which named segment contains DATA_BYTE. The answer is DSEG, so MASM then looks to see if it has a current ASSUMEption about a register which can be used to address that segment. In this case, one such exists thanks to ASSUME ES:DSEG, so ES can be used to address the segment containing DATA_BYTE. But INC uses the DS register as default, so MASM automatically generates a segment override and in this case assembles INC DATA_BYTE as INC ES:DATA_BYTE.

Pseudo-ops ORG, EVEN and INCLUDE

Table 9.5 contains a summary of all the pseudo-ops common to MASM and ASM, excluding those for controlling assembler printouts, which are dealt with in the next section. It contains two other entries for memory-related pseudo-ops (ORG and EVEN) and the five program linkage pseudo-ops (NAME, END, PUBLIC, EXTRN and INCLUDE) of which only INCLUDE has not been encountered before.

ORG allows the assembly language programmer access to the assembler's internal **location counter** which keeps a record of the next free address where an instruction or data item may be stored. Thus, as we saw in Chapter 3,

```
ORG 200H
```

sets the location counter to 200H relative to the start of the segment containing it.

MASM and ASM allow the programmer to refer to the current value of the location counter by using the dollar sign ($). Thus expressions such as

```
ORG $+2
```

are allowed and, in the program fragment below, PROC_LENGTH will be set to the number of bytes occupied by CSEG.

```
CSEG SEGMENT
START_COUNTER = $
      MOV AX,DS
       :
       :
       :
PROC_LENGTH = $-START_COUNTER+1
CSEG ENDS
```

EVEN causes the location counter to go to an even-numbered address. This is especially useful with an 8086 processor, where all memory access begins with an even-numbered address. INCLUDE is designed to eliminate the need to repeat a sequence of statements that are common to several source files – perhaps a set of research data expressed as a data segment. If these statements were in a file called STMENTS.ABC then

```
INCLUDE STMENTS.ABC
```

Table 9.5 Summary of pseudo-ops common to MASM and ASM (see Section 9.4 for pseudo-ops to control assembler printout).

Pseudo-op	Purpose
Data definition	
name LABEL type	Defines a name.
DB, DW, DD, DQ, DT	Reserves and initializes variables.
name EQU expression	Defines a symbolic constant.
name = expression	Defines a name which can be redefined.
Memory	
name PROC NEAR. . .name ENDP	Procedure definition.
name PROC FAR. . .name ENDP	Procedure definition.
name SEGMENT align-type combine-type class-name	Segment definition.
$\vdots$	
name ENDS	
name GROUP segname1, segname2, . . . , segnamet	Collects the named segments under the given group name.
ASSUME segment-register:name, segment-register:name, etc. ASSUME segment-register:NOTHING	Tells the assembler which segment register is to be used for accessing the given segments.
ORG expression	Defines location counter value.
EVEN	Sets location counter to next even address.
Program linkage	
NAME module-name	Defines a module name.
END expression	Specifies the end of the source code. The optional expression specifies the start of the source program.
PUBLIC symbol1, symbol2, . . , symbolt	Defines global names.
EXTRN name1:type1, name2:type2, etc.	Allows you to reference global names defined in another module.
INCLUDE filename	Inserts the contents of filename into the current program.

would cause the assembler to copy them into the assembly language program at the point where the INCLUDE directive appears.

EXERCISES 9.3

1. Using INCLUDE and the $ option of the ORG pseudo-op, write and test an 8088 assembly language program which, given a set of 8088 instructions in the file INSTRUCT.SET, will print out in decimal the number of locations occupied by those instructions. Assume that the only explicit references to memory data locations concern the word variables MY_WORD_1, MY_WORD_2 and MY_WORD_3 and declare these in the data segment of your own program.

2. Rewrite the following program by adding ASSUME statements and removing segment overrides only, so that no explicit segment overrides are required in the program.

```
SEG1 SEGMENT
DATA1 DW ?
TIME1 DW ?
SEG1 ENDS

SEG2 SEGMENT
DATA2 DW ?
TIME2 DW ?
SEG2 ENDS

SEG3 SEGMENT
DATA3 DW ?
TIME3 DW ?
SEG3 ENDS

SSEG SEGMENT STACK
          DB 100H DUP(?)
SSEG ENDS

CSEG SEGMENT
                ASSUME CS:CSEG,DS:SEG1,ES:SEG2,SS:SSEG
                MOV AX,ES:DATA3
                MOV DATA1,AX
                MOV AX,DATA2
                MOV ES:DATA3,AX

                ADD AX,ES:TIME3
                MOV SEG2:TIME3,AX
                MOV AX,DS
                MOV ES,AX
                MOV DS,BX
                MOV AX,ES:DATA2
```

```
                            MOV DS:TIME1,AX
            CSEG ENDS
            END
```

9.4   CONTROLLING ASSEMBLER PRINTOUT

MASM and ASM supply a range of facilities to assist the programmer in producing well laid out and fully titled printouts of programs. PAGE is used to set the length and width of the page, since the former will depend upon the paper being used and the latter on the make and type of printer being used, as well as its current settings (many printers allow a choice of page width). PAGE takes two operands separated by a comma. The first operand controls the page length and can be a number in the range 10 to 255. If a page length is not explicitly stated, the default is 66 lines per page. Each page of the printout produced by the assembler contains a chapter number and a page number (e.g. 3-2 is Chapter 3, page 2). The page number is incremented when a page is full or when PAGE is used with no operands (which also causes the printer to go to the top of a new page). To increment the chapter number, the PAGE+ version of the pseudo-op is used, indicating also that the page number is to be reset to 1. Operand two of PAGE specifies the page width, the default setting of which is 80 characters. It may be any number in the range 60 to 132.

TITLE allows the programmer to specify a program title which will be reproduced on the first line of each page of the program printout. SUBTTL similarly allows a subtitle to be printed on the line after the title in each page heading. In both cases the text displayed is limited to 60 characters, for example:

```
    TITLE PASCAL COMPILER VERSION 1.1
    SUBTTL SYNTAX ANALYSIS ROUTINES
```

If no NAME pseudo-op is used and the first six characters of the program title form a valid name, then those six characters are taken as the module name. Subtitling is turned off by the use of the SUBTTL pseudo-op without a text string. A subsequent SUBTTL with a different text string could be used to give another subtitle, more relevant to the particular part of the assembly language program in which the pseudo-op occurs.

Output from the assembler to the file containing the printout can be controlled by the .LIST and .XLIST pseudo-ops. The default is .LIST. When a .XLIST is encountered, the formation of a printout by the assembler is stopped until a .LIST pseudo-op is encountered. When working on a large program this is a useful facility, for .LST files are large, as you will no doubt have discovered.

The %OUT pseudo-op allows messages to be displayed on the screen at programmer selected points during a long assembly whenever a %OUT is encountered. Thus, when the assembler reaches the pseudo-op

```
%OUT ABOUT TO ASSEMBLE CALC PROCEDURE
```

the message ABOUT TO ASSEMBLE CALC PROCEDURE will be
displayed on the PC screen.

EXERCISE 9.4

Type in the following program, assemble it observing the display
screen during assembly and inspect the .LST file produced by the
assembler.

```
PAGE    10,60
TITLE   PRINTOUT CONTROL ILLUSTRATION PROGRAM
SUBTTL DATA SEGMENT
%OUT    STARTING DSEG ASSEMBLY
DSEG SEGMENT
        FIRST_QUANTITY DB ?
        SECOND_QUANTITY   DB ?
DSEG ENDS
PAGE
SUBTTL STACK SEGMENT
SSEG SEGMENT STACK
        DB 100H DUP(?)
SSEG ENDS
%OUT FINISHED SSEG ASSEMBLY
PAGE+
SUBTTL MAIN PROGRAM
CSEG SEGMENT
        ASSUME CS:CSEG,DS:DSEG,SS:SSEG
        .XLIST
                MOV AL,FIRST_QUANTITY
                ADD AL,SECOND_QUANTITY
        %OUT IN MIDDLE OF CSEG NOW
                MOV FIRST_QUANTITY,AL
CSEG ENDS
END
```

9.5 ASSEMBLER PASSES, RELOCATABLE CODE AND THE LINKER

The diligent reader who has completed Exercise 9.4 will have noticed that
the three %OUT messages are in fact displayed twice:

```
STARTING DSEG ASSEMBLY
FINISHED SSEG ASSEMBLY
IN MIDDLE OF CSEG NOW
STARTING DSEG ASSEMBLY
```

```
FINISHED SSEG ASSEMBLY
IN MIDDLE OF CSEG NOW
```

This is because the assembler actually makes two passes through any assembly language program during conversion to machine code. On pass one, the value of each name, variable or label used in the source program is calculated and kept in a symbol table, so that the relative offset of each source instruction is known ready for pass two. In pass two, the assembler uses these offsets to generate the output. For example, on pass one when assembling

```
        CR EQU ODH
           :
           :
        CSEG SEGMENT
            ASSUME CS:CSEG
            MOV AH,1
            INT 21H
            CMP AL,40H
            JA   DONT_PRINT
            MOV DL,CR
            CMP AL,DL
            JNE DONT_PRINT
            MOV AH,2
            INT 21H
    DONT_PRINT:
               :
               :
```

the assembler forms a table associating the symbol CR with the value 0DH and the symbol DONT_PRINT with the value 0012 determined by the location counter, since each of the instructions before DONT_PRINT has a 2-byte representation. On pass two it generates the equivalent sequence of machine code:

```
B4 01
CD 21
3C 40
77 0A
B2 0D
3A C2
75 04
B4 02
CD 21
```

This entire section of code is **relocatable** i.e. is not dependent on being in certain absolute memory locations. Comparatively few programs do depend on being in a precise place in memory (we shall see some in

Chapter 12), it being the *relative* positions of data and instructions within a segment which is important. Thus, given

```
DSEG SEGMENT
        DATE DW ?
        TIME DB ?
           :
           :
DSEG ENDS
CSEG SEGMENT
        ASSUME CS:CSEG,DS:DSEG
        MOV   AL,TIME
        MOV   BL,5
        IMUL BL
        MOV   DATE,AX
           :
           :
```

a printout of the assembled equivalent shows that MOV AL,TIME is assembled as A0 0002R and MOV DATE,AX as A3 0000R, so that DATE corresponds to 0000R, the R indicating a relocatable address at offset 0000 from the start of the DSEG segment, and TIME corresponds to a relocatable location at offset 0002 from the start of DSEG. The linker finally decides which absolute addresses are used, having made appropriate reference to any memory and program linkage pseudo-ops in the source program. It is for this reason that even a program consisting of just a single module must be submitted to the linker.

Because pass one must keep track of these relative offsets as it examines each source instruction, certain references must be known on pass one. The MASM and ASM manuals give full details of these but they include expressions appearing in the following pseudo-ops:

ORG expression
.RADIX expression
expression DUP (. . .)

Hence ORG OFFSET LATER+15 in

```
ORG  OFFSET LATER+15
        MOV AL,5
           :
           :
LATER:MOV AX,DX
           :
```

would generate the assembler error message

```
MUST BE DECLARED IN PASS 1
```

since the OFFSET of LATER cannot be known until it has been calculated after pass one has moved on from the ORG pseudo-op. However,

```
MOV AL,5
    :
    :
LATER:MOV AX,DX
ORG OFFSET LATER+15
    :
```

is perfectly correct, since this time pass one will know the value of OFFSET LATER when it comes to the ORG pseudo-op.

9.6   THE RECORD PSEUDO-OP

MASM (but *not* ASM) provides the RECORD pseudo-op which, among other things, is extremely useful when implementing sets within a Pascal compiler. Given, for example, the declarations

> **type** *colours* = (*brown, yellow, green, red, orange*);
> *palette* = *set of colours*;
> **var**   *davinci, rubens, renoir:palette*;

then possible values of davinci are [red, green], [orange], [brown, yellow, red] and [brown . . red]. Since the base type has five values, the number of possible values of a variable of type palette is $2^5 = 32$. Indeed, if the base type has n possible values, the number of possible values for a set of that type is 2^n. If n is just 64 then this number is an unbelievable

$$2^{64} = 18,446,744,073,709,551,616$$

This accounts for the tight limits on the maximum number of elements in a set in microcomputer implementations of Pascal (in OMSI Pascal it's 64, in UCSD Pascal 4080 – just 512 in the Apple version – and in Pascal/Z 256). It also accounts for the choice of a single bit to represent the presence (bit set to 1) or absence (bit set to 0) of each possible element of a set.

Thus, in the example above, five bits – one for each colour – are adequate to represent a variable of type palette:

Set	Representation
[red, green]	00110
[orange]	00001
[brown, yellow, red]	11010
[brown. .red]	11110

The RECORD pseudo-op can take the following general form:

> rec-name   RECORD   field1:width1, field2:width2, . . . , etc.

where rec-name gives a name to RECORDs of this type; field1, field2 etc. give the names of the fields; and width1, width2 etc. specify the number of bits in the field (allowed range − 1 to 16D inclusive). Thus:

```
PALETTE RECORD BROWN:1, YELLOW:1, GREEN:1, RED:1, ORANGE:1
```

implements the Pascal type palette.

In a RECORD the first field declared goes into the most significant bits, and successively declared fields are placed in the succeeding bits to the right. If the total number of bits is less than 8 (byte) or 16 (word), the fields are right-justified into the least significant bit positions of the byte or word. Thus, in the above example, a byte is used by the assembler for each palette RECORD and the least significant five bits of this byte contain the data of interest.

To assign values to a RECORD the same method as for DB, DD etc. is used. Thus:

```
DAVINCI PALETTE <1,1,0,1,0>
```

associates the MASM name DAVINCI with a byte of storage associated with a PALETTE RECORD and initialized to ???11010. Given also

```
RUBENS PALETTE <0,1,0,1,1>
RENOIR PALETTE <1,1,0,0,1>
```

then the Pascal

rubens := davinci

is implemented by the 8088 instructions

```
MOV AL,DAVINCI
MOV RUBENS,AL
```

To isolate the individual fields of a RECORD, there are three operators: shift count, WIDTH and MASK. The shift count operation is brought into effect by using the field-name. Thus

```
MOV CL,GREEN
```

would be assembled by MASM into an instruction equivalent to

```
MOV CL,2
```

since the GREEN field (sorry!) must be right-shifted two bits to be right-justified. The WIDTH operator brings the width operation into effect and returns the width of a field in a record. Thus

```
MOV CL,WIDTH ORANGE
```

assembles into an instruction equivalent to

```
MOV CL,1
```

Finally, MASK returns a bit-mask for the bit positions occupied by a field. For example

```
MOV CL,MASK YELLOW
```

assembles as

```
MOV CL,00001000B
```

An 8088 implementation of the Pascal

davinci := [*yellow*, *red*]

is easy using the RECORD operations:

```
MOV AL,1
MOV CL,YELLOW
SHL AL,CL
MOV DAVINCI,AL
MOV AL,1
MOV CL,RED
SHL AL,CL
OR  AL,DAVINCI
MOV DAVINCI,AL
```

(There are many other approaches. As ever, ours is but one possible solution.)

EXERCISE 9.5

Given

```
DATE RECORD MONTH:4, DAY:5, YEAR:7
BIRTHDAY DATE <1,27,76>
```

what will be in registers AX, BX, CX, DX and in the locations labelled BIRTHDAY after running the following program extract:

```
MOV AX,BIRTHDAY
MOV BX,0
MOV CL,DAY
MOV DL,YEAR
ADD DL,WIDTH MONTH
SHR AX,CL
AND AX,0FFFEH
SHL AX,CL
MOV BIRTHDAY,AX
MOV BX,NOT MASK MONTH
```

Check your answer using a computer.

Set operations

In Pascal these include the relational operators:

    =   set equality
    <>   set inequality
    <=   is contained in
    >=   contains

and the set operations:

    +   set union
    *   set intersection
    −   set difference
    in   set membership

Let us give examples of the implementation of some of these in our present context. The remainder will appear in the exercises!

Set union e.g. *renoir := davinci + rubens*

```
MOV AL,DAVINCI
OR  AL,RUBENS
MOV RENOIR,AL
```

Set intersection e.g. *renoir := davinci * rubens*

```
MOV AL,DAVINCI
AND AL,RUBENS
MOV RENOIR,AL
```

Set inclusion e.g. *davinci <= rubens*

Here we observe that, given sets a and b, a $<=$ b if and only if a $*$ b = a. Hence

```
MOV AL,DAVINCI
AND AL,RUBENS
XOR AL,DAVINCI
```

leaves AL set to zero if davinci $<=$ rubens and set to non-zero otherwise.

EXERCISES 9.6

1. Complete implementations of all the remaining Pascal set operations similar to those given above.

2. Using records with record-name DATE where DATE is defined by:

    ```
    DATE RECORD MONTH:4,DAY:5,YEAR:7
    ```

    write a program which asks its user for his or her date of birth in an appropriate form and compares it with your own birthday. If the program user's birthday has the day, month or year in common with your own, print messages such as 'CONGRATULATIONS. YOU WIN A PRIZE BECAUSE YOUR BIRTHDAY IS ON THE SAME DAY AS THE PROGRAMMER'S'.

9.7 THE STRUC PSEUDO-OP

In Section 7.5 we saw how based addressing facilitates the implementation of Pascal records in 8088 assembly language. Pascal offers the convenience of records to programmers because these aid efficient program development. Now 8088 assembly language is also a programming language of sorts, so its designers decided to include a means of structuring data equivalent to Pascal's records so that similar efficiency gains could be made. Thus, MASM (but not ASM) provides the STRUC pseudo-op. It takes the general form

```
structure-name STRUC
              :
              :
              :
structure-name ENDS
```

The STRUC equivalent of field-names is assigned by using DB, DW etc. to set default values to the various fields. For example:

```
ADDRESS STRUC
NAME    DB 'THE OCCUPIER'
STREET  DB 'IF UNDELIVERED PLEASE RETURN'
CITY    DB 'TO SENDER'
CODE    DB 'AB12 3DE'
COUNTRY DB 'UK'
ADDRESS ENDS
```

so that STREET labels a field of the ADDRESS STRUC which is 28 bytes wide and has the default value IF UNDELIVERED PLEASE RETURN.

Having defined ADDRESS we can initialize variables of this type in the same way as with DB, DW etc. but using < and > to enclose initial values. Thus

```
HOME1 ADDRESS
<'MR J.B.BLOGGS','14 RAILWAY CUTTINGS','LONDON','NW10 2AG','GB'>
```

or, using the default values for the NAME and COUNTRY fields

```
HOME2 ADDRESS <,'27 BLACK STREET','BRIGHTON','BL5 3TW',>
```

Likewise, given

```
STUDENT  STRUC
NAME     DB 'ABCDEFGHIJ'
ADDRESS  DB 'ABCDEFGHIJKLMN'
AGE      DB 19
```

```
BIRTHDAY DW 1969
MARKS    DB 40 DUP(?)
STUDENT  ENDS
```

we could have

```
GOODPUPIL STUDENT <'JONES ', 'CARDIFF ', 1971,>
BADPUPIL  STUDENT <'BROWN ', 'CARDIFF ', 1970,>
```

In this case, there are no realistic settings of the 'default' values. Rather, these were used merely to specify the field sizes.

Fields within a STRUC are of two types – **overridable**, when an object of that type is defined, and **not overridable**. A field with only one entry is overridable (DUP expressions don't count as one entry) whereas a field with multiple entries is not overridable. Thus, in STUDENT, NAME, ADDRESS, AGE and BIRTHDAY are overridable whereas MARKS is not. If the field contains a string, it may be overridden with another string; however, if the overriding string is shorter than the initial string, the assembler will pad the space to the right with blanks.

Within a MASM program, access to the fields of a structure is gained via the *structure-name.field-name* convention similar to that used for records in Pascal. Thus we could have, for example:

```
MOV AL,GOODPUPIL.AGE
```

or

```
MOV AL,[BX].AGE
```

if BX was pointing to the beginning of GOODPUPIL. As we shall see in the following example, some fields in a STRUC may not be named, in which case they are not accessible in this way.

An example program using STRUC

Given information about four students and their performance in maths, physics and chemistry exams our program will print out a summary of the grades obtained by all students and, for each subject, calculate the average grade for that subject on the basis that grade A counts 1, grade B counts 2 etc. We shall use

```
GRADE_CARD   STRUC
      NUMBER DB '1234'
             DB '$'
        NAME DB '123456789ABCDEF'
             DB '$'
       MATHS DB 0
     PHYSICS DB 0
   CHEMISTRY DB 0
GRADE_CARD   ENDS
```

wherein the field NUMBER will be used to store a 4-digit student number, the NAME field will contain the student's name (up to 15 characters), and the MATHS, PHYSICS and CHEMISTRY fields will contain the ASCII code for the grade the student obtained in that subject (one of A, B, C, D, E or F). The two fields without names are there to make programming easier. By defining them to have '$' values as default, the values of the NUMBER and NAME fields can be printed out using the PRINTSTRING subroutine (function 9 of INT 21H).

The data for the program is supplied as GRADE_CARD definitions in the data segment:

```
STUDENT   GRADE_CARD  <'1237',,'WILSON A.J.     ',,'A','E','D'>
          GRADE_CARD  <'2107',,'SMITH-JONES R. ',,'B','D','D'>
          GRADE_CARD  <'8095',,'CUNNINGHAM M.R.',,'C','C','C'>
          GRADE_CARD  <'5184', 'FEATHERSTONE B.',,'A','F','C'>
AVERAGES  GRADE_CARD  <'     ',' ','AVERAGE GRADES',,,,>
```

Here, the AVERAGES structure is another programming device and saves us trouble organizing layout.

An outline of the program (see Fig. 9.5) is now easy to write. We build up totals of the numerical equivalents of the grades for each subject in the array SUM which is initialized to zero in the data segment.

(In the outline, **spaces** is a procedure which takes a single argument – a non-negative whole number n – and prints n spaces on the screen.)

Implementing this outline in 8088 assembly language is fairly straight-forward. We have divided it up into two modules. The first (in a file called GRADE.ASM) contains the main program. The second (in a file called PRINTRTS.ASM) contains subroutines PRINTCHAR, PRINTSTRING, PRINT_NEWLINE and SPACES, most of which we have met before and which can now be tucked away in the PRINTRTS module for use when needed. These two modules are given in Figs 9.6 and 9.7.

There is just one minor (and easily solved) problem, however. PRINTSTRING requires the address of the string to be printed to be in register DX. We want to use it to print the NAME fields of the GRADE_CARDs for each student. Now if BX is set to point to STUDENT (the starting address of the first of the four GRADE_CARDs) as can easily be done via

```
MOV BX,OFFSET STUDENT
```

then the NAME component of the first GRADE_CARD is specified by [BX].NAME and so we want an instruction which is equivalent to the ILLEGAL:

```
MOV DX,OFFSET [BX].NAME ;illegal instruction
```

A solution is provided by the 8088 instruction **LEA** (Load Effective Address):

set up for return to the operating system;
establish data segment addressability;
print headings;
for *i := 1* **to** *4* **do**
    begin
    write(grade_card of student[i]);
    spaces(3);
    write(student[i].maths);
    sum[0] := sum [0] + student[i].maths;
    spaces(6);
    write(student[i].physics);
    sum[1] := sum[1] + student[i].physics;
    spaces(9);
    writeln(student[i].chemistry);
    sum[2] := sum[2] + student[i].chemistry
    end;
write(averages heading);
for *i := 0* **to** *2* **do** *sum [i] := round(sum[i]/3);*
spaces(3);
print the maths average;
spaces(6);
print the physics average;
spaces(9);
print the chemistry average;
print a new line;
return to the operating system

Fig. 9.5   Pseudo-Pascal outline of student marks program.

```
LEA DX,[BX].NAME
```

LEA is more powerful than using OFFSET in an instruction such as

```
MOV reg,OFFSET name
```

because an index or base register can be used to form the effective address.
Thus

```
MOV AX,OFFSET MY_VARIABLE
```

and

```
LEA AX,MY_VARIABLE
```

are exactly equivalent whereas

```
MOV AX,OFFSET SUM[SI] ;is illegal
LEA AX,SUM[SI]        ;is legal
```

```
        EXTRN PRINTSTRING:FAR
        EXTRN PRINTCHAR:FAR
        EXTRN PRINT_NEWLINE:FAR
        EXTRN SPACES:FAR
        GRADE_CARD STRUC
                NUMBER    DB '1234'
                          DB '$'
                NAME      DB '123456789ABCDEF'
                          DB '$'
                MATHS     DB 0
                PHYSICS   DB 0
                CHEMISTRY DB 0
        GRADE_CARD ENDS
        DSEG SEGMENT
        STUDENT  GRADE_CARD <'1237',,'WILSON A.J.     ',,'A','E','D'>
                 GRADE_CARD <'2107',,'SMITH-JONES R. ',,'B','D','D'>
                 GRADE_CARD <'8095',,'CUNNINGHAM M.R.',,'C','C','C'>
                 GRADE_CARD <'5184',,'FEATHERSTONE B.',,'A','F','C'>
        AVERAGES GRADE_CARD <'    ',' ','AVERAGE GRADES',,,,>
        HEADING DB '        STUDENT NAME    MATHS PHYSICS CHEMISTRY','$'
        SUM DB 3 DUP(0)
        DSEG ENDS
        SSEG SEGMENT STACK
                DB 100H DUP(?)
        SSEG ENDS
        CSEG SEGMENT
                ASSUME CS:CSEG,DS:DSEG,SS:SSEG
        START PROC FAR
        ;set up for return to operating system
                PUSH DS
                MOV  AX,0
                PUSH AX
        ;establish data segment addressability
                MOV  AX,DSEG
                MOV  DS,AX
        ;print heading
                MOV  DX,OFFSET HEADING
                CALL PRINTSTRING
                CALL PRINT_NEWLINE
        ;for i := 1 to 4 do
                MOV  CX,4
                MOV  BX,OFFSET STUDENT
            ;begin
            ;write(grade_card of student[i])
        NEXT_STUDENT: LEA  DX,[BX].NUMBER
                      CALL PRINTSTRING
```

Fig. 9.6 Contents of the file GRADE.ASM.

```
                MOV   AL,1
                CALL  SPACES
                LEA   DX,[BX].NAME
                CALL  PRINTSTRING
        ;spaces(3)
                MOV   AL,3
                CALL  SPACES
        ;write(student[i].maths)
                MOV   DL,[BX].MATHS
                CALL  PRINTCHAR
        ;sum[0] := sum[0] + student[i].maths
                SUB   DL,40H
                ADD   SUM[0],DL
        ;spaces(6)
        ;write(student[i].physics)
                MOV   AL,6
                CALL  SPACES
                MOV   DL,[BX].PHYSICS
                CALL  PRINTCHAR
        ;sum[1] := sum[1] + student[i].physics
                SUB   DL,40H
                ADD   SUM[1],DL
        ;spaces(9)
                MOV   AL,9
                CALL  SPACES
        ;writeln(student[i].chemistry)
                MOV   DL,[BX].CHEMISTRY
                CALL  PRINTCHAR
                CALL  PRINT_NEWLINE
        ;sum[2] := sum[2] + student[i].chemistry
                SUB   DL,40H
                ADD   SUM[2],DL
        ;end
                ADD   BX,SIZE STUDENT
                LOOP  NEXT_STUDENT
;write(averages)
        MOV   DX,OFFSET AVERAGES
        CALL  PRINTSTRING
    ;for i := 0 to 2 do sum[i] := round(sum[i]/4)
                MOV   CX,3
                MOV   SI,0
NEXT_AVERAGE: MOV   AL,SUM[SI]
                CBW
                MOV   BL,4
                DIV   BL
                CMP   AH,2
                JNE   DONT_ROUND
                INC   AL
   DONT_ROUND: MOV   SUM[SI],AL
                INC   SI
```

Fig. 9.6   (*continued*)

```
                        LOOP NEXT_AVERAGE
;spaces(3)
            MOV   AL,3D
            CALL  SPACES
;print(maths average);
            MOV   DL,SUM[0]
            ADD   DL,40H
            CALL  PRINTCHAR
;spaces(6)
            MOV   AL,6
            CALL  SPACES
;print(physics average)
            MOV   DL,SUM[1]
            ADD   DL,40H
            CALL  PRINTCHAR
;spaces(9)
            MOV   AL,9
            CALL  SPACES
;print(chemistry average)
            MOV   DL,SUM[2]
            ADD   DL,40H
            CALL  PRINTCHAR
            CALL  PRINT_NEWLINE
            RET
START ENDP

CSEG ENDS
END START
```

Fig. 9.6   (*continued*)

```
CR EQU 0DH
LF EQU 0AH
SPACE EQU 20H

CSEG SEGMENT
ASSUME CS:CSEG
PUBLIC PRINTSTRING,PRINTCHAR,PRINT_NEWLINE,SPACES

PRINTSTRING PROC FAR
MOV AH,9
INT 21H
RET
PRINTSTRING ENDP

PRINTCHAR PROC FAR
MOV AH,2
INT 21H
RET
PRINTCHAR ENDP
```

Fig. 9.7   Contents of the file PRINTRTS.ASM.

```
PRINT_NEWLINE PROC FAR
PUSH DX
MOV   DL,CR
CALL PRINTCHAR
MOV   DL,LF
CALL PRINTCHAR
POP   DX
RET
PRINT_NEWLINE ENDP

SPACES PROC FAR
        PUSH CX
        MOV   CH,0
        MOV   CL,AL
NEXT_SPACE:MOV   DL,SPACE
        CALL PRINTCHAR
        LOOP NEXT_SPACE
        POP   CX
        RET
SPACES ENDP

CSEG ENDS
END
```

Fig. 9.7 (*continued*)

EXERCISES 9.7

1. Modify the example program so that: i) it will accept the grades of
ten students not just four; ii) it will also accept grades for biology
and calculate the average biology grade for all students. Test your
answers on a computer.

2. Wongway Flights Inc. is a small airline operating four flights a day:

        09.50   LONDON $\to$ NEW YORK   11.50
        13.00   LONDON $\to$ MARSEILLES 17.00
        15.50   LONDON $\to$ ZAGREB   22.50
        18.00   LONDON $\to$ NEW YORK   20.00

Write and test a program which, given a required flight time and
destination, will print out complete details of the nearest available
flight to the specified time. Use MASM STRUC pseudo-ops to
represent the flight timetable.

3. Using a modified version of the pseudo-random number generator
of Section 7.9 (or otherwise), write a program to simulate the game
of SNAP with an ordinary pack of playing cards. (If you and I play
snap, we each have one half of the pack. I turn over my top card,
you turn over yours. If the turned-over cards belong to the same

suit the first person to say SNAP wins. If they belong to different suits the two cards are added to a pile on the table which is also collected by the next person who first says SNAP when the suits of the turned-over cards agree. The first person to run out of cards is the loser.) Represent each card as a STRUC of the form:

```
CARD STRUC
     NUMBER DB 0
     SUIT   DB 0
CARD ENDS
```

10 Macros and Conditional Assembly

AIMS

This chapter concerns two important MASM features not available in ASM which aid programmer productivity. The MASM **macro** facility allows the programmer to name a group of statements and have them placed in the assembly language program automatically whenever that name is invoked, so that they are assembled in place. Thus, if a program frequently requires a range check on an input character the programmer has a choice either of implementing a subroutine (and the attendant parameter passing) to carry out this check and then CALLing the subroutine each time the check is needed or of forming the instructions for this into a macro and invoking the macro to perform each check.

Conditional assembly allows groups of assembly language statements in a program to be included or excluded from the assembly process, depending on the values of certain parameters. In effect, a conditional assembly statement allows the programmer to say things such as: IF the value of MEMORY_EXTENSION_PRESENT is TRUE then assemble the following group of statements . . . . . . ELSE assemble the following statements. . . . . . One assembly language program could therefore contain all the code for two versions: one for an IBM PC with extended memory, and one for the basic (64K memory) machine. All the programmer has to do is change the setting of MEMORY_EXTENSION_PRESENT and the assembler arranges that only the appropriate instructions are assembled. This is more convenient than having two distinct versions of the same program, and generally produces a smaller object program than if the production version contained code for both possibilities.

10.1 MACROS

Let us consider the construction of an example macro which is a sequence of 8088 instructions to check that, given two locations, the unsigned contents of

```
        MOV  AL,FIRST_LOCATION
        CMP  AL,SECOND_LOCATION
        JNB  IN_ORDER
        XCHG AL,SECOND_LOCATION
        MOV  FIRST_LOCATION,AL
IN_ORDER:
```

Fig. 10.1 Program fragment to check location contents are in order.

the first location are larger than or equal to the contents of the second location and, if not, swaps these so that this is true. The program fragment in Fig. 10.1 does this for FIRST_LOCATION and SECOND_LOCATION.

Making this program fragment into a macro is easy. The general form of a macro definition is

name MACRO dummylist
:
:
:
ENDM

where **dummylist** is a list of names for the macro's parameters – rather like **myvar** and **total** are dummy parameters in the Pascal procedure declaration which begins

```
PROC PAYCALCS(VAR MYVAR:INT;TOTAL:REAL);
```

Figure 10.2 shows the macro SWAP_IF_NEEDED with dummy parameters FIRST_LOCATION and SECOND_LOCATION.

The complete program in Fig. 10.3 uses this macro definition. Three characters are read from the keyboard, their ASCII codes are put into TOTAL, SUM and MILES and the contents of these locations are rearranged into non-ascending order.

```
SWAP_IF_NEEDED MACRO FIRST_LOCATION,SECOND_LOCATION
               LOCAL IN_ORDER
               MOV   AL,FIRST_LOCATION
               CMP   AL,SECOND_LOCATION
               JNB   IN_ORDER
               XCHG  AL,SECOND_LOCATION
               MOV   FIRST_LOCATION,AL
       IN_ORDER:
               ENDM
```

Fig. 10.2 The SWAP_IF_NEEDED macro definition.

```
SWAP_IF_NEEDED MACRO FIRST_LOCATION,SECOND_LOCATION
               LOCAL IN_ORDER
               MOV   AL,FIRST_LOCATION
               CMP   AL,SECOND_LOCATION
               JNB   IN_ORDER
               XCHG  AL,SECOND_LOCATION
               MOV   FIRST_LOCATION,AL
        IN_ORDER:
               ENDM
DSEG SEGMENT
     TOTAL DB ?
     SUM   DB ?
     MILES DB ?
DSEG ENDS

SSEG SEGMENT STACK
     DB 100H DUP(?)
SSEG ENDS

CSEG SEGMENT
ASSUME CS:CSEG,DS:DSEG,SS:SSEG
        MOV    AX,DSEG
        MOV    DS,AX
        CALL   READCHAR
        MOV    TOTAL,AL
        CALL   READCHAR
        MOV    SUM,AL
        CALL   READCHAR
        MOV    MILES,AL
        SWAP_IF_NEEDED TOTAL,SUM
        SWAP_IF_NEEDED SUM,MILES
        SWAP_IF_NEEDED TOTAL,SUM
        HLT
READCHAR: MOV    AH,1
          INT    21H
          RET

CSEG ENDS
END
```

Fig. 10.3 A complete example program using a macro.

When assembled, this program will produce the sequence of instructions shown in the extract from an assembler listing in Fig. 10.4. Assembly language statements which are the result of expanding a macro are denoted on the listing by a + sign. From the listing, three things should be noted in particular: the difference between a subroutine CALL and use of a MACRO; the replacement of the macro's LOCAL label IN_ORDER by a unique label in each of its three expansions (??0000,??0001, and ??0002

```
 1              SWAP_IF_NEEDED MACRO FIRST_LOCATION,SECOND_LOCATION
 2                             LOCAL IN_ORDER
 3                             MOV   AL,FIRST_LOCATION
 4                             CMP   AL,SECOND_LOCATION
 5                             JNB   IN_ORDER
 6                             XCHG  AL,SECOND_LOCATION
 7                             MOV   FIRST_LOCATION,AL
 8                      IN_ORDER:
 9                             ENDM
10
11 0000                       DSEG SEGMENT
12 0000 ??                        TOTAL DB ?
13 0001 ??                        SUM   DB ?
14 0002 ??                        MILES DB ?
15 0003                       DSEG ENDS
16
17 0000                       SSEG SEGMENT STACK
18 0000 0100    [                  DB 100H DUP(?)
19                     ??
20                   ]
21
22 0100                       SSEG ENDS
23
24 0000                       CSEG SEGMENT
25                            ASSUME CS:CSEG,DS:DSEG,SS:SSEG
26 0000 B8    ----   R        MOV   AX,DSEG
27 0003 8E    D8              MOV   DS,AX
28
29 0005 E8    0048   R        CALL READCHAR
30 0008 A2    0000   R        MOV   TOTAL,AL
31 000B E8    0048   R        CALL READCHAR
32 000E A2    0001   R        MOV   SUM,AL
33 0011 E8    0048   R        CALL READCHAR
34 0014 A2    0002   R        MOV   MILES,AL
35                            SWAP_IF_NEEDED TOTAL,SUM
36 0017 A0    0000   R  +         MOV   AL,TOTAL
37 001A 3A    06    0001  R +     CMP   AL,SUM
38 001E 77    07          +       JNB   ??0000
39 0020 86    06    0001  R +     XCHG  AL,SUM
40 0024 A2    0000   R    +       MOV   TOTAL,AL
41 0027                   +       ??0000:
42                            SWAP_IF_NEEDED SUM,MILES
43 0027 A0    0001   R    +       MOV   AL,SUM
44 002A 3A    06    0002  R +     CMP   AL,MILES
45 002E 77    07          +       JNB   ??0001
46 0030 86    06    0002  R +     XCHG  AL,MILES
47 0034 A2    0001   R    +       MOV   SUM,AL
48 0037                   +       ??0001:
49                            SWAP_IF_NEEDED TOTAL,SUM
```

Fig. 10.4 An extract from the assembler printout after assembly
of the program in Fig. 10.3.

```
50 0037 A0   0000  R      +         MOV   AL,TOTAL
51 003A 3A   06   0001  R +         CMP   AL,SUM
52 003E 77   07           +         JNB   ??0002
53 0040 86   06   0001  R +         XCHG  AL,SUM
54 0044 A2   0000  R      +         MOV   TOTAL,AL
55 0047                   +         ??0002:
56 0047 F4                      HLT
57
58 0048 B4   01                 READCHAR: MOV   AH,1
59 004A CD   21                           INT   21H
60 004C C3                                RET
61
62 004D                         CSEG ENDS
63                              END
```

Fig. 10.4   (*continued*)

respectively); and the replacement of the dummy parameters FIRST_
LOCATION and SECOND_LOCATION by the corresponding actual
parameter pairs in each expansion (TOTAL,SUM; SUM,MILES; and
TOTAL,SUM respectively).

Macro parameters

Dummy parameters in macro definitions are not confined to variable names.
They may also be used to represent registers, instructions, 8088 op-codes,
strings or numerical values. The statements in the macro definition in
Fig. 10.5 have the same effect as the SWAP_IF_NEEDED macro, but in
this case the register to be used is supplied as a dummy parameter.
    The invocations of SWAP_IF_NEEDED in the program of Fig. 10.3
could thus be replaced by

```
NEW_SWAP_IF_NEEDED MACRO TEMP_REG,FIRST_LOCATION,SECOND_LOCATION
                   LOCAL IN_ORDER
                   MOV   TEMP_REG,FIRST_LOCATION
                   CMP   TEMP_REG,SECOND_LOCATION
                   JNB   IN_ORDER
                   XCHG  TEMP_REG,SECOND_LOCATION
                   MOV   FIRST_LOCATION,TEMP_REG
          IN_ORDER:
                   ENDM
```

Fig. 10.5   The macro NEW_SWAP_IF_NEEDED.

```
NEW_SWAP_IF_NEEDED AL,TOTAL,SUM
```

etc.

By way of illustration of the use of numbers as macro parameters, let us now write two macros – FORDO and ENDFOR – which, when used in conjunction, provide the Pascal programming structure:

for $i := lower$ **to** $upper$ **do begin**

$$\vdots$$
$$\vdots$$

end

FORDO will have five dummy parameters: *lower*, *upper*, two labels to control looping and the name of a register which is to be used for the loop counter i. ENDFOR has just two dummy parameters, both of them labels used to control looping. Thus, given

```
MY_ARRAY DB 100H DUP(41H)
```

the sequence

```
FORDO 1,100H,BEGINADD,ENDADD,SI
ADD MY_ARRAY[SI],5D
ENDFOR BEGINADD, ENDADD
```

would, when expanded, be a sequence of 8088 instructions to add 5D to each element of MY_ARRAY. Figure 10.6 gives the definitions of FORDO and ENDFOR, from which it can be seen that the expansion of these three MASM statements is

```
+              MOV SI,100H
+              SUB SI,1
+              JB  ENDADD
+              INC SI
+ BEGINADD: CMP SI,0
+              JE  ENDADD
+              DEC SI
               ADD MY_ARRAY[SI],5D
+              JMP BEGINADD
+    ENDADD:
```

Notice that, as in Pascal proper, a check is made that *lower* is not greater than *upper*.

The following program fragment illustrates the use of string parameters in a macro invocation and uses FORDO, ENDFOR and the PRINTCHAR subroutine of Chapter 5 to print Z, z, Y, y, . . . , A, a:

```
FORDO 'A','Z',BEGINPRINT,ENDPRINT,DL
;macro definition implies DL contains next letter
```

```
    FORDO    MACRO LOWER,UPPER,START_ADD,STOP_ADD,CALC_REG
             MOV CALC_REG,UPPER
             SUB CALC_REG,LOWER
             JB  STOP_ADD
             INC CALC_REG
START_ADD:   CMP CALC_REG,0
             JE  STOP_ADD
             DEC CALC_REG
             ENDM


    ENDFOR   MACRO START_ADD,STOP_ADD
             JMP START_ADD
STOP_ADD:
             ENDM
```

Fig. 10.6 Definitions of FORDO and ENDFOR.


```
CALL PRINTCHAR
ADD  DL,20H
CALL PRINTCHAR
SUB  DL,20H
ENDFOR BEGINPRINT,ENDPRINT
```

Dummy parameters in macro definitions may be instructions but cannot themselves be macros. However, macro definitions may be nested, as the following definition illustrates:

```
DOLOTS MACRO NUMBER,COUNTREG,INSTRUCTION,OPERAND
       FORDO 1,NUMBER,BEGINDOLOTS,ENDDOLOTS,COUNTREG
       INSTRUCTION OPERAND
       ENDFOR BEGINDOLOTS,ENDDOLOTS
       ENDM
```

The invocation

```
DOLOTS 27D,AH,INC,BX
```

would, on assembly, be expanded into 8088 instructions which will perform INC BX a total of 27D times.

Because macros are really a string replacement facility, the order of definition does not matter. Thus, MASM doesn't mind whether DOLOTS is defined before or after FORDO and ENDFOR in an assembly language program. However, as a programmer one's greatest concern is always to produce programs that someone else will find easy to follow, so this should not be taken as a licence for obscurity!

EXERCISES 10.1

1. Using the FORDO and ENDFOR macros, write and test assembly language programs to carry out the following tasks. In each program use at least one other macro.

   a) Calculate the sum of the squares of the first 30D whole numbers.

   b) Given the day of the week on which the first of the month falls and the number of days in the month, print out a calendar for the month in the form:

M	Tu	W	Th	F	Sa	Su
	1	2	3	4	5	6
7	8	9	10	11	12	13
14	15	16	17	18	19	20
21	22	23	24	25	26	27
28	29	30	31			

2. Write macro equivalents of the WHILE and REPEAT loop constructs of Pascal. Use them as appropriate in programs to carry out the following tasks:

   a) Input a sequence of brackets – (and) – and determine whether the sequence is well formed, i.e if there are equal numbers of (and), and the number of) read never exceeds the number of (read.

   b) Find all four-digit decimal whole numbers equal to the sum of the cubes of their digits.

   $$\text{e.g. } 153 = 1^3 + 5^3 + 3^3$$

10.2 USING MACROS TO DEFINE TABLES

In Chapter 5 (Section 5.6) we defined a table of powers of ten. Using a macro can save a lot of repetitive work in setting up tables of this sort. To illustrate, suppose we want a set of double words containing increasing powers of ten which can be individually addressed as TEN1 (containing 10D), TEN2 (containing 100D) and so on. We shall use the macro TEN_POWER defined as follows:

```
TEN_POWER MACRO LABEL_COUNT,VALUE
          TEN&LABEL_COUNT DD VALUE
          ENDM
```

The invocation TEN_POWER 1,10 would produce the assembly language statement

```
TEN1 DD 10
```

since the special macro symbol & in the definition of TEN_POWER indicates that the string TEN is to be concatenated with the actual parameter corresponding to the dummy parameter LABEL_COUNT.

It is also possible to use symbols defined in an EQU or = MASM pseudo-op as parameters in macro invocations. Thus, given:

```
THIS_POWER = 100
EXPONENT   =   2
```

the invocation TEN_POWER %EXPONENT %THIS_POWER would result in

```
TEN2 DD 100
```

because the macro % symbol indicates that EXPONENT and THIS_POWER are expressions which must be evaluated to a number before string substitution takes place.

To complete a table of powers of ten in a single macro we need to use one of three pseudo-ops MASM provides for repeating blocks of statements (which may or may not be macros). The simplest of these has the general form

REPT expression

    :

    : block of statements to be repeated

    :

ENDM

Thus, the first eight powers of ten could be defined via the macro TEN_POWERS_TABLE which has the following definition:

```
TEN_POWERS_TABLE MACRO
                 REPT   8
                 EXPONENT=EXPONENT+1
                 THIS_POWER=THIS_POWER*10
                 TEN_POWER %EXPONENT,%THIS_POWER
                 ENDM
                 ENDM
```

Here the REPT. .ENDM pseudo-op directs MASM to repeat the enclosed statements eight times so that the sequence

```
THIS_POWER = 1
EXPONENT   = 0
TEN_POWERS_TABLE
```

will be expanded to yield the set of statements

```
THIS POWER = 1
EXPONENT   = 0
TEN1 DD 10
TEN2 DD 100
```

```
TEN3 DD 1000
     :
     :
TEN8 DD 100000000
```

Often, tables do not contain a sequence of values so easily related by formulae. Consider, for example, the problem of setting up a table of the unsigned 8-bit equivalents of the first ten prime numbers by using a macro. In this case an easy solution is offered by the IRP pseudo-op, which has the general form

IRP dummy, <arg1,arg2, . . . , argN>
:
: block of statements to be repeated
:
ENDM

and which directs the assembler to repeat the statements within the IRP. . . ENDM block N times. Starting with arg1, on each repetition MASM replaces the dummy parameter with an actual parameter from the parameter list. Our FIRST_10_PRIMES macro can thus be defined:

```
FIRST_10_PRIMES MACRO
                IRP APRIME,<2,3,5,7,11,13,17,19,23,29>
                COUNT=COUNT+1
                PRIME&COUNT DB APRIME
                ENDM
                ENDM
```

so that the statements

```
COUNT=0
FIRST_10_PRIMES
```

would be expanded on assembly to

```
COUNT=0
PRIME1   DB   2
PRIME2   DB   3
PRIME3   DB   5
           :
           :
PRIME10 DB 29
```

Similarly

```
SAVE_REGS MACRO
          IRP REGISTER,<AX,BX,CX,DX,SI,DI,BP>
          PUSH REGISTER
          ENDM
          ENDM
```

would enable a copy of the registers AX, BX, CX, DX, SI, DI and BP to be saved on the stack via the single invocation

```
SAVE_REGS
```

since MASM actually views each argument as a character string.

The IRPC pseudo-op is a variation of IRP and takes the general form

```
IRPC dummy, string
:
: block of statements to be repeated
:
ENDM
```

In this case the statements within an IRPC. . .ENDM block are repeated once for each character in the string with the dummy parameter taking successive character values from the string, starting with the left-most character. Thus

```
IRPC CODE,CXPRLMNYZTUABVDIJKEFGHOQSW
DB '&CODE&'
ENDM
```

would be expanded into

```
DB 'C'
DB 'X'
 :
 :
DB 'W'
```

representing, perhaps, a secret code in which the letter A is coded as a letter C, a B as an X and so on. (Notice that use of REPT, IRP and IRPC is not confined to within the body of a macro. They are pseudo-ops in their own right and consequently our use of IRPC to define a table of codes would be perfectly acceptable as it stands in the data segment of a program.)

EXERCISES 10.2

1. Use REPT, IRP or IRPC as appropriate to initialize variables as follows:

   a) The squares of the first ten non-zero whole numbers in unsigned 8-bit form labelled SQUARE1, SQUARE2 etc.

   b) The number of days in each month labelled MONTH1, MONTH2 etc., starting with January and in unsigned 8-bit form.

   c) Twenty-six variables labelled A, B, C, . . . , Z and initialized to an indeterminate byte value.

   d) The first 30 powers of 2, labelled TWO1, TWO2 etc., in unsigned 64-bit form.

2. Write and test a macro SPACES which takes one parameter – a non-negative whole number – and produces instructions for printing that number of spaces.

3. Examine the FORDO macro of Section 10.1. Is it possible to rewrite the definition, omitting the parameters START_ADD and STOP_ADD? If not, explain why in detail. If so, verify your new definition on a computer.

10.3   MORE MACRO PSEUDO-OPS

Table 10.1 gives a summary of the MASM macro pseudo-ops. Of the special symbols only ! and ;; remain to be discussed. Most macro definitions will require comments (following our pseudo-Pascal convention, of course) but, more often than not in practice, one does not require these comments to be reproduced at every macro expansion in the main body of the program. Indeed, the whole purpose behind the use of a macro is often to free oneself from one level of complexity (for example, manipulating the statements to control a FOR loop as in FORDO). Those comments in a macro definition prefaced with ;; will therefore not be reproduced in each invocation expansion whereas those prefaced with a single ; *will* be reproduced. This is illustrated in Fig. 10.7.

The .LALL, .SALL and .XALL pseudo-ops control the levels of printout of macro expansions. Thus .LALL lists the complete macro text for all expansions – though comments prefaced by ;; still do not appear. .SALL suppresses listing of all text and object code produced by the macros and .XALL is the default condition – a source line is listed only if it generates object code (this will appear a more sensible choice of default after you have read Section 10.4).

As a special macro character, the ! character indicates that the character following it in a list of arguments is to be taken literally. Thus

```
IRP DUMMY, <!,,a,B>
    DB '&DUMMY&'
ENDM
```

produces

```
DB ','
DB 'a'
DB 'B'
```

because the ! symbol informs MASM that the following comma is not to be taken as a parameter separator in the normal way as with an IRP pseudo-op, but is to be taken literally.

Macros can be redefined in the course of an assembly language program, the most recently defined version being used for a given invocation. The PURGE pseudo-op, however, deletes a macro definition

Table 10.1 Macro pseudo-ops.

Pseudo-op	Purpose
name MACRO dummylist $\vdots$ $\vdots$ ENDM	Defines a macro.
REPT expression $\vdots$: block of statements to be repeated $\vdots$ ENDM	Statements are repeated the number of times determined by the expression.
IRP dummy,<arg1,arg2, . . . ,argN> $\vdots$: block of statements to be repeated $\vdots$ ENDM	Statements are repeated N times with dummy being substituted by arg1,arg2, . . . ,argN.
IRPC dummy,string $\vdots$: block of statements to be repeated $\vdots$ ENDM	Statements are repeated once for each character in the string, with each repetition substituting the next string character for dummy.
LOCAL dummy1,dummy2, . . . ,dummyN	The assembler creates a unique identifier for each of dummy1, . . . ,dummyN and substitutes this for each occurrence in the containing macro. If LOCAL statements are used, they must be the first statements in the macro body.
PURGE macro-name1, . . . ,macro-nameN	Removes the definition of the named macros from the assembler's list of macros.
EXITM	Used in conjunction with conditional pseudo-ops to terminate macro expansion (see Section 10.4).
Special symbols string1&string2	Concatenates two strings.
%expression	Causes the expression to be evaluated to a number.
!character	Indicates that the character is to be treated literally as an argument.
;;string	Comments following ;; are not reproduced on each macro invocation expansion.

```
QUIETMAC MACRO DUMMY
         ;;save working register
         PUSH AX
         ;;PC-DOS function
         MOV  AH,DUMMY
         INT  21H
         ;;restore working register
         POP  AX
         ENDM
LOUDMAC MACRO
         ;double AX
         ADD  AX,AX
         ;add BX
         ADD  AX,BX
         ENDM
           :
           :
         CSEG SEGMENT
           :
         QUIETMAC 2
+        PUSH AX
+        MOV  AH,2
+        INT  21H
+        POP  AX
           :
           :
         LOUDMAC
+        ;double AX
+        ADD  AX,AX
+        ;add BX
+        ADD  AX,BX
           :
           :
```

Fig. 10.7 Extract from an assembler listing showing use of the ;; special symbol.

entirely so that subsequent references to a PURGEd macro will cause an error. PURGE has the general format:

PURGE macro-name1,macro-name2, ...

Since the name of a macro can be the same as a pseudo-op (except for TITLE and COMMENT) or an 8088 instruction, it is possible to write your own version of assembler pseudo-ops with macros. If the name of an 8088 instruction is used, care is needed, because macro definitions may be recursive (see Section 10.5), but this can be a useful facility on occasion. By way of an example, the following macro redefines the 8088 ADD instruction:

```
ADD MACRO NUMBER
    ADC AX,NUMBER
ENDM
```

PURGE may subsequently be used to delete this new version, allowing the original meaning of ADD to become effective.

In the next section, we shall discuss conditional pseudo-ops which permit statements and macros to be included or excluded from the assembly process, depending on the settings of certain variables. It is therefore possible that a macro invocation must be terminated prior to reaching the ENDM pseudo-op. EXITM allows this premature termination and will be discussed more fully in the next section.

EXERCISES 10.3

1. Give two distinct reasons why COMMENT (see Section 4.4) cannot be redefined as a macro. (Try doing it and assemble your attempt if necessary.)

2. Examine the calculator simulator program in Appendix II and decide where -- if at all – macros could be used to advantage. Rewrite the program and assemble and test the new version.

3. Repeat Exercise 2 above for the text editor program of Appendix III.

10.4 CONDITIONAL ASSEMBLY

Conditional assembly allows the production of one large assembly language program covering various possibilities – for example, presence or absence of the 8087 Numeric Data Processor; available memory size; operating system being used (PC-DOS or CP/M86) – which at assembly time can be tailored to just one of these possibilities. In this way the actual machine code supplied to a given user of a PC with given facilities is not cluttered up with memory-consuming unnecessary alternatives, and the programmer does not have the bother of maintaining multiple versions of a piece of software. Suppose, for example, we want to cater for users who prefer CP/M86 to PC-DOS when writing our character input and output routines. CP/M86 uses function calls for this in a very similar way to PC-DOS, except that the function number must be in register CL and the INTerrupt number is 224D for CP/M86. By incorporating both possibilities in a macro, the greater part of the program can be written without reference to either operating system:

```
READ_CHARACTER MACRO
    IF CPM86
        MOV CL,1
        INT 224D
```

```
          ELSE
             MOV AH,1
             INT 21H
          ENDIF
          ENDM
```

To include the relevant section the value of CPM86 is set to 1 (denotes TRUE) or 0 (denotes FALSE) as appropriate. The IF statement checks the value of CPM86 and, if it is 1, includes the statements

```
   MOV CL,1
   INT 224D
```

in assembly, and otherwise includes the statements

```
   MOV AH,1
   INT 21H
```

Figure 10.8 shows an extract from an assembly listing in which the macro READ_CHARACTER is used.

Another difference between CP/M86 and PC-DOS is that CP/M86 functions preserve SS and SP but do not automatically preserve registers not directly involved: the programmer must arrange this. Hence, two macros are

```
   CPM86=1
   READ_CHARACTER MACRO
                  IF    CPM86
                        MOV CL,1
                        INT 224D
                  ELSE
                        MOV AH,1
                        INT 21H
                  ENDIF
                  ENDM
       :
       :
   CSEG SEGMENT
       :
       :
   READ_CHARACTER
 + MOV   CL,1
 + INT   224D
   SUB   AL,30H
   MOV   AH,0
   IMUL  BX
       :
       :
```

Fig. 10.8   Extract from an assembly listing showing conditional assembly.

required which can save (and restore) some or all of the registers AX, BX, CX, DX, SI, DI, BP, DS and ES on (or from) the stack. Let's call these macros PUSH_REGS and POP_REGS. To define PUSH_REGS we use another conditional assembly pseudo-op

   IFB <argument> . . . ELSE . . . ENDIF

which includes the statements before the ELSE in the assembly IF argument is Blank, but otherwise includes the statements after the ELSE:

```
PUSH_REGS   MACRO   R1,R2,R3,R4,R5,R6,R7,R8,R9
                IRP   REGISTER,<R9,R8,R7,R6,R5,R4,R3,R2,R1>
                    IFB <REGISTER>
                    ;;if REGISTER is blank do nothing
                    ELSE
                        PUSH REGISTER
                    ENDIF
                ENDM
            ENDM
```

On the invocation

```
PUSH_REGS BX,CX,DX
```

dummy parameters R4, R5, . . . , R9 are set to blank so that the following expansion will result:

```
PUSH DX
PUSH CX
PUSH BX
```

It is an exercise for the reader to write the corresponding macro POP_REGS. Once that is complete the macro READ_CHARACTER can be rewritten along the following lines, depending upon which actual registers need be saved:

```
READ_CHARACTER MACRO
        IF CPM86
          PUSH_REGS BX,CX,SI,DI,BP,DS,ES
          MOV   CL,1
          INT   224D
          POP_REGS ES,DS,BP,DI,SI,CX,BX
        ELSE
          MOV   AH,1
          INT   21H
        ENDIF
        ENDM
```

Using the

   IFDEF symbol . . . ELSE. . .ENDIF

pseudo-op we can illustrate how one might allow for different memory sizes on users' machines. IFDEF symbol . . . is TRUE if either symbol is defined in the program containing the IFDEF statement or is declared as external via the EXTRN pseudo-op. Hence in

```
MINMEMORY EQU 64
  :
  :
IFDEF MINMEMORY
        USER_WORK_SPACE DB   2000H DUP(?)
ELSE
        USER_WORK_SPACE DB 0A000H DUP(?)
ENDIF
  :
  :
```

the statement

```
USER_WORK_SPACE DB 2000H DUP(?)
```

would be assembled. Notice that, as with all the conditional pseudo-ops, use of IFDEF is not limited to within a macro. However, any argument to a conditional must be known on pass one to avoid errors and incorrect evaluation, since macro definitions are recorded by MASM on pass one.

The pseudo-ops IF1. . . and IF2. . . are similar in format and use to IFB except that neither takes an argument. In

```
IF1
 %OUT NOW DOING PASS 1
ENDIF
IF2
 %OUT AND NOW DOING PASS 2
END1F
```

one message is sent to the display on each assembler pass, since the statements between IF1 and ENDIF are assembled only IF it is assembler pass one, and the statements between IF2 and END1F only IF it is assembler pass two.

It is possible to keep a library of macros (see Section 11.4) in a separate file called, for instance, MACRO.LIB, which can then be incorporated into the main program via an INCLUDE pseudo-op. One often wants to do this for macros which would clearly be of use in contexts other than the problem in hand. If the INCLUDE is executed only on pass one, both operations and print time will be accelerated. This can be done as follows:

```
IF1
   INCLUDE MACRO.LIB
ENDIF
```

IF1 and IF2 are a dangerously special tool, really beyond the scope of this book. The power which they seem to offer the programmer is tempered by the difficulty of avoiding phase errors during assembly, wherein values calculated by the assembler on pass one do not agree with corresponding values calculated on pass two.

A generalized MOVE instruction

The final forms of MASM conditional pseudo-op are the **IFIDN** (IF IDeNtical) and **IFDIF** (IF DIFferent) pseudo-ops. IFIDN takes the general form

IFIDN <arg1>,<arg2>

    :

    : block of statements (1)

    :

ELSE

    :

    : block of statements (2)

    :

ENDIF

in which statements (1) are assembled if the string arg1 is identical to the string arg2, and statements (2) otherwise. IFDIF is similar, except that statements (1) are assembled if the string arg1 is different from the string arg2, and statements (2) otherwise.

We shall use IFIDN to write a macro MOVE16, a generalized form of the 8088 16-bit MOV instruction which, additionally, will allow the exchange of data between two memory locations. Register AX will be used as temporary store for these transfers but will be saved beforehand and restored afterwards. The definition of MOVE16 uses another macro, ISREG, which decides if its single argument is one of the 8088's 16-bit registers and sets IS_A_ REGISTER to 1 if so and to 0 if not:

```
ISREG MACRO REGISTER
IS_A_REGISTER=0
IRP   REG,<AX,BX,CX,DX,BP,SP,DI,SI,CS,DS,ES,SS>
IFIDN <REG>, <REGISTER>
    IS_A_REGISTER=1
ENDIF
ENDM
ENDM
```

Because of the IRP pseudo-op, REG takes successive values of 8088 16-bit register names. IFIDN then compares the value of REGISTER to see if it is identical with REG and sets IS_A_REGISTER to 1 if this is the case. Otherwise IS_A_REGISTER is left set to 0.

Once a correspondence between the value of REGISTER and one of the instances of REG has been found, there is no point in checking through

```
MOVE16 MACRO TO,FROM
       ISREG TO
       IFE IS_A_REGISTER
               ISREG FROM
               IFE IS_A_REGISTER
                       PUSH AX
                       MOV  AX,FROM
                       XCHG AX,TO
                       MOV  FROM,AX
                       POP  AX
               ELSE
                       MOV  TO,FROM
               ENDIF
       ELSE
              MOV TO,FROM
       ENDIF
ENDM
```

Fig. 10.9   MOVE16: a generalization of the 8088 MOV instruction.

the remainder of the list of possible values for REG since we know a match will be impossible. It would be an improvement, therefore, to rewrite ISREG using the EXITM pseudo-op discussed briefly at the end of Section 10.3. EXITM is used when you want to terminate a REPT, IRP, IRPC or MACRO invocation once some test proves that the remainder of that expansion is not required. When an EXITM is executed, the expansion or repetition is terminated immediately at that level, but expansion in any containing pseudo-ops is allowed to continue. Here, then, is our thus improved version of ISREG:

```
ISREG MACRO REGISTER
  IS_A_REGISTER=0
  IRP REG,<AX,BX,CX,DX,BP,SP,DI,SI,CS,DS,ES,SS>
  IFIDN <REG>,<REGISTER>
    IS_A_REGISTER=1
    EXITM
  ENDIF
  ENDM
  ENDM
```

MOVE16 is now easy to complete (see Fig. 10.9) using the IFE. . . conditional pseudo-op:

IFE expression

 :

 : block of statements (1)

 :

ELSE

:

: block of statements (2)

:

ENDIF

in which statements (1) are assembled IF, when evaluated, the expression is Equal to zero.

Figure 10.10 contains an extract from an assembly listing of a program in which MOVE16 was used.

Debugging complicated macros such as MOVE16 is facilitated by using the non-default .LALL macro expansion printout control. Since the existence of MOVE16 slows down the assembly process considerably,

```
50                        MOVE16 AX,BX
51 0008 8B C3        +              MOV   AX,BX
52                        MOVE16 AX,[BX]
53 000A 8B 07        +              MOV   AX,[BX]
54                        MOVE16 AX,MY
55 000C A1 0000   R  +              MOV   AX,MY
56                        MOVE16 [BX],AX
57 000F 89 07        +              MOV   [BX],AX
58                        MOVE16 MY,AX
59 0011 A3 0000   R  +              MOV   MY,AX
60                        MOVE16 [BX],[BP]
61 0014 50           +              PUSH  AX
62 0015 8B 46 00     +              MOV   AX,[BP]
63 0018 87 07        +              XCHG  AX,[BX]
64 001A 89 46 00     +              MOV   [BP],AX
65 001D 58           +              POP   AX
66                        MOVE16 [BX],MY
67 001E 50           +              PUSH  AX
68 001F A1 0000   R  +              MOV   AX,MY
69 0022 87 07        +              XCHG  AX,[BX]
70 0024 A3 0000   R  +              MOV   MY,AX
71 0027 58           +              POP   AX
72                        MOVE16 MY,[BX]
73 0028 50           +              PUSH  AX
74 0029 8B 07        +              MOV   AX,[BX]
75 002B 87 06 0000 R +              XCHG  AX,MY
76 002F 89 07        +              MOV   [BX],AX
77 0031 58           +              POP   AX
```

Fig. 10.10 Expansion of MOVE16 invocations in an assembly listing.

judicious use of %OUT can reassure the anxious programmer that assembly has not gone into an infinite loop thanks to a typing error.

General format of conditional pseudo-ops

MASM conditional pseudo-ops are summarized in Table 10.2 (in fact IF, IFE, IF1, IF2, IFIDN and IFDIF are allowed in ASM assembly language, though not with macros which ASM does not support). They may all take one of two forms, either:

    IFxxx expression
      :
      : block of statements (1)
      :
    ELSE
      :
      : block of statements (2)
      :
    ENDIF

or the simpler:

    IFxxx expression
      :
      : block of statements (3)
      :
    ENDIF

Table 10.2   MASM conditional pseudo-ops.

IFxxx	*Condition under which statements (1) or (3) are assembled (see text)*
IF expression	If expression evaluates to a non-zero number.
IFE expression	If expression evaluates to zero.
IF1	If encountered on assembly pass one.
IF2	If encountered on assembly pass two.
IFDEF symbol	If symbol is defined or has been declared external via EXTRN.
IFNDEF symbol	If symbol is undefined or not declared external via EXTRN.
IFB<argument>	If argument is blank.
IFNB<argument>	If argument is not blank.
IFIDN<arg1>,<arg2>	If the string arg1 is identical to the string arg2.
IFDIF<arg1>,<arg2>	If the string arg1 is different from the string arg2.

where the xxx represents some condition which the expression is to satisfy and, if it does, statements (1) (first format) or statements (3) (second format) are assembled. If the expression does not satisfy the condition then, in the first format, statements (2) are assembled whereas in the second format no statements are assembled as a result of this pseudo-op.

EXERCISES 10.4

1. Write and test MASM macros which perform the following tasks:

a) A macro MADD which generalizes the ADD instruction to allow multiple operands. Thus

```
MADD AX,BX,CX,[BX]
```

would generate

```
ADD AX,BX
ADD AX,CX
ADD AX,[BX]
```

b) A macro MSHL which generalizes the SHL instruction so that, for example:

```
MSHL AH,4
```

would generate

```
PUSH CX
MOV  CL,4
SHL  AH,CL
POP  CX
```

c) A macro MEM which allows register to register and memory to memory unsigned 8-bit addition, subtraction, multiplication and division. Thus, an invocation

```
MEM ADD,[BX],[BP]
```

should be expanded to 8088 instructions which add [BX] and [BP] and leave the result in [BX]. Similarly:

```
MEM SUB,[BX],[BP]
MEM MUL,[BX],MY_LOC
MEM DIV,TOTAL,MY_LOC
```

should each produce corresponding expansions.

Make sensible simplifying assumptions and use auxiliary macro definitions to structure and simplify the task.

2. In order to better understand the problems of assembly phase error, incorporate the macro MYORG, defined below, into a program which reads two characters from the keyboard and prints them out

using subroutines READCHAR and PRINTCHAR of Chapter 5. Invoke MYORG immediately after the first character is read:

```
.LALL
   :
CSEG SEGMENT
      :
      :
      CALL READCHAR
      MYORG PRINTCHAR
      :
      :
READCHAR: .......
PRINTCHAR: .......
      :
      :
END
```

The definition of MYORG is as follows:

```
MYORG MACRO MYLABEL
IF1
IFNDEF MYLABEL
   ORG $+30H
ENDIF
ENDIF
ENDM
```

Try to assemble the resulting program and study the contents of the .LST file in order to explain what has gone wrong.

3. Write and test a set of macros which mimic the string manipulation facilities available in Pascal. Assume that all string arguments for these macros are terminated by a $ character. Your macros should include, for example, one called LENGTH so that the invocation

```
LENGTH [BX]
```

would expand to 8088 instructions which left the length of the string pointed to by BX in register AX; a string insertion macro INSERT; a substring deletion macro DELETE; and a string concatenation macro CONCAT.

10.5 RECURSIVE MACROS

Macro definitions can be recursive. The following examples illustrate the format of recursive macro definitions and the resulting expansion of a typical invocation.

Factorials

Macro FACT expands to code which calculates the factorial of the unsigned number in AX and leaves the result in AX.

Definition

```
FACT MACRO N
     IF N-1
         MOV  BX,N-1
         MUL  BX
         FACT N-1
     ENDIF
     ENDM
```

Typical invocation

```
NUM  EQU 5
MOV  AX,NUM
FACT %NUM
```

Resulting expansion

```
MOV BX,4
MUL BX
MOV BX,3
MUL BX
MOV BX,2
MUL BX
MOV BX,1
MUL BX
```

Sum of the whole numbers 1 to *N*

Macro SUM expands to code which calculates $1 + 2 + 3 + \ldots + N$ and leaves the result in AX assuming N is in AX before an invocation.

Definition

```
SUM MACRO N
    IF N-1
        ADD AX,N-1
        SUM N-1
    ENDIF
    ENDM
```

Typical invocation

```
NUM EQU 4
MOV AX,NUM
SUM %NUM
```

Resulting expansion

```
ADD AX,4-1
ADD AX,4-1-1
ADD AX,4-1-1-1
```

Raising *M* to the power *N*

Macro POWER expands to code which raises the positive whole number M to the positive whole number power N, assuming M is in AX before an invocation.

Definition

```
POWER MACRO M,N
          IF    N-1
          MOV   BX,M
          MUL   BX
          POWER M,N-1
       ENDIF
       ENDM
```

Typical invocation

```
NUM    EQU 2
MOV    AX,NUM
POWER  %NUM,3
```

Resulting expansion

```
MOV BX,2
MUL BX
MOV BX,2
MUL BX
```

It should be clear from these examples that the programmer needs to control the use of recursively defined macros very carefully. The use of any of them to calculate with just medium-sized numbers (10! for example) will consume vast quantities of program memory space and, in general, will cause the program to run very much more slowly than non-recursively produced coding for a given task.

EXERCISES 10.5

1. Make a detailed comparison of the procedure FACT defined in Section 7.8 with the code produced by the macro FACT in terms of memory requirements and execution time. Complete the following table:

	FACT procedure		FACT macro	
N	Store	Time	Store	Time
1				
2				
3				
4				
5				
10				
20				
100				

2. Write and test a recursively defined macro FIB for which the invocation

    FIB N

will generate code to leave the Nth Fibonacci number in AX (see Section 7.8 for a definition of the Fibonacci series).

11 Disk Files

AIMS

PC-DOS allows the programmer to handle disk storage via operating system function calls much like those we first met in Chapter 4 for keyboard input and printing to the screen. In this chapter we shall study the use of PC-DOS disk handling facilities in detail, and construct four complete example programs: for dumping the contents of a file onto the display screen; storing keyboard input in a disk file; a file copy utility; and a random access read utility. Macros will often be used to implement the file handling operations as further practical illustration of the content of the last chapter.

11.1 DISK FILE HANDLING WITH INT 21H

The disk file handling functions provided by INTerrupt 21H assume each file to have a name conforming to the appropriate conventions, i.e. that file names are of the form

<first name>.<second name>

where the <first name> begins with a letter and consists of between one and eight characters and <second name> is blank or up to three characters in length. (There are further conventions regarding the characters which can be involved in <first name> and <second name>. Letters and digits are quite safe, but the reader unfamiliar with these conventions will have to consult the manual before using more exotic characters.)

PC-DOS regards a file as being made up of smaller chunks called **records**, each (by default) consisting of exactly 128 bytes of data. When data is transferred between the computer's main memory and a disk, one record is transferred at a time. This aids efficiency, for it takes an appreciable amount of time for the mechanical placing of the disk drive read/write head at the point where data is to be stored or retrieved. If transference were allowed in units of a single byte, the whole storage/retrieval operation would be slowed down to mechanical speed rather than electronic speed.

Thanks to INT 21H function calls, all the programmer has to do in order to read from or write to a disk file is: provide in a certain place in memory the name of the file to be acted on; nominate 128 bytes in main memory which *either* contain data to be written to the disk file of the given name *or* are to be used to store the next 128 bytes read from the named file; and specify which record in the file is to be the object of the transfer. This is done by giving a pair of numbers which uniquely specify the record concerned. The first number specifies which **block** the record is in and the second gives the relative **record number** within that block. (Compare this with the familiar method of specifying which day in a year it is by giving first the month, then the day relative to that month.)

Block numbers are kept in signed 16-bit form. Relative to that block number, the record number is stored in signed 8-bit form so that, just as in most months there are 31 days, so in all blocks there are 128 records numbered from 0 to 127. It follows that in one block there are 128 * 128 = 16 Kbytes – room for about ten A4 pages of double spaced typing. This information is summarized below:

1.   A file consists of one or more blocks.

2.   Each block consists of up to 128 records.

3.   Each record consists of 128 bytes. One record at a time is transferred between main memory and a disk.

File control blocks

For applications involving serial file access, the programmer has only to set the block number and relative record number once. This is done using the **file control block** mechanism. The programmer provides the operating system functions with the file name, block and record number by entering them into certain locations in an area of memory specially reserved for the task. This area of memory is known as the File Control Block (FCB) for the given file. If a program uses several files then several FCBs (one for each file) have to be maintained. Each FCB consists of 36D bytes of data which are used as shown in Table 11.1.

11.2   ACCESSING THE RECORDS OF A FILE SEQUENTIALLY – WRITING A FILE DUMP UTILITY

Specification

Our aim in this section is to describe the steps involved in reading successive records from a disk file in the order they occur in the file. In order to be specific, we shall write a program which will take as input the name of any

Table 11.1 Structure of a file control block.

Byte number	Use
0	A code indicating which disk drive is to be used for the file operation. code 0 denotes the default drive code 1 denotes drive A code 2 denotes drive B etc.
1–8 (inclusive)	The file's <first name> in ASCII codes, left-justified and with trailing blanks, i.e. if the <first name> involves less than eight characters the remaining bytes are filled with the ASCII 'space' character (20H).
9–11 (inclusive)	The file's <second name> in ASCII codes, filled out with ASCII 'space' characters as necessary.
12–13	The number of the block containing the data record.
14–15	Logical record size in bytes. The default is 128 bytes, requiring no action by the programmer.
16–19	File size in bytes.
20–21	Date the file was created or last updated, coded as follows: byte 21 byte 20 yyyyyyym mmmddddd where yyyyyyy is a 7-bit unsigned number in the range 0–119D corresponding to 1980–2099; mmmm a 4-bit unsigned number in the range 1–12; and ddddd is a 5-bit unsigned number covering the range 1–31.
22–31	Reserved for use by the operating system.
32	Contains the record number relative to the block number given in bytes 12 and 13.
33–35 (inclusive)	Used for random access to the records of the file. If the programmer changes the default record size to less than 64 bytes per record, a further byte is used in the FCB to provide two words, making an FCB of 37 bytes in total.

existing file and display the records of that file on the screen in hexadecimal format. Once the program is started up, the first 128-byte record of the file will be displayed. To have the second record displayed the user must press any key other than keys such as shift or control. If the user presses the X key then the program stops and exits to the operating system. After the second record has been displayed, pressing any sensible key again gives the next record (except that X causes an exit). And so on. When eventually the last record in the file has been printed we automatically exit to the operating system.

As usual, the assembly language program to carry out this task must be put into a file having the second name ASM. Since the object of the program is to dump the contents of any chosen file on the screen, we shall put the program to do this in a file called DUMP.ASM. After the program has been written, tested and debugged, its machine code equivalent will be contained in a file DUMP.EXE and the program can then be called into action in the normal way for machine code programs, i.e. just by typing the <first name> of the file which contains it. However, for programs which act on a disk file you are allowed to name the file to be affected at the same time. Thus, typing

```
DUMP ASAMPLE.XYZ
```

after the A> prompt would bring the machine code version of our program into action on the file ASAMPLE.XYZ. PC-DOS enables this by the convention that, if a file name is given in such a context, the bare bones of a file control block are automatically initialized for that file at locations 05CH and following, relative to the PC-DOS initialized value of DS for program DUMP. It follows, therefore, that if after the A> operating system prompt we type

```
DUMP ASAMPLE.XYZ
```

then the operating system would automatically arrange that, *before execution* of the machine code program in the file DUMP.EXE, we should have:

Location	5C	5D	5E	5F	60	61	62	63	64	65	66	67
Contents	0	41	53	41	4D	50	4C	45	20	58	59	5A

where both addresses and contents are given in hexadecimal notation and all addresses are relative to the DS register. Notice that, because up to eight characters are allowed for a file's <first name>, the eighth location reserved for it (64H) has been filled with an ASCII space (20H) character. Also, as no disk drive was explicitly named with the file name ASAMPLE.XYZ, the drive code in location 5CH is 0 (for 'use the current default drive').

EXERCISE 11.1

Suppose that in a file called SPELL.EXE there is a machine code program to check the spelling of all the words used in a file containing text. To bring the program into action on the file DIARY.VI the user types

```
SPELL DIARY.VI
```

after the A> operating system prompt. What will the operating system store in locations 05CH–67H inclusive (relative to the PC-DOS initialized value of DS) as the bare bones of a file control block for the file DIARY.VI?

The method

Thanks to PC-DOS, our file dump program may therefore assume that the 36D locations from address 05CH (relative to the initialized value of DS) contain a skeletal file control block for the file whose contents are to be dumped onto the screen, with the disk drive code, <first name> and <second name> sections already filled in. As a result, a pseudo-Pascal outline of our program looks as follows:

> *try to open the file specified by the file control block at*
> *location 5CH and following;* (*AL := 0FFH if not successful*)
> **if** *AL < > 0FFH* **then**
>   **begin**
>   *block_number := 0;*
>   *current_record := 0;*
>   **repeat** *read next record;* (*AL := 0 if no error*)
>   **if** *AL = 0* **then**
>   **begin**
>   *PUSH AX*
>   *print the record;*
>   *read(char);*
>   *print(newline);*
>   *POP AX*
>   **end**
>   **until** *AL < > 0* **or** *char = 'X';*
> *return to PC-DOS*

Attempting to *open* a file specified by a file control block causes the operating system to scan the disk in the disk drive specified by location 05CH of that file control block. If a file with the <first name> and <second name> given in the file control block is found on the disk, the operating system fills in many of the remaining entries in the file control block. If such a file cannot be found, register AL is set to 0FFH, otherwise it is set to zero.

If the file has been opened successfully, since we want to dump successive records of the named file starting with the first, the block number and relative record number fields of the file control block at 05CH must now both be set to zero.

Having done so, we *read* the next 128 byte record from the file specified by the file control block at location 05CH and following. The record to be read is specified by the block number and record number fields of that file control block. Transferring the data from the disk is carried out by function 14H of INT 21H (see Table 11.2) which will only do so if the relevant file has already been opened. (It is not necessary to open the file before every 'read', but an unopened file cannot be read.) Having made the transfer, the operating system will add 1 to the record count held in the file control block by adjusting the block number and relative record number fields as necessary. (Except in the case of files larger than 16 Kbytes, this will simply involve adding 1 to the record number field.) If the read was successful, register AL is set to 0, otherwise register AL is set to 01H to indicate no data in the record (i.e. the record specified in the FCB doesn't exist); to 03H to indicate that a partial record was read and has been filled out with zeros; and to 02H to indicate that there was not enough space in the disk transfer area to read one record, so the transfer was ended.

If the read was successful, the 128 bytes read are, by default, left in locations 80H–0FFH inclusive, relative to DS. Because location 80H gives us access to the file's records in this way, address 80H is referred to as the (default) Disk Transfer Area – the **DTA** – address. Displaying the record just read on the screen in hexadecimal format now boils down to printing the contents of each of locations 80H–0FFH (inclusive) in hexadecimal.

If we haven't reached the end of the file to be dumped, we wait for a key to be pressed and then repeat the read . . . print cycle, unless it was the X key. If it was, we stop and return control to the operating system.

It can be seen, therefore, that PC-DOS functions 0FH and 14H of INT 21H do all the work. Their actions are summarized in Table 11.2. As with previous operating system functions, these two are brought into action by loading register AH with the function number and executing an INT 21H.

The dump program

The complete program is given in Fig. 11.1. In the data segment we label the start of the file control block, the block and record number locations within that file control block, and the DTA address, using the ORG pseudo-op. The code segment follows the above method closely. Each record is printed by using the LODS string primitive to bring the record byte by byte into AL, and the subroutine PRINT_AL_IN_HEX is then employed to print the contents of AL in hexadecimal. To see how it works, suppose AL contains 01010111. After executing the

```
MOV CL,4
ROR AL,CL
```

instructions the contents of AL will be 01110101 (75H); the digits in the hexadecimal representation of the initial contents of AL (57H) have been swapped round. The PRINT_AL_IN_HEX subroutine now calls the subroutine PRINT_ONE_HEX_DIGIT, which first masks out the second digit of the original contents of AL via the AND AL,0FH instruction, leaving 00000101 in AL. Then we add 30H or 37H as necessary to convert the digit into ASCII ready for printing, print the digit (5) and return from this subroutine call. We now POP the saved initial value of AL off the stack, which in our example leaves 01010111 in AL. After AND AL,0FH, register AL contains 00000111 and we add 30H or 37H as necessary to convert this to ASCII and print the result (7).

Table 11.2 A summary of INT 21H disk file handling functions (the PC-DOS manual contains a complete list in Appendix D).

Function number	Function name	What it does
0FH	open-file	Opens the file specified by the file control block which starts at the address given in register DX (relative to the DS register). If the file is successfully opened, register AL is set to 0. If the file cannot be found, register AL is set to 0FFH.
10H	close-file	This function must be called after writing to a file to ensure that all directory information is updated. DX must contain the address (relative to DS) of an FCB for the file to be closed. If the 'close' is successful, AL is set to 0, otherwise AL is set to 0FFH.
13H	delete-file	If DX contains the address (relative to DS) of an FCB for an unopened file, that file is deleted. If no corresponding file exists AL is set to 0FFH, otherwise AL is set to 0.
14H	sequential read	This function works only if the file with the file control block starting at the address in DX (relative to DS) has either been opened by function 0FH or newly created by the create function, 16H. Provided that this has been done, the 128-byte record specified by the block number and relative record number fields of the file control block pointed to by DX will be read into memory starting at the DTA address (80H by default). If the read operation is successful, AL is set to 0. Otherwise AL is set to:
		01H – no data in the record
		03H – partial record read and filled with zeros
		02H – not enough space in DTA
15H	sequential write	Given that DS:DX points to an FCB for an opened file, the record specified by the current block and record number fields is written from the DTA address. The block and relative record number fields are then updated in the FCB to point to the next record. AL is set to 0 if the write was successful; to 01H if the diskette is full; and to 02H if there was insufficient space in the DTA.
16H	create-file	Given that DS:DX points to an FCB for an unopened file, a corresponding new file is created (if a file with that name already exists it is destroyed). On successful file creation AL is set to 0.
21H	read-random	Given that DX contains the address (relative to DS) of a file control block, this function reads from the appropriate file the record specified by bytes 33D, 34D and 35D of that file control block. The record is read into the DTA area of memory. If the read is successful

Table 11.2   (*continued*)

Function number	Function name	What it does
		AL is set to 0. Otherwise AL is set to a non-zero value, indicating the reason for failure as for function 14H.
22H	write-random	This works in a similar way to function 21H except that the 128 bytes at the DTA address and following are written as the specified record number of the file determined by the file control block pointed to by DX. AL is set to 0 if the write is successful. Otherwise it is set to a non-zero value as for function 14H.

Debugging programs which involve files

DEBUG provides facilities to name the file or files on which a program being debugged is to operate. Thus a debugging session involving the machine code version of DUMP would begin in the normal way with the programmer typing DEBUG DUMP.EXE. Suppose the file to be dumped is called TESTDATA.FEB. Then issuing the command

```
NTESTDATA.FEB
```

to DEBUG will result in a file control block being initialized at 05CH relative to DS in just the same way as if the DUMP program had been called into action by typing

```
DUMP TESTDATA.FEB
```

after the A> operating system prompt. (N is the 'Name file(s) to operate on' command.)

EXERCISES 11.2

1. Improve the user-friendliness of the DUMP utility just written. If the file for which a DUMP has been requested cannot be opened – or some other error has occurred when we have tried to open it – assume that the file does not exist and print out the message 'FILE DOESN'T EXIST – TYPING ERROR IN FILENAME?' When all the records of a particular file have been DUMPed, display the message 'ALL RECORDS NOW DUMPED' before exiting to the operating system.

2. Write an 8088 assembly language program which performs in exactly the same way as our DUMP program but which prints out each record in ASCII format whenever possible. (In other words, for each byte of a record, if that byte is the ASCII code for a printable character, then display that character else display a full stop.) Store the program in a file called ASCIDUMP.ASM.

```
DSEG SEGMENT
ORG  5CH
     FCB DB 0
ORG  68H
     BLOCK_NUMBER DW 0
ORG  7CH
     RECORD_NUMBER DB 0
ORG  80H
     DTA DB 0
DSEG ENDS

SSEG SEGMENT STACK
     DB 100H DUP(?)
SSEG ENDS

OPENFILE MACRO FCB              ;;open the file with given fcb
         MOV  AH,0FH
         MOV  DX,OFFSET FCB
         INT  21H
         ENDM
READNEXTRECORD MACRO FCB
         MOV  AH,14H
         MOV  DX,OFFSET FCB
         INT  21H
         ENDM
CSEG SEGMENT
ASSUME CS:CSEG,DS:DSEG,SS:SSEG
START PROC FAR
      PUSH DS    ;save address for return to PC-DOS
      MOV  AX,0
      PUSH AX    ;save offset for return to PC-DOS
;open the file
      OPENFILE FCB
;if AL <> 0FFH then
      CMP  AL,0FFH
      JZ   DONE
      ;begin
      ;block_number := 0; record_number := 0;
            MOV  BLOCK_NUMBER,0
            MOV  RECORD_NUMBER,0
      ;repeat read next record
        NEXT_RECORD:READNEXTRECORD FCB
            ;if AL = 0 then
                        CMP  AL,0
                        JNZ  UNTILCHECK
                ;begin
                        PUSH AX
                ;print out record just read in hex
                        CALL HEX_RECORD_PRINT
                ;read(char); print(newline)
                        MOV  AH,1
                        INT  21H
                        MOV  CL,AL
                        CALL PRINT_NEWLINE
```

Fig. 11.1 The complete DUMP program.

```
                                    POP   AX
                          ;end
          ;until AL <> 0 or char = 'X'
      UNTILCHECK:CMP   CL,'X'
                  JZ    DONE
                  CMP   AL,0
                  JNZ   DONE
                  JMP   NEXT_RECORD
          ;end
;return to PC-DOS
DONE: RET
HEX_RECORD_PRINT PROC NEAR
                  MOV   SI,OFFSET DTA
                  MOV   CX,80H
          PRINTING:  LODSB
                  PUSH CX     ;preserve CX so we don't lose count
                  CALL PRINT_AL_IN_HEX
                  POP   CX
                  LOOP PRINTING
                  CALL PRINT_NEWLINE
                  RET
HEX_RECORD_PRINT ENDP
PRINT_AL_IN_HEX PROC NEAR
                      PUSH AX
                      MOV   CL,4
                      ROR   AL,CL
                      CALL PRINT_ONE_HEX_DIGIT
                      POP   AX
PRINT_ONE_HEX_DIGIT:  AND   AL,0FH
                      ADD   AL,30H
                      CMP   AL,3AH
                      JB    DISPLAY_IT
                      ADD   AL,7H
          DISPLAY_IT: MOV   DL,AL
                      MOV   AH,2H
                      INT   21H
                      RET
PRINT_AL_IN_HEX ENDP
PRINT_NEWLINE PROC NEAR
                  PUSH AX
                  MOV   AH,2H
                  MOV   DL,0DH
                  INT   21H
                  MOV   DL,0AH
                  INT   21H
                  POP   AX
                  RET
PRINT_NEWLINE ENDP
START ENDP
CSEG ENDS
END
```

Fig. 11.1   (*continued*)

11.3 PUTTING DATA INTO FILES

When putting data into files there has to be a way of saying 'that's the end of the data'. By convention the CTRL-Z character (ASCII code 1AH) is used for this. Thus it is up to the programmer to watch out for ASCII code 1AH and, when it is encountered, to write the last record into the file and close access to the file. Before writing the last record, the remainder of that 128-byte record should be filled up with CTRL-Z characters.

Closing the file is carried out by operating system function number 10H. This function *must* be called after writing to a file has finished or the data written to the file will not be permanently recorded on disk. Given the address of a file control block in DX (relative to DS), data held on the disk concerning the relevant file is updated and the new file made permanent. If all is well AL is set to zero after the file has been closed. If an error occurs, AL is set to 0FFH.

Prior to writing to a *new* file, it is first necessary to *create* an entry for that file in the file directory held on the appropriate disk. This is done by a call to function number 16H. Given the address of a file control block in register DX (relative to DS), this function amends the appropriate disk directory and initializes the file control block in the same manner as a call to the open-file function. For this reason, a file need not be opened after it has been created which, in effect, means that before gaining access to a file it is necessary to *open* it if the file already exists, or to *create* it if the file is new. If an error occurs during a call to the create-file function (because there is no room left in the directory, for example) then register AL is set to 0FFH. If all is well, AL is set to zero.

Operating system function number 15H will *write* the 128 bytes in the DTA area to the disk file named in the file control block beginning at the location given in register DX (relative to DS). The 128-byte record is written at a position in the file determined by the block number and record number fields of the file control block. After writing, the record number is increased by one (and the block number adjusted if necessary). If the write was successful, AL is set to zero, otherwise AL is set to a non-zero value.

Table 11.2 contains a summary of these and all the other INT 21H file handling functions.

DATAGRAB – an example of file input

By way of illustration of the process involved in writing data into a file, we shall now construct a program which will accept an arbitrary number of characters typed at the keyboard and store the ASCII codes for those characters in a disk file. Input is accepted until a CTRL-Z character is typed. We shall assume that the program itself is in a file called DATAGRAB.ASM. The file in which the typed characters are to be stored will be named at the same time as calling the program into action. Thus typing DATAGRAB MYCHARS.ABC after the A> operating system

```
DSEG SEGMENT
ORG  5CH
     FCB DB 0
ORG  68H
     BLOCK_NUMBER  DW 0
ORG  7CH
     RECORD_NUMBER DB 0
ORG  80H
     DTA           DB 0
ORG  0FFH
     LAST_OF_DTA   DB 0
DSEG ENDS
SSEG SEGMENT STACK
     DB 100H DUP(?)
SSEG ENDS
MAKEFILE MACRO FCB
         MOV  AH,16H
         MOV  DX,OFFSET FCB
         INT  21H
         ENDM
WRITERECORD MACRO FCB
         MOV  AH,15H
         MOV  DX,OFFSET FCB
         INT  21H
         ENDM
CLOSEFILE MACRO FCB
         MOV  AH,10H
         MOV  DX,OFFSET FCB
         INT  21H
         ENDM
CSEG SEGMENT
ASSUME CS:CSEG,DS:DSEG,SS:SSEG
START PROC FAR
;set up to return to operating system
     PUSH DS
     MOV  AX,0
     PUSH AX
;try to make new file's entry in directory (*AL := 0 if OK*);
     MAKEFILE FCB
;block_number := 0; record_number := 0;
     MOV  RECORD_NUMBER,0
     MOV  BLOCK_NUMBER,0
;if AL = 0 then
     CMP  AL,0
     JNZ  DONE
```

Fig. 11.2 The complete DATAGRAB program.

```
                ;begin
                ;repeat
                    READ_RECORD: CLD
                            ;count := 80H
                            MOV   CX,80H
                            MOV   DI,OFFSET DTA
                            ;repeat read(ch)
                NEXT_DATA_BYTE: CALL READ_A_CHARACTER
                                ;next available DTA location := ch
                                STOSB
                            ;until count = 0 or ch = 1AH
                            CMP   AL,1AH
                            LOOPNZ NEXT_DATA_BYTE   ;LOOP does count := count-1
                            ;if ch = 1AH then fill up DTA with CTRL-Zs
                            CMP   AL,1AH
                            JNZ   WRITE_RECORD
                            REP STOSB ;last instruction left CX,DI set up
                            ;write record in DTA to file (*AL := 0 if OK*)
                WRITE_RECORD: WRITERECORD FCB
                    ;until last byte in DTA = 1AH or AL <> 0
                        CMP   AL,0
                        JNZ   CLOSE
                        MOV   AL,LAST_OF_DTA
                        CMP   AL,1AH
                        JNZ   READ_RECORD
                    ;close file
                    CLOSE: CLOSEFILE FCB
                    ;end;
                ;return to PC-DOS
                DONE: RET

                READ_A_CHARACTER PROC NEAR
                                MOV   AH,1
                                INT   21H
                                RET
                READ_A_CHARACTER ENDP
                START ENDP
                CSEG ENDS
                END
```

Fig. 11.2   (*continued*)

prompt will allow the user of our program to enter an arbitrary number of characters into the new file MYCHARS.ABC. As before, the operating system sets up the bare bones of a file control block for that file at location 5CH relative to the PC-DOS initialization of the DS register for the DATAGRAB program.

Once again the method consists of a few simple steps:

try to create the new file's directory entry; (*AL := 0 if OK*)
block_number := 0;
record_number := 0;
if *AL = 0* **then**
    begin
    repeat *count := 80H*;
        repeat *read(ch)*;
            next available DTA location := ch;
            count := count−1
        until *count = 0* **or** *ch = 1AH*;
        if *ch = 1AH* **then** *fill up DTA with CTRL-Zs*;
        write record in DTA to file (*AL := 0 if OK*)
    until *last byte in DTA = 1AH* **or** *AL <> 0*;
    close file
    end;
return to PC-DOS

Figure 11.2 shows the complete DATAGRAB program, in which register CX has been used for the variable count in the above outline. The reader is invited to type in the program and verify that it works, using the DUMP program of Section 11.2 to check the contents of files created using DATAGRAB.

EXERCISES 11.3

1. If you have tried to inspect the contents of files created using DATAGRAB with the PC-DOS TYPE instruction, some very strange results will have been obtained if the RETURN key was pressed during data input to the file. The RETURN key has code 0DH (carriage return) which is dutifully entered into the file by DATAGRAB. However, when printing out the contents of your file, TYPE displays *exactly* what is in the file and therefore prints just a carriage return and no line feed. As a result the subsequent line overprints the previous one.

   Alter DATAGRAB so that TYPE prints out the contents of a text file correctly. One way of doing this would be to replace every RETURN typed by a user inputting a file via DATAGRAB with two code bytes, 0AH (line feed) and 0DH.

2. Add more informative error messages to the DATAGRAB program. If a new file cannot be created because there would then be too many entries in the disk's directory, display the error message 'TOO MANY FILES ON THE DISK'. If an error occurs whilst a record is being written then display 'WRITE ERROR – EXECUTION STOPPED'.

3. One unfortunate consequence of the DATAGRAB program is that, if the file named to hold the characters entered already exists, the contents of that file will be overwritten. One way of avoiding this

difficulty is to try to open the named file before doing a make function call. If the open is successful the file already exists, so the DATAGRAB program should print the error message 'FILE ALREADY EXISTS' and execution should finish. On the other hand, if the open is unsuccessful the creation operation can proceed safely. Add this precaution to DATAGRAB.

4. Write an 8088 assembly language program which will allow its user to store as many numbers as he or she wants in the range 0–100 (inclusive) in a disk file. Any number which is out of range should be rejected and a suitable error message printed. Input is terminated when the user presses CTRL-Z. Store the program in a file called NUMGRAB.ASM.

11.4 COPYING FILES

Our aim in this section is to write a program, the assembly language version of which will be held in a file called FILECOPY.ASM. This program will be called into action by typing a command of the form

```
FILECOPY MYFILE.OLD YOURFILE.NEW
```

after the A> operating system prompt. A copy of the existing file MYFILE.OLD will then be made in the new file YOURFILE.NEW.

On receiving a command of the form

FILECOPY <first file> <second file>

our helpful operating system sets up the bare bones of *two* file control blocks, one for <first file> at 5CH and one for <second file> at 6CH relative to the PC-DOS initialized value of DS. Now between locations 05CH and 06CH there are 06CH−05CH = 10H (i.e. 16D) locations. But a full file control block occupies 36D locations. Hence, if we open the file whose file control block is at 5CH, the operating system will complete that file control block to 36D bytes and so rub out the partial file control block for the <second file>. So the first thing our file copy program needs to do is to copy the bare bones file control block for the <second file> to another, safe, place in memory. Having done that, the method is, more or less, straightforward:

error := false;
try to open the source file;
if *AL < > 0* **then** *error := true*;
DX := address of 'open' error message;
if not *error* **then**
    begin
    delete old object file (if it exists);
    create new object file;

if *AL* < > *0* **then** *error* := *true*;
DX := *address of 'create' error message*
end;
if not *error* **then repeat** *read a source file record*;
     BL := *AL*;
     write a record to the object file;
     if *AL* < > *0* **then** *error* := *true*;
     DX := *address of 'write' error message*
     until *BL* < > *0* **or** *error*;
if not *error* **then**
  begin
  close object file;
  DX := *address of 'close' error message*;
  if *AL* < > *0FF* **then** *DX* := *address of 'normal end' message*
  end;
print the message addressed by DX;
return to PC-DOS

Deletion of an already existing second file is carried out using operating system function number 13H (see Table 11.2). It removes the disk directory entry for the file specified by the bare bones file control block at the address in DX (relative to DS). If the file doesn't exist register AL is set to 0FFH, whereas if a file is actually deleted register AL is set to zero. (No harm is done by attempting to delete a non-existent file.)

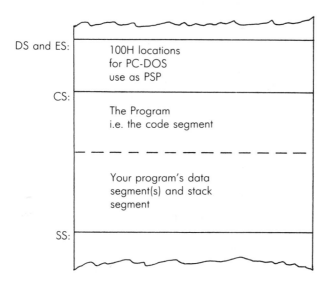

Fig. 11.3   Register initialization by PC-DOS.

Storage allocation by the operating system

When the operating system loads one of our programs into memory ready to be executed, storage is allocated according to the linker's instructions by initializing the CS, DS, SS and ES registers to certain values. Until now it hasn't been necessary to know the relationship between these values, but the file copy program requires a more detailed knowledge of this initialization, which is shown in Fig. 11.3.

The DS register is initialized to a value determined by PC-DOS and the first 100H locations of the data segment thus defined are reserved as a **Program Segment Prefix** (PSP) for PC-DOS use, including a file control block area at 5CH (relative to DS) and a default DTA area at 80H (relative to DS). The CS register is set to point to the location 100H from the start of the data segment, and the SS register to point to the first possible location

```
           READ_NEXT_RECORD MACRO FCB
                            MOV DX,OFFSET FCB
                            MOV AH,14H
                            INT 21H
                            ENDM
           WRITE_NEXT_RECORD MACRO FCB
                            MOV DX,OFFSET FCB
                            MOV AH,15H
                            INT 21H
                            ENDM
           OPEN_A_FILE MACRO FCB
                       MOV DX,OFFSET FCB
                       MOV AH,OFH
                       INT 21H
                       ENDM
           CLOSE_A_FILE MACRO FCB
                        MOV DX,OFFSET FCB
                        MOV AH,10H
                        INT 21H
                        ENDM
           MAKE_A_FILE MACRO FCB
                       MOV DX,OFFSET FCB
                       MOV AH,16H
                       INT 21H
                       ENDM
           DELETE_A_FILE MACRO FCB
                         MOV DX,OFFSET FCB
                         MOV AH,13H
                         INT 21H
                         ENDM
```

Fig. 11.4 Contents of the file FILEMACS.LIB.

after the end of your program's code and data segments; ES is set to the same value as DS.

In FILECOPY, in order to access the file control blocks easily and to avoid repeatedly changing the value of DS we copy the entire file control block area from before the code segment into the data segment. Also, since it is a classic instance of the advantages of such an approach, we shall assume that all the necessary file handling macros are held in a macro library called FILEMACS.LIB. (A macro library simply contains the assembly language forms of macros which are of use in more than one application.) A busy 8088 assembly language programmer would gradually add to this library to avoid continual reinvention of the wheel (and its vital attendant and time-consuming commitment to testing). Figure 11.4 shows the contents of FILEMACS.LIB used in our FILECOPY program.

The FILECOPY program (Fig. 11.5) uses an INCLUDE pseudo-op so that these macro definitions are incorporated into the program at assembly time.

Debugging programs which act on two files

For debugging purposes the names of the two files operated on by FILECOPY – the original and the one to hold the copy – could be specified using the DEBUG command N. Thus

```
NMYFILE.OLD YOURFILE.NEW
```

sets up two skeletal file control blocks, one for MYFILE.OLD at 5CH and

```
CR EQU 0DH
LF EQU 0AH
DSEG SEGMENT
ORG  5CH
     FCB DB 0
ORG  OFFSET FCB+12D
     BLOCK_NUMBER        DW 0
ORG  OFFSET FCB+32D
     RECORD_NUMBER       DB 0
ORG  OFFSET FCB+36D
     FCB2                DB 0
ORG  OFFSET FCB2+12D
     FCB2_BLOCK_NUMBER   DW 0
ORG  OFFSET FCB+32D
     FCB2_RECORD_NUMBER DB 0
;error messages
NO_SUCH_FILE          DB 'NO SUCH FILE EXISTS',CR,LF,'$'
DIRECTORY_FULL        DB 'CANNOT CREATE A NEW FILE — TOO MANY'
                      DB 'FILES ON THE DISK',CR,LF,'$'
DISK_FULL             DB 'NO ROOM LEFT ON THE DISK',CR,LF,'$'
DISK_WRITE_PROTECTED DB 'DISK WRITE PROTECTED',CR,LF,'$'
```

Fig. 11.5 The FILECOPY program.

```
        NORMAL_END              DB 'COPY COMPLETED',CR,LF,'$'
        DSEG ENDS
        SSEG SEGMENT STACK
            DB 100H DUP(?)
        SSEG ENDS
        INCLUDE FILEMACS.LIB
        CSEG SEGMENT
        ASSUME CS:CSEG,DS:DSEG,SS:SSEG
        START PROC FAR
                PUSH DS
                MOV  AX,0
                PUSH AX
                CLD
        ;initialize file control area;
                MOV  AX,DSEG
                MOV  ES,AX
                MOV  CX,10H
                MOV  SI,5CH
                MOV  DI,OFFSET FCB
                REP  MOVSB
                MOV  CX,10H
                MOV  DI,OFFSET FCB2
                REP  MOVSB
        ;establish data segment addressability;
                MOV  AX,DSEG
                MOV  DS,AX
        ;zero block number and record number fields of FCB2;
                MOV  FCB2_BLOCK_NUMBER,0
                MOV  FCB2_RECORD_NUMBER,0
        ;error := false;
                MOV  BH,0
        ;try to open source file;
                OPEN_A_FILE FCB
        ;if AL <> 0 then error := true;
                CMP  AL,0
                JZ   OPEN_OK
                MOV  BH,1
        ;DX := address of 'open' error message;
        OPEN_OK: MOV  DX,OFFSET NO_SUCH_FILE
        ;if not error then
                CMP  BH,0
                JNZ  READ_BLOCK
                ;begin
                ;delete old object file;
                        DELETE_A_FILE FCB2
                ;create new object file;
                        MAKE_A_FILE FCB2
```

Fig. 11.5 (*continued*)

```
       ;if AL <> 0 then error := true;
               CMP   AL,0
               JZ    CREATE_OK
               MOV   BH,1
          ;DX := address of 'create' error message
   CREATE_OK:  MOV   DX,OFFSET DIRECTORY_FULL
          ;end;
;if not error then
        READ_BLOCK: CMP BH,0
                    JNZ END_OF_FILE_BLOCK
                    READ_NEXT_RECORD FCB

                    MOV   BL,AL
               ;repeat read a source file record;
               ;write a record to the object file;
                    WRITE_NEXT_RECORD FCB2
               ;if AL <> 0 then error := true;
                    CMP   AL,0
                    JZ    WRITE_OK
                    MOV   BH,1
               ;DX := address of 'write' error message
           WRITE_OK: MOV   DX,OFFSET DISK_FULL
               ;until BL <> 0 or error;
                    CMP   BL,0
                    JNZ   END_OF_FILE_BLOCK
                    CMP   BH,0
                    JNZ   END_OF_FILE_BLOCK
                    JMP   READ_BLOCK
;if not error then
END_OF_FILE_BLOCK:CMP   BH,0
                  JNZ   DONE
        ;begin
        ;close object file;
        END_OF_FILE: CLOSE_A_FILE FCB2
        ;DX := address of 'close' error message;
               MOV   DX,OFFSET DISK_WRITE_PROTECTED
        ;if AL <> 0FFH then DX := add of 'normal end' mess
               CMP   AL,0FFH
               JZ    DONE
               MOV   DX,OFFSET NORMAL_END
        ;end;
;print message addressed by DX;
DONE: MOV   AH,09H
      INT   21H
;return to PC-DOS
      RET
START ENDP
CSEG ENDS
END
```

Fig. 11.5 (*continued*)

one for YOURFILE.NEW at 6CH (both relative to DS) just as if the command

```
FILECOPY MYFILE.OLD YOURFILE.NEW
```

had been issued.

EXERCISES 11.4

1. If the file which is to contain the copy already exists, FILECOPY rubs it out without warning the user that it is about to do so. Amend the program so that the user is asked if he or she really does wish to have an existing program rubbed out. If the user doesn't, return control to the operating system.

2. Write an 8088 assembly language program which is to be called up by a command of the form

```
CHANGE PRIVATE.OLD PUBLIC.NEW
```

and which copies the file PRIVATE.OLD into the file PUBLIC.NEW but replaces every occurrence of the string LTD by the string PLC.

3. Write a utility program COUNT which counts the number of occurrences in a file of an alphabetic string of between one and eight characters. This number is then printed on the screen and control is returned to the operating system. For example, to obtain the number of occurrences of the string HUMPTY in the file NURSERY.RYM the program would be called up by the command

```
COUNT NURSERY.RYM HUMPTY
```

11.5 RANDOM ACCESS FILES

The PC-DOS functions for reading and writing files which we have met so far access the files sequentially. That is, they expect us to start at the beginning of a file and step through the file record by record. If access to the records is to be on a more random basis – perhaps we want the customer record for J.BLOGGS and then for R.SMITH and finally for T.ALBANS – then the **random-read** and **random-write** functions should be used.

Both of these require that the record to be accessed is specified in bytes 33D, 34D and 35D of a file control block for the file concerned (provided the default record size of 128 bytes per record has not been altered – see Table 11.2). Records are numbered from zero and record numbers are unsigned 24-bit numbers stored with least significant digits in the first byte, next least significant digits in the next byte and so on. Thus, to access record 13FH of a file, bytes 33D, 34D and 35D of a file control block for that file should be set as follows:

File control block byte	33D	34D	35D
Contents	3FH	01H	00H

Having set the record number, the relevant random access file function can be called up (21H is read-random, 22H is write-random – see Table 11.2) to perform the read or write using that record.

A random access read utility

We shall now write a program which will allow its users to look at any of the first ten records of a (text) file in any order. The assembly language version of the program will be stored in a file called RANDREAD.ASM and will be called into action on a file called MY.TEX by typing the command

```
RANDREAD MY.TEX
```

after the A> operating system prompt. Typing a number n in the range zero to nine inclusive will then cause the nth record of the file MY.TEX to be printed on the display screen. If there is no nth record in the file a question mark (?) will be displayed and the program will wait for another record number to be typed in. The question mark error symbol is likewise displayed if any character other than a digit 0, 1, . . . , 9 is typed, except that typing X terminates the execution of the program.

The method involves glueing together the necessary function calls:

open the file;
if *AL < > 0FFH* **then**
    begin
    read(ch); *print(newline)*;
    while *ch < > 'X'* **do**
        begin
        if *ch in ['0' . .'9']* **then**
            begin
            read the ch-th record;
            if *AL = 0* **then** *print the record*
            end
        else *print error message*;
        read(ch); *print(newline)*
        end;
    end;
return to PC-DOS

An implementation of this pseudo-Pascal outline is given in Fig. 11.6.

```
CR EQU 0DH
LF EQU 0AH
DSEG SEGMENT
ORG  5CH
     FCB                     DB 0
ORG  7DH
     RANDOM_RECORD_NUMBER DW 0
     RANDOM_BLOCK_NUMBER  DB 0
     DTA                     DB 0
DSEG ENDS
SSEG SEGMENT STACK
     DB 100H DUP(?)
SSEG ENDS
OPEN_FILE MACRO FCB
     MOV  AH,0FH
     MOV  DX,OFFSET FCB
     INT  21H
     ENDM

RANDOM_READ MACRO FCB
     MOV  AH,21H
     MOV  DX,OFFSET FCB
     INT  21H
     ENDM
CSEG SEGMENT
     ASSUME CS:CSEG,DS:DSEG,SS:SSEG
START PROC FAR
     PUSH DS
     MOV  AX,0
     PUSH AX
;open the file
OPEN_FILE FCB
;if the file exists then
     CMP  AL,0FFH
     JZ   DONE
    ;begin
    ;read(ch); print(newline);
     MOV  AH,1
     INT  21H
     CALL PRINT_NEWLINE
    ;while ch <> 'X' do
A_RECORD: CMP  AL,'X'
          JZ   DONE
             ;begin
             ;if ch in ['0' .. '9'] then
                 ;begin
                     SUB  AL,30H
                     JAE  CHECK_UPPER_LIMIT
```

Fig. 11.6 The RANDREAD program.

```
                              JMP   KEY_IN
          CHECK_UPPER_LIMIT: CMP   AL,10D
                              JNB   KEY_IN
                      ;read the ch-th record;
                              MOV   AH,0
                              MOV   RANDOM_RECORD_NUMBER,AX
                              MOV   RANDOM_BLOCK_NUMBER,0
                              RANDOM_READ FCB
                      ;if AL = 0 then print the record
                              CMP   AL,0
                              JNZ   KEY_IN
                              CLD
                              MOV   CX,80H
                              MOV   SI,OFFSET DTA
             NEXT_CHARACTER: LODSB
                              CMP   AL,1AH
                              JNZ   PRINT_IT
                              CALL  PRINT_NEWLINE
                              JMP   NEXT
                  PRINT_IT:MOV   DL,AL
                              CALL  PRINT_A_CHARACTER
                              LOOP  NEXT_CHARACTER
                      ;end
                              JMP   READ_NEXT_INS
              ;else print error message;
              KEY_IN: CALL ERROR_MESSAGE
              ;read(ch); print(newline)
       READ_NEXT_INS: CALL PRINT_NEWLINE
                      MOV   AH,1
                      INT   21H
                      CALL  PRINT_NEWLINE
              ;end
               NEXT: JMP   A_RECORD
        ;end
;return to PC-DOS
DONE: RET

PRINT_A_CHARACTER PROC NEAR
      MOV   AH,2
      INT   21H
      RET
PRINT_A_CHARACTER ENDP
PRINT_NEWLINE PROC NEAR
      PUSH AX
      MOV   AH,2
      MOV   DL,CR
      INT   21H
      MOV   DL,LF
      INT   21H
      POP   AX
```

Fig. 11.6   (*continued*)

```
        RET
PRINT_NEWLINE ENDP
ERROR_MESSAGE PROC NEAR
        MOV   AH,2
        MOV   DL,'?'
        INT   21H
        RET
ERROR_MESSAGE ENDP
START ENDP
CSEG ENDS
END
```

Fig. 11.6   (*continued*)

EXERCISES 11.5

1. The error messages in RANDREAD are primitive to say the least. Add more informative error messages to it as well as the ability to display records 0 to 99 inclusive.

2. Construct the counterpart, RANDWRIT, to RANDREAD which operates in much the same way, except that, when digit n is typed, the program then waits for the user to type in 128 characters which are to be stored as record n of the file named when RANDWRIT was called up. Use RANDREAD to check that RANDWRIT works!

12 Device Drivers

AIMS

Pascal compilers are very machine specific as far as I/O is concerned, the 'standard' Pascal I/O features – including read(. . .) and write(. . .) – having to be mapped onto the particular features of the hardware on which the compiler is to run. In this chapter we discuss the programming of some of the IBM PC I/O devices – monochrome and colour display (for alphanumerics and graphics), keyboard, disk drive, printer and speaker – keeping in mind the elementary techniques needed by both compiler writer and operating system designer. Since the 8088 microprocessor must be supported by a number of other device-specific chips to handle interrupts, timing and the display, and so on, we shall necessarily be involved with the programming of these chips. In particular we shall examine examples using the 8259 Interrupt Controller, the 8255 Programmable Peripheral Interface, the 8253 Timer Chip and the 6845 Display Controller. Programmed control of the disk drives at the support chip level is beyond the scope of this book, and so the PC's BIOS is used to access disks at a lower level than that afforded by the DOS INT 21H.

12.1 THE IBM PC PARALLEL PRINTER INTERFACE

To understand how to program the transmission of data to a remote device such as a printer, it is first necessary to remind ourselves that all communication between the various internal parts of a microcomputer is carried out via the **system bus**. This is a sort of motorway for electrons, since electronic signals can travel along the bus in two directions and at very high speeds. All communication must involve the system bus, so sending the character whose ASCII code is in register AL to a printer connected to a microcomputer involves putting the byte in AL onto the system bus. One possibility now is to connect the printer directly to the system bus, but this is impractical in two respects. First, the amount of electrical power used to send signals along the bus is very, very low. This means that using a cable longer than a few centimetres is out of the question – there just isn't enough driving force to push the bits along. The second impracticality arises from the fact that there would then be a direct electrical path from the printer to the microprocessor and other parts of the microcomputer. Consequently, if something were to go wrong with the printer so that a relatively high voltage was suddenly sent back along the bus, it would be possible for the microprocessor and other chips to be destroyed.

External devices are therefore almost always connected not directly to the system bus but to an **interface**. The IBM PC printer interface that we shall describe comes on the Monochrome Display and Printer Adapter, which plugs into a slot inside the back of the IBM PC and allows you to connect both a monochrome monitor and a printer requiring a parallel interface of the Epson type (Epson is the brand name for a variety of computer printer).

The printer interface in the Monochrome Display and Printer Adapter transmits data to the printer in parallel mode. Parallel transmission of the letter A (ASCII code 01000001) to a printer is illustrated in Fig. 12.1. Sections 12.6 and following discuss the programming of the monochrome display circuits in this adapter.

Peripheral interface chips

Some devices which are external to the main microcomputer are capable of both receiving and sending data. Thus a disk drive is, by design, external to the main computer but may receive data to write onto a disk and may also send data read from a disk to an area of memory. If the external device is a printer, communication is one way only as far as our data is concerned. But if we are to be able to take 'intelligent' actions (such as stopping the computer from sending out data to be printed when the printer has run out of paper), some primitive form of two-way communication is essential.

Most interfaces are designed so that a range of such possibilities can be catered for, leaving the programmer to specify his or her requirements. This

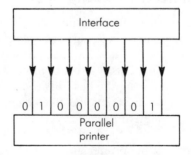

Fig. 12.1 Parallel transmission of the ASCII code for 'A' – eight bits are transmitted at a time, so eight data lines are necessary.

is done by setting certain registers in the **peripheral interface chip** used by the interface. Because of the possible confusion with the main registers of the 8088, peripheral interface chip registers are usually referred to as **ports**. A typical interface may have three or more ports associated with it: a control port, the setting of which will determine if the interface is to send or receive; a data port for the data element to be transmitted or to hold a data element received; and a status port which can be used to obtain information such as 'printer out of paper, don't send any more data' or, for a serial transmission, 'all the bits of the data element haven't yet been received'. Any interface will have at least a data port, but the functions of status port and control port may be combined into one port for a simple interface. On the other hand, sophisticated interfaces may have several control and status ports.

Input and output instructions

Just as locations in memory are referred to by their numeric addresses, so the various ports attached to an 8088-based microcomputer are numbered. There is provision for ports numbered 0 to 0FFFFH. Which port is given which number is more or less determined by the designer of a particular microcomputer. The parallel printer interface on the IBM PC has three 8-bit ports as shown below.

Port function	IBM PC port number
data	3BCH
output control	3BEH
printer status	3BDH

Port number 3BCH is the data port. If this port is set to the ASCII code for a character, and the output control and printer status registers are set correctly, that character will be printed wherever printing last left off.

Setting the data port is accomplished by the 8088 OUT instruction. It has the general formats:

i)   OUT DX, accumulator

ii) OUT port_number, accumulator

where 'accumulator' denotes AL or AX depending on whether an 8-bit or 16-bit port is involved. If the port number is between 0 and 0FFH inclusive then format ii) can be used and the contents of the named register are copied thereby into the specified port. In all other cases format i) must be used, in which case the contents of the named register are copied into the port whose number is given in register DX. Thus the sequence

```
MOV AL,42H
MOV DX,3BCH
OUT DX,AL
```

would set the data port of the parallel printer interface in the Monochrome Display and Printer Adapter to the ASCII code for the letter B.

Having set up the data port we must next check the printer status before telling the printer to print the data. Reading the printer status is carried out by the 8088 IN instruction, which has two general formats corresponding to those for the OUT instruction:

IN accumulator, DX
IN accumulator, port_number

Thus the sequence

```
MOV DX,3BDH
IN   AL,DX
```

copies the contents of the printer status port into AL. The setting of the eight bits in the resulting value signify various printer conditions, as shown in Fig. 12.2 for both the output control and the printer status ports.

To test if the printer is busy we can use the TEST instruction. Remembering that 80H = 10000000B:

```
TEST AL,80H
```

sets the Z-flag if the printer is busy but does not change the contents of AL. If the printer is busy we simply have to wait until it is ready:

```
                MOV   DX,3BDH
TEST_IF_BUSY: IN    AL,DX
                TEST AL,80H
                JZ    TEST_IF_BUSY
```

Each character is sent to the printer following a timing pulse. Once we know that the printer is ready, we use the output control port to send signals which we can therefore regard as being to start and stop the printing of the character in the data port. Since the printer can capture the character from the data port very quickly, the stop and start instructions can come one after another. To start printing the right-most bit of the contents of the output control port must be set to 1; to stop printing it is set back to 0. This must be done for each and every character printed. Lastly, bits 5 and 6 (numbering left to right) must always be set to 1 during printing.

Thus, given that 0DH = 00001101B and that 0CH = 00001100B, the following instruction sequence prints the character whose ASCII code is in the data port, provided the printer is not busy:

```
MOV DX,3BEH
MOV AL,0DH
OUT DX,AL    ;start printing
MOV AL,0CH
OUT DX,AL    ;stop printing
```

Before beginning a session the printer must be initialized by setting bit 6 of

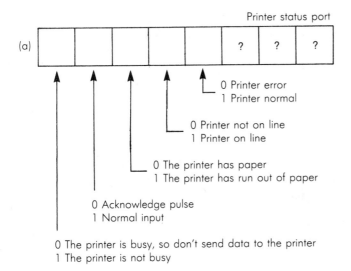

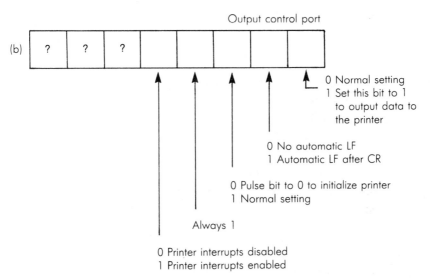

Fig. 12.2 Output control and printer status port configurations.

the output control register to 0 for at least 50 microseconds (0.000050 seconds) and then setting it back to 1. This wait can be timed by executing 50D NOP instructions, which will take longer than 50 microseconds even with the fastest possible 8088 clock.

Putting all this together we can easily construct (Fig. 12.3) the skeleton of a program which will cause the printer to print those printable characters typed at the keyboard. Flesh out the skeleton and test run the resulting program.

```
;initialize the printer
          MOV   DX,3BEH
;set bit 6 of output control port to 0
          MOV   AL,08H
          OUT   DX,AL
          MOV   AL,0CH
          MOV   CX,50D
;wait at least 50 microseconds
     WAIT: NOP
          LOOP WAIT
;repeat read a character from the keyboard
     READ: CALL READCH
     ;transfer character to data port
               MOV   DX,3BCH
               OUT   DX,AL
     ;check if the printer is busy
               MOV   DX,3BDH
TEST_IF_BUSY: IN    AL,DX
               TEST AL,80H
               JZ    TEST_IF_BUSY
     ;now print the character
               MOV   DX,3BEH
               MOV   AL,0DH
     ;start printing
               OUT   DX,AL
               MOV   AL,0CH
     ;stop printing
               OUT   DX,AL
;forever
     JMP   READ
```

Fig. 12.3 Parallel printer control program.

EXERCISES 12.1

1. Enhance the program fragment in Fig. 12.3 so that if the printer runs out of paper a suitable message is displayed on the screen and the program waits until more paper has been inserted. Once this has been done the program should return to normal execution.

2. The bit in position 4 of the printer status port is set to 1 if the printer is on-line (i.e. it is switched on and capable of receiving data from the computer and not left in some printer test mode). If the printer is not on-line this bit is set to 0. Amend the program fragment in Fig. 12.3 so that a suitable message is displayed on the screen if the printer is not on-line, and so that the program waits until it is.

12.2 INTERRUPTS AND TRAPS

Chapter 11 demonstrated the labour-saving advantages of interrupts such as INT 21H, which allows programmers access to file handling routines within the DOS section of PC-DOS. Interrupts are used to access these and other system software resources because they avoid dependence on particular addresses. Thus, if a new version of PC-DOS is issued, programs which we write and which access routines within PC-DOS will still work without alteration if access is through interrupts, whereas if subroutine calls or jump instructions were used (both of which require actual addresses), our programs would require modification to run under the updated PC-DOS. In this and the subsequent two sections we shall examine the 8088 interrupt mechanism in detail and study more of the available PC-DOS interrupt-accessed routines.

A program fragment which watches out for a special condition to occur (such as arithmetic overflow or division by zero) illustrates the concept of a trap. Indeed, we refer to such program fragments as 'trap on overflow', 'trap on division by zero' etc. The trap facility is specially associated with the flag register's trap flag. No instructions are provided for setting and clearing the trap flag directly, but it can be set by modifying the flag register as in

```
PUSHF
POP    AX
OR     AX,0100H
PUSH   AX
POPF
```

which sets the trap flag to 1.

If the trap flag is set to 1, the 8088 causes a type 1 interrupt to occur after each and every instruction has been executed, a facility which can be useful when debugging hardware systems using the 8088 (DEBUG provides this facility for software development).

All interrupts cause an automatic transfer to a location where an **interrupt service routine** is stored. The interrupt service routine is executed and sequential execution resumes from where it left off before the interrupt. Software interrupts are caused by executing an INT instruction which has the general format

INT interrupt-type

where interrupt-type is a whole number between 0 and 255. For a software interrupt of a given type, the 4-byte address of the interrupt service routine – the **interrupt vector** – is stored at an address calculated by multiplying the interrupt type by 4. Hence, the interrupt vector for INT 21H will be found at location (21*4)H, i.e. 84H. Figure 12.4 illustrates this mechanism.

All the first 400H absolute locations in memory are thus taken up with interrupt vectors, most of which are reserved for PC-DOS or BASIC use,

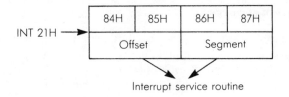

Fig. 12.4 The software interrupt mechanism.

but the programmer can employ vectors at addresses 100H–1FFH (absolute) for his or her own purposes (these correspond to interrupt types 40H–7FH). For example, execution of INT 5 will cause a transfer of control to the address given in the interrupt vector at absolute locations 14–17H inclusive where there is code to send the screen contents to the printer. Table 12.1 summarizes PC-DOS interrupt types and their functions.

On executing an INT instruction, the flag register and offset and segment addresses of the interrupted program are saved on the stack, the trap and interrupt-enable flags are cleared (thus prohibiting further interrupts), and CS and IP are loaded with the address of the interrupt service routine. In detail, the action is:

1. Decrement SP by 2.
2. Push flag register onto stack.
3. Clear trap and interrupt-enable flags, thus disabling further interrupts.
4. Decrement SP by 2.
5. Push current CS onto stack.
6. Load CS with segment address from interrupt vector.
7. Decrement SP by 2.
8. Push current IP onto stack.
9. Load IP with offset address from interrupt vector.

Following execution of an interrupt service routine, a return to the program which was interrupted is effected by the **IRET** (Interrupt RETurn) instruction, which pops the top two stack bytes into IP, the next two stack bytes into CS and the succeeding two stack bytes into the flags register.

Hardware interrupts

Software interrupts aid programmer productivity in a way which doesn't increase program maintenance costs as a computer manufacturer upgrades its operating system. But the principal reason for having interrupts is to provide an efficient way for external devices to get the attention of the 8088. Rather than us having to check at regular intervals whether a key on the keyboard has been pressed, the keyboard hardware itself can send a pulse

Table 12.1 Summary of PC-DOS interrupt types and their functions.

Type	Vector address		Interrupt purpose
0	0–3	8088	Division by zero
1	4–7	interrupts	Single step
2	8–B		Non-maskable interrupt (NMI)
3	C–F		Breakpoint
4	10–13		Overflow
5	14–17		Print screen
6, 7	18–1B		Reserved
8	20–23	8259	Timer
9	24–27	hardware	Keyboard
A, B, C, D	28–37	interrupts	Reserved
E	38–3B		Disk
F	3C–3F		Reserved
10	40–43	Software	Display I/O
11	44–47	interrupts	Equipment check
12	48–4B	to BIOS	Memory size check
13	4C–4F		Disk I/O
14	50–53		Communication I/O
15	54–57		Cassette I/O
16	58–5B		Keyboard input
17	5C–5F		Printer I/O
18	60–63	Software	ROM BASIC
19	64–67	interrupts	Bootstrap from disk
1A	68–6B		Time of day
1B	6C–6F		Keyboard break
1C	70–73		Timer strobe
1D	74–77	Table pointers	Video table pointer
1E	78–7B		Disk table pointer
1F	7C–7F		Graphics character table pointer
20	80–83	Interrupts	Terminate program
21	84–87	to DOS	Function calls
22	88–8B		Program termination address
23	8C–8F		CTRL-BREAK exit address
24	90–93		Fatal error
25	94–97		Absolute disk read
26	98–9B		Absolute disk write
27	9C–9F		End program, remain resident
28–3F	A0–FF		Reserved: used by DOS
40–7F	100–1FF	User interrupts	
80–F0	200–3C3	BASIC interrupts	

along the interrupt line of the 8088 to demand attention. The mechanism is the same as for a software interrupt, except that the hardware arranges that the 8088 knows the type of interrupt the electrical pulse has signalled. On the IBM PC keyboard, pressing or releasing a key causes an interrupt equivalent to executing the INT 9 instruction. When such an interrupt is received, the 8088 can break off from its current task – though note that, with all interrupts, the current instruction being executed is first completed – service the keyboard, and return to the original task. Because both hardware interrupts and INT disable further interrupts within an interrupt service routine, that routine is executed without interruption unless we so wish. Often there has to be a priority order in which interrupts are dealt with, the keyboard coming higher in priority than other external devices so that, for example, CTRL-BREAK and CTRL-ALT-DELETE can be used to return control to the operating system or reboot whilst a user program is running.

Non-maskable interrupts use a special line into the 8088 to signal an interrupt which takes overriding priority, even when interrupts have otherwise been disabled. For example, the type 2 interrupt is non-maskable for it signals a memory parity error indicating a hardware misfunction.

Enabling and disabling interrupts within an 8088 assembly language program is carried out via the **STI** (SeT Interrupt-enable flag) and **CLI** (CLear Interrupt-enable flag) instructions. STI enables all maskable interrupts, CLI disables them.

Figure 12.5 contains a complete program example using interrupts. In it, we reset the type 0 interrupt vector so that instead of pointing to the DOS routine for a division-by-zero error the vector points to our own interrupt service routine. This simply sets register AX to 0FFFFH and then returns from the interrupt. The main program reads two digits from the keyboard (having numeric equivalent, say, a and b), and prints out the result of a **div** b. If b is zero so that the divide-by-zero interrupt has set AX to 0FFFFH, a letter X is printed to denote exceptional circumstances.

Notice that we disable interrupts whilst the divide-by-zero error interrupt vector is reset. Were interrupts allowed during this process, a divide-by-zero error occurring somewhere deep in the operating system's code would crash the system trying to access an interrupt service routine at a garbled address.

There are two special interrupt instructions. **INTO** (INTerrupt on Overflow) generates a type 4 interrupt if the overflow flag is set to 1. It is up to the programmer to provide an appropriate interrupt service routine – if required – and to set the type 4 vector to point to that routine: DOS initializes this to point to a single IRET instruction. On the other hand, a type 3 interrupt is special because it has both a normal 2-byte op-code like all instructions of the form INT n and a single byte op-code. This is because a type 3 interrupt can be used to provide program breakpoints, i.e. addresses at which it is desired to discontinue program execution, probably for the purpose of debugging.

```
DSEG SEGMENT
ZERO_DIVISOR DW ?
DSEG ENDS

SSEG SEGMENT STACK
      DB 100H DUP(?)
SSEG ENDS

CSEG SEGMENT
ASSUME CS:CSEG,DS:DSEG,SS:SSEG
START PROC FAR
              PUSH DS
              MOV  AX,0
              PUSH AX
;change interrupt vector
              MOV  AX,0
              MOV  ES,AX
;disable interrupts while resetting the interrupt vector
              CLI
              MOV  ES:ZERO_DIVISOR,OFFSET OUR_ZERO_DIVISOR_ROUTINE
              MOV  ES:ZERO_DIVISOR+2,SEG OUR_ZERO_DIVISOR_ROUTINE
;enable interrupts again
              STI
;read a character from the keyboard
              MOV  AH,1
              INT  21H
;convert it to numeric form: a
              SUB  AL,30H
              MOV  BL,AL
;read another character
              MOV  AH,1
              INT  21H
;convert it to numeric form: b
              SUB  AL,30H
;calculate a/b
              MOV  AH,0
              XCHG AL,BL
              DIV  BL
;result now in AL
              CMP  AX,0FFFFH
              JNZ  DIVISION_OK
              MOV  AL,'X'
              JMP  PRINT_RESULT
  DIVISION_OK: ADD  AL,30H
PRINT_RESULT: MOV  DL,AL
              MOV  AH,2
              INT  21H
              RET
START ENDP
OUR_ZERO_DIVISOR_ROUTINE: MOV  AX,0FFFFH
                          IRET
CSEG ENDS
END
```

Fig. 12.5 Program to change the divide-by-zero interrupt.

To implement a breakpoint, the first byte of the instruction at the breakpoint address is replaced with the single-byte type 3 interrupt instruction. This causes an interrupt to occur when an attempt is made to execute the instruction which starts at that location, and the interrupt service routine can now display the status of registers and memory as required. Typically, the instruction byte replaced by the type 3 interrupt will have been saved so that it can be restored and executed when the debugging routine allows the program to continue.

The single-byte form is essential when replacing single-byte instructions at breakpoints, since otherwise an earlier jump to the location following the breakpoint might be corrupted.

EXERCISES 12.2

1. Edit the program in Fig. 12.5 so that everything remains the same except for the statements which reset the division-by-zero vector. Remove these and re-assemble, link and run the program for the following trial pairs of operands: (6, 3), (1, 4), (8, 0).

2. Write a mini-version, MINDEBUG, of DEBUG which uses type 1 and type 3 interrupts to offer its users the following facilities.

   Assuming a program is loaded in memory starting at CS:IP, it should accept any number of commands of two types: *either* the command S which executes one single step of the given program, *or* a breakpoint address in the range 0–0FFH. By repeating S commands the user should be able to work through the program looking at the contents of registers AX, BX, CX and DX on the way. Once a breakpoint has been set, execution resumes from the previous breakpoint (or the beginning of the program) until that breakpoint is reached. Then the contents of registers AX, BX, CX and DX are displayed.

3. Write a program similar to that in Fig. 12.5, providing an overflow error interrupt service routine which prints ARITHMETIC OVERFLOW and sets DX to 0FFFFH if the overflow flag is set to 1, and a main program which accepts a digit typed in at the keyboard and adds its numeric value to 7CH via an ADD BL,AL instruction and either prints out the result in hexadecimal if there is no overflow, or prints the letter X otherwise, thereafter returning to the operating system.

WAIT, ESC, HLT and LOCK

HLT and WAIT suspend the execution of instructions pending electronic (i.e. not software) interruptions of some kind. Thus the **HLT** instruction HaLTs the processor until a hardware interrupt is received by the 8088, after which normal execution resumes, while the **WAIT** instruction halts pending either a hardware interrupt or the arrival of the appropriate electronic signal on the TEST input of the 8088 chip, after which the wait state resumes.

The **ESC** (ESCape) instruction has the format

ESC external op-code,source

and causes no action to be taken as far as the 8088 is concerned. Rather it is used to initiate action by another attached processor (e.g. the 8087 Numeric Data Processor), for the 6-bit op-code specified as part of the instruction is placed on the system bus for examination by another processor. Once it has been fetched, the source operand (which may be in memory or a register) is also placed on the bus.

LOCK is useful in resource scheduling and synchronization, for example when several independent 8088 processors share the same memory. To prevent one processor accessing a location in shared memory while another processor is changing the contents of that location, the LOCK instruction – used as a prefix to a main instruction – sends an electronic signal from the LOCK output of the 8088.

12.3 BIOS AND DOS

The IBM PC **BIOS** (Basic Input Output System) is a set of 8088 programs which are held in ROM and which initialize the entire system when the PC is turned on. In addition, these programs provide the minimum software support necessary to control the various devices that may be attached to the computer.

On power up, the 8088 enters its reset state wherein CS is set to 0FFFFH and IP to 0. Hence, the first instruction the 8088 will execute is at absolute address 0FFFF0H which is part of the memory allocated to ROM. Through this instruction the BIOS gains control, interrogates the various I/O ports to determine which devices are attached, initializes those which are, emits a beep from the speaker and then sets up the interrupt service routine address table. Since this table contains addresses within the BIOS itself we can access them via the INT instruction. Table 12.2 lists some of the BIOS routines and corresponding INT types. More complete information can be obtained from the complete listing of the BIOS to be found in the IBM PC technical manual.

If the BIOS discovers that a disk drive is attached to the system, it will bootstrap the DOS. DOS fills in additional entries in the interrupt vector table before issuing the 'Enter Date' command. With DOS booted, the memory-map of the PC is as shown in Fig. 12.6.

Apart from INT 21H (the facilities offered by which, it should be noted, are at a much higher level than those of the BIOS interrupt service routines in Table 12.1), DOS provides seven other interrupts which may be of use to the programmer. These are summarized in Table 12.3. Full details can be found in the DOS manual, Appendix D.

Table 12.2 Some BIOS routines and their interrupt types.

Interrupt	Register settings	Registers altered	Effect
INT 10H	Display output AH = 0. AL = 0: 40 * 25 black and white AL = 1: 40 * 25 colour AL = 2: 80 * 25 black and white AL = 3: 80 * 25 colour AL = 4: 320 * 200 colour AL = 5: 320 * 200 black and white AL = 6: 640 * 200 black and white	AX, SI, DI, BP	Sets display to the mode specified by the AL register.
	AH = 2, BH = 0 DH = row DL = column	AX, SI, DI, BP	Set cursor on screen to position specified. Row 0, column 0 is upper left corner.
	AH = 14, BX = 0 AL = character	AX, SI, DI, BP	Display character specified on screen at current cursor position and advance cursor.
INT 13H	Disk I/O AH = 0	AX	Reset disk system. AH = disk status
	AH = 1	AX	Read disk status. AH = disk status
	AH = 2 DL = drive (0–3) DH = side (0–1) CH = track (0–39) CL = sector (1–8) AL = number of sectors (1–8) BX = address of area to be filled within extra segment	AX	Read the specified sector(s) into memory. AH = disk status CF = 0 if successful CF = 1 if error
	AH = 3 DL = drive (0–3) DH = side (0–1) CH = track (0–39) CL = sector (1–8) AL = number of sectors (1–8) BX = address of area containing data to be written, within extra segment	AX	Write the specified sector(s) from memory. AH = disk status CF = 0 if successful CF = 1 if error

Table 12.2   (*continued*)

Interrupt	Register settings	Registers altered	Effect
INT 16H	Keyboard input		
	AH = 0	AX	Read character from keyboard into AL.
	AH = 1	AX	Set ZF = 0 if any key has been pressed, otherwise ZF = 1.
	AH = 2	AX	Return shift key status in the bits of AL register: Bit 1 = INSERT key Bit 2 = CAPS LOCK Bit 3 = NUM LOCK Bit 4 = SCROLL LOCK Bit 5 = ALT SHIFT Bit 6 = CTRL SHIFT Bit 7 = left SHIFT Bit 8 = right SHIFT (numbering left to right)
INT 17H	Printer output		
	AH = 0, DX = 0 AL = character	AH	Print character specified in AL register.
	AH = 1, DX = 0	AH	Initialize printer.
	AH = 2, DX = 0	AH	Return printer status in the bits of the AH register: 1: set to 1 if busy 2: acknowledge signal 3: 1 if out of paper 4: select signal 5: 1 if error 6, 7: unused 8: 1 if timeout (numbering left to right)

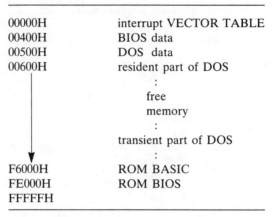

00000H	interrupt VECTOR TABLE
00400H	BIOS data
00500H	DOS data
00600H	resident part of DOS
	:
	free
	memory
	:
	transient part of DOS
	:
F6000H	ROM BASIC
FE000H	ROM BIOS
FFFFFH	

Fig. 12.6   The PC memory map under DOS.

EXERCISES 12.3

1. Without using any software interrupts other than BIOS INT 16H and INT 10H, write a program which simply copies what is typed at the keyboard onto the display screen. Be sure that upper and lower case are faithfully displayed. For control keys, display an exclamation mark (!).

2. Under the same constraints as in Exercise 1 above, write a program which allows its users to type in the abbreviations on the left of the following list and displays their full equivalent shown on the right-hand side:

Abbreviation	Full equivalent
E.	ERASE
D.	DIRECTORY
R.	RENAME
T.	TYPE

12.4   SYSTEM SUPPORT CHIPS

System support chips undertake a variety of tasks which enable the computing power derivable from the 8088 microprocessor to be maximized. For example, the 8237 DMA controller chip effectively allows the 8088 direct memory access, i.e. the 8088 can program this chip with an iteration count and a memory start address, command an I/O device to begin a read or write sequence, and the data transfer will take place without using any more of the 8088's time. The 8237 allows up to four independent DMA

Table 12.3 DOS interrupts.

Interrupt	Function
20H	Program termination.
21H	Function call.
22H	Terminate and transfer control to termination address.
23H	Activated when CTRL-BREAK is pressed.
24H	Fatal error.
25H	Absolute disk read – select by sectors.
26H	Absolute disk write – select by sectors.
27H	Terminate current program but keep it in memory.
28H–35H	Reserved for DOS use.

operations to take place at the same time. One of these operations is the continuous process of refreshing the RAM chips so that the data they hold is not forgotten, and another is used by the disk drive interface. Apart from the 8237, the most important of the control chips used on the PC system board are the 8259 interrupt controller chip, the 8253 timer chip (see Section 12.8) and the 8255 programmable peripheral interface chip. All of these chips are programmable, each of them containing one or more internal registers which can be accessed via the IN and OUT instructions using an appropriate port address as given in Table 12.4.

On power-up, the BIOS configures the 8259 internally to correspond to its physical connections on the PC system board. Because the 8088 has just one input line on which to receive a normal (i.e. not a non-maskable) interrupt, the task of the 8259 is to queue up interrupts from all the eight

Table 12.4 I/O addresses for the 8259, 8253 and 8255 chips.

8259 interrupt controller	
20H	Interrupt command register
21H	Interrupt mask register
8253 timer chip	
40H	Timer channel 0 latch register access
41H	Timer channel 1 latch register access
42H	Timer channel 2 latch register access
43H	Timer command register
8255 programmable peripheral interface	
60H	Input port, PA
61H	Input/output port, PB
62H	Input port, PC
63H	Command register

Table 12.5   Type codes associated with 8259 interrupt sources
(lower codes have higher priority).

Interrupt source	Type code	Corresponding interrupt mask register bit (numbering left to right)
8253 timer chip	08H	8
Keyboard	09H	7
Colour/graphics*	0AH	6
Unused	0BH	5
RS232 serial interface*	0CH	4
Unused	0DH	3
Disk interface	0EH	2
Printer	0FH	1

*denotes 'if present in system as configured'.

possible sources – keyboard, disk drive etc. – and present them one by one
to the 8088 along with a unique interrupt type as shown in Table 12.5.

Thanks to BIOS initialization, programming the 8259 consists of either
enabling or disabling each interrupt source by outputting a value to the
interrupt mask register or signalling the end of an interrupt service routine
by sending 20H to the interrupt command register within the 8259 –
essential so that the next queued interrupt in order of priority can be passed
on to the 8088. The 8259 interrupt mask register is a 1-byte register accessed
through I/O port 21H; setting a given bit to 1 disables (or masks) interrupts
from the corresponding source, and setting that bit to 0 enables interrupts
from that source. Table 12.5 shows the correspondence. Thus, the fragment

```
MOV AL,7FH
OUT 21H,AL
```

disables interrupts from all devices except the printer and, since the
interrupt command register is at I/O port 20H,

```
MOV AL,20H
OUT 20H,AL
```

signals the end of an interrupt service routine.

The 8255 Programmable Peripheral Interface Chip contains three
registers of interest to us – PA, PB and PC – located at I/O ports 60H, 61H
and 62H respectively. There is also a 1-byte command register on the chip
which the BIOS initializes so that PA and PC are configured for input and
PB for output. Figure 12.7 shows the significance of the bits in these
registers, the situation being slightly complicated by the ability to select two
sources of input to each of PA and PC by setting certain bits to PB. Note
that we can read back the last value which was written to PB by inputting
from PB.

Port PA (60H) PB bit 1 set to 0

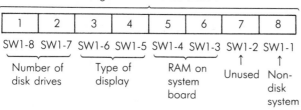

Port PA (60H) PB bit 1 set to 1

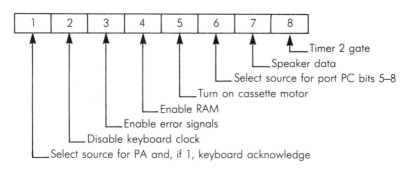

Port PB (61H)

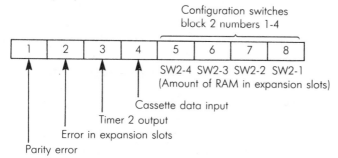

Port PC (62H) PB bit 6 set to 1

Fig. 12.7 8255 registers PA, PB and PC.

Port PC (62H) PB bit 6 set to 0

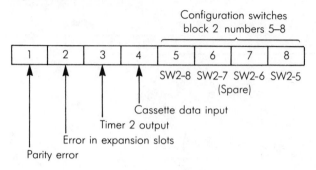

Fig. 12.7   (*continued*)

EXERCISE 12.4

The following program fragment leaves in AL the number of disk drives attached to the system:

```
IN   AL,61H
OR   AL,80H ;set bit 1 of PB
OUT  61H,AL
IN   AL,60H ;examine PA
NOT  AL
MOV  CL,6
SHR  AL,CL  ;isolate the relevant bits of PA
```

Using this and similar fragments, write a program which prints on the display screen the number of disk drives attached to the system and the amoûnt of RAM on the system board. (Codings for switch settings can be found in the manual.)

12.5   A SIMPLE KEYBOARD DRIVER

The PC keyboard is interfaced to the rest of the system through the interrupt mechanism and ports PA and PB of the 8255. In this section we shall program this interface to produce our own keyboard support software. In fact, we shall turn the PC into a sort of typewriter (!), but, as always, it is the principles involved which are important here, not the real world usefulness of our example program. Although we shall use the BIOS INT 10H interrupt to display characters typed in, all the handling of keyboard input will be performed by our software.

Within the keyboard itself is hardware which receives its basic power and clock signals from the main PC system board and which scans for and detects any change in the state of the keys. It is enabled by setting bits 1 and 2 (numbering from left to right) of port PB to 0 and 1 respectively. If this is done, the keyboard will send an interrupt to the 8259 whenever any key is

Function keys

F1	59	F5	63	F9	67
F2	60	F6	64	F10	68
F3	61	F7	65		
F4	62	F8	66		

Alphanumeric and punctuation keys

1	2	Y	21	'	40
2	3	U	22	#	41
3	4	I	23	\	43
4	5	O	24	Z	44
5	6	P	25	X	45
6	7	{	26	C	46
7	8	}	27	V	47
8	9	A	30	B	48
9	10	S	31	N	49
0	11	D	32	M	50
-	12	F	33	,	51
=	13	G	34	.	52
Q	16	H	35	/	53
W	17	J	36	PrtSc	55
E	18	K	37	SPACE BAR	57
R	19	L	38		
T	20	;	39		

Numeric keypad area

7	71	5	76	3	81
8	72	6	77	0	82
9	73	+	78	.	83
−	74	1	79		
4	75	2	80		

Control keys

ESC	1	TAB	15	Right SHIFT	54
BACKSPACE	14	ENTER	28	ALT	56
NUM LOCK	69	CTRL	29	CAPS LOCK	58
SCROLL LOCK	70	Left SHIFT	42		

Fig. 12.8 Keyboard scan codes (in decimal).

pressed or released. After that, it sends a 1-byte **scan code** to the system board and waits for an acknowledge signal. The programmer provides this by setting bit 1 of port PB to 1 momentarily.

Dealing with the keyboard interrupt is also the responsibility of the keyboard support software. The scan code transmitted to the system board can be obtained by reading port PA of the 8255 chip. It will be a number between 1 and 83 (there are 83 keys on the PC keyboard) uniquely identifying which key changed state and whether the key was pressed or released. Figure 12.8 shows the decimal scan codes associated with each keyboard key. In 8-bit binary forms the highest order bit is set to 0 to indicate that the key was pressed and to 1 to indicate that the key was released.

The specification of our simple keyboard driver program

Since the scan code can be interpreted in any way we please, the meaning of each key is decided by the keyboard support software. Of course, the usual meaning of a given key depends on whether the SHIFT or CTRL key is also being pressed and on whether the CAPS LOCK key has been pressed. To focus better on the essential processes involved, our example program will ignore such factors and give a single response (if any) to each key depression, that is if a key normally corresponds to a printable character then that character will be displayed on the screen, otherwise nothing happens.

Taking special action on the simultaneous depression of two keys such as CTRL and A requires the software to store sequences of scan codes and react accordingly. Indeed, a buffer of the order of 100 bytes in length is normally employed to give users a 'type-ahead' facility. Once again we shall simplify the programming task by employing a 1-byte buffer, and the reader will be invited to expand our simple example into a more realistic program in Exercises 12.5. In this 1-byte buffer, we shall store the rogue value 0FFH whenever we are waiting for a keyboard interrupt to arrive.

Figure 12.9 gives the complete keyboard driver program. As usual, the reader is invited to type in the complete program and to try it out. Because of our 1-byte buffer and response to scan-codes, the important control key combinations CTRL-BREAK and CTRL-ALT-DEL are ignored by our keyboard driver program. Consequently, running it will lock up the machine and the only way to exit is to turn the machine off.

EXERCISES 12.5

1. Augment the buffer in our keyboard driver to a (circular) queue of length 50H.

2. Using the version with larger buffer from Exercise 1 above, alter the interpretation of scan-codes so that upper and lower case are correctly displayed.

3. Add to the version prepared in Exercise 2 above the facility to recognize CTRL codes. If, for example, CTRL-Z is pressed then ^Z should be printed on the screen.

4. Add to the version prepared in Exercise 3 above the ability to return to PC-DOS if CTRL-BREAK is pressed.

```
LF EQU 0AH
CR EQU 0DH

DSEG SEGMENT
KEYBOARD_CHARACTER DB 0FFH
SCAN_TABLE DB 0,0,'1234567890-=',8,0
           DB 'QWERTYUIOP{}',0DH,0
           DB 'ASDFGHJKL;',0,0,0,0
           DB 'ZXCVBNM,./',0,0,0
           DB ' ',0,0,0,0,0,0,0,0,0,0,0,0,0
           DB '789-456+1230'
DSEG ENDS

SSEG SEGMENT STACK
           DB 100H DUP(?)
SSEG ENDS

CSEG SEGMENT
ASSUME CS:CSEG,DS:DSEG,SS:SSEG
;establish data segment addressability
     MOV AX,DSEG
     MOV DS,AX
;set up our own keyboard interrupt service routine (KISR)
;disable all interrupts
     CLI
;set ES register to segment address of KISR
     MOV AX,0
     MOV ES,AX
;set DI to offset of vector for INT 09H
     MOV DI,09H*4
;set AX to offset address of our own KISR
     MOV AX,OFFSET KISR
;place new KISR in the interrupt vector table
     CLD
     STOSW
     MOV AX,CS
     STOSW
;program the 8259 to allow timer and keyboard interrupts only
     MOV AL,0FCH
     OUT 21H,AL
;enable interrupts to the 8088
     STI
;main program loop
;repeat
FOR_EVER: CALL GET_CHAR
          PUSH AX
          CALL DISPLAY_CHAR
          POP  AX
          ;if character read was a CR
          CMP  AL,CR
```

Fig. 12.9 The keyboard driver program.

```
                    JNZ   REPEAT_LOOP
                    ;then print an LF as well
                    MOV   AL,LF
                    CALL DISPLAY_CHAR
     ;forever
     REPEAT_LOOP: JMP FOR_EVER
     ;********************************************************
         GET_CHAR:    CLI
                      ;while KEYBOARD_CHARACTER = OFFH do
                      CMP   KEYBOARD_CHARACTER,OFFH
                      JNZ   RESET_ROGUE_VALUE
                          ;wait
                          STI
                          JMP GET_CHAR
                      ;return scan code for key in AL
     RESET_ROGUE_VALUE: MOV   AL,KEYBOARD_CHARACTER
                      ;reset rogue value
                      MOV   KEYBOARD_CHARACTER,OFFH
                      RET
     ;********************************************************
     KISR: PUSH BX
           PUSH AX ;save registers which will be altered
           ;read the keyboard input from 8255 port PA
           IN    AL,60H
           PUSH AX
           ;read 8255 port PB
           IN    AL,61H
           ;set keyboard acknowledge signal
           OR    AL,80H
           ;send keyboard acknowledge signal
           OUT   61H,AL
           ;reset keyboard acknowledge signal
           AND   AL,7FH
           ;restore original 8255 port PB
           OUT   61H,AL
           ;decode the scan code received
           POP   AX
           ;if it is not a key being released then
           TEST AL,80H
           JNZ   SEND_EOI
               ;begin
               ;convert scan code to ASCII
               MOV BX,OFFSET SCAN_TABLE
               XLATB
               ;if it is printable ASCII then
               CMP AL,0
               JZ  SEND_EOI
               ;then put it into KEYBOARD_CHARACTER
               MOV KEYBOARD_CHARACTER,AL
```

Fig. 12.9 (*continued*)

```
                  ;end;
             ;indicate the end of interrupt to the 8259
SEND_EOI: MOV   AL,20H
          OUT   20H,AL
          ;restore altered registers
          POP   AX
          POP   BX
          IRET
;*******************************************************
DISPLAY_CHAR: PUSH BX
              MOV  BX,0
              MOV  AH,14
              INT  10H
              POP  BX
              RET

CSEG ENDS
END
```

Fig. 12.9   (*continued*)

12.6   THE MONOCHROME DISPLAY

The Monochrome Display and Printer Adapter supports an 80-column by 25-line screen image, thus allowing $80 * 25 = 2000$ characters to be displayed at the same time. It contains 4 Kbytes of memory, addressable by the 8088 at absolute locations 0B0000H and following. Starting at 0B0000H, each location having an even-numbered address contains a character representation for a character to be displayed in the corresponding screen position, and each odd-numbered location contains an **attribute byte**, specifying the manner in which the associated character is to be displayed (normal video, reverse video, blinking etc.). Figure 12.10 shows the possible settings for the attribute byte.

The correspondence between display memory location and screen position is as follows. Rows are numbered 0–24, with row 0 at the top of the screen, and columns 0–79, with column 0 at the left of the screen. If we wish to place a character on the screen in row y and column x, then the (ASCII) code for that character must be placed in location 0B0000H + ($y * 160D$) + ($x * 2$) and its attribute byte in the following location. Hence, to display a character in the top left-hand corner of the screen (row 0, column 0), the two corresponding memory bytes are in locations 0B0000H + (0 * 160D) + (0 * 2) = 0B0000H and 0B0000H + 1. Likewise, to display a character in the bottom right-hand corner (row 24, column 79), the two corresponding bytes are in locations 0B0000H + (24 * 160D) + (79 * 2) = 0B0F9EH and 0B0F9EH + 1.

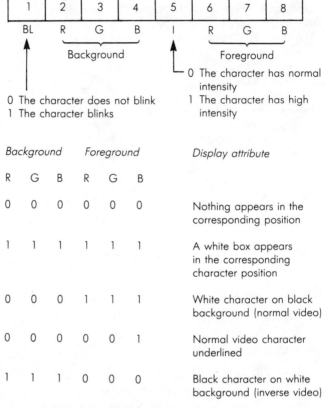

Fig. 12.10   Monochrome display attribute byte settings.

Each character displayed can be one of 256 images, since the monochrome display adapter uses an extended ASCII code. Thus, whilst the second table in Appendix I shows the images of characters with codes 20H to 7EH, higher (non-control) codes give fancier characters such as Greek letters, French and German accents, and teletext-like block graphics. Figure 12.11 contains a complete program which displays all possible character images. There are eight possible (non-blank) display attributes, so the user is expected to enter a digit in the range 1–8, in which case all the character images are displayed with a corresponding attribute. Pressing any other key (except keys such as SHIFT and CTRL) clears the screen and returns control to PC-DOS. If a digit in the given range was entered and all the character images have been displayed, then entering another digit causes the cycle to be repeated, but for the new attribute value. Note that this program may not work with a colour display – it depends on the settings of the configuration switches inside the PC.

```
DSEG SEGMENT
ATTRIBUTES EQU THIS BYTE
NORMAL                  DB 07H
UNDERLINE               DB 01H
REVERSE                 DB 70H
INTENSE                 DB 0FH
BLINK                   DB 87H
INTENSE_AND_BLINK       DB 8FH
REVERSE_AND_BLINK       DB 0F0H
REV_AND_INT_AND_BLINK DB 0F8H
DSEG ENDS

SSEG SEGMENT STACK
        DB   100H DUP(?)
SSEG ENDS

CSEG SEGMENT
ASSUME CS:CSEG,DS:DSEG,SS:SSEG
START PROC FAR
;set up for return to PC-DOS
        PUSH DS
        MOV  AX,0
        PUSH AX
;establish data segment addressability
        MOV  AX,DSEG
        MOV  DS,AX
;set ES to point to display memory
        MOV  AX,0B000H
        MOV  ES,AX
;clear the screen
        CLD
        MOV  DI,0
        MOV  AL,' '
        MOV  AH,NORMAL
        MOV  CX,2000D
        REP  STOSW
;read(ch) through the BIOS so no screen echo
        MOV  AH,0
        INT  16H
;while ch in ['1' .. '8'] do
IN_RANGE: CMP  AL,31H
        JC   DONE
        CMP  AL,39H
        JNC  DONE
        ;begin
```

Fig. 12.11 A program to display all possible character images.

```
                        ;set the attribute value in AH
                                SUB   AL,31H
                                MOV   BL,AL
                                MOV   BH,0H
                                MOV   AH,ATTRIBUTES[BX]
                        ;DI := start of row 1
                        ;display character code(AL) := 0
                                MOV   DI,(1*160D)+(0*2)
                                MOV   AL,0
                        ;column count(DH) := 0
                                MOV   DH,0
                        ;repeat display char with code in AL, attribute in AH
                NEXT_CHARACTER: MOV   ES:[DI]+1,AH
                                MOV   ES:[DI],AL
                            ;miss a column before next character
                                ADD   DI,4
                                ADD   DH,2
                            ;if we're now beyond column 79
                                CMP   DH,79D
                                JB    NEXT_CODE
                            ;then begin
                            ;skip a line
                                ADD   DI,160
                            ;reset column counter
                                MOV   DH,0
                            ;end;
                            ;next character code
                    NEXT_CODE: INC   AL
                ;until code in AL is 0H
                            CMP   AL,0H
                            JZ    NEXT_ATTRIBUTE
                            JMP   NEXT_CHARACTER
        ;read(ch) through BIOS so no screen echo
        NEXT_ATTRIBUTE: MOV   AH,0
                        INT   16H
                        JMP   IN_RANGE
        ;blank out screen
        DONE: MOV   DI,0
              MOV   AL,' '
              MOV   AH,NORMAL
              MOV   CX,2000D
              REP   STOSW
        ;return to PC-DOS
              RET

        START ENDP
        CSEG ENDS
        END
```

Fig. 12.11   (*continued*)

12.7 A MONOCHROME DISPLAY DRIVER

The 6845 CRT controller

The main component responsible for the positioning of the cursor within the ,
Monochrome Display and Printer Adapter is the 6845, the Cathode Ray
Tube Controller (CRTC) chip. Just as in an ordinary television, the image
on the PC display is built up by an electron beam which scans the screen line
by line from the top downwards. The designers of the IBM PC decided that,
on the monochrome display, each character should be nine scan lines high
with a further five scan lines providing 'blank' space between lines of display
text. In fact, each character can be regarded as consisting of a collection of
dots (see Fig. 12.12): nine dots high (corresponding to the nine scan lines)
and seven dots wide (with two further dots providing the space between
successive characters).

Apart from cursor positioning, it is the responsibility of the 6845 to
select each character code to be displayed from the adapter memory, to
select which scan row of a character should be displayed, to synchronize
operations between the other components in the monochrome display
adapter and to generate the cursor image.

Table 12.6 shows a list of the 6845 ports and their functions. In fact a
total of 16 registers within the 6845 have to be accessed through two ports.
Thus, if we want to access the cursor start register of the 6845, we must
first place its register number (10D) in port 3B4H; outputting to port 35BH
will then in fact be setting the cursor start register.

The horizontal registers determine the number of characters per line
and the width of each character, and the vertical registers the number of
characters per column and the number of scan lines per character. These are

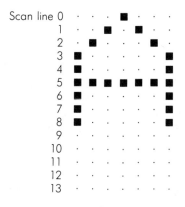

Fig. 12.12 Display of the letter A with the monochrome display adapter.

Table 12.6 The 6845 ports and corresponding registers.

PC port address	6845 register	Register number	Description
3B4H	Address register		
3B5H	Horizontal registers	0–3	Control horizontal characteristics of the display.
	Vertical registers	4–9	Control vertical display characteristics.
	Cursor start	10	Define cursor image as in Fig. 12.13.
	Cursor end	11	
	Start address high	12	Determine which part of the adapter
	Start address low	13	memory is used.
	Cursor address high	14	Determine the display position of the
	Cursor address low	15	cursor.

initialized by the BIOS and it is beyond the scope of this book to discuss their use. Interested readers may like to consult the BIOS listing in the PC Technical Manual.

Figure 12.13 shows the significance of bits in the cursor start and cursor end registers.

Since the adapter circuit board generates the cursor blink, the blinking cannot be turned off and neither can the blink rate bits be used. However, the following program fragment stops the display of a cursor:

```
;address the cursor start register in the 6845
        MOV DX,3B4H
        MOV AL,10D
        OUT DX,AL
;set the 6845 data register to 'no cursor displayed' code (20H)
        MOV DX,3B5H
        MOV AL,20H
        OUT DX,AL
```

The values for the cursor-start and cursor-end addresses determine which scan lines contain the cursor and the height and position of the cursor within the scan lines allocated to each character. Normally these are set to 11 and 12 respectively to give the familiar underline-shaped PC cursor as shown in Fig. 12.14, which also gives some other examples based on 14 scan lines per character.

The start address registers in the 6845 (12D and 13D) choose where, in the 16K of memory the 6845 can address, the code for the first character to be displayed is located. Since the monochrome display and printer adapter card contains only 2K of memory for the 2000D character codes to be displayed and a separate 2K of memory for the attributes, the start-address registers are not important when programming the monochrome adapter.

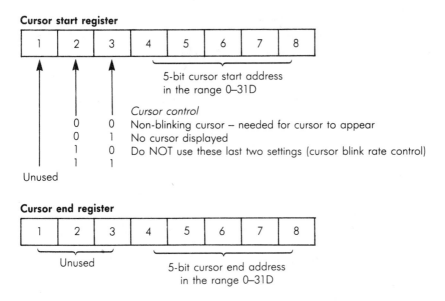

Fig. 12.13   6845 cursor-start and cursor-end register.

If we place the monochrome adapter memory address of the appropriate character code into the cursor-address registers, the cursor can be positioned over a specific character display position. The only slight complication is that, as has already been hinted, the 6845 views the memory on the adapter card as being in two distinct blocks – 2K for character codes and 2K for attribute codes. In fact a 0 bit is appended to a character code address

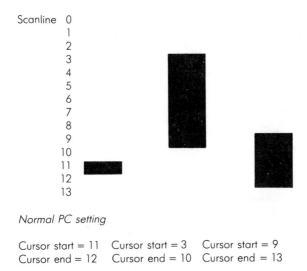

Fig. 12.14   Illustration of cursor-start and cursor-end address settings.

generated by the 6845 (thus giving the 'correct' even 8088 address) and a 1 bit is appended to attribute code addresses generated by the 6845 (giving, similarly, the 'correct' odd 8088 address). From the programming point of view, this simply means that if we want to position the cursor on row y, column x using 6845 cursor-address registers, then the corresponding offset from the start of the 2K character code memory is given by

$$(y * 80D) + x$$

Assuming definitions

```
COLUMN DW ?
ROW    DB ?
```

then the following subroutine will position the cursor on the screen at the column specified by the (unsigned) contents of COLUMN and at the row specified by the (unsigned) contents of ROW – we assume both numbers are within the appropriate ranges.

```
POSITION_CURSOR PROC NEAR
;BX := the 6845 cursor address
        MOV AL,80D
        MUL ROW
        ADD AX,COLUMN
        MOV BX,AX
;set the 6845 address register to access register 14D
        MOV DX,3B4H
        MOV AL,14D
        OUT DX,AL
;set cursor address (high)
        MOV DX,3B5H
        MOV AL,BH
        OUT DX,AL
;set 6845 address register to access register 15D
        MOV DX,3B4H
        MOV AL,15D
        OUT DX,AL
;set cursor address (low)
        MOV DX,3B5H
        MOV AL,BL
        OUT DX,AL
        RET
POSITION_CURSOR ENDP
```

The display driver

We now turn to the problem of writing a monochrome display driver program or, rather more precisely, to the problem of writing a program which emulates the action of the BIOS INT 10H function when AH is set to

14 (see Table 12.2) and which accepts characters typed in at the keyboard via BIOS INT 16H and uses the emulator to display them at the current cursor position, then moving the cursor to a new position. A backspace character will move the cursor back one column on the same line unless the cursor is already in column zero, in which case no action will be taken. If the emulator receives a carriage return character it will move the cursor to the beginning of the same line, whereas a line feed causes a move down one line to the same column position. Once the cursor is on the bottom line, the display is scrolled up instead of the cursor being moved down. In other words, the contents of the top line of the display is replaced with the contents of the second line, those of the second by the contents of the third, and so on. Then the last line of the display is blanked out, so that the cursor is now in the correct column of a blank line.

The complete program, which uses the POSITION_CURSOR sub-routine, is given in Fig. 12.15. By way of illustration, the program uses the LES instruction which, together with its counterpart LDS, can be useful when either of the registers DS or ES is to be loaded with a segment address and another register loaded with an offset. The format of these instructions is

```
LDS  reg,double-word pointer
LES  reg,double-word pointer
```

and on execution, for example,

```
LES BX,ROW
```

is equivalent to the three instructions

```
MOV BX,OFFSET ROW
MOV AX,SEG ROW
MOV ES,AX
```

If the DD pseudo-op is used to redefine a variable as in

```
MY_ADDRESS DD ROW
ROW        DB 0
```

then locations MY_ADDRESS and MY_ADDRESS+1 contain the offset of ROW and the next two locations the segment base value of ROW. In the program we have taken a slightly different approach.

EXERCISES 12.6

1. Amend the program in Fig. 12.15 so that a backspace character not only moves the cursor back but also erases the character the cursor was on before the backspace was received.

2. Write a display driver and main program to use the driver similar to that in the text but which uses only rows 0 to 12 and columns 0 to 39 of the display, thus producing a sort of windowing effect.

```
BS EQU 08H
LF EQU OAH
CR EQU ODH
DSEG SEGMENT
MDA EQU THIS DWORD
START_OF_DISPLAY DW 0
MDA_SEGMENT       DW 0B000H
NORMAL_ATTRIBUTE DB 07H
COLUMN DW 0
ROW    DB 0
TWO    DW 2
DSEG ENDS
SSEG SEGMENT STACK
        DB 100H DUP(?)
SSEG ENDS
CSEG SEGMENT
ASSUME CS:CSEG,DS:DSEG,SS:SSEG
;establish data segment addressability
            MOV   AX,DSEG
            MOV   DS,AX
;point ES to monochrome display adapter memory and DI to
;offset of start of display
            LES   DI,MDA
;clear the display
            MOV   AL,' '
            MOV   AH,NORMAL_ATTRIBUTE
            MOV   CX,2000D
            CLD
            REP   STOSW
;position cursor at top left of screen (column = 0, row = 0)
            CALL POSITION_CURSOR
;repeat read(ch)
    NEXT_CHAR:   MOV   AH,0
                 INT   16H
                 PUSH AX
    ;display(ch)
                 CALL DISPLAY_DRIVER
                 POP   AX
    ;if ch = CR then display an LF also
                 CMP   AL,CR
                 JNZ   SKIP_LF
                 MOV   AL,LF
                 CALL DISPLAY_DRIVER
;forever
    SKIP_LF: JMP   NEXT_CHAR

POSITION_CURSOR PROC NEAR
;BX := the 6845 cursor address
```

Fig. 12.15 Program containing a monochrome display device driver.

```
                MOV   AL,80D
                MUL   ROW
                ADD   AX,COLUMN
                MOV   BX,AX
;set the 6845 address register to access register 14D
                MOV   DX,3B4H
                MOV   AL,14D
                OUT   DX,AL
;set cursor address (high)
                MOV   DX,3B5H
                MOV   AL,BH
                OUT   DX,AL
;set 6845 address register to access register 15D
                MOV   DX,3B4H
                MOV   AL,15D
                OUT   DX,AL
;set cursor address (low)
                MOV   DX,3B5H
                MOV   AL,BL
                OUT   DX,AL
                RET
POSITION_CURSOR ENDP


DISPLAY_DRIVER PROC NEAR
;case AL of ...
                CMP   AL,BS
                JZ    DO_BS
                CMP   AL,LF
                JZ    DO_LF
                CMP   AL,CR
                JZ    DO_CR
                CALL DISPLAY_CHAR
                JMP   END_CASE
        DO_BS:  CALL BACKSPACE
                JMP   END_CASE
        DO_LF:  CALL LINE_FEED
                JMP   END_CASE
        DO_CR:  MOV   COLUMN,0
;reposition cursor
    END_CASE:   CALL POSITION_CURSOR
                RET
DISPLAY_DRIVER ENDP


BACKSPACE PROC NEAR
;if column <> 0 then column := column-1
                CMP   COLUMN,0
                JZ    DO_NOTHING
                DEC   COLUMN
  DO_NOTHING:   RET
BACKSPACE ENDP
```

Fig. 12.15   (*continued*)

```
LINE_FEED PROC NEAR
;if row <> 24 then row := row-1
                CMP    ROW,24
                JZ     SCROLL
                INC    ROW
                JMP    DONE_LF
;else begin
     SCROLL: PUSH DS
        ;set ES and DS to adapter memory
                MOV    AX,MDA_SEGMENT
                MOV    DS,AX
        ;start the block move with the 2nd display line
                MOV    SI,(160D*1)+(2*0)
        ;relocate the block starting at the first display line
                MOV    DI,0
        ;move 24D rows of 80D characters
                MOV    CX,24D*80D
        ;do the move
                REP    MOVSW
        ;now blank out the bottom line of the screen
                MOV    AL,' '
                MOV    AH,NORMAL_ATTRIBUTE
                MOV    CX,80D
                REP    STOSW
                POP    DS
     DONE_LF: RET
LINE_FEED ENDP

DISPLAY_CHAR PROC NEAR
;save AL in BL
                MOV    BL,AL
;AX := offset of current cursor position from 6845 point of view
                MOV    AL,80D
                MUL    ROW
                ADD    AX,COLUMN
;double this to get address from 8088 point of view
                MUL    TWO
;display the character in BL
                MOV    DI,AX
                MOV    ES:[DI],BL
;column := column + 1
                INC    COLUMN
;if column = 80D then
                CMP    COLUMN,80D
                JNZ    DONE_DISPLAY
                ;begin
                        MOV    COLUMN,0
                        CALL LINE_FEED
                ;end
```

Fig. 12.15   *(continued)*

```
DONE_DISPLAY: RET
DISPLAY_CHAR ENDP

CSEG ENDS
END
```

Fig. 12.15 (*continued*)

12.8 THE 8253 TIMER CHIP

At the device driver level, most timing and counting functions are performed by the 8253 timer chip, which has three independent timing channels. Basic clock pulses are fed to the 8253 from a 1.19318 MHz clock (1,193,180 pulses every second). Using these pulses and the resulting output from channel 0 of the 8253, the BIOS can keep track of the time of day provided suitable initialization is carried out on power-up. Channel 0 is also used indirectly for disk motor timing, which depends on the BIOS time of day clock. The output of channel 1 is used to issue a signal periodically to the DMA channel which is responsible for memory refresh, whilst the output of channel 2 goes to the PC speaker to generate sound effects.

Each of the three channels can operate in six different modes. The contents of the timer command register (PC port number 43H – see Table 12.4 and Fig. 12.16) determine which channel and which mode are

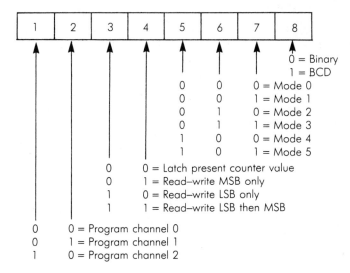

Fig. 12.16 8253 timer command register configuration.

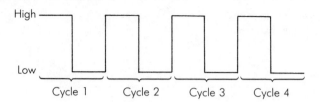

Fig. 12.17 Electrical output from timer channel 2 in mode 3.

used as well as specifying how transfers are to be made into the selected
channel's counter register (port 42H). Thus:

```
MOV AL,0B6H
OUT 43H,AL
```

sets channel 2 to mode 3 and allows us to initialize the channel 2 counter
register in two successive byte transfers using OUT.

In mode 3, the timer counts down from the value set in the counter
register, subtracting one from an internal copy of this value every time it
gets a clock pulse. Once zero is reached, another internal copy is taken and
the whole process is repeated. During the countdown to zero, the electrical
output of the channel is held high until the internal copy has been
decremented to half the initial value, at which point the electrical output
becomes low. Over a period of time, the electrical output from channel 2 in
mode 3 is thus a square wave, as in Fig. 12.17.

Feeding this into the PC speaker will produce a 'musical' note, since the
speaker and its amplifier cannot respond to the sharp edges of the square
wave and the waveform will thus be rounded off at the corners. The pitch of
the musical note will depend on the frequency of the wave, as shown in
Table 12.7. Table 12.7 also contains the required counter value to obtain a
given frequency. Since clock pulses come at 1,193,180 pulses per second,

Table 12.7 Frequencies and counter values for musical notes.

Musical note	Frequency (cycles per second)	Counter value required
low C	131	9108
D	147	8116
E	165	7231
F	175	6818
G	196	6088
A	220	5423
B	247	4831
middle C	262	4554

this is obtained simply by dividing 1,193,180 by the desired frequency.

The timer channel 2 output is not fed directly to the speaker. If the least significant bit of the 8255 output port PB is set, then the timer channel is connected to the speaker via an AND gate, the other signal of which comes from the speaker data bit (bit 7, numbering left to right) of 8255 port PB. This is illustrated in Fig. 12.18.

Provided, then, that 8255 port PB is set to 03H, the 8253 timer command register set to 0B6H and the timer channel 2 counter register set to 9108D then we should get the musical note C played through the loud speaker.

Figure 12.19 contains a complete program example which uses these ideas to turn the digit keys 1–8 into part of a piano keyboard capable of playing the notes low C, D, E, F, G, A, B and middle C respectively. Notice that the timer channel 2 count register (port 42H) is loaded in two successive OUT instructions, the lower byte being loaded first.

EXERCISES 12.7

1. The program in Fig. 12.19 plays each note until a different key is pressed. Rewrite the program so that a note is played only whilst a given key is held down.

2. Given that the black notes of the piano in the range low C to middle C have the following frequencies:

    C sharp 139
    D sharp 156
    F sharp 185
    G sharp 208
    A sharp 233

rewrite the program of Fig. 12.19 so that the keys

    ·W E   Y U I
    A S DF G H JK

can be used to mimic the normal piano keyboard more closely.

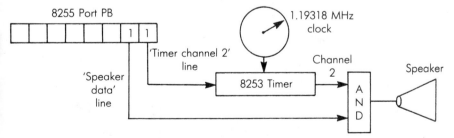

Fig. 12.18 Producing musical notes from the 8255 output port PB.

```
DSEG SEGMENT
NOTES DW 9108D,8116D,7231D,6818D,6088D,5423D,4831D,4554D
DSEG ENDS

SSEG SEGMENT STACK
        DB 100H DUP(?)
SSEG ENDS

CSEG SEGMENT
ASSUME CS:CSEG,DS:DSEG,SS:SSEG
;establish data segment addressability
        MOV AX,DSEG
        MOV DS,AX
;repeat get a note from the keyboard
NEXT_NOTE: MOV AH,0
           INT 16H
    ;set SI to offset of corresponding counter value
           SUB AL,31H
           MOV CL,2
           MUL CL
           MOV SI,AX
    ;set DX to desired note counter value
           MOV DX,NOTES[SI]
    ;set up 8255 port
           IN  AL,61H
    ;turn on speaker data and timer gate 2 signals
           OR  AL,3
           OUT 61H,AL
    ;set timer channel 2
           MOV AL,0B6H
           OUT 43H,AL
    ;set counter value least significant byte
           MOV AL,DL
           OUT 42H,AL
    ;set counter value most significant byte
           MOV AL,DH
           OUT 42H,AL
;forever
JMP NEXT_NOTE
CSEG ENDS
END
```

Fig. 12.19 Converting the digit keys into a mini-piano keyboard.

12.9 DISK INPUT/OUTPUT

Programming disk operations at the level of the controlling chips is very complicated indeed and definitely not within the scope of this introductory book. However, Table 12.2 shows some of the functions available under BIOS INT 13H, which are one level further down ('nearer' the hardware) than the INT 21H DOS functions.

Under normal circumstances, DOS resets the disk system on initialization. However, should an error occur during disk I/O, the reset function of INT 13H must be used before disk I/O can be attempted again. The read and write functions of INT 13H actually allow disk transfer to take place. Data is transferred sector by sector (see Fig. 12.20), each sector containing 512 bytes. A single function call can transfer between one and eight sectors. For each transfer, BX contains the starting address of the group of memory locations which will be used, relative to ES.

Unlike DOS, which is self-contained with regard to error detection, BIOS requires the programmer to perform error detection and recovery. Each of the functions of INT 13H returns a status value in AH. The significance of this value is shown in Table 12.8.

Because the disk drive motor takes about half a second to reach full speed it may be the case that, the first time a read function is issued, an error is reported even though there is nothing wrong with the disk itself or the drive hardware. Consequently, it is normal practice to attempt any read function at least three times before accepting that an error really exists. If, on one of these three attempts, an error status is returned, the reset function must be executed before further disk I/O attempts are made. Since the write function waits automatically for the motor to gain its full speed, no retries are necessary in that case. Indeed, any error returned from a write function definitely arises from a genuine fault.

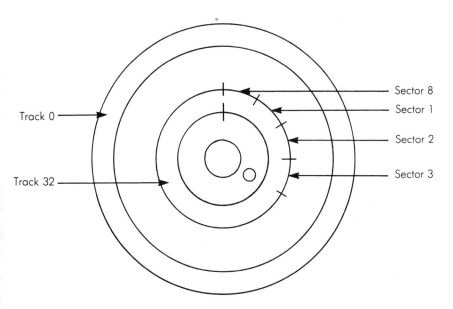

Fig. 12.20 Disk tracks and sectors.

Table 12.8 Status values after INT 13H and their meanings.

Value	Meaning	Likely cause
0	No error	
2	Address mark not found	Bad disk
3	Can't write on disk due to write protection	Protected disk
4	Sector not found	Bad disk
8	DMA error	Bad disk adapter card
10H	CRC error	Bad disk
20H	EDC error	Bad disk adapter card
40H	Seek error	Bad disk drive
80H	Time-out error	Bad disk drive or disk drive not ready

The program in Fig. 12.21 uses BIOS INT 13H to allow its users to inspect the text content of the disk in drive A, sector by sector. When the program is started up, the text content of the first sector is displayed (non-text characters are replaced with a period(.)). Pressing the space bar displays successive sectors. To terminate the program, press any key other than the SPACE BAR or keys such as SHIFT and CTRL.

EXERCISES 12.8

1. Modify the program in Fig. 12.21 so that a user can type in a track number (in the range 0–39) and a sector number (1–8) and have the text content of that sector displayed on the screen.

2. When a file is erased by PC-DOS, its directory entry is removed but the actual contents remain on the disk until the sectors they occupy are re-used. Write a file utility RECOVER which, when brought into action by typing

   ```
   RECOVER MYFILE.ABC
   ```

   would enable its user to locate the disk sectors containing an accidentally erased file and copy their contents into the new file MYFILE.ABC.

12.10 THE COLOUR/GRAPHICS MONITOR ADAPTER

The Colour/Graphics Monitor Adapter is similar to the monochrome display adapter in that they both use a 6845 to control the images produced and they both contain memory from which the display image is formed. In

```
DSEG SEGMENT
TRACK_NO   DB 0
SECTOR_NO DB 1
SECTOR     DB 512D DUP(?)
DSEG ENDS

SSEG SEGMENT STACK
        DB 100H DUP(?)
SSEG ENDS

CSEG SEGMENT
ASSUME CS:CSEG,DS:DSEG,SS:SSEG
START PROC FAR
;set up to return to PC-DOS
          PUSH DS
          MOV  AX,0
          PUSH AX
;establish data and extra segment addressability
          MOV  AX,DSEG
          MOV  DS,AX
          MOV  ES,AX
;repeat
          ;repeat CX := 3
     NEXT_SECTOR: MOV  CX,3
               ;repeat read current track
            READ_AGAIN: PUSH CX
                        MOV  AH,2
                        MOV  DL,0
                        MOV  DH,0
                        MOV  CH,TRACK_NO
                        MOV  CL,SECTOR_NO
                        MOV  AL,1
                        MOV  BX,OFFSET SECTOR
                        INT  13H
                        POP  CX
            ;until no carry or CX = 0
                JNC   READ_DONE
                LOOP READ_AGAIN
          ;if CX <> 0 then begin
          READ_DONE: CMP  CX,0
                     JZ    ERROR
                ;display the sector
                        CALL DISPLAY_SECTOR
                ;increment sector
                        INC  SECTOR_NO
                ;if sector = 9 then
                        CMP  SECTOR_NO,9
                        JNZ  NO_NEW_TRACK
                        ;begin
                                MOV SECTOR_NO,1
```

Fig. 12.21 A program which uses BIOS INT 13H.

```
                                        INC  TRACK_NO
                            ;end;
                    ;read(ch)
              NO_NEW_TRACK: MOV  AH,0
                            INT  16H
              ;end
;until ch <> space or track_no = 40D or CX = 0
ERROR: CMP  CX,0
       JZ   DONE
       CMP  AL,' '
       JNZ  DONE
       CMP  TRACK_NO,40D
       JZ   DONE
       JMP  NEXT_SECTOR
DONE: RET
START ENDP

   DISPLAY_SECTOR: PUSH CX
                   MOV  SI,OFFSET SECTOR
                   MOV  CX,512D
          NEXT_CH: LODSB
          ;if AL does not contain a text char
                   CMP  AL,20H
                   JB   REPLACE
                   CMP  AL,7FH
                   JNC  REPLACE
                   JMP  ALREADY_PRINTABLE
             ;then replace it with a period
             REPLACE: MOV  AL,'.'
             ;print it
ALREADY_PRINTABLE: PUSH SI
                   MOV  AH,14D
                   MOV  BX,0
                   INT  10H
                   POP  SI
                   LOOP NEXT_CH
                   POP  CX
                   RET
   CSEG ENDS
   END
```

Fig. 12.21 (*continued*)

the case of the colour adapter, this memory is located at absolute locations 0B8000H and following, there being a total of 16K memory locations on the adapter card. As with the monochrome adapter, two bytes are used for each character to be displayed – one for the character itself and one for the display attributes.

Alphanumeric modes

As can be seen from Table 12.2, the 6845 is programmed to interact with this memory to provide several different display modes which we shall select using BIOS INT 10H. If one of the alphanumeric modes is selected (25 rows of 40 columns of text in black and white or colour, or 25 rows of 80 columns of text in black and white or colour) then several complete displays, or **pages**, of text can be kept in the adapter memory: four pages of 80 * 25 display; eight pages of 40 * 25. Pages are placed sequentially in memory so that, for an 80 * 25 display, page 0 occupies absolute locations 0B8000H to 0B8FFFH inclusive (4K in all), page 1 occupies 0B9000H to 0B9FFFH, and so on. For a 40 * 25 display each page is 2K long. Which page is displayed is determined by the value in the start-address registers in the 6845. By altering the 6845 start-address registers and thus advancing the beginning of the displayed page by one line of character images (40 * 2 = 80 bytes for the 40 * 25 display and 160 bytes for the 80 * 25 display), the display image can be scrolled faster than by moving characters around in memory. This is **hardware scrolling**.

If a black and white image is selected, all the attributes – except for underlining – available from the Monochrome Display/Printer Adapter (see Fig. 12.10) are also obtainable from the Colour/Graphics Monitor Adapter. For colour images there are 16 foreground colours (for the text characters themselves) and eight possible background colours (for the screen surrounding each text character) as shown in Table 12.9. Background colours may be selected from either the first eight or last eight colours, but

Table 12.9 Colours available in alphanumeric mode.

I	R	G	B	Colour
0	0	0	0	Black
0	0	0	1	Blue
0	0	1	0	Green
0	0	1	1	Cyan
0	1	0	0	Red
0	1	0	1	Magenta
0	1	1	0	Brown
0	1	1	1	Light grey
1	0	0	0	Dark grey
1	0	0	1	Light blue
1	0	1	0	Light green
1	0	1	1	Light cyan
1	1	0	0	Light red
1	1	0	1	Light magenta
1	1	1	0	Yellow
1	1	1	1	White

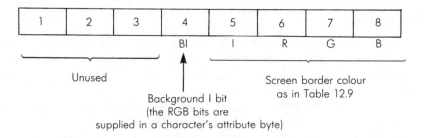

Fig. 12.22 Colour-select register configuration in alphanumeric mode.

colours from the two different groups of eight cannot be displayed as backgrounds simultaneously.

After mode selection, the colour-select register (port 3D9H) must be initialized to set the screen border colour and to determine whether the first eight or last eight colours in Table 12.9 are to be used for backgrounds. Its configuration is shown in Fig. 12.22.

From the 8088 point of view the offset addresses from the start of the colour adapter memory for a character in row y column x are given by:

$$(160 * x) + (2 * y) \qquad (80 * 25 \text{ display})$$
$$(80 \, * x) + (2 * y) \qquad (40 * 25 \text{ display})$$

the attribute byte occupying the next location in each case. The configuration of an attribute byte is shown in Fig. 12.23.

For the colour adapter, the 6845 address register is port 3D4H and all the other 6845 registers are at port 3D5H. As before, display and attribute bytes are addressed separately by the 6845, since the hardware adds 0 or 1 to the least significant end of a 6845 address before communication with the 8088.

The program in Fig. 12.24 displays the letter A in every possible foreground colour and with every possible background colour in the first eight of the list in Table 12.9. One letter A is displayed and then another A in a different colour combination appears on the next line when a key (not

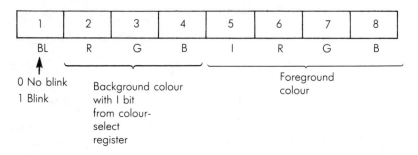

Fig. 12.23 Display attribute byte for colour/graphics monitor adapter.

```
DSEG SEGMENT
FOREGROUND DB 0
BACKGROUND DB 0
DSEG ENDS

SSEG SEGMENT STACK
          DB 100H DUP(?)
SSEG ENDS

CSEG SEGMENT
ASSUME CS:CSEG,DS:DSEG,SS:SSEG
START PROC FAR
;set up for return to PC-DOS
    PUSH DS
    MOV  AX,0
    PUSH AX
;establish data segment addressability
    MOV  AX,DSEG
    MOV  DS,AX
;initialize the colour adapter to 40*25 colour mode
    MOV  AH,0
    MOV  AL,1
    INT  10H
;select blue screen border via colour select register
    MOV  AL,1
    MOV  DX,3D9H
    OUT  DX,AL
;set ES to address colour adapter memory
    MOV  AX,0B800H
    MOV  ES,AX
;blank out screen and the whole memory with blue on blue
    MOV  DI,0
    MOV  AL,' '
    MOV  AH,1*16D+0
    MOV  CX,8000D
    CLD
    STOSW
;DI := column 20D
    MOV  DI,40D
;for foreground := 0 to 15 do
;for background := 0 to 7 do begin
    MOV  FOREGROUND,0
    MOV  BACKGROUND,0
       ;store an A ready for display in those colours
DO_NEXT: MOV  BYTE PTR ES:[DI],'A'
         MOV  AL,16D
         MUL  BACKGROUND
         ADD  AL,FOREGROUND
         MOV  ES:[DI]+1,AL
         ADD  DI,80D
```

Fig. 12.24 Program to display 'A' in every colour combination.

```
             INC   BACKGROUND
             CMP   BACKGROUND,8
             JNZ   DO_NEXT
             MOV   BACKGROUND,0
             INC   FOREGROUND
             CMP   FOREGROUND,15
             JNZ   DO_NEXT
         ;end
 ;set cursor address to the first character
     MOV  BX,0
 ;set 6845 address register to access register 14D
     MOV  DX,3D4H
     MOV  AL,14D
     OUT  DX,AL
 ;set cursor address (high)
     MOV  DX,3D5H
     MOV  AL,BH
     OUT  DX,AL
 ;set 6845 address register to access register 15D
     MOV  DX,3D4H
     MOV  AL,15D
     OUT  DX,AL
 ;set cursor address (low)
     MOV  DX,3D5H
     MOV  AL,BL
     OUT  DX,AL
 ;repeat read(ch)
 NEXT_CH: MOV  AH,0
          INT  16H
       ;scroll down one line
          ADD  BX,40D
       ;set 6845 address register to access register 12D
          MOV  DX,3D4H
          MOV  AL,12D
          OUT  DX,AL
       ;set start address (high)
          MOV  DX,3D5H
          MOV  AL,BH
          OUT  DX,AL
       ;set 6845 address register to access register 13D
          MOV  DX,3D4H
          MOV  AL,13D
          OUT  DX,AL
       ;set start address (low)
          MOV  DX,3D5H
          MOV  AL,BL
          OUT  DX,AL
 ;until BX = 40*127
     CMP  BX,40D*127D
     JNZ  NEXT_CH
```

Fig. 12.24   (*continued*)

```
        RET
START ENDP
CSEG ENDS
END
```

Fig. 12.24 (*continued*)

SHIFT, CTRL, etc.) is pressed, and so on. When the bottom of the screen is reached, a hardware scroll is performed. After every combination has been displayed the program returns control to PC-DOS.

EXERCISE 12.9

Write a program to display the poem:

> The egg and the duck
> Didn't have much luck
> When the river flooded
> Both were stuck
> In the water
> Which was cold

in eight different colour presentations using the colour adapter memory. The user is to select a presentation by keying a digit 1–8, at which point the display scrolls backwards or forwards to the next screen. When the program is started up, presentation 1 automatically appears.

12.11 COLOUR GRAPHICS MODE

In graphics mode, two resolutions are possible: 320 * 200 plottable points in black and white or colour; and 640 * 200 plottable points in black and white only. Using colour, each point or dot in a given display can be one of four colours. Having chosen the first (background) colour from Table 12.9, the other three colours may either be red, green and yellow, or cyan, magenta and white. To emphasize: a given graphics display can contain only four colours; and the combinations of colours are restricted.

Once again we shall use the BIOS INT 10H to set up a (colour) graphics display. When we have done so, the colour-select register is used to select the working colour-set. Figure 12.25 shows the configuration of this register in graphics mode.

Addressing an actual point is complicated by the desire to restrict the amount of memory used to control each point. In fact, two bits are used to represent each point on the colour graphics screen, the setting of these two bits determining the colour displayed at that point as follows:

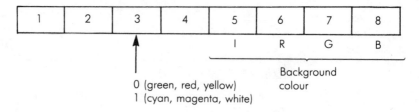

Fig. 12.25   Colour-select register configuration for graphics mode.

0	0	background colour
0	1	green or cyan
1	0	red or magenta
1	1	yellow or white

depending on the choice of colour set. Since a dot displayed in the 00 form will be in the background colour it will not be distinguishable from the background.

Mapping every point in the 200 row, 320 column display down to two bits in the adapter memory is carried out as follows. Even row numbers (0,2,4, . . . ,198) map to the memory starting at offset address 0; odd row numbers map to memory starting at offset address 2000H. Each row of 320 dots needs 320 * 2 bits or 80 bytes of display memory. Hence to place a dot at row y, column x, the group of 80 bytes representing row y has offset

$(y \text{ div } 2) * 80$

from the appropriate start address. Similarly the expression

$(x*2) \text{ div } 8 = x \text{ div } 4$

will give the number of the byte containing the appropriate two bits for a given dot and

$x \bmod 4$

specifies which of the four groups of two bits in a byte (numbering most significant two bits as pair 0, next most significant two bits as pair 1 etc.) represent that column. Most of this calculation can be accomplished by shift operations as is done in the example program, Fig. 12.26.

This program allows its user to doodle on the screen. When it is run, a yellow dot appears on a blue background. The user can move the yellow dot around using the U (UP), D (DOWN), L (LEFT) and R (RIGHT) keys and thus doodle on the screen. When reading through the program, note that, when a dot within a byte is changed, the other dots represented by that byte must be preserved.

```
DSEG SEGMENT
ROW        DW  100D
COLUMN     DW  160D
MASKS      DB  11000000B
           DB  00110000B
           DB  00001100B
           DB  00000011B
YELLOW     DB  11111111B
EIGHTY     DB  80D
DSEG ENDS

SSEG SEGMENT STACK
           DB  100H DUP(?)
SSEG ENDS

CSEG SEGMENT
ASSUME CS:CSEG,DS:DSEG,SS:SSEG
;set up data segment addressability
           MOV  AX,DSEG
           MOV  DS,AX
;set mode using BIOS for 320*200 colour image
           MOV  AH,0
           MOV  AL,4
           INT  10H
;use colour-select register for yellow on blue
           MOV  DX,3D9H
           MOV  AL,01H
           OUT  DX,AL
;set ES to address adapter memory
           MOV  AX,0B800H
           MOV  ES,AX
;place dot in centre of screen (row 100, column 160)
           CALL DRAW_DOT
;repeat read(ch)
    NEXT_CH: MOV  AH,0
             INT  16H
    ;case ch of ...
             CMP  AL,'U'
             JZ   DO_U
             CMP  AL,'D'
             JZ   DO_D
             CMP  AL,'L'
             JZ   DO_L
             CMP  AL,'R'
             JZ   DO_R
             JMP  DONE_COMMAND
        DO_U: CMP  ROW,0
              JZ   SKIP_U
              DEC  ROW
              CALL DRAW_DOT
```

Fig. 12.26 A colour graphics doodle drawing program.

```
        SKIP_U:  JMP   DONE_COMMAND
          DO_D:  CMP   ROW,199D
                 JZ    SKIP_D
                 INC   ROW
                 CALL  DRAW_DOT
        SKIP_D:  JMP   DONE_COMMAND
          DO_L:  CMP   COLUMN,0
                 JZ    SKIP_L
                 DEC   COLUMN
                 CALL  DRAW_DOT
        SKIP_L:  JMP   DONE_COMMAND
          DO_R:  CMP   COLUMN,319D
                 JZ    DONE_COMMAND
                 INC   COLUMN
                 CALL  DRAW_DOT
;forever
DONE_COMMAND:  JMP   NEXT_CH


DRAW_DOT PROC NEAR
;preserve value of ROW
         PUSH ROW
;if least significant bit of ROW is 1
         SHR  ROW,1
         JNC  EVEN
;then DI := 2000H
         MOV  DI,2000H
         JMP  ROW_OFFSET
;else DI := 0;
   EVEN: MOV  DI,0
;calculate the row offset
ROW_OFFSET: MOV  AX,ROW
            MUL  EIGHTY
            ADD  DI,AX
;DX := within row offset
            MOV  DX,COLUMN
            SHR  DX,1
            SHR  DX,1
            ADD  DI,DX
;SI := within byte offset
            MOV  SI,COLUMN
            AND  SI,03H
;get colour mask for this position
            MOV  AL,MASKS[SI]
            MOV  BL,YELLOW
            AND  BL,AL
            NOT  AL
;get byte containing dot to be changed
            MOV  AH,ES:[DI]
```

Fig. 12.26 (*continued*)

```
;select the dot
              AND   AH,AL
;turn the yellow dot on
              OR    AH,BL
;store it in the adapter memory
              MOV   ES:[DI],AH
;restore original value of ROW
              POP   ROW
              RET
DRAW_DOT ENDP

CSEG ENDS
END
```

Fig. 12.26 (*continued*)

EXERCISES 12.10

1. Modify the program in Fig. 12.26 so that pressing one of the letters G (Green), B (Blue), Y (Yellow), R (Red) means that the movable dot becomes the corresponding colour. Change the control keys so that the arrow keys on the numeric keypad are used to move the dot around the screen.

2. High-level language interfaces to graphical display often allow users to specify two points and then have a straight line drawn between them. Write an 8088 assembly language program to provide such a facility, assuming the two given points are specified in variables COLUMN1, ROW1 and COLUMN2, ROW2.

APPENDIX I

ASCII Codes

CONTROL CODES

Character		Binary	Hex	Decimal
NUL	Null	00000000	00	0
SOH	Start of heading	00000001	01	1
STX	Start of text	00000010	02	2
ETX	End of text	00000011	03	3
EOT	End of transmission	00000100	04	4
ENQ	Enquiry	00000101	05	5
ACK	Acknowledge	00000110	06	6
BEL	Bell	00000111	07	7
BS	Backspace	00001000	08	8
HT	Horizontal tabulation	00001001	09	9
LF	Line feed	00001010	0A	10
VT	Vertical tabulation	00001011	0B	11
FF	Form feed	00001100	0C	12
CR	Carriage return	00001101	0D	13
SO	Shift out	00001110	0E	14
SI	Shift in	00001111	0F	15
DLE	Data link escape	00010000	10	16
DC1	Device control 1	00010001	11	17
DC2	2	00010010	12	18
DC3	3	00010011	13	19
DC4	4	00010100	14	20
NAK	Negative acknowledge	00010101	15	21
SYN	Synchronous idle	00010110	16	22
ETB	End of transmission block	00010111	17	23
CAN	Cancel	00011000	18	24
EM	End of medium	00011001	19	25
SUB	Substitute	00011010	1A	26
ESC	Escape	00011011	1B	27
FS	File separator	00011100	1C	28
GS	Group separator	00011101	1D	29
RS	Record separator	00011110	1E	30
US	Unit separator	00011111	1F	31
DEL	Delete	01111111	7F	127

THE PRINTABLE CHARACTER CODES

Character	Binary	Hex	Dec	Character	Binary	Hex	Dec
SPACE	00100000	20	32	P	01010000	50	80
!	00100001	21	33	Q	01010001	51	81
"	00100010	22	34	R	01010010	52	82
#	00100011	23	35	S	01010011	53	83
$	00100100	24	36	T	01010100	54	84
%	00100101	25	37	U	01010101	55	85
&	00100110	26	38	V	01010110	56	86
'	00100111	27	39	W	01010111	57	87
(	00101000	28	40	X	01011000	58	88
)	00101001	29	41	Y	01011001	59	89
*	00101010	2A	42	Z	01011010	5A	90
+	00101011	2B	43	[	01011011	5B	91
,	00101100	2C	44	\	01011100	5C	92
–	00101101	2D	45	]	01011101	5D	93
.	00101110	2E	46	^	01011110	5E	94
/	00101111	2F	47	_	01011111	5F	95
0	00110000	30	48	$	01100000	60	96
1	00110001	31	49	a	01100001	61	97
2	00110010	32	50	b	01100010	62	98
3	00110011	33	51	c	01100011	63	99
4	00110100	34	52	d	01100100	64	100
5	00110101	35	53	e	01100101	65	101
6	00110110	36	54	f	01100110	66	102
7	00110111	37	55	g	01100111	67	103
8	00111000	38	56	h	01101000	68	104
9	00111001	39	57	i	01101001	69	105
:	00111010	3A	58	j	01101010	6A	106
;	00111011	3B	59	k	01101011	6B	107
<	00111100	3C	60	l	01101100	6C	108
=	00111101	3D	61	m	01101101	6D	109
>	00111110	3E	62	n	01101110	6E	110
?	00111111	3F	63	o	01101111	6F	111
@	01000000	40	64	p	01110000	70	112
A	01000001	41	65	q	01110001	71	113
B	01000010	42	66	r	01110010	72	114
C	01000011	43	67	s	01110011	73	115
D	01000100	44	68	t	01110100	74	116
E	01000101	45	69	u	01110101	75	117
F	01000110	46	70	v	01110110	76	118
G	01000111	47	71	w	01110111	77	119
H	01001000	48	72	x	01111000	78	120
I	01001001	49	73	y	01111001	79	121
J	01001010	4A	74	z	01111010	7A	122
K	01001011	4B	75	{	01111011	7B	123
L	01001100	4C	76	|	01111100	7C	124
M	01001101	4D	77	}	01111101	7D	125
N	01001110	4E	78	~	01111110	7E	126
O	01001111	4F	79					

APPENDIX II

The Calculator Simulator Program

```
LF EQU OAH
CR EQU ODH

DSEG SEGMENT
POWERS_TABLE DD 10000000
             DD 1000000
             DD 100000
             DD 10000
             DD 1000
             DD 100
             DD 10
             DD 1
ZERO_DIV_MESS DB 'DIVISION BY ZERO NOT ALLOWED',CR,LF,'$'
ILLEGAL_MESS DB 'ILLEGAL CHARACTER - RESTART CALCULATION',CR,LF,'$'
TOO_BIG_MESS DB 'NUMBER TOO BIG - RESTART CALCULATION',CR,LF,'$'
DSEG ENDS

SSEG SEGMENT STACK
     DW 100H DUP(?)
SSEG ENDS

CSEG SEGMENT
ASSUME CS:CSEG,DS:DSEG,SS:SSEG
;establish data segment addressability
MOV AX,DSEG
MOV DS,AX
;digits_read := 5;
START:MOV CH,5
;while digits_read = 5 or code <> 1 do
TEST:CMP CH,5
    JZ READ_FIRST_DECIMAL
    CMP CL,1
    JNZ READ_FIRST_DECIMAL
    JMP READ_SECOND_DECIMAL
```

```
                ;begin
                ;print(newline);
                READ_FIRST_DECIMAL:CALL PRINT_NEWLINE
                                   CALL GET_OK_NUM_AND_TERM_NON_SPACE_CHAR
                ;if digits_read = 5 then print(too long);
                                   CMP   CH,5
                                   JNZ   TRY_CODE
                                   CALL  TOO_LONG
                ;if code <> 1 then print(illegal character);
                           TRY_CODE:CMP   CL,1
                                   JZ    NO_NUM_BEFORE_OPERATOR
                                   CALL  ILLEGAL_CHAR
                ;if digits_read = 0 and code = 1 then
         NO_NUM_BEFORE_OPERATOR:CMP   CL,1
                                   JNZ   END_FIRST_WHILE
                                   CMP   CH,0
                                   JNZ   END_FIRST_WHILE
                                   ;begin
                                   ;print(illegal character);
                                       CALL ILLEGAL_CHAR
                                   ;code := 0
                                       MOV CL,0
                                   ;end
END_FIRST_WHILE:JMP TEST
;preserve operator and operand on the stack
;call GET_OK_NUM_AND_TERM_NON_SPACE_CHAR
READ_SECOND_DECIMAL:PUSH AX
                   PUSH BX
                   CALL GET_OK_NUM_AND_TERM_NON_SPACE_CHAR
;if digits_read = 5 then begin clear stack; print(too long) end
            CMP CH,5
            JNZ TRY_DO_SUM
            POP BX
            POP AX
            CALL TOO_LONG
            JMP REPEAT_LOOP
;else if digits_read <> 0 and code = 2 then begin
    TRY_DO_SUM:CMP CH,0
            JZ NO_DIGITS
            CMP CL,2
            JNZ NO_DIGITS
    ;pop operand and operator
            POP AX
            POP DX           ;operand into DL
    ;case operator of ...
            CMP  DL,'+'
```

```
                JZ    PLUS
                CMP   DL,'-'
                JZ    MINUS
                CMP   DL,'*'
                JZ    STAR
                CMP   DL,'/'
                JZ    SLASH
                JMP   REPEAT_LOOP
           PLUS:CALL  DOPLUS
                JMP   REPEAT_LOOP
          MINUS:CALL  DOSUB
                JMP   REPEAT_LOOP
           STAR:CALL  DOMULT
                JMP   REPEAT_LOOP
          SLASH:CALL  DODIVISION
                JMP   REPEAT_LOOP
       ;else begin clear stack; print(illegal character) end
NO_DIGITS:POP AX
          POP BX
          CALL ILLEGAL_CHAR
;forever
REPEAT_LOOP:JMP START
; ******************************************************************
     DOPLUS:CALL ADDITION
            CALL PRINTOUT
            RET
; ******************************************************************
        DOSUB:CALL SUBTRACTION
        ;check if result was negative
              JNB   RESULT_NOT_NEG
        ;if so print minus sign
              PUSH DX
              MOV  DL,'-'
              CALL PRINTCHAR
              POP  DX
        ;then negate DX,CX
              MOV  BX,DX
              MOV  AX,CX
              MOV  DX,O
              MOV  CX,O
              CALL BIG_SUB
          ;now convert to decimal and print
RESULT_NOT_NEG:CALL PRINTOUT
              RET
; ******************************************************************
```

```
    DOMULT:CALL MULTIPLY
           CALL PRINTOUT
           RET
; *********************************************************************
    DODIVISION: CMP  BX,0      ;check for division by zero
                JZ   DIVISION_ERROR
           ;otherwise do the division
               CALL DIVIDE
           ;print the quotient
               PUSH AX               ;preserve remainder
               PUSH BX               ;on stack
               CALL PRINTOUT
               MOV  DL,'R'
               CALL PRINTCHAR        ;print R for Remainder
               POP  BX
               POP  AX               ;now restore and print
               MOV  DX,BX            ;remainder
               MOV  CX,AX
               CALL PRINTOUT
               JMP  DONE_DIV
 DIVISION_ERROR:CALL DIVISION_BY_ZERO    ;prints error message
       DONE_DIV:RET
; *********************************************************************
ADDITION:ADD AX,BX
         MOV CX,AX
         MOV DX,OH
         RET
; *********************************************************************
SUBTRACTION:SUB AX,BX
            CWD
            MOV CX,AX
            RET
; *********************************************************************
MULTIPLY:IMUL BX
         MOV CX,AX
         RET
; *********************************************************************
DIVIDE:MOV DX,0
       IDIV BX
       MOV CX,AX
       MOV AX,DX
       MOV DX,0
       MOV BX,0
       RET
; *********************************************************************
```

```
GET_OK_NUM_AND_TERM_NON_SPACE_CHAR:MOV  BX,OH
;digits_read := 0;
     MOV CH,O
;repeat read(char) until char <> ' ';
SKIP_SPACES:CALL READCHAR
           CMP  AL,' '
           JZ   SKIP_SPACES
;while char in ['0'..'9'] and digits_read <> 4 do
CHECK_NUMERIC:  CMP  AL,'0'
                JB   MISS_TRAIL_SPACES
                CMP  AL,'9'
                JA   MISS_TRAIL_SPACES
                CMP  CH,4
                JZ   MISS_TRAIL_SPACES
                ;begin
                ;digits_read := digits_read + 1;
                INC CH
                ;BX := BX * 10D + binary_value_of (char)
                MOV  CL,AL  ;copy the contents of AL for safe keeping
                MOV  AX,10D
                IMUL BX
                MOV  BX,AX  ;BX now contains 10D times its previous
                                   ;contents
                MOV  AL,CL  ;restore AL
                SUB  AL,30H ;retrieve numeric value from character
                MOV  AH,OH  ;prepare AX for 16-bit addition
                ADD  BX,AX
                ;read(char)
                CALL READCHAR
                ;end
                JMP  CHECK_NUMERIC
;while char = ' ' do read(char)
MISS_TRAIL_SPACES:CMP  AL,' '
                  JNZ  IS_THIS_FIFTH_DIGIT
                  CALL READCHAR
                  JMP  MISS_TRAIL_SPACES
;if char in ['0'..'9'] then digits_read := digits_read + 1
IS_THIS_FIFTH_DIGIT:CMP AL,'0'
                  JB  TRY_OPERATOR
                  CMP AL,'9'
                  JA  TRY_EQUALS
                  INC CH
                  JMP DONE_THIS
;else if char in ['+', '-', '*', '/'] then CL := 1
TRY_OPERATOR:CMP AL,'+'
             JZ  GOT_OPERATOR
```

```
                CMP AL,'-'
                JZ  GOT_OPERATOR
                CMP AL,'*'
                JZ  GOT_OPERATOR
                CMP AL,'/'
                JZ  GOT_OPERATOR
;else if char = ' = ' then CL := 2
  TRY_EQUALS:CMP AL,' = '
                JNZ DONE_THIS
                MOV CL,2
                JMP DONE_THIS
GOT_OPERATOR:MOV CL,1
  DONE_THIS:RET
; ************************************************************************
;power := 7;
PRINTOUT:MOV  BP,7
         MOV  SI,OFFSET  POWERS_TABLE
;digit_printed_yet := false;
         MOV  BH,0
;repeat count := 0
   NEXT_POWER:MOV  BL,0
     ;while DX,CX >= 0 do begin
  REMOVE_POWER:MOV  AX,DX
               RCL  AX,1
               JB   ADD_BACK
         ;DX,CX := DX,CX-10^power;
               PUSH BX
               MOV  AX,[SI]
               MOV  BX,2[SI]
               CALL BIG_SUB
         ;count := count + 1
               POP  BX
               INC  BL
         ;end;
               JMP REMOVE_POWER
     ;DX,CX := DX,CX + 10^power;
ADD_BACK:PUSH BX
         MOV  AX,[SI]
         MOV  BX,2[SI]
         CALL BIG_ADD
     ;count := count-1;
         POP  BX
         DEC  BL
     ;if count <> 0 then begin
         CMP BL,0
         JZ  TRY_COUNT_ZERO
```

```
                ;digit_printed_yet := true;
                    MOV BH,1
                ;print(count)
                    ADD  BL,30H
                    PUSH DX
                    MOV  DL,BL
                    CALL PRINTCHAR
                    POP  DX
                ;end;
        ;if count = 0 and (digit_printed_yet or (power = 1)) then
TRY_COUNT_ZERO:CMP BL,0
            JNZ DONE_THIS_POWER
            CMP BP,0
            JZ  PRINT_THIS_ZERO
            CMP BH,1
            JZ  PRINT_THIS_ZERO
            JMP DONE_THIS_POWER
            ;begin
            ;print(count);
PRINT_THIS_ZERO:PUSH DX
                    MOV  DL,BL
                    ADD  DL,30H
                    CALL PRINTCHAR
                    POP  DX
                ;digit_printed_yet := true
                    MOV BH,1
                ;end;
        ;power := power-1
DONE_THIS_POWER:ADD SI,4
                    SUB BP,1
;until power = 0
        JAE NEXT_POWER
DONE_ALL_DIGITS:RET
; *******************************************************************
BIG_ADD:CLC
        ADD CX,AX
        ADC DX,BX
        RET
; *******************************************************************
BIG_SUB:CLC
        SUB CX,AX
        SBB DX,BX
        RET
; *******************************************************************
```

```
ILLEGAL_CHAR:CALL  PRINT_NEWLINE
             MOV   AH,O9H
             MOV   DX,OFFSET ILLEGAL_MESS
             INT   21H
             RET
; ********************************************************************
TOO_LONG:CALL  PRINT_NEWLINE
         MOV   AH,O9H
         MOV   DX,OFFSET TOO_BIG_MESS
         INT   21H
         RET
; ********************************************************************
DIVISION_BY_ZERO:CALL  PRINT_NEWLINE
                 MOV   AH,O9H
                 MOV   DX,OFFSET ZERO_DIV_MESS
                 INT   21H
                 RET
; ********************************************************************
READCHAR:MOV  AH,1H
         INT  21H
         RET
; ********************************************************************
PRINTCHAR:MOV  AH,2H
          INT  21H
          RET
; ********************************************************************
PRINT_NEWLINE:MOV   DL,CR
              CALL  PRINTCHAR
              MOV   DL,LF
              CALL  PRINTCHAR
              RET
; ********************************************************************
CSEG ENDS
END
```

APPENDIX III

The Text Editor Program

```
LF EQU OAH
CR EQU ODH
STAR EQU '*'
DOLLAR EQU '$'


DSEG SEGMENT
START_OF_TEXT DB 675D DUP(?)
READ_LINE_BUFFER DB 50H DUP(?)
LINE_LENGTHS    DB 0,0,0,0,0,0,0,0,0

ILLEGAL_MESS DB 'ILLEGAL CHARACTER IN INPUT',CR,LF,DOLLAR
NO_SUCH_LINE DB 'NO SUCH LINE EXISTS. '
             DB 'ILLEGAL CHARACTER IN LINE NUMBER?',CR,LF,DOLLAR
RETURN_ERROR DB 'A COMMAND MUST BE TERMINATED BY '
             DB 'PRESSING THE RETURN KEY',CR,LF,DOLLAR
TOO_LONG     DB 'STRING TOO LONG',CR,LF,DOLLAR
SEARCH_ERROR DB '%SIGN(S) MISSING IN FIND COMMAND',CR,LF,DOLLAR
FIND_OK      DB 'SEARCH COMPLETED',CR,LF,DOLLAR
SWAP_OK      DB 'SWAP COMPLETED',CR,LF,DOLLAR
DELETE_OK    DB 'DELETION COMPLETED',CR,LF,DOLLAR
DSEG ENDS

SSEG SEGMENT STACK
        DW 100H DUP(?)
SSEG ENDS

CSEG SEGMENT
        ASSUME DS:DSEG,SS:SSEG,CS:CSEG

MAIN PROC FAR
;set up stack for return to PC-DOS
        PUSH DS
        MOV  AX,0
        PUSH AX
```

352

```
;address our program data segment
        MOV AX,DSEG
        MOV DS,AX
        MOV ES,AX               ;for string manipulation instructions

;initialize storage for the text lines
  CALL INITIALIZE
;print(prompt)
  MOV   DL,'*'
  CALL PRINTCHAR
;read(char1, char2);
  CALL READCHAR
  MOV   CL,AL
  CALL READCHAR             ;CL = char1, AL = char2
;while char1 <> E or char2 <> CR do
PROCESS:CMP CL,'E'
        JNZ NOT_END
        CMP AL,CR
        JNZ NOT_END
        JMP DONE
    ;begin
    ;if char1 = P and char2 = CR
        NOT_END:CMP  CL,'P'
                JNZ  TRY_LINE
                CMP  AL,CR
                JNZ  TRY_LINE
    ;then print all the text
                CALL PRINT_ALL_TEXT
                JMP  GET_COMMAND
    ;else if char1 = P then print a line
      TRY_LINE:CMP  CL,'P'
                JNZ  TRY_S
                CALL PRINT_A_LINE
                JMP  GET_COMMAND
    ;else if char1 = S then call swap
        TRY_S:CMP  CL,'S'
                JNZ  TRY_N
                CALL SWAP
                JMP  GET_COMMAND
    ;else if char1 = N then call new_text
        TRY_N:CMP  CL,'N'
                JNZ  TRY_D
                CALL NEW_TEXT
                JMP  GET_COMMAND
```

```
           ;else if char1 = D then call delete
               TRY_D:CMP   CL,'D'
                     JNZ   TRY_F
                     CALL  DELETE
                     JMP   GET_COMMAND
           ;else if char1 = F then call find
               TRY_F:CMP   CL,'F'
                     JNZ   ILLEGAL
                     CALL  FIND
                     JMP   GET_COMMAND
           ;else print(illegal character);
              ILLEGAL:CALL ILLEGAL_CHARACTER
           ;print(newline);
         GET_COMMAND:CALL PRINT_NEWLINE
           ;print(prompt);
                     MOV   DL,'*'
                     CALL  PRINTCHAR
           ;read(char1, char2);
                     CALL  READCHAR
                     MOV   CL,AL
                     CALL  READCHAR
           ;end;
                     JMP   PROCESS
       ;return to PC-DOS
          DONE:RET

       MAIN ENDP

       ; ********************************************************************

       INITIALIZE PROC NEAR
       ;for i := 1 to 9 do text-line[i] := blank;
                 MOV   CX,9
                 MOV   SI,OFFSET START_OF_TEXT
        INIT_NEXT:MOV   BYTE PTR  [SI],CR
                 MOV   BYTE PTR 1[SI],LF
                 MOV   BYTE PTR 2[SI],DOLLAR
                 ADD   SI,75D
                 LOOP  INIT_NEXT
                 RET
       INITIALIZE ENDP

       ; ********************************************************************
```

```
PRINT_ALL_TEXT PROC NEAR
;for i := 1 to 9 do print(text-line[i]);
          CALL PRINT_NEWLINE
          MOV   CX,9
          MOV   DX,OFFSET START_OF_TEXT
NEXT_LINE:CALL PRINT_STRING
          ADD   DX,75D              ;set address pointer to next line
          LOOP NEXT_LINE
          RET
PRINT_ALL_TEXT ENDP

; **********************************************************************

VERIFY_RANGE_AND_FORMAT PROC NEAR
;if char2 not in ['1'..'9'] then
        CMP AL,'1'
        JB  OUT_OF_RANGE
        CMP AL,'9'
        JBE IN_RANGE
    ;begin
    ;set DX to address of error message
OUT_OF_RANGE:MOV DX,OFFSET NO_SUCH_LINE
    ;set AH to indicate error
            MOV AH,OFFH
    ;end
            JMP RF_ERROR
;else begin
      ;read(char3)
IN_RANGE:MOV BL,AL        ;char2 now in BL
         CALL READCHAR
;if char3 <> CR then
         CMP AL,CR
         JZ RF_OK
         ;begin
         ;set DX to address of error message
            MOV DX,OFFSET RETURN_ERROR
         ;set AH to indicate error
            MOV AH,OFFH
         ;end
         JMP RF_ERROR
;else set AH to indicate OK
   RF_OK:MOV AH,0
RF_ERROR:RET
VERIFY_RANGE_AND_FORMAT ENDP

; **********************************************************************
```

```
PRINT_A_LINE PROC NEAR
          CALL VERIFY_RANGE_AND_FORMAT
          CALL PRINT_NEWLINE
;if AH <> OFFH then DX := address of text-line[BL-30H];
          CMP  AH,0FFH
          JZ   PRINT_DONE
          SUB  BL,31H
          MOV  AL,75D
          IMUL BL
          MOV  DX,AX
          ADD  DX,OFFSET START_OF_TEXT
PRINT_DONE:CALL PRINT_STRING
          RET
PRINT_A_LINE ENDP


; ********************************************************************


READCHAR PROC NEAR
        MOV AH,1
        INT 21H
        RET
READCHAR ENDP


; ********************************************************************


PRINTCHAR PROC NEAR
        MOV AH,2
        INT 21H
        RET
PRINTCHAR ENDP


; ********************************************************************


PRINT_NEWLINE PROC NEAR
        PUSH AX
        PUSH DX
        MOV  DL,CR
        CALL PRINTCHAR
        MOV  DL,LF
        CALL PRINTCHAR
        POP  DX
        POP  AX
        RET
PRINT_NEWLINE ENDP


; ********************************************************************
```

```
PRINT_STRING PROC NEAR
        PUSH AX
        MOV  AH,9
        INT  21H
        POP  AX
        RET
PRINT_STRING ENDP

; ***********************************************************************

ILLEGAL_CHARACTER PROC NEAR
        MOV  DX,OFFSET ILLEGAL_MESS
        CALL PRINT_STRING
        RET
ILLEGAL_CHARACTER ENDP

; ***********************************************************************

NEW_TEXT PROC NEAR
                CALL VERIFY_RANGE_AND_FORMAT
                CALL PRINT_NEWLINE
;if AH = OFFH then print error message
                CMP  AH,OFFH
                JNZ  OBEY_NEW
                CALL PRINT_STRING
                JMP  NEW_DONE
;else begin
        ;print(colon prompt)
        OBEY_NEW:CLD
                MOV  DL,':'
                CALL PRINTCHAR
        ;CX := 73D;DI := address of READ_LINE_BUFFER
                MOV  DI,OFFSET READ_LINE_BUFFER
                MOV CX,73D
        ;repeat read(char)
READ_MORE:      CALL READCHAR
        ;store char in buffer
                STOSB
        ;until CX = 0 or char = CR
                CMP AL,CR
                LOOPNZ READ_MORE
        ;if char = CR
                JZ END_OF_LINE
```

```
                    ;then print TOO_LONG message
                        MOV DX,OFFSET TOO_LONG
                        CALL PRINT_NEWLINE
                        CALL PRINT_STRING
                        JMP NEW_DONE
              ;else begin
                        ;add LF and DOLLAR to end of text in buffer
        END_OF_LINE:    MOV BYTE PTR [DI],LF
                        INC DI
                        MOV BYTE PTR [DI],DOLLAR
                        ;calculate starting address of text's destination
                        SUB BL,31H
                        MOV AL,75D
                        IMUL BL                 ;address now in AX
                        ;calculate and store length of this text
                        MOV DI,AX
                        ADD DI,OFFSET START_OF_TEXT
                        MOV SI,OFFSET READ_LINE_BUFFER
                        MOV DX,75D
                        SUB DX,CX
                        MOV CX,DX
                        MOV BH,0        ;BX now contains the line no. - 1
                        ADD BX,OFFSET LINE_LENGTHS
                        SUB DL,3        ;remove CR, LF, DOLLAR from count
                        MOV [BX],DL             ;store line length
                        ;move the text into place
                        REP MOVSB
                  ;end
              ;end
    NEW_DONE:           RET
    NEW_TEXT ENDP


    ; ********************************************************************

    FIND PROC NEAR
    ;if AL <> '%' then DX := address of SEARCH_ERROR message
            CMP AL,'%'
            JZ READ_SEARCH_STRING
            MOV DX,OFFSET SEARCH_ERROR
            JMP FIND_DONE
        ;else begin
            ;count := 73D;
    READ_SEARCH_STRING:MOV CX,73D
                ;point DI to start of READ_LINE_BUFFER
                MOV DI,OFFSET READ_LINE_BUFFER
```

```
              ;repeat
MORE_STRING:CALL READCHAR
                  ;store char
                  STOSB
              ;until char = % or count = 0
              CMP AL,'%'
              LOOPNZ MORE_STRING
              ;if count = 0 then DX := address of TOO_LONG message
              JZ END_OF_STRING
              MOV DX,OFFSET TOO_LONG
              JMP FIND_DONE
                    ;else begin
                        ;read(char);
              END_OF_STRING:CALL READCHAR
                        ;if char <> CR then DX := address of RETURN_ERROR
                        CMP AL,0DH
                        JZ START_SEARCH
                        MOV DX,OFFSET RETURN_ERROR
                        JMP FIND_DONE
                              ;else begin
                                  ;BX := length of search text
                        START_SEARCH:MOV BX,73D
                                  SUB BX,CX
                                  DEC BX          ;ignore final %
                                  ;if BX <> 0 then
                                      CMP BX,0
                                      JZ  FIND_DONE
                                          ;begin
                                          MOV BP,BX
                                          CALL PRINT_NEWLINE
                                          CALL LOCATE
                                          ;end
                                  ;end
                        ;end
              ;DX := address of FIND_OK message
  FIND_DONE:MOV DX,OFFSET FIND_OK
              ;end;
CALL PRINT_NEWLINE
CALL PRINT_STRING
RET
FIND ENDP

; ***********************************************************************
```

```
LOCATE PROC NEAR
;for DL := 8 downto 0  do
  MOV DL,8
        ;begin
        ;AX := length of line DL + 1
SEARCH_NEXT_LINE:MOV BX,OFFSET LINE_LENGTHS
        MOV AL,DL
        XLAT BX
        MOV AH,0
        ;if AX <= BP then AX := 0
        CMP AX,BP
        JAE SET_SCANS
        MOV AX,0
        JMP SET_ADDRESS
        ;else AX := max number of scans necessary of this line
SET_SCANS:SUB AX,BP
        INC AX
        ;BX := start address of the (DL + 1)th line  of text
SET_ADDRESS:PUSH AX
        MOV BL,DL
        MOV AL,75D
        IMUL BL
        ADD AX,OFFSET START_OF_TEXT
        MOV BX,AX
        POP AX
        ;found := false
        MOV CL,0FFH
        ;while not found and AX <> 0 do
CHECK_THIS_LINE:CMP AX,0
        JZ END_FOR
        CMP CL,0FFH
        JNZ END_FOR
                ;begin
                PUSH AX
                PUSH CX
                ;CX := length of search string
                MOV CX,BP
                ;set DI to start of text being searched
                ;DI := AX + BX-1
                DEC AX
                ADD AX,BX
                MOV DI,AX
                ;set SI to start of search text
                MOV SI,OFFSET READ_LINE_BUFFER
                ;compare the strings
                REPZ CMPSB
```

```
                        ;if strings equal then
                        JNZ TRY_FURTHER_ALONG
                                ;begin
                                ;print line number DL + 1
                                ADD DL,31H
                                CALL PRINTCHAR
                                CALL PRINT_NEWLINE
                                SUB DL,31H
                                ;found := true
                                POP CX
                                MOV CL,0
                                POP AX
                                DEC AX
                        ;end
                                JMP END_WHILE
                        ;else begin
TRY_FURTHER_ALONG:POP CX
                        POP AX
                        DEC AX
                        ;end
        ;end (*of while*)
END_WHILE:JMP CHECK_THIS_LINE
        ;end (*of for loop*)
END_FOR:SUB DL,1
        JB LOCATE_DONE
        JMP SEARCH_NEXT_LINE
;set DX to address of completion message
LOCATE_DONE:MOV DX,OFFSET FIND_OK
        RET
LOCATE ENDP

; ********************************************************************
DELETE PROC NEAR
     CALL VERIFY_RANGE_AND_FORMAT
     CALL PRINT_NEWLINE
;if AH = OFFH then print error message
     CMP  AH,OFFH
     JNZ  DO_DELETE
     MOV  DX,OFFSET NO_SUCH_LINE
     CALL PRINT_STRING
     JMP  DELETE_DONE
;else begin
     ;find start address of line to be deleted
DO_DELETE:SUB  BL,31H  ;our line is this many 75D blocks
                       ;from start
        MOV  AL,75D
```

```
        IMUL BL
        ADD  AX,OFFSET START_OF_TEXT;
    ;start address now in AX
    ;insert CR, LF, DOLLAR at beginning of line with this address
        MOV  SI,AX
        MOV  BYTE PTR [SI],CR
        MOV  BYTE PTR 1[SI],LF
        MOV  BYTE PTR 2[SI],DOLLAR
    ;reset line length to zero
        MOV  SI,OFFSET LINE_LENGTHS
        MOV  BH,OH
        ADD  SI,BX
        MOV  [SI],BH
    ;print deletion OK message
        MOV  DX,OFFSET DELETE_OK
        CALL PRINT_STRING
DELETE_DONE:RET
DELETE ENDP


; ***********************************************************************

SWAP PROC NEAR
;if AL not in ['1'..'9'] then print NO SUCH LINE
    CMP  AL,'1'
    JB   TOO_LOW
    CMP  AL,'9'
    JBE  LINE_NO_OK
TOO_LOW:MOV  DX,OFFSET NO_SUCH_LINE
        CALL PRINT_STRING
        JMP  SWAP_DONE
;else begin
        MOV  CL,AL
    ;read(char)
        CALL READCHAR
        CALL VERIFY_RANGE_AND_FORMAT
    ;if AH = OFFH then print error message
        CMP  AH,OFFH
        JNZ  DO_THE_SWAP
        MOV  DX,OFFSET NO_SUCH_LINE
        CALL PRINT_STRING
        JMP  SWAP_DONE
    ;else begin
    ;swap the recorded line lengths
  DO_THE_SWAP:  SUB  CL,31H
                SUB  BL,31H
                CALL LENGTH_SWAP
```

```
              ;DX := address of first text line
                        MOV   AL,75D
                        IMUL BL
                        ADD   AX,OFFSET START_OF_TEXT
                        MOV   DX,AX
              ;AX := address of second text line
                        MOV   AL,75D
                        IMUL CL
                        ADD   AX,OFFSET START_OF_TEXT
              ;move string addressed by AX into READ_LINE_BUFFER
                        MOV   SI,AX
                        MOV   DI,OFFSET READ_LINE_BUFFER
                        MOV   CX,75D
                        REP   MOVSB
              ;move string addressed by DX into locations addressed by AX
                        MOV   SI,DX
                        MOV   DI,AX
                        MOV   CX,75D
                        REP   MOVSB
              ;copy string in READ_LINE_BUFFER to locations addressed by DX
                        MOV   SI,OFFSET  READ_LINE_BUFFER
                        MOV   DI,DX
                        MOV   CX,75D
                        REP   MOVSB
              ;print(swap complete)
                        MOV   DX,OFFSET SWAP_OK
                        CALL PRINT_NEWLINE
                        CALL PRINT_STRING
                  ;end
    ;end
SWAP_DONE: RET
SWAP ENDP


; ***********************************************************************

  LENGTH_SWAP PROC NEAR
;preserve BL on the stack
  PUSH  BX
  MOV   SI,OFFSET LINE_LENGTHS
  MOV   CH,0
  MOV   BH,0
  ADD   BX,SI  ;start address of 2nd line now in BX
  ADD   SI,CX  ;start address of 1st line now in SI
  MOV   AL,[SI]
  XCHG  AL,[BX]
  MOV   [SI],AL
```

```
    POP    BX
    RET
LENGTH_SWAP ENDP
```

; **

```
CSEG ENDS
END
```

APPENDIX IV

8088 Instruction Set Summary

Flag registers

AF=Auxiliary carry   PF=Parity
CF=Carry   SF=Sign
DF=Direction   TF=Trap
IF=Interrupt   ZF=Zero
OF=Overflow

Legend for flag conditions

A=Altered to reflect results of operation
R=Replaced from storage
U=Undefined
0=Unconditionally cleared to 0
1=Unconditionally set to 1
None=No flags affected

AAA (no operands) – ASCII adjust for addition			
Operands	Bytes	Example	Flags
none	1	AAA	AF=A PF=U CF=A SF=U OF=U ZF=U

AAD (no operands) – ASCII adjust for division			
Operands	Bytes	Example	Flags
none	2	AAD	AF=U PF=A CF=U SF=A OF=U ZF=A

AAM (no operands) – ASCII adjust for multiply			
Operands	Bytes	Example	Flags
none	1	AAM	AF=U PF=A CF=U SF=A OF=U ZF=A

AAS (no operands) – ASCII adjust for subtraction			
Operands	Bytes	Example	Flags
none	1	AAS	AF=A PF=U CF=A SF=U OF=U ZF=U

ADC destination,source – Add with carry

Operands	Bytes	Example	Flags
register,register	2	ADC AX,SI	AF=A
register,memory	2-4	ADC DX,BETA [SI]	PF=U
memory,register	2-4	ADC ALPHA [BX] [SI],DI	CF=A
register,immediate	3-4	ADC BX,256	SF=U
memory,immediate	3-6	ADC GAMMA,30H	OF=U
accumulator,immediate	2-3	ADC AL,5	ZF=U

ADD destination,source – Addition

Operands	Bytes	Example	Flags
register,register	2-4	ADD CX,DX	AF=A
register,memory	2-4	ADD DI,[BX],ALPHA	PF=U
memory,register	3-4	ADD TEMP,CL	CF=A
register,immediate	3-6	ADD CL,2	SF=U
memory,immediate	2-3	ADD ALPHA,2	OF=U
accumulator,immediate		ADD AX,200	ZF=U

AND destination,source – Logical AND

Operands	Bytes	Example	Flags
register,register	2	AND AL,BL	AF=U
register,memory	2-4	AND CX,FLAG WORD	PF=A
memory,register	2-4	AND ASCII [DI],AL	CF=0
register,immediate	3-4	AND CX0,F0H	SF=A
memory,immediate	3-6	AND BETA,01H	OF=0
accumulator,immediate	2-3	AND AX,01010000B	ZF=A

CALL target – Call a procedure

Operands	Bytes	Example	Flags
near-proc	3	CALL NEAR_PROC	none
far-proc	5	CALL FAR_PROC	
memptr 16	2-4	CALL PROC_TABLE [SI]	
regptr 16	2	CALL AX	
memptr 32	2-4	CALL [BX.].TASK [SI]	

CBW (no operands) – Convert byte to word

Operands	Bytes	Example	Flags
none	1	CBW	none

CLC (no operands) – Clear carry flag

Operands	Bytes	Example	Flags
none	1	CLC	CF=0

CLD (no operands) – Clear direction flag

Operands	Bytes	Example	Flags
none	1	CLD	DF=0

CLI (no operands) – Clear interrupt flag

Operands	Bytes	Example	Flags
none	1	CLI	DF=0

CMC (no operands) – Complement Carry Flag

Operands	Bytes	Example	Flags
none	1	CMC	CF=A

CMP destination,source – Compare destination to source

Operands	Bytes	Example	Flags
register,register	2	CMP BX,CX	AF=A
register,memory	2-4	CMP DH.ALPHA	PF=A
memory,register	2-4	CMP [BP + 2],SI	CF=A
register,immediate	3-4	CMP BL,02H	SF=A
memory,immediate	3-6	CMP [BX] RADAR [DI],3420H	OF=A
accumulator,immediate	2-3	CMP AL,00010000B	ZF=A

CMPS dest-string,source-string – Compare string

Operands	Bytes	Example	Flags
dest-string,source-string	1	CMPS BUFF1,BUFF2	AF=A PF=A
(repeat) dest-string,source-string	1	REPE CMPS ID,KEY	CF=A SF=A OF=A ZF=A

CWD (no operand) – Convert word to doubleword

Operands	Bytes	Example	Flags
none	1	CWD	none

DAA (no operand) – Decimal adjust for addition

Operands	Bytes	Example	Flags
none	1	DAA	AF=A PF=U CF=A SF=U OF=U ZF=U

DAS (no operand) – Decimal adjust for subtraction

Operands	Bytes	Example	Flags
none	1	DAS	AF=A PF=A CF=A SF=A OF=A ZF=A

DEC destination – Decrement by 1

Operands	Bytes	Example	Flags
reg16	1	DEC AX	AF=A SF=A
reg8	2	DEC AL	OF=A ZF=A
memory	2-4	DEC ARRAY [SI]	PF=A

DIV source – Division, unsigned

Operands	Bytes	Example	Flags
reg8	2	DIV CL	AF=U PF=U
reg16	2	DIV BX	CF=U SF=U
mem8	2-4	DIV ALPHA	OF=U
mem16	2-4	DIV TABLE [SI]	ZF=U

ESC external-op code,source – Escape

Operands	Bytes	Example	Flags
immediate,memory	2-4	ESC 6,ARRAY [SI]	none
immediate,register	2	ESC 20,AL	

HLT (no operands) – Halt

Operands	Bytes	Example	Flags
none	1	HLT	none

IDIV source – Integer division

Operands	Bytes	Example	Flags
reg8	2	IDIV BL	AF=U PF=U
reg16	2	IDIV CX	CF=U SF=U
mem8	2-4	IDIV DIVISOR BYTE [SI]	OF=U
mem16	2-4	IDIV [BX],DIVISOR_WORD	ZF=U

IMUL source – Integer multiplication

Operands	Bytes	Example	Flags
reg8	2	IMUL CL	AF=U PF=U
reg16	2	IMUL BX	CF=A SF=U
mem8	2-4	IMUL RATE_BYTE	OF=A ZF=U
mem16	2-4	IMUL RATE_WORD[BP] [DI]	

IN accumulator,port – Input byte or word

Operands	Bytes	Example	Flags
accumulator,immed8	2	IN AL,0FFEAH	none
accumulator,DX	1	IN AX,DX	

INC destination – Increment by 1

Operands	Bytes	Example	Flags
reg19	1	INC CX	AF=A SF=A
reg8	2	INC BL	OF=A ZF=A
memory	2-4	INC ALPHA [DI] [BX]	PA=A

INT interrupt-type – Interrupt

Operands	Bytes	Example	Flags
immed8(type=3)	1	INT 3	IF=0
immed8(type≠3)	2	INT 67	TF=0

INTO (no operands) – Interrupt if overflow

Operands	Bytes	Example	Flags
none	1	INTO	IF=0 TF=0

IRET (no operands) – Interrupt return

Operands	Bytes	Example	Flags
none	1	IRET	AF=R PF=R CF=R SF=R DF=R TF=R IF=R ZF=R

JA/JNBE short-label – Jump if above/Jump if not below or equal

Operands	Bytes	Example	Flags
short-label	2	JA ABOVE	none

JAE/JNB short-label – Jump if above or equal/Jump if not below

Operands	Bytes	Example	Flags
short-label	2	JAE ABOVE_EQUAL	none

JB/JNAE short-label – Jump if below/Jump if not above nor equal

Operands	Bytes	Example	Flags
short-label	2	JB BELOW	none

JBE/JNA short-label – Jump if below or equal/Jump if not above

Operands	Bytes	Example	Flags
short-label	2	JNA NOT ABOVE	none

JC short-label – Jump if carry

Operands	Bytes	Example	Flags
short-label	2	JC CARRY SET	none

JCXZ short-label – Jump if CX is zero

Operands	Bytes	Example	Flags
short-label	2	JCXZ COUNT DONE	none

JE/JZ short-label – Jump if equal/Jump if zero

Operands	Bytes	Example	Flags
short-label	2	JZ ZERO	none

JG/JNLE short-label – Jump if greater/Jump if not less than

Operands	Bytes	Example	Flags
short-label	2	JG GREATER	none

JGE/JNL short-label – Jump if greater or equal/Jump if not less

Operands	Bytes	Example	Flags
short-label	2	JGE GREATER EQUAL	none

JL/JNGE short-label – Jump if less/Jump if not greater nor equal

Operands	Bytes	Example	Flags
short-label	2	JL LESS	none

JLE/JNG short-label – Jump if less or equal/Jump if not greater

Operands	Bytes	Example	Flags
short-label	2	JNG NOT GREATER	none

JMP target – Jump

Operands	Bytes	Example	Flags
short-label	2	JMP SHORT	none
near-label	3	JMP WITHIN SEGMENT	
far-label	5	JMP FAR LABEL	
memptr16	2-4	JMP [BX],TARGET	
regptr16	2	JMP CX	
memptr32	2-4	JMP OTHER SEG [SI]	

JNC short-label – Jump if not carry

Operands	Bytes	Example	Flags
short-label	2	JNC NOT CARRY	none

JNE/JNZ short-label – Jump if not equal/Jump if not zero

Operands	Bytes	Example	Flags
short-label	2	JNE NOT EQUAL	none

JNO short-label – Jump if not overflow

Operands	Bytes	Example	Flags
short-label	2	JNO NO OVERFLOW	none

JNP/JPO short-label – Jump if not parity/Jump if parity ODD

Operands	Bytes	Example	Flags
short-label	2	JPO ODD PARITY	none

JNS short-label – Jump if not sign

Operands	Bytes	Example	Flags
short-label	2	JNS POSITIVE	none

JO short-label – Jump if overflow			
Operands	**Bytes**	**Example**	**Flags**
short-label	2	JO SIGNED_OVRFLW	none

JP/JPE short-label – Jump if parity/Jump if parity even			
Operands	**Bytes**	**Example**	**Flags**
short-label	2	JPE EVEN_PARITY	none

JS short-label – Jump if sign			
Operands	**Bytes**	**Example**	**Flags**
short-label	2	JS NEGATIVE	none

LAHF (no operands) – Load AH from flags			
Operands	**Bytes**	**Example**	**Flags**
none	1	LAHF	none

LDS destination,source – Load pointer using DS			
Operands	**Bytes**	**Example**	**Flags**
reg16,mem32	2-4	LDS SI,DATA.SEG[DI]	none

LOCK (no operands) – Lock bus			
Operands	**Bytes**	**Example**	**Flags**
none	1	LOCK XCHG FLAG.AL	none

LODS source-string – Load string			
Operands	**Bytes**	**Example**	**Flags**
source-string	1	LODS CUSTOMER NAME	none
(repeat) source-string	1	REP LODS NAME	

LOOP short-label – Loop			
Operands	**Bytes**	**Example**	**Flags**
short-label	2	LOOP AGAIN	none

LOOPE/LOOPZ short-label – Loop if equal/Loop if zero			
Operands	**Bytes**	**Example**	**Flags**
short-label	2	LOOPE AGAIN	none

LOOPNE/LOOPNZ short-label – Loop if not equal/Loop if not zero			
Operands	**Bytes**	**Example**	**Flags**
short-label	2	LOOPNE AGAIN	none

LEA destination,source – Load effective address

Operands	Bytes	Example	Flags
reg16,mem16	2-4	LEA BX,[BP] [DI]	none

LES destination,source – Load pointer using ES

Operands	Bytes	Example	Flags
reg16,mem32	2-4	LES DI,[BX].TEXT_BUFF	none

MOV destination,source – MOVE

Operands	Bytes	Example	Flags
memory,accumulator	3	MOV ARRAY [SI],AL	none
accumulator,memory	3	MOV AX,TEMP_RESULT	
register,register	2	MOV AX,CX	
register,memory	2-4	MOV BP,STACK_TOP	
memory,register	2-4	MOV COUNT [DI],CX	
register,immediate	2-3	MOV CL,2	
memory,immediate	3-6	MOV MASK [BX][SI],2CH	
seg-reg,reg16	2	MOV ES,CX	
seg-reg,mem16	2-4	MOV DS,SEGMENT_BASE	
reg16,seg-reg	2	MOV BP,SS	
memory,seg-reg	2-4	MOV [BX].SEG_SAVE,CS	

MOVS dest-string,source-string – MOVE string

Operands	Bytes	Example	Flags
dest-string,source-string	1	MOVS LINE_EDIT_DATA	none
(repeat)	1	REP MOVS	
dest-string,source-string		SCREEN,BUFFER	

MOVSB/MOVSW (no operands) – Move string (byte/word)

Operands	Bytes	Example	Flags
none	1	MOVSB	none
(repeat) none	1	REP MOVSW	

MUL source – Multiplication, unsigned

Operands	Bytes	Example	Flags
reg8	2	MUL BL	AF=U PF=U
reg16	2	MUL CX	CF=A SF=U
mem8	2-4	MUL MONTH [SI]	OF=A ZF=U
mem16	2-4	MUL BAUD-RATE	

NEG destination – Negate

Operands	Bytes	Example	Flags
register	2	NEG AL	AF=A PF=A
memory	2-4	NEG MULTIPLIER	CF=1*
			SF=A OF=A ZF=A

NOP no operands – No operation

Operands	Bytes	Example	Flags
none	1	NOP	none

NOT destination – Logical not

Operands	Bytes	Example	Flags
register	2	NOT AX	none
memory	2-4	NOT CHARACTER	

OR destination,source – Logical inclusive OR

Operands	Bytes	Example	Flags
register,register	2	OR AL,BL	AF=U
register,memory	2-4	OR DX,PORT ID [DI]	PF=A
memory,register	2-4	OR FLAG BYTE.CL	CF=0
accumulator,immediate	2-3	OR AL,0110110B	SF=A
register,immediate	3-4	OR SC,01FH	OF=0
memory,immediate	3-6	OR [BX] CMD WORD,0CFH	ZF=A

OUT port,accumulator – Output byte or word

Operands	Bytes	Example	Flags
immed8.accumulator	2	OUT 44.AX	none
DX.accumulator	1	OUT DX.AL	

POP destination – Pop word off stack

Operands	Bytes	Example	Flags
register	1	POP DX	none
seg-reg (CS illegal)	1	POP DS	
memory	2-4	POP PARAMETER	

POPF (no operands) – Pop flags off stack

Operands	Bytes	Example	Flags
none	1	POPF	AF=R PF=R CF=R SF=R DF=R TF=R IF=R ZF=R

PUSH source – Push word onto stack

Operands	Bytes	Example	Flags
register	1	PUSH SI	none
seg-reg (CS legal)	1	PUSH ES	
memory	2-4	PUSH PARAMETER	

PUSHF (no operands) – Push flags onto stack

Operands	Bytes	Example	Flags
none	1	PUSHF	none

RCL destination,count – Rotate left through carry

Operands	Bytes	Example	Flags
register,1	2	RCL CX,1	CF=A
register,CL	2	RCL AL,CL	OF=A
memory,1	2-4	RCL ALPHA,1	
memory,CL	2-4	RCL [BP].PARM,CL	

RCR destination,count – Rotate right through carry

Operands	Bytes	Example	Flags
register,1	2	RCR BX,1	CF=A
register,CL	2	RCR BL,CL	OF=A
memory,1	2-4	RCR [BX],STATUS,1	
memory,CL	2-4	RCR ARRAY [DI],CL	

REP (no operands) – Repeat string operation

Operands	Bytes	Example	Flags
none	1	REP MOVS DEST.SRCE	none

REPE/REPZ (no operands) – Repeat string operation equal/while zero

Operands	Bytes	Example	Flags
none	1	REPE CMPS DATA.KEY	none

REPNE/REPNZ (no operands) – Repeat string operation not equal/not zero

Operands	Bytes	Example	Flags
none	1	REPNE SCAS INPUT LINE	none

RET optional-pop-value – Return from procedure

Operands	Bytes	Example	Flags
(intra-segment,no pop)	1	RET	none
(intra-segment,pop)	3	RET 4	
(inter-segment,no pop)	1	RET	
(inter-segment,pop)	3	RET 2	

ROL destination,count – Rotate left

Operands	Bytes	Example	Flags
register,1	2	ROL BX,1	CF=A
register,CL	2	ROL DI,CL	OF=A
memory,1	2-4	ROL FLAG BYTE[DI],1	
memory,CL	2-4	ROL ALPHA,CL	

ROR destination,count

Operands	Bytes	Example	Flags
register,1	2	ROR AL,1	CF=A
register,CL	2	ROR BX,CL	OF=A
memory,1	2-4	ROR PORT STATUS,1	
memory,CL	2-4	ROR CMD WORD,CL	

SAHF (no operands) – Store AH into flags			
Operands	Bytes	Example	Flags
none	1	SAHF	AF=A SF=R CF=R ZF=R PF=R

SAL/SHL destination,count – Shift arithmetic left/Shift logical left			
Operands	Bytes	Example	Flags
register,1	2	SAL AL,1	CF=A
register,CL	2	SHL DI,CL	OF=A
memory,1	2-4	SHL [BX].OVERDRAW,1	
memory,CL	2-4	SAL STORE_COUNT,CL	

SAR destination,source – Shift arithmetic right			
Operands	Bytes	Example	Flags
register,1	2	SAR DX,1	AF=U PF=A
register,CL	2	SAR DI,CL	CF=A SF=A
memory,1	2-4	SAR N BLOCKS,1	OF=A ZF=A
memory,CL	2-4	SAR N BLOCKS,CL	

SBB destination,source – Subtract with borrow			
Operands	Bytes	Example	Flags
register,register	2	SBB BX,CX	AF=A
register,memory	2-4	SBB DI,[BX].PAYMENT	PF=A
memory,register	2-4	SBB BALANCE,AX	CF=A
accumulator,immediate	2-3	SBB AX,2	SF=A
register,immediate	3-4	SBB CL,1	OF=A
memory,immediate	3-6	SBB COUNT[SI],10	ZF=A

SCAS dest-string – Scan string			
Operands	Bytes	Example	Flags
dest-string	1	SCAS INPUT_LINE	AF=A PF=A
(repeat string)	1	REPNE SCAS BUFFER	CF=A SF=A
			OF=A ZF=A

SHR destination,count – Shift logical right			
Operands	Bytes	Example	Flags
register,1	2	SHR SI,1	CF=A
register,CL	2	SHR SI,CL	OF=A
memory,1	2-4	SHR ID BYTE [SI][BX],1	
memory,CL	2-4	SHR INPUT WORD,CL	

STC (no operands) – Set carry flag			
Operands	Bytes	Example	Flags
none	1	STC	CF=1

STD (no operand) – Set direction flag

Operands	Bytes	Example	Flags
none	1	STD	DF=1

STI (no operands) – Set interrupt enable flag

Operands	Bytes	Example	Flags
none	1	STI	IF=1

STOS dest-string – Store byte or word string

Operands	Bytes	Example	Flags
dest-string	1	STOS PRINT LINE	none
(repeat) dest-string	1	REP STOS DISPLAY	

SUB destination,source – Subtraction

Operands	Bytes	Example	Flags
register,register	2	SUB XC.BX	AF=U
register,memory	2-4	SUB DX,MATH_TOTAL[SI]	PF=A
memory,register	2-4	SUB [BP+2],CL	CF=A
accumulator,immediate	2-3	SUB AL,10	SF=A
register,immediate	3-4	SUB SI,5280	OF=A
memory,immediate	3-6	SUB [BP].BALANCE,1000	ZF=A

TEST destination,source – Test or non-destructive logical AND

Operands	Bytes	Example	Flags
register,register	2	TEST SI,DI	AF=U
register,memory	2-4	TEST SI,END_COUNT	PF=A
accumulator,immediate	2-3	TEST AL,00100000B	CF=0
register,immediate	3-4	TEST BX,0CC4H	SF=A
memory,immediate	3-6	TEST RETURN CODE,01H	OF=0
			ZF=A

WAIT (no operands) – Wait while TEST pin not asserted

Operands	Bytes	Example	Flags
none	1	WAIT	none

XCHG destination,source – Exchange

Operands	Bytes	Example	Flags
accumulator,reg16	1	XCHNG AX,BX	none
memory,register	2-4	XCHG SEMAPHORE,AX	
register,register	2	XCHG AL,BL	

XLAT source-table – Translate

Operands	Bytes	Example	Flags
source-table	1	XLAT ASCII_TAB	none

XOR destination,source — Logical exclusive OR			
Operands	**Bytes**	**Example**	**Flags**
register,register	2	XOR CX,BX	AF=U
register,memory	2-4	XOR CL,MASK BYTE	PF=A
memory,register	2-4	XOR ALPHA [SI],DX	CF=0
accumulator,immediate	2-3	XOR AL,01000010B	SF=A
register,immediate	3-4	XOR SI,00C2H	OF=0
memory,immediate	3-6	XOR RETURN CODE.0D2H	ZF=A

APPENDIX V

8088 Instruction Set Encoding

8088
Register Model

AX:	AH	AL	Accumulator
BX:	BH	BL	Base
CX:	CH	CL	Count
DX:	DH	DL	Data

General Register File

SP	Stack Pointer
BP	Base Pointer
SI	Source Index
DI	Destination Index

IP	Instruction Pointer
FLAGSH · FLAGSL	Status Flags

CS	Code Segment
DS	Data Segment
SS	Stack Segment
ES	Extra Segment

Segment Register File

Instructions which reference the flag register file as a 16-bit object use the symbol FLAGS to represent the file:

15								7							0
X	X	X	X	OF	DF	IF	TF	SF	ZF	X	AF	X	PF	X	CF

x = Don't Care

AF: Auxiliary Carry - BCD
CF: Carry Flag
PF: Parity Flag   — 8080 Flags
SF: Sign Flag
ZF: Zero Flag

DF: Direction Flag (Strings)
IF: Interrupt Enable Flag
OF: Overflow Flag (CF ⊕ SF)   — 8088 Flags
TF: Trap - Single Step Flag

Operand Summary

"reg field Bit Assignments:

16-Bit (w=1)	8-Bit (w=0)	Segment
000 AX	000 AL	00 ES
001 CX	001 CL	01 CS
010 DX	010 DL	10 SS
011 BX	011 BL	11 DS
100 SP	100 AH	
101 BP	101 CH	
110 SI	110 DH	
111 DI	111 BH	

Second Instruction Byte Summary

mod	xxx	r/m

mod	Displacement
00	DISP=0*. disp-low and disp-high are absent
01	DISP=disp-low sign-extended to 16-bits. disp-high is absent
10	DISP=disp-high: disp-low
11	r/m is treated as a "reg" field

r/m	Operand Address
000	(BX) + (SI) + DISP
001	(BX) + (DI) + DISP
010	(BP) + (SI) + DISP
011	(BP) + (DI) + DISP
100	(SI) + DISP
101	(DI) + DISP
110	(BP) + DISP*
111	(BX) + DISP

DISP follows 2nd byte of instruction (before data if required).
*except if mod = 00 and r/m = 110 then EA = disp-high: disp-low.

Memory Segmentation Model

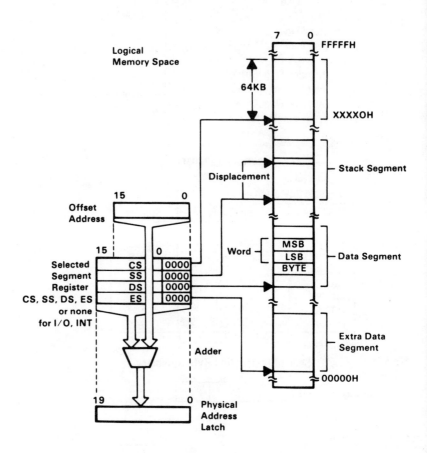

Segment Override Prefix

| 0 0 1 reg 1 1 0 |

Use of Segment Override

Operand Register	Default	With Override Prefix
IP (Code Address)	CS	Never
SP (Stack Address)	SS	Never
BP (Stack Address or Stack Marker)	SS	BP + DS or ES, or CS
SI or DI (not including strings)	DS	ES, SS, or CS
SI (Implicit Source Address for Strings)	DS	ES, SS, or CS
DI (Implicit Destination Address for Strings)	ES	Never

Data Transfer

MOV = Move
Register/memory to/from register

1 0 0 0 1 0 d w	mod reg r/m

Immediate to register/memory

1 1 0 0 0 1 1 w	mod 0 0 0 r/m	data	data if w=1

Immediate to register

1 0 1 1 w reg	data	data if w=1

Memory to accumulator

1 0 1 0 0 0 0 w	addr-low	addr-high

Accumulator to memory

1 0 1 0 0 0 1 w	addr-low	addr-high

Register/memory to segment register

1 0 0 0 1 1 1 0	mod 0 reg r/m

Segment register to register/memory

1 0 0 0 1 1 0 0	mod 0 reg r/m

PUSH = Push
Register/memory

1 1 1 1 1 1 1 1	mod 1 1 0 r/m

Register

0 1 0 1 0 reg

Segment register

0 0 0 reg 1 1 0

POP = Pop
Register/memory

1 0 0 0 1 1 1 1	mod 0 0 0 r/m

Register

0 1 0 1 1 reg

Segment register

0 0 0 reg 1 1 1

XCHG = Exchange
Register/memory with register

1	0	0	0	0	1	1	w	mod	reg	r/m

Register with accumulator

1	0	0	1	0	reg

IN = Input to AL/AX from
Fixed port

1	1	1	0	0	1	0	w	port

Variable port (DX)

1	1	1	0	1	1	0	w

OUT = Output from AL/AX to
Fixed port

1	1	1	0	0	1	1	w	port

Variable port (DX)

1	1	1	0	1	1	0	w

XLAT = Translate byte to AL

1	1	0	1	0	1	1	1

LEA = Load EA to register

1	0	0	0	1	1	0	1	mod	reg	r/m

LDS = Load pointer to DS

1	1	0	0	0	1	0	1	mod	reg	r/m

LES = Load pointer to ES

1	1	0	0	0	1	0	0	mod	reg	r/m

LAHF = Load AH with flags

1	0	0	1	1	1	1	1

SAHF = Store AH into flags

1	0	0	1	1	1	1	0

PUSHF = Push flags

1	0	0	1	1	1	0	0

POPF = Pop flags

1	0	0	1	1	1	0	1

Arithmetic

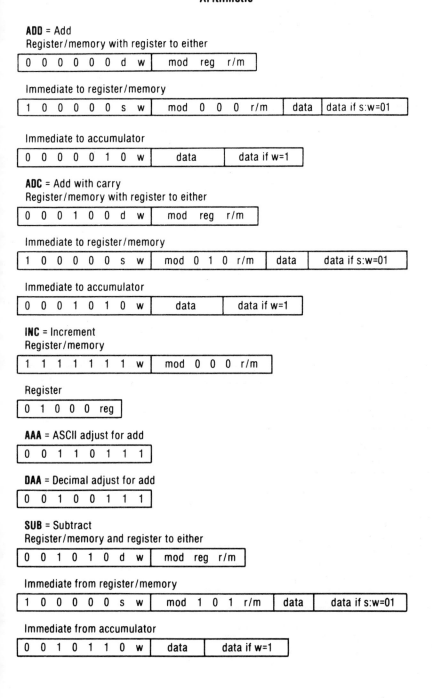

ADD = Add
Register/memory with register to either

0 0 0 0 0 0 d w	mod reg r/m

Immediate to register/memory

1 0 0 0 0 0 s w	mod 0 0 0 r/m	data	data if s:w=01

Immediate to accumulator

0 0 0 0 0 1 0 w	data	data if w=1

ADC = Add with carry
Register/memory with register to either

0 0 0 1 0 0 d w	mod reg r/m

Immediate to register/memory

1 0 0 0 0 0 s w	mod 0 1 0 r/m	data	data if s:w=01

Immediate to accumulator

0 0 0 1 0 1 0 w	data	data if w=1

INC = Increment
Register/memory

1 1 1 1 1 1 1 w	mod 0 0 0 r/m

Register

0 1 0 0 0 reg

AAA = ASCII adjust for add

0 0 1 1 0 1 1 1

DAA = Decimal adjust for add

0 0 1 0 0 1 1 1

SUB = Subtract
Register/memory and register to either

0 0 1 0 1 0 d w	mod reg r/m

Immediate from register/memory

1 0 0 0 0 0 s w	mod 1 0 1 r/m	data	data if s:w=01

Immediate from accumulator

0 0 1 0 1 1 0 w	data	data if w=1

SBB = Subtract with borrow
Register/memory and register to either

0 0 0 1 1 0 d w	mod reg r/m

Immediate from register/memory

1 0 0 0 0 0 s w	mod 0 1 1 r/m	data	data if s:w=01

Immediate from accumulator

0 0 0 1 1 1 0 w	data	data if w=1

DEC = Decrement
Register/memory

1 1 1 1 1 1 1 w	mod 0 0 1 r/m

Register

0   1   0   0   1   reg

NEG = Change sign

1 1 1 1 0 1 1 w	mod 0 1 1 r/m

CMP = Compare
Register/memory and register

0 0 1 1 1 0 d w	mod reg r/m

Immediate with register/memory

1 0 0 0 0 0 s w	mod 1 1 1 r/m	data	data if s:w=01

Immediate with accumulator

0 0 1 1 1 1 0 w	data	data if w=1

AAS = ASCII adjust for subtract

0   0   1   1   1   1   1   1

DAS = Decimal adjust for subtract

0   0   1   0   1   1   1   1

MUL = Multiply (unsigned)

1 1 1 1 0 1 1 w	mod 1 0 0 r/m

IMUL = Integer multiply (signed)

1 1 1 1 0 1 1 w	mod 1 0 1 r/m

AAM = ASCII adjust for multiply

1 1 0 1 0 1 0 0	0 0 0 0 1 0 1 0

DIV = Divide (unsigned)

1 1 1 1 0 1 1 w	mod 1 1 0 r/m

IDIV = Integer divide (signed)

1 1 1 1 0 1 1 w	mod 1 1 1 r/m

AAD = ASCII adjust for divide

1 1 0 1 0 1 0 1	0 0 0 0 1 0 1 0

CBW = Convert byte to word

1 0 0 1 1 0 0 0

CWD = Convert word to double word

1 0 0 1 1 0 0 1

Logic

NOT = Invert

1 1 1 1 0 1 1 w	mod 0 1 0 r/m

SHL/SAL = Shift logical/arithmetic left

1 1 0 1 0 0 v w	mod 1 0 0 r/m

SHR = Shift logical right

1 1 0 1 0 0 v w	mod 1 0 1 r/m

SAR = Shift arithmetic right

1 1 0 1 0 0 v w	mod 1 1 1 r/m

ROL = Rotate left

1 1 0 1 0 0 v w	mod 0 0 0 r/m

ROR = Rotate right

1 1 0 1 0 0 v w	mod 0 0 1 r/m

RCL = Rotate through carry left

1 1 0 1 0 0 v w	mod 0 1 0 r/m

RCR = Rotate through carry right

1 1 0 1 0 0 v w	mod 0 1 1 r/m

AND = And
Register/memory and register to either

0 0 1 0 0 0 d w	mod reg r/m

Immediate to register/memory

1 0 0 0 0 0 0 w	mod 1 0 0 r/m	data	data if w=1

Immediate to accumulator

0 0 1 0 0 1 0 w	data	data if w=1

TEST = And function to flags, no result
Register/memory and register

1	0	0	0	0	1	0	w	mod	reg	r/m

Immediate data and register/memory

1	1	1	1	0	1	1	w	mod 0 0 0 r/m	data	data if w=1

Immediate data and accumulator

1	0	1	0	1	0	0	w	data	data if w=1

OR = OR
Register/memory and register to either

0	0	0	0	1	0	d	w	mod	reg	r/m

Immediate to register/memory

1	0	0	0	0	0	0	w	mod 0 0 1 r/m	data	data if w=1

Immediate to accumulator

0	0	0	0	1	1	0	w	data	data if w=1

XOR = Exclusive or
Register/memory and register to either

0	0	1	1	0	0	d	w	mod	reg	r/m

Immediate to register/memory

1	0	0	0	0	0	0	w	mod 1 1 0 r/m	data	data if w=1

Immediate to accumulator

0	0	1	1	0	1	0	w	data	data if w=1

String Manipulation

REP = Repeat

1	1	1	1	0	0	1	z

MOVS = Move String

1	0	1	0	0	1	0	w

CMPS = Compare String

1	0	1	0	0	1	1	w

SCAS = Scan String

1	0	1	0	1	1	1	w

LODS = Load String

1	0	1	0	1	1	0	w

STOS = Store String

1	0	1	0	1	0	1	w

Control Transfer

CALL = Call
Direct within segment

1 1 1 0 1 0 0 0	disp-low	disp-high

Indirect within segment

1 1 1 1 1 1 1 1	mod 0 1 0 r/m

Direct intersegment

1 0 0 1 1 0 1 0	offset-low	offset-high
	seg-low	seg-high

Indirect intersegment

1 1 1 1 1 1 1 1	mod 0 1 1 r/m

JMP = Unconditional Jump
Direct within segment

1 1 1 0 1 0 0 1	disp-low	disp-high

Direct within segment-short

1 1 1 0 1 0 1 1	disp

Indirect within segment

1 1 1 1 1 1 1 1	mod 1 0 0 r/m

Direct intersegment

1 1 1 0 1 0 1 0	offset-low	offset-high
	seg-low	seg-high

Indirect intersegment

1 1 1 1 1 1 1 1	mod 1 0 1 r/m

RET = Return from CALL
Within segment

1 1 0 0 0 0 1 1

Within segment adding immediate to SP

1 1 0 0 0 0 1 0	data-low	data-high

Intersegment

1 1 0 0 1 0 1 1

Intersegment, adding immediate to SP

1 1 0 0 0 0 1 0	data-low	data-high

JE/JZ = Jump on equal/zero

0 1 1 1 0 1 0 0	disp

JL/JNGE = Jump on less/not greater or equal

0 1 1 1 1 1 0 0	disp

JLE/JNG = Jump on less or equal/not greater

0 1 1 1 1 1 1 0	disp

JB/JNAE = Jump on below/not above or equal

0 1 1 1 0 0 1 0	disp

JBE/JNA = Jump on below or equal/not above

0 1 1 1 0 1 1 0	disp

JP/JPE = Jump on parity/parity even

0 1 1 1 1 0 1 0	disp

JO = Jump on overflow

0 1 1 1 0 0 0 0	disp

JS = Jump on sign

0 1 1 1 1 0 0 0	disp

JNE/JNZ = Jump on not equal/not zero

0 1 1 1 0 1 0 1	disp

JNL/JGE = Jump on not less/greater or equal

0 1 1 1 1 1 0 1	disp

JNLE/JG = Jump on not less or equal/greater

0 1 1 1 1 1 1 1	disp

JNB/JAE = Jump on not below/above or equal

0 1 1 1 0 0 1 1	disp

JNBE/JA = Jump on not below or equal/above

0 1 1 1 0 1 1 1	disp

JNP/JPO = Jump on not parity/parity odd

0	1	1	1	1	0	1	1	disp

JNO = Jump on not overflow

0	1	1	1	0	0	0	1	disp

JNS = Jump on not sign

0	1	1	1	1	0	0	1	disp

LOOP = Loop CX times

1	1	1	0	0	0	1	0	disp

LOOPZ/LOOPE = Loop while zero/equal

1	1	1	0	0	0	0	1	disp

LOOPNZ/LOOPNE = Loop while not zero/not equal

1	1	1	0	0	0	0	0	disp

JCXZ = Jump on CX zero

1	1	1	0	0	0	1	1	disp

8088 Conditional Transfer Operations

Instruction	Condition	Interpretation
JE or JZ	ZF = 1	"equal" or "zero"
JL or JNGE	(SF xor OF) = 1	"less" or "not greater or equal"
JLE or JNG	((SF xor OF) or ZF) = 1	"less or equal" or "not greater"
JB or JNAE or JC	CF = 1	"below" or "not above or equal"
JBE or JNA	(CF or ZF) = 1	"below or equal" or "not above"
JP or JPE	PF = 1	"parity" or "parity even"
JO	OF = 1	"overflow"
JS	SF = 1	"sign"
JNE or JNZ	ZF = 0	"not equal" or "not zero"
JNL or JGE	(SF xor OF) = 0	"not less" or "greater or equal"
JNLE or JG	((SF xor OF) or ZF) = 0	"not less or equal" or "greater"
JNB or JAE or JNC	CF = 0	"not below" or "above or equal"
JNBE or JA	(CF or ZF) = 0	"not below or equal" or "above"
JNP or JPO	PF = 0	"not parity" or "parity odd"
JNO	OF = 0	"not overflow"
JNS	SF = 0	"not sign"

*"Above" and "below" refer to the relation between two unsigned values, while "greater" and "less" refer to the relation between two signed values.

INT = Interrupt
Type specified

1	1	0	0	1	1	0	1		type

INTO = Interrupt on overflow

1	1	0	0	1	1	1	0

Type 3

1	1	0	0	1	1	0	1

IRET = Interrupt return

1	1	0	0	1	1	1	1

Processor Control

CLC = Clear carry

1	1	1	1	1	0	0	0

STC = Set carry

1	1	1	1	1	0	0	1

CMC = Complement carry

1	1	1	1	0	1	0	1

NOP = No operation

1	0	0	1	0	0	0	0

CLD = Clear direction

1	1	1	1	1	1	0	0

STD = Set direction

1	1	1	1	1	1	0	1

CLI = Clear interrupt

1	1	1	1	1	0	1	0

STI = Set interrupt

1	1	1	1	1	0	1	1

HLT = Halt

1	1	1	1	0	1	0	0

WAIT = Wait

1	0	0	1	1	0	1	1

LOCK = Bus lock prefix

1	1	1	1	0	0	0	0

ESC = Escape (to external device)

1	1	0	1	1	x	x	x	mod	x	x	x	r/m

Footnotes:
if d = 1 then "to"; if d = 0 then "from"
if w = 1 then word instruction; if w = 0 then byte instruction
if s:w = 01 then 16 bits of immediate data from the operand
if s:w = 11 then an immediate data byte is sign extended to form the 16-bit operand
if v = 0 then "count" = 1; if v = 1 then "count" in (CL)
x = don't care
z is used for some string primitives to compare with ZF FLAG
AL = 8-bit accumulator
AX = 16-bit accumulator
CX = Count register
DS = Data segment
DX = Variable port register
ES = Extra segment
Above/below refers to unsigned value
Greater = more positive;
Less = less positive (more negative) signed values

8088 Instruction Set Matrix

HI \ LO	0	1	2	3	4	5	6	7
0	ADD b,f,r/m	ADD w,f,r/m	ADD b,t,r/m	ADD w,t,r/m	ADD b,ia	ADD w,ia	PUSH ES	POP ES
1	ADC b,f,r/m	ADC w,f,r/m	ADC b,t,r/m	ADC w,t,r/m	ADC b,i	ADC w,i	PUSH SS	POP SS
2	AND b,f,r/m	AND w,f,r/m	AND b,t,r/m	AND w,t,r/m	AND b,i	AND w,i	SEG =ES	DAA
3	XOR b,f,r/m	XOR w,f,r/m	XOR b,t,r/m	XOR w,t,r/m	XOR b,i	XOR w,i	SEG =SS	AAA
4	INC AX	INC CX	INC DX	INC BX	INC SP	INC BP	INC SI	INC DI
5	PUSH AX	PUSH CX	PUSH DX	PUSH BX	PUSH SP	PUSH BP	PUSH SI	PUSH DI
6								
7	JO	JNO	JB/JNAE	JNB/JAE	JE/JZ	JNE/JNZ	JBE/JNA	JNBE/JA
8	Immed b,r/m	Immed w,r/m	Immed b,r/m	Immed is,r/m	TEST b,r/m	TEST w,r/m	XCHG b,r/m	XCHG w,r/m
9	NOP	XCHG CX	XCHG DX	XCHG BX	XCHG SP	XCHG BP	XCHG SI	XCHG DI
A	MOV m AL	MOV m AL	MOV AL m	MOV AL m	MOVS b	MOVS w	CMPS b	CMPS w
B	MOV i AL	MOV i CL	MOV i DL	MOV i BL	MOV i AH	MOV i CH	MOV i DH	MOV i BH
C			RET (i+SP)	RET	LES	LDS	MOV b,i,r/m	MOV w,i,r/m
D	Shift b	Shift w	Shift b,v	Shift w,v	AAM	AAD		XLAT
E	LOOPNZ/LOOPNE	LOOPZ/LOOPE	LOOP	JCXZ	IN b	IN w	OUT b	OUT w
F	LOCK		REP	REP z	HLT	CMC	Grp 1 b,r/m	Grp 1 w,r/m

b = byte operation	m = memory
d = direct	r/m = EA is second byte
f = from CPU reg	si = short intrasegment
i = immediate	sr = segment register
ia = immed. to accum.	t = to CPU reg
id = indirect	v = variable
is = immed. byte, sign ext.	w = word operation
l = long ie. intersegment	z = zero

8088 Instruction Set Matrix

HI \ LO	8	9	A	B	C	D	E	F
0	OR b,f,r/m	OR w,f,r/m	OR b,t,r/m	OR w,t,r/m	OR b,i	OR w,i	PUSH CS	
1	SBB b,f,r/m	SBB w,f,r/m	SBB b,t,r/m	SBB w,t,r/m	SBB b,i	SBB w,i	PUSH DS	POP DS
2	SUB b,f,r/m	SUB w,f,r/m	SUB b,t,r/m	SUB w,t,r/m	SUB b,i	SUB w,i	SEG= CS	DAS
3	CMP b,f,r/m	CMP w,f,r/m	CMP b,t,r/m	CMP w,t,r/m	CMP b,i	CMP w,i	SEG= CS	AAS
4	DEC AX	DEC CX	DEC DX	DEC BX	DEC SP	DEC BP	DEC SI	DEC DI
5	POP AX	POP CX	POP DX	POP BX	POP SP	POP BP	POP SI	POP DI
6								
7	JS	JNS	JP/ JPE	JNP/ JPO	JL/ JNGE	JNL/ JGE	JLE/ JNG	JNLE/ JG
8	MOV b,f,r/m	MOV w,f,r/m	MOV b,t,r/m	MOV w,t,r/m	MOV sr,t,r/m	LEA	MOV sr,f,r/m	POP r/m
9	CBW	CWD	CALL l,d	WAIT	PUSHF	POPF	SAHF	LAHF
A	TEST b,i	TEST w,i	STOS b	STOS w	LODS b	LODS w	SCAS b	SCAS w
B	MOV i AX	MOV i CX	MOV i DX	MOV i BX	MOV i SP	MOV i BP	MOV i SI	MOV i DI
C			RET l,(i+SP)	RET l	INT Type 3	INT (Any)	INTO	IRET
D	ESC 0	ESC 1	ESC 2	ESC 3	ESC 4	ESC 5	ESC 6	ESC 7
E	CALL d	JMP d	JMP l,d	JMP si,d	IN v,b	IN v,w	OUT v,b	OUT v,w
F	CLC	STC	CLI	STI	CLD	STD	Grp 2 b,r/m	Grp 2 w,r/m

where:

mod▭r/m	000	001	010	011	100	101	110	111
Immed	ADD	OR	ADC	SBB	AND	SUB	XOR	CMP
Shift	ROL	ROR	RCL	RCR	SHL/SAL	SHR	—	SAR
Grp 1	TEST	—	NOT	NEG	MUL	IMUL	DIV	IDIV
Grp 2	INC	DEC	CALL id	CALL l,id	JMP id	JMP l,id	PUSH	—

Index